ANTHONY D. SMITH

Theories of Nationalism

A TORCHBOOK LIBRARY EDITION
Harper & Row, Publishers
New York, Evanston, San Francisco, London

First TORCHBOOK LIBRARY EDITION published 1971

Standard Book Number (cloth): 06–136069–4

Library of Congress Catalog Card Number: 73–181528

Contents

Acknowledgments

Although the responsibility for the views expressed in this work is mine alone, I should like to record my gratitude to the many people who have helped me; to the Library Staffs of the London School of Economics, Chatham House, the British Museum and the School of Oriental and African Studies; to my students at the Borough Polytechnic and University of York for their stimulation; to many colleagues for their valuable comments, including Professor J. E. T. Eldridge, Dr. L. Sklair, Mr. A. Brittan, Mr. J. Winckler, Miss E. P. Taylor, and Mr. S. Brett; to Mr. M. Hickox for several useful discussions; and to Professor R. P. Dore, Dr. P. Cohen, Professor E. Kedourie and Mr. W. G. Forrest for their illuminating suggestions. I am particularly grateful to Mr. E. de Kadt, who made many helpful comments on some early drafts of portions of this work. I should like to record my special thanks to Professor Ernest Gellner, not only for his many suggestions and criticisms, but especially for his untiring help in matters of style and presentation. My shortcomings in these and other respects are not for lack of advice.

It is the business of the legislature to follow the spirit of the nation, when it is not contrary to the principles of government; for we do nothing so well as when we act with freedom, and follow the bent of our natural genius.

Montesquieu, *The Spirit of the Laws* 19

At tibi fortassis, si—quod mens sperat et optat—
Es post me victura diu, meliora supersunt
Secula; non omnes veniet Letheus in annos
Iste sopor! Poterunt discussis forte tenebris
Ad purum priscumque iubar remeare nepotes.

(For you however, if you should long outlive me, as my soul hopes and wishes, there is perhaps a better age in store; this slumber of forgetfulness will not last forever. After the darkness has been dispelled, our grandsons will be able to walk back into the pure radiance of the past.)

Petrarch, *Africa* IX

Behold, I will bring them from the north country, and gather them from the coasts of the earth, and with them the blind and the lame, the woman with child and her that travaileth with child together: a great company shall return thither.

They shall come with weeping, and with supplications will I lead them: I will cause them to walk by the rivers of waters in a straight way, wherein they shall not stumble: for I am a father to Israel, and Ephraim is my firstborn.

Jeremiah 31 (Authorised Version)

Introduction

> Our Rwenzururu, our Rwenzururu
> Our Rwenzururu, the land we cry for
> Where are you now?
> When we think of how you were
> Tears flow.
> Rwenzururu National Anthem

In 1962, a schoolteacher, Isaga Mukirane, established the Rwenzururu Kingdom Government in the southern mountains of the Toro District of Western Uganda. Rwenzururu was the name of the proposed separate District for which the inhabitants, the tribes of the Konzo and Amba, had vainly petitioned the Toro and Uganda governments.[1] So that Rwenzururu is part of the Toro District, which is itself part of Uganda. The whole area contained, in 1959, 103,868 Konzo, 32,866 Amba and 183,492 Toro, and the two minority tribes had resented Toro domination since the British introduced indirect rule by the Toro Agreement of 1900. The Toro supplied the officials, the majority of the teachers and doctors; they held the best coffee-growing land; and the Toro language was used in courts and councils, schools and churches.

When the Toro Agreement came up for revision with the coming of Ugandan independence, and the Konzo and Amba petition was refused, a walk-out was staged from the local parliament and violence followed. This escalated into a full revolt, which had to be suppressed by the central government; and in 1967 all that remained was a handful of rebels in the inaccessible mountains, plus Mukirane's administrative system. The majority of the Konzo sympathised with the rebels, for in their eyes the word Rwenzururu symbolised freedom from the Toro.

This rebellion is typical of many 'failed' group revolts against foreign domination. It exhibits, in telescoped fashion, all the main features and stages of such rebellions. In the first phase, the Konzo are powerless. They dream of a justice in heaven which is denied them on earth—a modern, Christian heaven. Then a new mood of defiance is nurtured by a study of the community and its history. Teachers, clerks and farmers join Mukirane's and Bakombe's 'The Bakonjo Life History Research Rwenzori', a cultural society founded in the mid-1950's. This leads to the reformist demand for equal status with the Toro, through constitutional means. The reformists still ape Toro manners in the hope of acceptance. Refusal brings violent reaction, and open rebellion marks the third stage. Finally, defeat begets a return to the old dream in the phase of withdrawal in the mountains and the Semliki forest; only this time, the Christian imagery has lost its power, and the rebels dream of justice in their kingdom promised at the end of the nineteenth century.

The Konzo revolt poses two questions: can we characterise it as another of the many nationalist movements throughout the centuries, from the Zealots and Marathon to Anguilla and al-Fatah? If so, why has it emerged at this particular time and in this form? How shall we explain the incidence and variety of all the movements for an ideal state of freedom and justice on earth, of which Rwenzururu is one example? In a dramatic form, the Konzo rebellion poses the problems of definition and explanation of nationalism. [2]

In the world today, there are well over a hundred actual Rwenzururus, if thereby we mean the member states of the United Nations. Each possesses its flag, anthem, administration, educational system, army, judicial system, legislature, citizenship rights, founding myth and constitution, coinage and capital. The nation-state is the norm of modern political organisation; and it is as ubiquitous as it is recent. The nation-state is the almost undisputed foundation of world order, the main object of individual loyalties, the chief definer of a man's identity. It is far more significant for the individual and for world security than any previous type of political and social organisation. It permeates our outlook so much that we hardly question its legitimacy today. The nation-state has become an indispensable prop in our thinking, and we tend to regard nations like skin-colour—as a 'natural' attribute of man. When we talk of 'society' today, we refer implicitly to 'nations'.

Plainly, nationalism is important—both as a social and political phenomenon, and as an object of sociological investigation. Add to this the obvious and critical role that nationalist movements have played in recent history—their impact on the political map, their utilisation in major and minor wars, the impetus they have given to social and economic development, and so on—and one can only be amazed at the comparative lack of sociological interest and research in this field. Sociologists from Comte and Marx to Parsons and Dahrendorf have neglected nationalism; and even today it has not become a major locus of sociological interest. Perhaps this is because the field was pre-empted by historians, or because the classical sociologists preceded the era of new states, which has aroused such curiosity among the political scientists. Perhaps the area seemed to be unpromising for a discipline that conceives its task to lie in producing far-ranging generalisations. Alternatively, the classical emphasis on stratification within societies diverted attention from the vertical differentiae which create national solidarities.

Of course, nationalism is by no means the only or most important force at work in contemporary politics or society. Men are motivated by many other considerations, and their allegiances are not exclusively directed to the nation-state. And even when they are, they often have a good deal of choice as to *which* state and nation is their true one. Even with the decline of the extended family in the West, the individual's attention and loyalty is bound up with other units—trade union, professional association, political party, church, social club, sub-culture, etc. But in recent history nationalism as a movement and ideology has become increasingly prevalent and perhaps dominant, even over communism.[3] The nation-state form of political organisation is not only the desired and normal unit of government and society, but has assumed an increasingly significant role in the lives of individuals and groups, through its regulative, cognitive and emotional attributes.

The question of the 'limits' of nationalism is closely related to attitudes of the observer towards the phenomenon. Perhaps in no field is it more necessary to take account of biases and value orientations in Weber's sense. I have indicated why I think the topic merits systematic and prolonged investigation. It is not always easy to avoid such biases in regard to some of the approaches and 'theories' of nationalism, which themselves take up rather extreme positions and attitudes. My choice of the whole subject has been influenced by the considerations outlined above and the belief that sociological theory can (and ought to) throw light on the causes and consequences of nationalism, as well as by experiences which have convinced me of the importance of the subject-matter in the social and political fabric of the contemporary world.

Despite the obvious difficulties in this field, I agree with Kedourie that it is illegitimate to categorise and judge the tenets of one ideology by those of another. [4] In any case, the main focus of this work is sociological: the relation of nationalism to economic development and social and cultural modernisation, in the conviction (which I hope to support) that nationalism is deeply embedded in this wider trend.

This is not the only reason for what the reader may consider a surprising omission—I mean, the absence of reference to Fascism. There is considerable difficulty in deciding whether Fascism and especially racism and Nazism are really just further developments of nationalism, or rather quite different ideological movements. Clearly one's overall attitude to nationalism will be affected by the decision. One factor in deciding against the inclusion of Fascism, etc., from the definition of nationalism has been the desire to limit the scope of this work. Fascism and Nazism pose a whole new range of questions for sociological theory, and this has been recognised by the separate treatments of Neumann, Lipset, Parsons and Kornhauser. There is no doubt that traditional nationalism is one ingredient of the Fascist constellation; but the other ingredients and the whole tenor of Fascist regimes and movements seem to me to be more important and even overriding (that is, where 'Fascism' is being used in a strict sense rather than as a term of abuse). Close inspection of the respective movements reveals the difference in their total outlooks and activities, their assumptions and character—both on an ideological and a sociological plane. For those reasons, Fascism requires separate consideration. It is a distinct movement, though linked with nationalism (see Appendix B).

In a work of this kind, it is even more important than usual to define the basic problem and delimit the field. The first man to deal with nationalism in any systematic manner was very conscious of this need. Of the subject 'of this Book' (Book 19 of *The Spirit of the Laws*, entitled 'Of Laws in Relation to the Principles which form the general spirit, the morals and the customs of a nation'), Montesquieu writes:

> This subject is very extensive. In that crowd of ideas which presents itself to my mind, I shall be more attentive to the order of things than to the things themselves. I shall be obliged to wander to the right and to the left, that I may investigate and discover the truth.[5]

In a field in which single case studies proliferate, and where the only really general studies have been narrative and chronological, we require a critical examination of approaches and of the forms of nationalism, pitched at a sufficiently abstract level to contribute to further research and suggest new connections. And if that goal is too ambitious at this stage, then perhaps the present work may at least lead others to question established conceptions and revise old approaches.

An important methodological assumption has guided the formulation of my basic problem. The plasticity of ideology has been a generally accepted sociological tenet. Ideologies are regarded largely as flexible legitimations for the activities of social groups, whose 'real' motivations lie in unsuspected places, inaccessible to all but sociologists. The view that men might actually fight wars or exclude each other from jobs and resources for the reasons they profess is only recently gaining a slight measure of respectability among sociologists. That ideological reasons might figure among these acceptable causes is still regarded as a concession to old-fashioned idealism. This may be a further ground why sociology, when it has concerned itself with our field, has been more interested in the growth of *nations* or national solidarities, as opposed to other kinds of integration, than with the impact and emergence of the ideological movement called *nationalism*.[6]

It may, of course, be asked whether the two processes, the growth of nations and the rise of nationalism, can be separated. I shall argue that it is both possible and desirable to do so—mainly on methodological grounds. Nationalism, in its main outlines, has shown remarkable staying power. It is an ideological movement which has continually reappeared in new guises—liberal, traditionalist, socialist, etc.—and won out. Nationalism has been one of the most influential of the various doctrinal constellations that have vied for men's loyalties since the erosion of traditional religion. Despite protean local variation, it has reappeared as a consistent set of demands and beliefs with regard to political and social arrangements.[7]

The nationalist movement, then, forms the referent for this investigation and review. Nationalism is treated as a distinct ideological variety of social and political movement, with a definite 'directional tendency', a recognisable profile and thrust.

The problem that forms the kernel of my argument can be formulated now as follows: Under what conditions and by what mechanisms do nationalist movements arise?

To explain the recurrent emergence in many parts of the world of such a movement, one must first, however, have formed a clear idea of the main features of such movements. One must therefore also ask:

What is the character of nationalism, as a movement? This is the familiar and vexing, but unavoidable, question of definition of nationalism, about which there has been so much theoretical debate. What matters is not the originality but the usefulness of the delineation of the main features of nationalist movements and whether it has heuristic utility and analytic clarity for the real problems of explanation which are the interesting ones; in particular, whether they illuminate the relationship between nationalism and that complex of trends and processes which can be conveniently labelled 'modernisation'.

The primary aim of this work is to demonstrate the intricate and profound nexus of relationships between types of nationalism and the processes of modernisation. For the variety of nationalist movements is one important indicator of the complexity of modernisation, while at the same time contributing to that complexity. To achieve credibility any theory of nationalism must take these processes as their indispensable starting-point. Beyond this very general contention, I have tried to select those aspects of the processes of modernisation which I think are most potent in generating certain nationalist ideologies and movements. Perhaps it may be possible to build upon these suggestions later and attempt to verify or specify them in concrete instances.

Chapter One

THE DOCTRINE AND ITS CRITICS

The prevailing image of nationalism in the West today is mainly
negative. As a result of two world wars and the Nazi horrors, it
has lost much of its former appeal. In the more secure Anglo-Saxon
countries, where there was no special need to emphasise a doctrine
of self-determination for the oppressed, the predominant long-
term trend is towards consolidation and retrenchment. Insofar
as nationalism is seen to be subversive of existing social structures
and political orders, it is regarded with increasing suspicion. Even
the initial wave of support for the anticolonial nationalism of the
new states of Africa and Asia has ebbed. The former democratic
regimes of these states have been overturned and replaced by
military or presidential dictatorships, and the initial sympathy
with the efforts of the underprivileged coloured peoples to throw
off colonial domination has cooled.

Critics of nationalism have grown more vociferous, and the
tone of the debate on the place of revolutionary activity in backward countries has become more acrimonious. This is largely
because the aspirations of nationalists have become part of the
larger struggle of the superpowers using an ideological language
which has little to do with nationalism. Nationalism in the
developing countries is increasingly the pawn in the global
struggle between sympathisers of communism of the Maoist

variety, and upholders of the pro-American traditional regimes. In Europe, on the other hand, nationalism is reviled as much as it is practised, because in the Cold War stalemate it is held to be unrealistic and passé—and politically dangerous. All of which is quiet testimony to the continued attraction it exerts for large numbers of people.

his negative evaluation, Tespecially among the Western intelligentsia, contrasts with the favourable attitude of nineteenth-century liberals and radicals, and later conservatives, towards the doctrine of national self-determination. This attitude is summed up in the famous passage of Mill:

> It is, in general, a necessary condition of free institutions that the boundaries of government should coincide in the main with those of nationality. . . . Where the sentiment of nationality exists in any force, there is a *prima facie* case for uniting all the members of the nationality under the same government, and a government to themselves apart. This is merely saying that the question of government ought to be decided by the governed. One hardly knows what any division of the human race should be free to do, if not to determine with which of the various collective bodies of human beings they choose to associate themselves.[1]

This favourable judgment, notwithstanding some qualifications, was also evinced by Renan in his equally celebrated essay of 1882, and it was translated into action in Wilson's Fourteen Points at the Versailles Peace Conference.[2]

The Conservative critique

The earliest warning on the dangers inherent in nationalist doctrine was given by Lord Acton. In his essay on Nationality (1862), he declared:

> Nationality does not aim at either liberty or prosperity, both of which it sacrifices to the imperative necessity of making the nation the mould and measure of the State. Its course will be marked with material as well as moral ruin, in order that a new invention may prevail over the works of God and the interests of mankind.[3]

Many historians have been guided by this Actonian tradition, and their views have received powerful expression in the recent attack on nationalism by Kedourie.

Kedourie regards nationalism as one of the most pernicious doctrines to have been inflicted on a long-suffering humanity. He holds that it is an antiquarian irrelevance, a baneful invention of some misguided German philosophers supported by the frustrations of obscure middle-class writers, low-born sons of artisans, farmers and pastors. True, there was the example of the French revolutionaries at hand; but the real doctrine of national self-determination was elaborated in the first decades of the nineteenth century by Fichte and his followers, in their egoistic and idealist emendations of Kant's notion of autonomy.

The new doctrine of nationalism is profoundly subversive of all political order. It introduces, according to Kedourie, an extremist style into politics. Formerly, conflicts had arisen over rival claims to territory or dynastic succession; they had been conflicts of interest, and therefore subject to compromise. Now nationalism 'represented politics as a fight for principles, not the endless composition of claims in conflict'.[4] Nationalism confuses principles with interests. It makes conflicts that much less amenable to a negotiated peace, because men will not compromise over principles. The results of nationalism are largely negative: instead of peace, prosperity and freedom 'it has created new conflicts, exacerbated tensions, and brought catastrophe to numberless people innocent of all politics'.[5] Nationalism, therefore, cannot survive what Kedourie considers the 'only criterion capable of public defence', namely, 'whether the new rulers are less corrupt and grasping, or more just and merciful, or whether there is no change at all . . .'.[6] This German doctrine is not to be confused, argues Kedourie, with what he calls the Whig doctrine of nationality, which is founded on Locke's idea of individual rights, and finds its classic expression in the passage of Mill quoted above. Whigs wanted self-government, because 'people who are self-governing are likely to be governed well'; whereas what Kedourie dubs the 'Continental theory' claimed self-determination, because 'people who live in their own national states are the only free people'. This is a crucial distinction which the peacemakers at Versailles blurred—with all-too familiar consequences.[7]

Kedourie's critique of nationalist doctrine does not stop at its pernicious consequences. Nationalism, he holds, is logically absurd. It claims that political boundaries should be determined by linguistic considerations. The boundaries of a state must be made to coincide with the boundaries of a group of people who speak the same language. The state must be coextensive with the 'nation', and the 'nation' can only be ascertained by a linguistic criterion. Hence the nineteenth-century passion for censuses, hence all the agitation of nationalists seeking to increase the number of those whom they could present as speaking the desired language.

But this kind of leap from anthropological premisses to political conclusions is unwarranted. Since when, asks Kedourie, has language been regarded as a relevant criterion for decisions about political arrangements? It is illegitimate to make political obliga-tion dependent on cultural criteria. It simply does not follow that men ought only to obey the government when it reflects the 'nation', i.e. when state and language-group are coextensive and the rulers speak the same language as their fellow-citizens. Is language in some sense more 'natural' than territory, religion, war or dynastic arrangement?

> There is no convincing reason why the fact that people speak the same language or belong to the same race should, by itself, entitle them to enjoy a government exclusively their own. For such a claim to be convincing, it must also be proved that similarity in one respect absolutely overrides differences in other respects.[8]

Language had never before been a political issue, and to make it one, is to make the orderly functioning of a society of states extremely difficult, because it opens the way to 'equivocal claims and ambiguous situations'.[9]

Sometimes, nationalists reveal the true nature of their doctrine. Achad Ha'am, the Zionist thinker, admits that what really counts for the definition of a nation is subjective feeling. A nation 'is what individuals feel in their hearts is the nation', and appeals to philology or biology are really superfluous. For Achad Ha'am, the spirit of nationality, once formed, is independent of

> external or objective actuality. If I feel the spirit of Jewish nation-ality in my heart so that it stamps all my inward life with its seal, then the spirit of Jewish nationality exists in me; and its existence is not at an end even if all my Jewish contemporaries should cease to feel it in their hearts.[10]

This reveals that nationalism is ultimately based on will; and will alone cannot serve as the foundation of a state. Renan is right: the nation is truly a 'daily plebiscite', and a 'political community which conducts daily plebiscites must soon fall into querulous anarchy, or hypnotic obedience'.[11] From this Kedourie concludes that 'national self-determination is, in the final analysis, a determination of the will, and nationalism is, in the first place, a method of teaching the right determination of the will'.[12] Nationalism annihilates freedom in the service of the state. It is a form of political messianism which 'looks inwardly away from and beyond the imperfect world'. Nationalism is 'a passionate assertion of the will, but at the core of this passion is a void, and all its activity is the frenzy of despair; it is a search for the unattainable which, once attained, destroys and annihilates'.[13]

Kedourie's portrait of the nationalist is sharply opposed to the nationalist self-portrait. Instead of the heroic educator of his people, we see a fanatic unable to come to terms with a corrupt world. In place of the leader entrusted with a sacred mission, addressing the erring, slumbering nation like some ancient prophet and inveighing against the psychic deformities induced by mechanical oppression and an overdose of artificial rationalism, we are faced with the secular successor of the messiahs of the millennial movements, trying to institute a reign of justice on earth, only to compound its miseries by raising more intractable problems. Heine's words were only too prophetic:

> There will be Kantians forthcoming who in the new world to come will know nothing of reverence for aught, and who will ravage without mercy, and riot with sword and axe through the soil of all European life to dig out the last root of the past; there will be well-weaponed Fichteans on the ground, who in the fanaticism of the Will, are not to be restrained by fear or self-advantage, for they live in the Spirit.[14]

The ethics of nationalism

This is a severe indictment of nationalism. So severe and contemptuous as to make one wonder why it has succeeded to the extent it has. But before turning to the question of explanation on which Kedourie has some original suggestions, I should like to consider briefly both the ethical and the logical criticisms of nationalism, and to show why I think they are founded on a fundamental confusion.

Let us, to begin with, take for granted Kedourie's portrait of nationalist doctrine as founded on the two ideas of language and the will of the people. To attribute to this doctrine purely iniquitous consequences is a grossly one-sided misrepresentation.

It assumes in the first place that the age preceding nationalism knew nothing of principles, and that its conflicts were simply motivated by gain—territorial, economic or political. This will hardly do for the Wars of Religion in the sixteenth and early seventeenth centuries. Nor for the Crusades, and the subsequent resistance to the Turks' encroachments in Eastern Europe. In all these cases, we see that typical intertwining of interest with ideology which characterises conflicts in the nineteenth century.[15] One thinks too of the many millenarian pogroms, the sectarian struggles of the Middle Ages, the use of imperial Rome to legitimate the actions of the Emperors. In the pre-classical ancient world, most wars were undertaken to increase the gods' power, and the modern cynicism of a Thucydides is exceptional even in ancient Greece. Political power was inextricably bound up with religious belief; if the latter did not have any hold over the mass of the population, why should rulers and rebels alike take such pains to invoke religious favour?

There is, therefore, no sharp contrast between a pre-modern age of 'interests' and a modern post-Revolutionary one of 'principles'. It is merely the *content* of the principles invoked that has dramatically changed.

The second criticism of Kedourie's picture of the effects of nationalism is that it overlooks completely the advantages and blessings of nationalist revivals. If we are going to attribute advantages and disadvantages to doctrines *tout court*, then we might as well recall the inspiration that patriotism and nationalism as a sentiment have provided in the field of culture. It has led to philological and historical research, and to literary renaissances; it has inspired composers and artists from Mussourgsky, Dvorak and Chopin to David and Delacroix. To pick upon the excesses of nationalism fervour, as Kedourie does, while ignoring its humanising and civilising influence, is misleading. The smaller-scale but noteworthy renaissances that have arisen in Africa, the Middle East and India, with nationalism as a constant leitmotif, are too important to be dismissed in this manner.[16]

Thirdly, Kedourie selects those features of nationalism—the movement and the ideology—which stress the elements of secret conspiracy, terrorism, ruthless reprisals against collaborators, and above all, a restless nihilism and totalitarianism. Nobody would dispute that these have been features of some nationalisms, particularly in the strife-torn Balkans. But it is only fair to recall the extreme situations in which they operated. The ruthlessness of the Dashnaks or the Macedonian IMRO or the Carbonari in Italy pales before that of the Austrian or Ottoman or Czarist police and bureaucracy. But beyond this, Kedourie forgets the uses of nationalism in developing countries, the way in which they can legitimate new regimes desirous of maintaining political stability and keeping a fissiparous population under a single and viable harness. He forgets too the examples of nationalism providing an impetus to constitutional reform, as in India or Ottoman Turkey, not to mention its uses in legitimating sweeping social change and modernisation; the obvious examples are Japan, China and Kemalist Turkey.

All these one-sided exaggerations spring, we may claim, from that tendency to reify nationalist doctrine of which Acton's indictment is a striking example. Kedourie takes the assertions of nationalists seriously, perhaps too seriously; and in doing so obscures the real message behind the florid appeals of nationalist rhetoric, to which I shall return.

Now it is true that systems of ideas are not without causal force. They are not immune to moral judgment—even if Kedourie's own criterion of the virtues of an ideology is not the only one 'capable of public defence'. From the standpoint of a nationalist, or of a liberal, Kedourie's criterion seems to assume the perpetuation of that very institution of unaccountable government which they set out to destroy. Nationalism, along with other modern ideologies, is indeed not concerned with the mercy of the new rulers, but with bridging the gulf between rulers and ruled which has induced this fatalistic passivity.

The real difficulty, however, for any ethical evaluation of 'nationalism' is its protean character which, as more than one scholar has noted, eludes easy and wholesale judgments. It is this that makes the classic inventories of the 'blessings and curses of nationalism' appear so banal and *simpliste*. This does not mean, of course, that the analyst can be exempted from the task of evaluation; but it does require him to exercise more caution in regard to so complex a phenomenon.

Since there is indeed hardly a field so heavily impregnated with the analyst's value-orientations (not to mention overt value-judgments) as nationalism and the study of ideology, this is perhaps the moment to indicate briefly my own position. Overall, the attitude adopted is one of ethical ambivalence. The reason is this: there is, as I hope to show, an 'original' or 'core' doctrine of nationalism, but this is not the romantic-linguistic version which Kedourie castigates. This 'core' doctrine is in itself 'incomplete' and 'unstable'. That is, most of the movements conventionally labelled 'nationalist' exhibit an uneasy combination of assumptions, which taken by themselves are insufficient to furnish a complete account of the group's situation, such that a clear course of action can emerge. One has therefore to round out the core doctrine with more specific theories directed to the particular situation of one's group. These latter 'theories', however, tend to accentuate in a rather one-sided fashion a particular strand of the original doctrine, and our judgments are addressed to these and not to the core doctrine.

Germany furnishes the classic example of this process of elaboration and accentuation. One of the original ideas of the 'core' doctrine of nationalism is that of the 'naturalness' of nations. The German writers emphasised this aspect through an analogy with organisms until it appeared as if nations were part of a fixed law of natural evolution. Such determinist and evolutionist accretions, when taken to their logical conclusion, come into conflict with another aspect of the original doctrine, namely, its voluntarism.

These later, additional 'theories' are then used to justify certain political actions; and the 'nationalism' we see and judge is the specific manifestation at a particular historical juncture. These political actions are morally highly variegated; and whether we adopt a conservative or socialist, liberal or Marxist standpoint, we shall be forced into contradiction, if we make a *simpliste* ascription of all these concrete manifestations to the *unmediated* effects of 'nationalism'.

But, taking the core doctrine as a whole and without reference to its real or alleged consequences, we can say that nationalism appears as a not unreasonable application of Enlightenment principles to the complexities of modern polities and societies. The core doctrine is schematic and tentative; yet it constitutes a necessary condition for the search for realistic conditions of liberty and equality, not to mention democracy, in an already divided world.

The German version

So far I have accepted Kedourie's definition of nationalist doctrine as founded on the two pillars of language and collective self-determination. I want now to go further and suggest that this definition is misleading, and that Kedourie has confused the German Romantic version of nationalism with the core doctrine itself. It is then an easy step to his overall negative ethical conclusion, for the German version lends itself to such an indictment.

The version of nationalism elaborated by the German Romantics—notably Fichte, Schlegel, Schleiermacher, Arndt, Jahn and Muller—might be more accurately called the 'organic version'. It holds that the subject of history is the nation, a phenomenon at once unique, 'natural' and 'objective'. The nation stands over and above the individuals who compose it, and the members possess common mental characteristics which are objectively ascertainable and mark them off from non-members. 'Nature' itself has ordained this cultural individuality, and the proof of this is to be found in the manifest differences of language, customs, history, institutions, descent and religion. From these external differences we must infer a distinctive 'spirit' of the nation, with its own independent causal power. Such a spirit welds the parts of a nation into an organic 'whole', which turns an aggregate of individuals and elements into a unique seamless pattern, on which the parts in turn depend for their life and form.

The self-moving national spirit emerges only gradually from the accretions of prehistory, with its mass of cross-cutting dynastic, local, class and religious allegiances. These loyalties and the sequences of events which reveal them, would be incomprehensible without this assumption about the activities of the national soul, whose 'history' these events really constitute. Minogue has made a felicitous comparison between the Romanticist's tale of the nation's awakening after its long sleep and the fairy-tale of the sleeping beauty.[17] It is the nationalist's historical and philological researches and his educational and political efforts which restore the nation's spirit to self-conscious activity on the stage of history. The parallel misses one point: not an alien prince, but the nation itself, in the Romantic theory, determines itself. It assures for itself the conditions of its own rebirth. At a certain point in the historical process, it enters into self-consciousness, and in the struggle for autoemancipation its fetters and the false sentiments and consciousness of its members fall away. As Jahn says:

> In the whole history of a people, its holiest moment is when it awakens from its unconsciousness, and for the first time thinks of its old holy rights. A people which grasps its sense of nationality with pleasure and love can always celebrate its rebirth.[18]

The life of the nation is continual struggle, but once it has achieved the sovereignty of statehood, it has 'realised' itself in all its uniqueness. Secure in its historic destiny, it can set forth on its historic mission for the liberation of mankind from the slavery of cosmopolitan tyranny. Only then can the individual become truly free, since his autonomy is but the expression of that of his nation-state.[19]

The German 'organic version' of nationalism, then, is based on the principle that nations possess 'the capacity to shape destiny by the historic workings of the national will'.[20] It embraces three distinct notions: (1) that of cultural diversity, i.e. Herder's idea that the world has been divided into unique organic 'nations' or language-groups, (2) the notion of national self-realisation through political struggle, and (3) the idea that the individual's will must be absorbed in that of the organic state—both of these latter ideas being the peculiar contribution of Fichte. The result is an exclusive emphasis on education, which for Fichte becomes a political instrument for injecting national spirit, 'a reliable and deliberate art for fashioning in man a stable and infallible good will'—in his reformulation of Rousseau's advice to the Poles.[21]

The core doctrine

This is the German Romantic version of nationalism, which has been so historically influential in the shaping of nationalist movements in Eastern Europe and the Middle East. And this is the doctrine which Kedourie equates with nationalism *tout court*.

In his opening words, Kedourie supplies us with a definition of nationalism:

> Nationalism is a doctrine invented in Europe at the beginning of the nineteenth century. It pretends to supply a criterion for the determination of the unit of population proper to enjoy a government exclusively its own, for the legitimate exercise of power in the state, and for the right organisation of a society of states. Briefly, the doctrine holds that humanity is naturally divided into

nations, that nations are known by certain characteristics which can be ascertained, and that the only legitimate type of government is national self-government.[22]

This is an interesting definition. It makes no mention of language; the characteristics in question might be those of religion, descent, history or common institutions. Nations here are not identified with language groups or even cultures. Nor is there any mention of the idea of collective will as a force in itself, external to the sum of the wills of its members. Later on, Kedourie admits that different writers stress different characteristics of national distinctiveness, such as race;[23] and as we saw, he even concedes, when discussing the passage of Achad Ha'am referred to above, that language and culture are irrelevant for nationalist doctrine—which, in the case of the broad category of culture, goes rather too far in the opposite direction.

The important point is that nationalist writers and nationalist movements have emphasised every kind of cultural and other criterion in staking out their claims for their 'nation'. Mazzini pointed to Italy's unique geography, Tilak to India's worship of Kali, Blyden and Senghor to the blackness and spirituality of the African; and the early French nationalists were more impressed by their common laws and institutions than by any linguistic homogeneity. Indeed, most of the Enlightenment thinkers, as Kemilainen's careful study reveals, made the fundamental assumption that the world is divided into distinct and natural entities called 'nations', even if many went on to deplore the fact;[24] at the same time, they did not identify the 'nation' with either a linguistic community or with a 'daily plebiscite' based on a collective will.

Sociologically, too, a review of the factors influencing the demands of nationalists shows that language has its limitations. In Africa, the identity of the nation with language communities is rarely claimed, not only to prevent further 'balkanisation', but because the factors that could turn language into an integrative force—such as a written tradition and textual educational system—have been largely absent. In other cases, such as Greece, Israel, Burma, Pakistan and Indonesia, religion has been a more potent self-definer, and has provided a more subtle and solid foundation for national identity.[25] In general, the linguistic criterion has been of sociological importance only in Europe and the Middle East (to some extent); and a good case can be made for the seminal influence of Rousseau and Mill rather than Fichte or Herder in Africa and India.[26]

Kedourie, then, would appear to accept (1) that there is a true or 'naked' doctrine of nationalism and later explanatory accretions or 'theories'—for example, the German 'organic' version or the Whig 'theory of nationality';[27] and (2) that the linguistic criterion, like the racial, is one of these more florid commentaries. But by identifying elsewhere the linguistic (i.e. German 'organic') version with the true doctrine of nationalism, Kedourie is able to castigate the latter for the sins of the former—a tactic that does scant justice to the nationalist doctrine.

For Kedourie then denudes the original doctrine of nationalism of every vestige of meaning, by an act of foreshortening, of truncating and reducing the scope of its contentions. One of these contentions is that the world is divided into 'natural' nations. Taken literally, this is absurd. But such a literalist reading misses the essential *political* point behind nationalist thinking—and nationalism is first and foremost a political doctrine.

Nationalists recognised that the exercise of individual 'will' could never ensure freedom or stability for the community.[28] But, fortunately, men were not like individual atoms. They were embedded in historical ('natural' by a mistaken transference from Enlightenment categories) communities, which had evolved distinctive traits and institutions, i.e. 'national character'. These communities of distinctive habits and character ensured just that political freedom and stability, which the exercise of 'will' on its own would continually jeopardise. And we have therefore to set Renan's celebrated metaphor of the daily plebiscite in its context: his careful definition of the nation as an historical and purposive collectivity.

For nationalists, will and aspiration are predicated of the pre-existent nation. It is not your will and my aspirations that matter; it is the nation's, however embryonic. To Burke, Rousseau, Zimmerman, Jefferson, Bolingbroke and Montesquieu, as well for the German romantics and African and Asian nationalists today, nations are distinct and natural entities, which thereby embody the collective will. This balance which the doctrine achieves between the assumptions of national individuality and collective will is well expressed in a passage of Rousseau's *Projet Corse*:

La première règle que nous avons à suivre, c'est le caractère national; tout peuple a, ou doit avoir, un caractère; s'il en manquait, il faudrait commencer par le lui donner.[29]

This is the same balance which Weber brings out when he stresses that the sense of ethnicity and nationality is both political and cultural. He argues that language community is an insufficient basis for sustaining national identity, as is belief in common ancestry. What is crucial in defining it is political action:

> It is primarily the political community, no matter how artificially organised, that inspires the belief in common ethnicity. This belief tends to persist even after the disintegration of the political community, unless drastic differences in the custom, physical type, or, above all, language exist among its members.[30]

Nations are distinguished by the fact that the objective of their social action can only be the 'autonomous polity', a sovereign state of their own; and they derive their sense of community from historically specific political actions.

Kedourie, then, has emphasised the linguistic basis of nationalist doctrine and of nationality at the expense of the political; and I think he has done this because he prefers to see nationalism as a coherent and well-elaborated doctrine, such as is apparent in the writings of the German 'organic' version. But such an intellectualist approach fails to differentiate between what is common to the majority of those who are labelled 'nationalist' (or style themselves nationalists) and the accretions to this common stock which arose under specific social and political conditions in the case of each nationalist movement.

For we can, I think, distinguish a body of assumptions common to most examples generally included under the rubric of 'nationalism', a kind of *sine qua non* for all nationalists. Over and above these assumptions, there is a series of more extravagant and ambitious interpretations of specific writers—the Romantic version, the Whig doctrine, the religio-geographical theory of Mazzini, Maurras' 'integral' nationalism, Mickiewicz's identification of Poland with the suffering Christ, along with such elaborations as national mission', national 'soul', volkish exclusiveness, etc.; such accretions are not shared by all nationalists, but originate in the aspirations and locations of particular movements and groups.

The core nationalist *doctrine*, on the other hand, is constructed from a few far-reaching propositions:

1 Humanity is naturally divided into nations
2 Each nation has its peculiar character
3 The source of all political power is the nation, the whole
   collectivity
4 For freedom and self-realisation, men must identify with a
   nation
5 Nations can only be fulfilled in their own states
6 Loyalty to the nation-state overrides other loyalties
7 The primary condition of global freedom and harmony is the
   strengthening of the nation-state.[31]

It will be immediately apparent from this list of propositions
that nationalism, unlike Marxism, does not furnish a complete
theory of social change or political action. It does not even define
the 'unit of population proper to enjoy a government exclusively
its own'. This is exactly the point at which supporting 'theories'
are needed, to suit the occasion; and I would contend that
we ought not to take these additions at their face-value, but
see in them lines of action adapted to the situation of their
proponents. To do anything else, to mistake for example the
linguistic or 'organic' version for the core doctrine of nationalism, is to risk tilting at windmills and imposing on
nationalism a unity and rigour and completeness which it does
not possess.[32]

This *caveat*, however, should not be taken to imply that we have
carte blanche in dealing with the phenomenon of 'nationalism'.
Sketchy and incomplete as is the doctrine, it nevertheless reminds
men of an important nexus of conditions, social, cultural, political
and psychological, obtaining in the modern world, which we
neglect at our peril, and which must be incorporated by any more
general theory of socio-political phenomena if we wish to provide
a coherent and realistic account of our era. Nationalism expresses
and draws attention to certain forces at work in the actions and
beliefs of large numbers of people in all parts of the world, and
prescribes in roughest outline a programme of action for their
satisfaction.

To this doctrine corresponds a movement with distinct concerns. Identity, purity, regeneration, the 'enemy', historical roots,
self emancipation, building the 'new man' and the 'new community', collective sovereignty and participation—these are some

of the themes that recur endlessly in the literature of nationalism. They provide the chief impetus for the peculiar activities of nationalist movements: those philological, anthropological and historical researches of small coteries of intellectuals, the secret societies pressing for reform and independence, the reliance on censuses, the concern with symbols of solidarity—flags, anthems, frontiers, military parades, services for fallen heroes, shrines and museums, history textbooks, the 'head of state', the name of the country and its constitution, oaths and mythologies, passports, sanctions against treason, even flower and animal totems.[33] And behind it all, a ceaseless evaluation and measuring of self and the present with the 'significant other', with the mythical Golden Age, with the vague intimations of social utopia.

For nationalism may be described as the myth of the historical renovation. Rediscovering in the depths of the communal past a pristine state of true collective individuality, the nationalist strives to realise in strange and oppressive conditions the spirit and values of that distant Golden Age. The roots of the individual are buried in the history and ethos of his group, in its culture and institutions; and from these, and these alone, he can draw purpose and strength for the heroic deeds of the future. The Golden Age is not a blue-print; it does not lie outside time and the world. It is an ideal state, not a primordial one. The admired time is bounded by nature and history. But it is chosen not by detached empirical analysis but for the satisfaction of present yearnings for an ideal community.

Nationalism is a vision of the future which restores to man his 'essence', his basic pattern of living and being, which was once his undisputed birthright. It is not a mechanical linking of past to future in the chain of generations, not an evolution of the traditional into the modern. It is an attack on tradition and modernity alike, insofar as they obscure and distort the genuine relationship of man with nature and with his fellow-man. The true bond is a 'fraternal' one. All men will be nationalists in the day when they will recognise their identity in the active enterprise of 'love'. As Aflaq puts it, nationalism, the joyful acceptance of one's nation—an identity like one's name or physiognomy—is a fact that exists apart from any subjective reasons for assenting to it.[34] We may say this fact is a relationship of brotherhood which underlies contrary appearances. This is not the universal fraternity of Schiller and Beethoven, but a brotherhood born among those who have grown and suffered together, of individuals who can pool their memories under a succession of common historical experiences. That elusive third ideal of the French revolutionaries, fraternity, turns out to entail a re-reading of history, or better, prehistory. But now it is not property relations and class antagonisms that have thwarted and stunted man's self-realisation; the 'alien' elements that debase and denaturalise men are defined as everything that does not spring directly from the consciousness and will of the subjected community. The fraternal tie, the ideal of the future, can only emerge from the autonomous will, denied by the past.

So that, in the eyes of the nationalists, men will be fit for citizenship, they will be 'lovers of their city', only when they have been purified from the tyranny and corruption of epochs in which they were without dignity or roots.[35] The recovery of self-respect must be preceded by a return to 'nature'—'as in the days of old', when the community mirrored the conditions of nature and produced 'natural men'.[36] Of course, the community of the future will not replicate that of the Golden Age, but it will recapture its spirit and set man free to be himself. Universal peace will not be assured till each man is liberated, that is, until he finds his roots within the communities of nature into which the world has been divided in the course of history. Then men will understand the beneficent purpose which their prehistory concealed, that in these communities or 'nations', and these alone, can men realise their autonomy, potential and 'essence', and that this recognition entails the acceptance of national differences. The fraternity of individuals within the nation entails the brotherhood of nations within the world.

This brief outline of the aspirations and reasonings of nationalists reveals, perhaps, that the core doctrine of nationalism is something more than a mere 'doctrine of the will', but rather less than the full-blown Romantic theory of the national 'soul' expressing itself in purity of language which is the object of Kedourie's scorn. Fundamentally, nationalism fuses three ideals: collective self-determination of the people, the expression of national character and individuality, and finally the vertical division of the world into unique nations each contributing its special genius to the common fund of humanity. The doctrine leaves open the form of the self-determination as well as the content of the expression of national individuality. And that is what has endowed nationalism with its tantalising amorphousness, its doctrinal sketchiness and the multifarious nature of the movements' activities and goals.

Part One

THEORIES OF NATIONALISM

Chapter Two

THE IMITATION OF KANT

Historical theories of nationalism are predominantly diffusionist. They treat nationalism as an ideology with specific roots in post-medieval Europe and trace its development from small beginnings to its present position as one of the dominant forces in the world. The precise date of nationalism's genesis is a matter of dispute: Kohn tends to favour 1642, Acton the 1772 Partition of Poland, Kedourie 1806, the date of Fichte's famous Addresses to the German Nation in Berlin. Most, however, opt for 1789—with the proviso that the Revolution served merely to bring together the elements of the nationalist idea, which were brewing up throughout the previous two centuries.

Clearly different definitions of the concept nationalism are being employed in this dispute. Yet common to all the historical theories is the assumption of a specific European origin for an idea which has since been carried to other parts of the world in an inexorable process. Nationalism is a single, fairly clear ideology, whose origins can be pinpointed in space and time, and whose subsequent development and diffusion from its birthplace it is the duty of the historian to unfold.

Underlying this conception, we meet a further assumption: that certain ideologies possess an independent causal force, which is so potent that well-established structures and beliefs must crumble beneath its onslaught. At the root of the historian's picture of nationalism is the idea that we are face to face with another religion, and that 'religion is like the Black Death'. For good or ill, its appearance leaves men naked amid the debris of their former social orders, victims of a force which few comprehend but all need.

Historians here share with others a basic psychological assumption: men need to belong to some group. There is a universal craving for solidarity and security, and 'tribalism', in Popper's sense, satisfies this urge. Given the dislocations of industrialisation and urbanisation, what can be more natural than that men should wish to replace the sense of lost community by creating other groups more adapted to the new conditions? The common state of man is the closed society of the 'tribe';[1] and we do not have to appeal to Le Bon's crowd psychology or Trotter's 'herd instinct' to understand the deep psychic satisfaction that nationalism affords. It is this universal craving for security and belonging that underlies the historian's explanation (as opposed to his description) of both the origins and the widespread appeal of nationalism today.[2]

The common historical view, then, of nationalism assumes the following:

1 All men crave security and desire to belong to a human group of some kind
2 Nationalism is an ideology which creates new groups, which can substitute for the lost security afforded by the old
3 Its success consists, not only in its group-creating propensity, but in its destructive power, before which other beliefs and structures wilt.

Given the assumption that there is a universal 'need to belong', the mechanics of the spread of nationalism depend on the faculty of 'imitation'. In an age of increased communications through travel and the press, men experience a need to experiment with the ideas they encounter. Nationalism's widespread success is the outcome of the desire to imitate new ideas and ways. Nationalism—like democracy, science and monogamy—is an importation from the West. Once planted, the seeds of nationalism are carried back to fertilise lands which till then were blissfully unaware of its existence. Or, on the still less favourable analogy, the plague once caught sweeps irresistibly outwards to taint and disrupt perfectly stable and well-adjusted ways and institutions.

How is this process of imitation and importation effected? By a wave-like outward movement of the ideology from its French and English heartlands, using the medium of the tiny educated elites of more backward areas. According to Trevor-Roper's formulation, the seed was first planted in Germany, Hungary and Italy. From these 'historic' cases of nationalism, the intelligentsias of eastern and southern Europe borrowed their images and concepts and slogans; they served as models for the 'secondary' nationalisms of Serbia, Greece, the Czechs and Slovaks, the Jews and Ukrainians, the Poles and Rumanians, etc.[3] From there the tide of nationalism swept east into the Middle East, India and the Far East, till finally even Africa fell under its sway.

This classic picture of the spread of nationalism emphasises its Western origins and the 'alienity' of its content from the thought and sentiments of the populations and lands to which it was carried. The ideology is a quite new-fangled notion—half-understood, misapplied, distorted. The political thinking of the indigenous intelligentsia is purely derivative, and on the whole out of place in the local setting. The customary laments over the failure of the Westminster model in Asia and Africa are closely bound up with this stereotype of foreign students imbibing Rousseau, Marx and Mill at the Sorbonne or London School of Economics, only to miss the subtleties and nuances of their thought. Theories are mistaken for political slogans, and hypotheses are treated as straitjacketing doctrines, when the student returns to his traditional setting. Instead of judiciously selecting those aspects of what he has been taught which might be useful in advancing his society along the road of westernisation, the graduate rashly seeks its immediate implementation through direct imitation of Western ways and patterns. Nationalism, a Western doctrine, is now turned against the West and its colonial representatives. Psychological snubs and occupational discrimination in the colony only ignite the students' nationalistic fervour still more. Above all, the discovery that the Western rulers don't really believe in the values of liberalism and Christianity which they profess, but only in their imperialist mission, evokes a reactive nationalism which has the force of a situational imperative.[4]

The mechanism of 'imitation' is given a more sociological twist by the political scientists. They stress the role of mass literacy which accompanies the introduction of Western domination and commerce. The vehicle of nationalism and other Western ideas is the press, and later radio and television. A fairly regular correlation can be observed between the rise of nationalism and the mushrooming of local journalism. For example, Egyptian nationalism's emergence from the late 1870's onwards coincides almost exactly with the influx of Syrian writers like Nimr, Ishaq and Sarruf, and with the growth of an Arabic popular press, starting with journals like *al-Muqattam* and *al-Muqtataf*.[5] In Central Asia, papers like *Taraqyiy*, founded by the Tatar social revolutionary, Ismail Abidiy, or *Khurshid*, the offspring of the founder of the first Uzbek *jadid maktab* in Tashkent, Munawwar Qari, were symptomatic of the Turkestani awakening in 1906 following the abortive Revolution.[6] Chapman's leadership of the early Ewe national movement immediately after the Second War was aided by his articles on Anlo society and Ewe orthography in the new Ewe newsletter.[7] The evolution of Serbian nationalism from the late eighteenth century outside Serbia was strongly related to the publication of Serbian books and newspapers, especially from the 1790's in Vienna, Pest and Novi Sad;[8] and the growth of independence in Serbia proper coincided with supremacy of Serbian cultural work over the Habsburg centres by 1848.[9]

There is little doubt that the new possibilities in the field of communications helped to spread all kinds of ideas and practices that would otherwise have been the preserve of particular societies. But opportunity alone is an inadequate explanation of the appeal of a particular doctrine, nationalism, to a certain social group, the intelligentsia. It is to this double task that Kedourie's *theory* of nationalism, as opposed to his *definition* of the doctrine, addresses itself. For we are dealing here with two questions simultaneously: why is it that the intelligentsia is particularly affected that *it* becomes the medium of imitation, and why is it nationalism that proves so potent and attractive?

Philosophy and politics

The best way to approach both questions, and understand the success of nationalism, argues Kedourie, is by searching out the origins of nationalism in Europe. In that way, one can best appreciate its unique, destructive character, and the disturbing and bewitching influence the doctrine has managed to exert. The power of nationalism must be sought in the far-reaching implications of certain ideas at the very heart of European philosophical developments from the time of Descartes.

Why did nationalism arise, and why at the end of the eighteenth century? Basically, answers Kedourie, because of a revolution in European philosophy, and a breakdown in European society.

The first was the work of Kant. In epistemology, he had set out to oppose both metaphysical dogmatism and Hume's radical scepticism; but he ended by completely separating appearance and reality. Our knowledge, Kant contended, is based on sensations emanating from things-in-themselves; and the perceiving self, 'with the help of categories inherent in it, imposes a synthetic intelligible unity on what would, otherwise, remain a chaos of unrelated and incoherent impressions'. Yet, because these categories (including time and space) are logically prior to and independent of experience, 'we can never know things as they really are, as they exist in themselves independent of our observation'.[10]

In ethics, too, Kant effected a similar separation. If liberty and virtue are not to be mere illusions based on opinions, morality cannot be based on knowledge of the phenomenal world. Neither the will of God nor the natural world can be the source of moral value, for then man's freedom would disappear and morality become meaningless. Virtue depends on a continual struggle against the natural inclinations, and upon a free choice to obey the inward moral law or categorical imperative. Hence Kant's 'new formula' in ethics amounts to this: 'the good will, which is the free will, is also the autonomous will'.[11] The individual is here the self-determining centre of the universe. Even the existence of God depends on man's need for moral freedom; and true religion becomes for Kant's followers, Schleiermacher and Schlegel, simply the intuitive quest for man's perfection, and the spontaneous expression of a free will.

The political consequences of this ethical and epistemological dualism are far reaching. Self-determination becomes the supreme good. Explaining the excesses of the French Revolution he so admired, Kant maintained:

> One must be free in order to learn how to use one's powers freely and usefully. To be sure, the first attempts will be brutal, and will bring about a more painful and more dangerous state than when one was under the orders, but also under the protection, of a third party. However, one never ripens into reason except through one's own experiences, and one must be free in order to be able to undergo them.[12]

It follows that republicanism is the sole possible form of government, for only in a republic can the laws express the autonomous will of the citizens. And, just as in ethics, a man must fight his inclinations, so in politics, social action and development depends on the citizen's activism.

Of course, Kant was not a nationalist, nor was he responsible for the emendations of his followers. It was, in fact, Fichte who 'resolved' the philosophical difficulties raised by the Kantian doctrine in favour of a 'subjectivist' interpretation. Men after all do know how to distinguish reality from fantasy; they do generally agree about the features of a world independent of the senses. Surely, he argued, it must be because that world is a product of a universal consciousness or Ego (as opposed to Kant's individual consciousnesses), which guarantees its rationality and stability. The world is coherent because it is a manifestation of the Ego, it is 'an organic whole, no part of which can exist without the existence of all the rest'.

Fichte's subjectivism, when applied to politics, results in an organic theory of the state. 'In an organised body, each part continuously maintains the whole, and in maintaining it, maintains itself also. Similarly, the citizen with regard to the state.'[13] Now it is in the State, the true aesthetic polity, not the mechanical examples which disfigured Germany, that a man can achieve self-realisation; and an 'aesthetic' state is one which expresses the individuality of a nation. Furthermore, according to Kedourie, Fichte follows Herder in identifying 'true' nations with 'natural' ones, that is, language groups whose languages are pure. Now Herder had assumed that the supreme good for men is the cultivation of their identities, for spontaneity and diversity are the laws of nature and progress. What is purer and more revealing of the inner self than language—providing it is unmixed with elements from other languages? The result; that fatal equation of language, state and nation, which is the cornerstone of the German version of nationalism...

But this transformation in the realm of ideas was only possible, and influential, because of the accompanying upheaval in social life. Kedourie points to the low social status of the German romantics, as sons of pastors, artisans, and small farmers, whose upward mobility was blocked at the time. Of much greater significance, however, is the wider breakdown in the transmission of social and political habits. These men were driven to import philosophy into politics because society and state in eighteenth-century Europe seemed cold and heartless; not just the caste-bound suffocation of 'the provincial, narrow, philistine society of the German principalities, or of a Prussia which for all its official enlightenment was, at bottom, dependent on the harsh will of a strict master',[14] but in Schiller's words:

> an ingenious enginery, in which a mechanical life forms itself as a whole, from the patchwork of innumerable but lifeless parts. The state and church, laws and customs, are now rent asunder; enjoyment is separated from labour, the means from the end, exertion from recompense.[15]

A sense of grievance and a deep estrangement engulfed a Mazzini and Mickiewicz as much as Fichte or Arndt. There was, of course, the example and legend of the French Revolution. But what really caused the restlessness of this generation was the 'breakdown in the transmission of political habits from one generation to the next. In societies suddenly exposed to the new learning and the new philosophies of the Enlightenment and of Romanticism, orthodox settled ways began to seem ridiculous and useless.'[16] Nationalists turn not only against the foreigner, but also against their fathers whose otherworldly passivity offends against life and the spirit. As their names (Young Italy, Young Egypt, Young Turkey) imply, nationalist movements are 'children's crusades', and they

> are seen to satisfy a need, to fulfil a want. Put at its simplest, the need is to belong together in a coherent and stable community. Such a need is normally satisfied by the family, the neighbourhood, the religious community. In the last century and a half such institutions all over the world have had to bear the brunt of violent social

and intellectual change, and it is no accident that nationalism was at its most intense where and when such institutions had little resilience and were ill-prepared to withstand the powerful attacks to which they were exposed.[17]

In this confusing situation, the youth failed to perceive the critical fact of the 'ultimate incompatibility of philosophical speculation with the civil order', for this only became apparent with the swift and cheap dissemination of ideas provided by printing and journalism. Philosophical speculations fed the dangerous musings of the youth, and these could not be controlled because they formed part of the logic of the situation. 'They were inherent in the nature of things: they emanated from the very spirit of the age.'[18]

Ideas and structure

This is a powerful and original thesis. Kedourie rightly insists that nationalism should not simply be treated as a sub-variety of 'ideology'. He also rejects all kinds of sociological reductionism. Ideas can only be understood in the context of an intellectual tradition; he subscribes to Durkheim's dictum that ideas, 'once born, have a life of their own'. We should take the nationalists' cultural models seriously, and analyse the 'logic' of their systems of belief.

This is related in turn to the scrutiny of the intelligentsia's alienated situation. The attempt is made to understand their dilemma not just as a case of thwarted career aspirations and blocked mobility in a traditional setting that can no longer satisfy the westernised; more significant is their sense of inner exclusion, of a lost cultural patrimony, so that it is not merely the world about them, but their inner being, which is cold and lifeless. Kedourie traces their drive for mastery over a state machine moulded according to their image of self and society, to this inner emptiness projected outside.

Finally, a sociological basis is sought for this psychic malaise in a broader context of the worldwide undermining of long-established orthodoxies and cherished institutions. Clearly, in the case of a phenomenon so varied and complex as nationalism, some more general sociological trends necessarily enter into the explicans—especially the decay of legitimating beliefs which leaves the structures they once made meaningful to appear at best irrelevant, at worst oppressive. The strength of Kedourie's thesis derives from the brilliant manner in which he suggests the impact of this wider context.

The moment, however, we forsake the realm of intelligibility, of 'adequacy at the level of meaning', and demand satisfaction according to the canons of causal explanation, we are beset by difficulties. Is Kedourie's thesis an explanation at all, or merely an illuminating empirical tautology? If 'self-determination' is the essence of nationalism, how can Kant's doctrine in ethics constitute a 'cause', let alone the chief one? We require something more than the assertion that nationalism (=self-determination) corrodes traditional institutions whose breakdown further disarms societies against the nationalist virus.

The circularity in the argument is not avoided by an appeal to the apparently universal 'need to belong', which drives men to replace disrupted communities, at no matter what cost. I am not competent to judge the validity of arguments for a 'territorial imperative'.[19] But, even if borne out, they appear at variance with historical evidence (e.g. the Jews, gypsies, etc.). More important, the 'need to belong' explains too much: it precludes an answer to the historical problem, why only at certain times and places it was the *nation* which replaced the family, the religious community, the village, etc. Why does this need to belong appear to affect some and not others in a given population? How can we measure it, in relation to other factors? In nationalist literature, belonging is merely one among several themes, and then only in a quasi-utopian setting. Without these tests, the argument is a piece of circular psychologism: the need to belong is inferred from cases of strong nationalism, and the latter are then derived from a need which lacks any independent confirmation.

But the general tenor of Kedourie's argument, unlike that of other historians, eschews any determinism of needs. Instead, we are given an historical determinism of *ideas*, of the 'spirit of the age'. This provides the locus for a number of objections. First, there is Gellner's complaint about the excessive role attributed to Kant in the genesis of nationalism.[20] Even if Kedourie's interpretation of Kant's doctrine of autonomy is right, he allows it too much significance in the overall doctrine of nationalism and forgets Kant's debt to Rousseau. It is perhaps a certain intellectualism which makes Kedourie give primacy to Kant and Fichte over Rousseau, Herder, Bolingbroke and Burke; just as it seems to be a certain historicism (in the pre-Popperian sense) which relegates the early enlighteners and nationalists of eastern European and non-European countries to something like pale reflections of the 'originals' which they imitate after contact through travel, reading or study abroad.

Secondly, this latter mechanism of 'imitation' seems rather superficial and threadbare. Why is it nationalism, from all that the 'West' has to offer, that so affects the intelligentsia? One can grant that the dialectic of exclusion and belonging fits these individuals rather more closely than it does their compatriots; but can we really believe that the 'demonstration effect' of an idea like nationalism should possess, on importation, such power to destroy and re-create?

Closer inspection of the 'imitation mechanism' in Kedourie and others reveals a curious uncertainty over the concept itself. When one talks of X imitating Y (person or object), there is no clue as to whether the action is done consciously or not. This is presumably related to the issue of voluntarism. Do the students in London, Paris and New York consciously and voluntarily select certain of the offerings purveyed by their teachers, or do they succumb unconsciously to the contagion of ideas to which they are so insalubriously exposed? If the latter, one is left in the dark as to why it should be nationalism, rather than, say, constitutionalism or welfare socialism or Christian humility, that possesses them so exclusively. On this account, they should be equally affected by every new idea that comes their way; or we still have to render a special explanation, over and above the 'imitation mechanism', for their addiction to nationalism.

But the same argument applies, if we adopt the conscious, voluntarist meaning of 'imitation'. What is so attractive about nationalism that our students should always opt for this ideology, and treat other 'isms' and notions as secondary? Isn't the assumption necessary and present in all these accounts of 'imitation', that the students and travellers come already attuned to certain ideas and values? If so, then all that study abroad does is to clarify and underline this state of attunement. There is no question of actually imitating what is already felt and known before alighting on the Western shore. All that is copied, or rather selectively borrowed, is method—the various techniques for putting into effect what has already been internalised in the indigenous setting.

Of course, not all non-Westerners arrive with a commitment to nationalism. Many arrive with a fervent desire to westernise born of a new-found sense of humanity. Some remain still convinced of an ideology which they arrived at before coming. Others, thinking about the actual state of affairs obtaining in the world, fail to find confirmation of this conviction, and return to their communities with new convictions born of both thought and observation. But my point is that, whichever path they ultimately choose, it is chosen through a complicated process of reasoning, feeling and observation; a process that owes most to their socialisation and indigenous traditions, and the conflict of those traditions with the new ways of perceiving the world and acting in it. The minds of foreign students are not *tabula rasa*, ready to be enslaved by new-fangled ideologies against which they have no defence. They come to Europe painfully aware of the dilemma into which they have been born, and hoping to find in the West a way out of this difficult and challenging situation.

Kedourie cites the case of Korais (1748–1833) as the prototype of the 'marginal man', the alienated intellectual, who forsakes Smyrna for Holland in 1772, and Paris in 1789. Now Smyrna was as much a Greek as a Muslim town and its population was therefore exposed to different cultural influences. It hardly needed contact with the Dutch clergy there to stir his interest in the classical Greek past, which became his model. To Korais, the much-admired West had simply imitated Athens; hence 'imitating the West' is for modern Greece simply a return to her glorious past. [21] If nationalism was just a consequence of the diffusion of ideas through imitation we could not explain why Korais should have sought his model in classical Greece, since the French nationalists of the time were not terribly interested in their own primeval past.

There is a further difficulty with the diffusionist thesis. Why does nationalism become so effective for other groups in the population? Do they likewise imitate their educated elites, for the sake of power and status, perhaps? Scattered hints hardly suffice for so important a phase in the explanation of nationalism's appeal. [22]

But the major objection remains Kedourie's 'idealist' methodology, which alone makes sense of the subordinate mechanisms of imitation, belonging and chronological derivation. Analytically, his total account derives nationalism from the convergence of three contingent causal chains: the Kantian philosophical dualism, the exclusion of the German intelligentsia from the affairs of state, and the breakdown of traditional ways and stable communities. In practice, however, it is the *first* chain which bears the greatest weight, both in significance and causally; the political and social chains become dependent on the intellectual. I think this results from postulating a gulf between thought and action, between philosophy and politics. Kedourie claims that chance rules in the realm of politics, perhaps in social life. It has little place in speculative thinking, which thereby assumes an appearance of logical coherence which belies its partly social origins. The very detachment of philosophical reasoning from the chaos of everyday life lends it an aura of force; it seems a doubly potent weapon against crabbed society. This sharp contrast between philosophy and life sets the stage for Kedourie's crucial thesis: it is modern secular thought which is the chief solvent of traditional institutions.[23] The social factors become contributory (e.g. journalism), or intervening (e.g. exclusion of the intelligentsia), variables in what amounts to a single-factor explanation.

Were Kedourie merely asserting that, as a matter of procedure, an excellent point of departure for the analysis of nationalism is change in philosophical perceptions, there could be no objection. It is the implicit claim, however, that these changes furnish a basis for an overall theory, not just of German, but of *all* cases of nationalism, that is completely unacceptable. And it is this claim that lies at the root of the subsequent errors in the characterisation and explanation of the doctrine. Not only does Kedourie treat the evolution of German thought (which he has traced in some detail) as the main cause of German nationalism, bringing in other factors in a purely secondary role; he assumes the wholesale adoption of the results of this specifically German philosophical development by the intellectuals of other, often remote, areas, to account for the rise of nationalism elsewhere. The Kantian revolution is enacted everywhere. But the procedure here is deductive, and the only evidence consists of isolated statements showing an imitative affinity with Fichtean sentiments. What Kedourie has done is to trace an empirical sequence (the German) then to utilise it as an ideal-type process, and finally suppose it to be exemplified, with the minimum of 'local' concession, in *all* cases of emergent nationalism. But the ideal-type base-line is too narrow to support the weight of the overall theory, and the comparison with the empirical cases too mechanical.

What lends this procedure plausibility is the backcloth portrayal of the 'spirit of the age', an age of despair, of passionate disorientation, impelling the youth to clutch at any doctrine of revolutionary violence and messianic comfort. At the same time, we are told that this age is one of 'the new learning and the new philosophies of the Enlightenment and of Romanticism'. Now these intellectual forces, which undermine traditional ways, are generally held to be informed by an essentially optimistic spirit, a commitment to 'modernity' and a belief in the perfectibility of the world through man's rational mastery over his environment (*pace* Becker).²⁴ The despair and disorientation of the youth resulted from the tenacious resistance of traditional institutions to the new forces rather than from any insecurity or 'failure' of cultural transmission. The traditional groupings seemed oppressive, the conceptions underlying them obscurantist.

If then we drop this implicit intellectual determinism and this simplified picture of the age, we are left with a doctrine of nationalism which is indeed revolutionary, at times even 'messianic', yet a product of a greater variety of interests and more complex background than Kedourie indicates. Even the German variant of nationalism did not arise in such uniformly oppressive and hopeless conditions: one recalls the rise of an independent German tradition in literature and music in the eighteenth century, the growth of the press, the rise in living standards of the Protestant middle classes. This is sufficient to warn against inferring a uniform 'spirit of the age' everywhere from the development of a collective will to self-determination.

Kedourie's critique raises, though it disqualifies itself from answering, the difficult question of the precise mechanisms whereby ideas help to undermine existing structures. Why the break in their 'meaning', their gradual or sudden 'irrelevance'? Granted a breakdown in transmission of political habits and religious beliefs, how did it occur and why did it assume such significance at this juncture? Social change, sometimes rapid, has occurred before; traditional institutions and orthodox ways have been criticised frequently by the younger generation. Why did nationalism appear so sporadically in earlier eras? Does the recent onslaught on tradition possess a unique character? Kedourie suggests an inverse connection between the success of doctrines like nationalism, and the degree of 'resilience' and 'preparedness' of family, neighbourhood and religious community in the face of such attacks. Since this is the only test he provides, we need to know the criteria for deciding the degree of these variables, and the manner in which they may be 'operationalised'. May not family and religious ties also contribute to the strength and permanence of the nationalist venture, as opposed to, say, the socialist? And, if so, under which conditions?

These are a few of the pertinent problems raised by this account of the genesis of nationalism. Until at least some of these questions are answered, the conservative critique remains largely ideological.

For its mode of explanation employs the same fundamental categories as its definition of the doctrine: moral judgments drawn from a religious framework. For Kedourie as for other conservatives, the real culprit in the birth of doctrines like nationalism is secular pride: the dangerous desire for epistemological and moral certainty which can satisfy human reason, in an imperfect world. Revolutionary rationalism is the genuine modern heir of the absurd, because inherently unattainable, chiliasm of the medieval millenarians dreaming of terrestrial social justice.[25] 'Pride', like 'will', is a religious, not a psychological concept, and it belongs to an entirely different mode of discourse to that of social and political analysis. It is redolent with the moral pessimism of traditional religious outlooks, with their low estimate of human nature and limited political horizons. The nationalist passion for the unattainable is 'empty' only because it dares to bridge the gulf between God and man and thereby destroy the traditional image of the cosmic order.

The failure to find a convincing explanation to support the conservative ideological critique is, I think, evidence of the deeper failure of communication between the religious and nationalist outlooks, which always sound so hollow and superficial when attempting to comprehend each other.

Chapter Three

THE RELIGION OF MODERNISATION

Contemporary sociological theories of nationalism start from the notion of 'modernisation'. Most of them see the movement as a subspecies of ideologies which erupt from and expand this overall process, and it is with these that I am concerned here. Those which emphasise the role of nationalism and the growth of nation-states as a *central* part of the process will receive more detailed treatment later.

A convenient point of departure is the familiar sociological distinction between the so-called 'integration model' of society and the so-called 'conflict model'.[1] Briefly, the former addresses itself to the problem of persistence: how can social forms and relationships endure? Logically the explanation of persistence entails that of change; therefore if we could only state the determinants of social structures, we would be in a position to account for movement, revolution and the birth of new structures. The conflict model, in contrast, assumes flux, movement and process as the social norm; inertia, not change, arrested development rather than revolution, require special explanation.

Theories of nationalism and modernisation which hold to the persistence perspective regard them as products of the breakdown of traditional communities. Nationalism is one of a class of sociopolitical movements whose matrix is the disintegration of traditional structures. Ideologically, 'disintegration' theorists share Kedourie's conservative assumptions; methodologically, however, their 'sociocentrism' stands at the opposite pole to his 'idealism'.

Differentiation

The disruption of traditional communities is often viewed as the inevitable outcome of the process of structural differentiation. Both Smelser and Eisenstadt hold that a high degree of role and functional specialisation is an essential attribute of a 'modern' structure.[2] In traditional communities, the same unit fulfils many functions. Role relationships are diffuse and face-to-face; statuses are largely ascriptive; and communities are small-scale, solidary and fairly isolated. The social cohesion and permanence of these communities depends on conditions of subsistence, an agrarian economy and a low, relatively stagnant level of technology. A modern society, by contrast, possesses a variety of organisations with highly specialised functions and roles. Men live in large, impersonal groups, loosely bound together by a complex division of labour. Relationships are 'segmental' and ephemeral; that is, only a part of the self is involved in any one relationship.[3] Status is largely achieved, values are, theoretically at least, universal. Modern society is based on large-scale mechanised industrial production and a market-oriented agriculture; and it supports an expanding population seeking urban employment.

Modernisation is the more or less painful transition from the 'traditional' to the 'modern' type of society. Modernisation can be broken down into three analytically distinct processes: differentiation, reintegration and disturbance. They can be defined as follows:

1 'Structural differentiation' is defined as

> a process whereby one social role or organisation . . . differentiates into two or more roles or organisations which function more effectively in the new historical circumstances.[4]

These new units are structurally distinct, but functionally equivalent to the original unit. Whereas a single unit performed many functions, now the latter are fulfilled by separate units.

2 If centrifugal differentiation continues unabated, there is a risk

that all social ties will disintegrate. To prevent this, modernisation creates mechanisms of 'reintegration' which coordinate the new units, norms and activities. New institutions, e.g. unions, parties, welfare agencies, arise to solve experimentally these problems of reintegration. Eisenstadt sees these 'mass consensual' tendencies as

> rooted in the growing impingement of broader strata on the centre, in their demand to participate in the sacred symbols of society and their formulation, and in the replacement of the traditional symbols by new ones that stress these participatory and social dimensions.[5]

3 Reintegration is not achieved without costs. Differentiation produces *dislocation* and conflict, especially national conflict. The new groups mass at the centre, they become more salient and visible for each other, and more estranged from the *status quo*. The result: panics, crazes, movements, even crystallised contracultures—every variety of 'dissensual formation'. Protest movements are no mere local rebellions. In modern society, they involve all major groups, and seek a total transformation of the society and its values. One important theme of protest is nationalism,

> a search for new common symbols in which various groups of the society could find some sense of personal and collective identity.[6]

Nationalism, for Eisenstadt, links the community's tradition with the modernising process. It does this by forging roles which unite universal with particularistic orientations to underpin the civil order.

Smelser's account is a little more elaborate. One can describe the modernising situation as a three-way tug-of-war between the forces of tradition, differentiation and integration. The experience of rapid change brings inevitable conflicts and violent discontinuities. It is people who are most dislodged from the securing ties of the traditional order who feel particularly drawn to collective movements, and this is because their promise of a new dispensation and ideal harmony is designed to short-circuit the very real problems of the situation.

One such promise is nationalism. As an impetus to economic development, it is more potent than the Protestant ethic. Smelser cites Davis' judgment approvingly:

> With the world organised as it is, nationalism is a *sine qua non* of industrialisation, because it provides people with an overriding, easily acquired, secular motivation for making painful changes. National strength or prestige becomes the supreme goal, industrialisation the chief means. The costs, inconveniences, sacrifices and loss of traditional values can be justified in terms of this transcending collective ambition. The new collective entity, the nation-state, that sponsors and grows from this aspiration is equal to the exigencies of industrial complexity; it draws directly the allegiance of every citizen, organising the population as one community; it controls the passage of persons, goods and news across the borders; it regulates economic and social life in detail. To the degree that the obstacles to industrialisation are strong, nationalism must be intense to overcome them.[7]

Smelser then distinguishes the early stages of nationalism when it fosters change and economic advance from its later tendency to retard growth by reaffirming traditional values, generating irrelevant anticolonialist sentiment and encouraging expectations of ready-made prosperity. Why is nationalism then so Janus-like? The clue lies in the logic of the differentiation process, not the analysts' value-orientations:

> In the early phases of modernisation, many traditional attachments must be modified to permit more differentiated institutional structures to be set up. Because the existing commitments and methods of integration are deeply rooted in the organisation of traditional society, a very generalised and powerful commitment is required to pry individuals from these attachments.[8]

But later, the very success of nationalism breeds the conditions of its demise. Further differentiation secularises society: the values of each of life's spheres gradually lose their sanction by religious and ideological values:

> As a society moves increasingly towards more complex social organisation, the encompassing demands of nationalistic commitment give way to more autonomous systems of rationality.[9]

Nationalism is an example of what Smelser terms 'value-oriented' movements. That is, it aims at a total reconstitution of the core values and underlying beliefs of the society, and not a partial reform of rules, norms and prescriptions. In order to mobilise those who suffer under an acute sense of deprivation, it employs a generalised belief, in which

> the environment is portrayed in terms of omnipotent forces, conspiracies and extravagant promises, all of which are immanent.[10]

These all-embracing beliefs only exercise sway in conditions of 'strain'. That is, the situation has to be sufficiently disruptive of established habits and ideas that groups of the 'unattached' crystallise and seek outlets for their frustrations and personality disequilibrium. The probability of extremist outbursts is maximised under vacillating rule and ambiguous social controls. But, in general, the responses of anxiety, hostility and fantasy which nationalism expresses so concisely, are at their most intense when the forces of tradition clash with the inexorable processes of differentiation and reintegration.

The natural community

Despite some differences of emphasis, Smelser and Eisenstadt belong to the 'neo-evolutionary functionalist' school of sociological thinking. Their model of modernisation shares certain assumptions:

1 Institutions have a built-in tendency to generate changes adaptive to the environment in the direction of increasing complexity

2 Modernisation implies a society's capacity for self-sustaining growth, and the absorption of the changes it generates through mechanisms of reintegration

3 The failure to modernise produces imbalances and 'malintegration' of the groups and sectors in a society; this in turn brings social eruptions and protest movements

4 Ideologies like nationalism can help to bridge the gap between a precontractual *Gemeinschaft* and a *Gesellschaft* based on calculation of interest; but their utility is in inverse ratio to their success.

The model has a distinguished ancestry. In Durkheim's theories, the division of labour is the fundamental element in the transition from a 'mechanical' to an 'organic' type of solidarity.[11] In the former type of society, men share a common set of beliefs, sentiments and values, which over the generations is congealed into the 'conscience collective'. The force of custom and tradition in solidary, small-scale communities allows little room for alternative loyalties and conceptions. On the other hand, 'organic' integration rests on the complementarity of tasks and role expectations in groups with a high degree of specialised labour; and it is this organisation which solves the problem of the perennial conflicts which spring from intense economic competition arising when the range and frequency of social relationships rapidly expands.

Yet this account appeared over-optimistic, when compared with the increasing problems of industrial society. These societies undoubtedly fell at the 'organic' pole of his ideal-typical continuum; why then the sectional and occupational conflicts, the economic fluctuations, the rise in divorce and especially suicide rates? Did this not indicate a profound state of anomie, a lack of regulation of desires and of normative authority, which threatened the very survival of such societies? Clearly, specialisation of labour was not a sufficient condition of social persistence. We cannot always assume complementary expectations and roles, and interest cannot bind individuals for long. The moral force of society must guarantee relations of contract. Already in *The Division of Labour*, Durkheim argues that, to survive, modern societies need the cohesive force of the reconstituted collective norms of the 'mechanical' type of society. To meet the changing needs, modern societies must reorganise themselves as modifications of the old communitas, or disintegrate.[12]

The communitarian ideal which Durkheim here acknowledges is one of the central themes of nationalism; yet it is simpler, more comforting and more elastic. In itself neither radical nor conservative, it fits both kinds of ideology admirably. At its heart is the notion of a single will or 'soul', representing and expressing all the trends, customs and habits of a people. It is an idea which Durkheim seems to have derived from Rousseau, the father of the radical varieties of communitarianism.[13] Durkheim's types of social integration, despite essential differences in style and intent, are foreshadowed in Rousseau's contrast between nature and civilisation. 'Organic solidarity', of course, only roughly resembles the 'civil state'—an interdependence of parts in a whole characterised by inequalities, conflicts of will and fleeting relationships— but the state of nature is more closely related to the Durkheimian 'mechanical solidarity' and 'conscience collective'. In both, we find the communitarian ideal of a fixed and constant orientation of minds and activities in a distinct direction, a persistent shared disposition of individuals. Both writers agree on the impermanence of relations based on interest alone, and oppose the cold competitive impersonality of modern aggregates. Both desire the restoration of emotionally satisfying face-to-face relationships.

They differ, however, in their proposals for a solution to the modern dilemma. Rousseau wants to link society's members directly and equally to the impersonal community, to escape the dependence of the citizens on each other which is the old tyranny. The true community, the real 'moi commun', is revealed in the sovereignty of the impersonal general will, with equal and un-mediated citizenship for all. Durkheim's solution is somewhat less radical. The division of labour is both beneficial and irrever-sible, but it is morally insufficient. To secure cohesion and loyalty, old norms and beliefs must be retained and adapted in new set-tings, notably in the form of occupational codes, as in the pro-fessions. Society will then form a network of functional groups regulated by the administrative state. This means, 'society' must be refashioned into a cohesive unit with a single focus of moral authority and system of beliefs, yet this new 'community' must be sufficiently flexible to allow some individual autonomy, and adaptive enough to cope with rapidly changing needs and circumstances.[14]

Political religion

Although Durkheim's account of social cohesion is sociologically far more penetrating than Rousseau's philosophical sketch, it contains one grave weakness which hinders it from providing an explanation of ideologies like nationalism. This is the separation of political power from social authority, and the subordination, even the absorption, of the former in the latter. Durkheim's distrust of political power and his explicit equation of the social with the moral and sacred elements, made it difficult to furnish an account of ideologies whose effects serve to strengthen the politi-cal state. Durkheim did realise that one of the most important conditions of the restoration of a free, and hence genuine, com-munitas, was the emergence of a satisfying collective system of values and beliefs; and at the end of his life, under the impact of the Great War, he placed great hopes in the integrative force of patriotism.[15] In The Elementary Forms of the Religious Life, the patriotism of the French Revolution is cited as an example of a secular religion, sharing with the primitive religion of the Arunta a set of emotionally effervescent and unifying rituals. Yet Durkheim's distrust of the State, to which he accorded only administrative functions, and his theoretical neglect of political forces, prevented him from developing these suggestions into a theory of political cohesion in modernising societies, such as might explain the appeal of nationalism.

In this respect, Rousseau possessed greater insight. His interest was the 'religion of the citizen', which unites State and Church, and

> embracing but a single country, gives it its deities, its proper and tutelary patrons. It has its dogmas and rituals, its external cult prescribed by law. Outside the single nation adhering to it, the rest of the world is unbelieving, foreign, barbarian.[16]

Rousseau counselled the Poles to develop their national character through a system of communal education and ritual, so that, like the Jews, they would prove unassimilable. He attacked the pseudo-cosmopolitanism of the *philosophes* whose rationalism belittled national differences, and emphasised the specific character and peculiar attributes of each nation. But he disagreed with Montesquieu's treatment of nationality as a political datum determined by natural factors like climate. National character can be created by suitable institutions, and this is eminently desirable:

> Ce sont les institutions nationales qui forment le génie, le caractère, les goûts et les moeurs d'un peuple . . . qui lui inspirent cet ardent amour de la patrie.[17]

In the long run, it is governments which mould peoples.

Recently, political scientists studying the formation of the new states in Africa and Asia have drawn on the suggestions of both Rousseau and Durkheim in their analyses. The equation of a 'nation' with the mores and customs, laws, constitutions and currents of opinion of a population and with the relation of the state to its members, underlies the modern concepts of 'nation-building', 'political development' and 'political religion' which form the theoretical scaffolding of these investigations. The argument has received one of its fullest elaborations in the writings of David Apter.[18] Rapid industrialisation and modernisation require a flexible political framework, one capable of engendering initiative and coping with unforeseen change. This requirement is in turn best served by an ideology which symbolically identifies the individual with the State. In non-Western contexts, this can be achieved in only one of two ways: by a political use of religion on the part of the traditional authority, as in the modernising theocracies (e.g. Meiji Japan, Buganda), or by a revolutionary new 'political religion' which hallows the regime's economic and technological goals and mobilises the people for sacrifices. 'Political religions' have the following features: the State is a moral, regenerative, dignifying force. It and its laws, together with the regime, become sacred. To maintain communal solidarity and the regime's legitimacy, a new mythology is erected around the rebirth of the purified nation bent on restoring a golden age soiled by oppressors. These 'mobilisation systems', as Apter calls the more revolutionary party-states of Africa (e.g. Nkrumah's Ghana, Guinea and Mali), operate the 'totalitarian' version of democracy; they are true successors of Jacobin political messianism.[19] In their eyes, the new nations are sinless; society is an organism in which every cleavage is unnatural; only political means can achieve its goals of harmony, progress and industrialisation; and any opposition to the State is a political crime.

The sources of these new religions are to be sought in the 'needs' of the new nations: the need to build a polity, the need to transcend 'primordial' ties of ethnicity, language and religion, to reconstitute a strong central authority, to develop economic rationality among a traditionally-minded citizenry; above all, the need for rapid material development. These needs drive men to sacrifice themselves to realise the ends of the society; their commitment parallels the sense of vocation and the urge for frugality and self-discipline of the early Puritans. Mobilisation systems manage to equate individual and national purposes to the extent that they fit individual moral ends into the demands of a dynamic technology and its organisational framework. Socialistic nationalism is the Calvinism of the Third World.[20]

The functionalist framework

The functionalist perspective on modernisation starts, as we see, from the suggestions in Rousseau, draws heavily on Durkheim's analysis of complex society, and ends by echoing Weber. The key to the argument is the idea of the 'imperatives' of a community of tradition, which are erected into criteria for the adequate conceptualisation of the modernisation process. To survive painful dislocation, societies must institutionalise new modes of fulfilling the principles and performing the functions with which earlier structures can no longer cope. To merit the title, a new 'society' must reconstitute itself in the image of the old. The baseline for the transition is provided by a stereotypical traditional community, the 'primitive' tribal society, and another stereotype of modernity, the nation-state of Western Europe and America. Mechanisms of reintegration and stabilisation can ease and facilitate the transition; among them are collective ideologies like nationalism which spring up naturally in periods of social crisis, and appear meaningful and effective for the participants of the situation.

There are really two basic flaws in the thinking of this school. The first is the oft-criticised failure of functionalism, even in its evolutionary phase, to provide satisfactory explanations, especially of social change. The second, and for my purposes more serious set of objections, concerns its vacuous treatment of the problem of ideology.

The former, theoretical, criticisms can be summarised as follows: functionalism operates with ethnocentric and crude stereotypes of 'tradition' and 'modernity'. It imputes teleological needs to societies undergoing transformation. This implies a retrospective determinism which makes analysis of actions and situations somewhat superfluous. Finally, it assumes that the motor of all structural change is continuous differentiation of roles and institutions to adapt to the environment.

1 The first argument is vital. It is, I think, true that functionalists tend to simplify and reify their ideal-types of 'tradition' and 'modernity'; as a number of critics have pointed out, the process of structural differentiation in the writings of Parsons, Bellah, Eisenstadt and others is often explicitly modelled on Western valuations. [21] Nothing, except confusion and misunderstanding, is gained by throwing discrete elements like parliamentary democracy and role differentiation into a single composite ideal-type of 'modernity'. There is no logical connection between American democracy and the 'mature' complexity of modern society, or between ethnicity and the simplicity of the traditional. What we have here is merely an ethnical analogy with individual character-formation: societies, like personalities, mature in successive stages of progressive effectiveness and flexibility vis-à-vis their environment from one fixed state, tradition, to another fixed state, modernity. The unit's potential is gradually unfolded from the simplest to the most highly developed patterns,

through a process of self-division followed by a synthesis of semi-autonomous, specialised parts.

2 The slide from treating 'tradition' and 'modernity' as heuristic devices to thinking of them as fixed empirical states of affairs of a rather uniform kind, is abetted by the functionalist propensity to reason in terms of final causes. Apter's argument is particularly open to the familiar charge of teleological explanation. His list of 'needs' (for polity-building, economic rationality, ethnicity transcendence, etc.) makes sense only as goals of the national elites in polyethnic states, or as value-judgments of the Western observer. Most of these goals are logically and historically posterior to the emergence of a nationalist conceptual framework, and so cannot be invoked to explain the 'political religion' of nationalism. Moreover, can the survival or 'effectiveness' of a society only be assured by a rousing 'political religion'? Once again, we are faced with the difficulty of basic definition of terms such as 'society', 'survival', etc. The assertion seems to be either true by definition, or empirically false—or at least uncertain and in need of criteria of testability. As it stands, this is just another instance of the functionalist deduction of institutional patterns of belief and activity from higher-order 'prerequisites' of 'society', which on inspection turn out to be little more than the extension of the complex of meanings associated with the term 'society' in the first place.

3 The result of deriving explanations largely from end-states is to turn attention away from the search for hypotheses about antecedents. The sense of alternatives and openness of choice for actors is diminished. For example, Smelser's analysis cannot escape retrospective determinism, because, arguing forwards to the occurrence of an ideological or social movement, he is led to assume an *inevitable* connection between differentiation, 'strain' and short-circuiting generalised beliefs. No allowance is made for the conceptions and attitudes of individuals and groups whose interpretations might redefine and modify their situations. There are, for example, a large number of cases of traditional communities subjected to differentiation and to external pressure, which nevertheless failed to develop any form of protest, let alone a significant movement. Yet, Smelser's analysis cannot cope with these 'exceptions'. As always, the observation of these trends depends only on the salience and visibility of cases manifesting the

developmental pattern, e.g. nationalism. Smelser is a determinist to the extent that the demand of systemic analysis for logical closure is paralleled by the assumption of empirical closure of a system of needs, implied by the functional equivalence of new units to the old ones. Nations *must* emerge to fulfil the functions and needs once satisfied by the old communities.

4 The same determinism permeates all functionalist explanations of social change. It would require lengthy discussion to deal with the familiar charge that functionalism cannot cope with social change. [22] Suffice it to say here that the latest so-called 'neo-evolutionary' phase of functionalism shows it up as much a theory of change as it is of social persistence; but it also reveals only too clearly the links between functionalism and its progenitor, classical evolutionism.

It certainly shares all the latter's defects. [23] Theoretically, the idea that the motor of all change lies in the tendency or 'need' of every structure to adapt to its environment through specialisation of its parts, or perish, cannot help us to explain *particular* transitions like modernisation. When we have discovered the reasons for such transitions, the general framework of stages of complex differentiation becomes superfluous; and when we don't know the reasons, it is inadequate. [24] At a more empirical level, the functionalist equation of modernisation with continuing differentiation of roles and structures assumes that all 'structural' change inevitably tends towards complexity; but, as the fusion of roles and institutions in China and Russia suggests, this assumption is untenable. [25]

Religion versus ideology

The real trouble with the functionalist perspective is that it is pitched at such a high level of generality that it entirely fails to relate even to a large-scale set of changes, like modernisation. The framework is cut off from the empirical world, and theory is stillborn. Can any suggestions, however, relating to our problem, be salvaged from this logical wreckage? How far can the analysis of social consequences, the *method* of functional analysis, help to illuminate the nature and causes of nationalism?

Unfortunately, the same weakness of vague over-generalisation filters over into the more empirical concerns. The treatment of ideology is schematic and one-sided. There is no chance of a refined analysis of differential ideological response to modernisation. Once again, the concept of 'reintegration' reveals the essential tautology of the position.

1 The functionalist conception of ideology is narrowly 'therapeutic'. It is a blanket response to emotional strain and social deprivation, when a society becomes disorganised and 'malintegrated' in its parts. Geertz, however, sees ideology performing a range of functions—justifying, morale-boosting, cathartic, solidarity-creating—and criticises the lack of causal connection in functionalist analysis between the situations of strain and their consequent attachment to symbols and belief systems.[26] Why does the patterned desperation of individuals assume collective shape at all? And why the elaboration of symbols?

2 One of the more interesting questions in this field concerns the range and saliency of ideological responses to external influences and indigenous pressures. Why was Pakistan's type of nationalism of the so-called 'neo-traditional' kind, whereas Turkey's was secularist? Why the Bolshevik response in Russia, the Fascist in Italy, the socialist in Yugoslavia and Israel? Why does one ideology succeed at one time and place, often in the teeth of bitter rivalry? These are questions which functionalism is precluded from answering, except in an *ad hoc* manner; and this is not merely because of the level of generality at which it attacks the problems, but an inevitable outcome of its fundamental 'sociologism'. Methodologically, it works forward from structural trends towards the ideological response, which is then invoked mechanically. Finally the appearance of the response is seen as a confirmation of the methodology.

Perhaps this is the main weakness of Smelser's 'value-added' schema of collective behaviour. We may grant, some structures permit, and others impede, mass actions, some situations of deprivation provoke, while others dampen, collective outbursts: yet, why does a 'powerful generalised belief' arise in some cases and not in others? Which beliefs galvanise social movements, which divert them? Which ideologies 'misfire', and why do others crystallise, even help to create revolutionary situations, as did Fichte's addresses in 1806, or the Negro American missionaries in the Central African situation of the Great War? By working inwards *only* from massive structural trends, one can never reach the target. [27]

3 In fact, the functionalist solution to the problem of ideology is to treat it as a sort of *deus ex machina* of cohesion. The very phrase, 'political religion', puts it concisely. Ideology is simply religion politicised, made relevant to the public issues of this world.

But why is ideology a form of religion for functionalists? Because it functions to 'reintegrate', which is the same thing as to 'remake society', i.e. to refashion the broken elements into a 'new community', to re-create order in what was fast becoming a welter of disparate relationships, to bind again.

Now this is exactly what 'religion', in Durkheim's usage, achieves. That which functions to create cohesion, it is suggested, in the realm of beliefs and activities, is 'religion'; therefore religion is necessary for society, and 'political religion' for modernising societies, so as to utilise the coercive power of the State to prevent further disintegration. Church and State acting together for identical ends in a defined territory, can ease the birthpangs of the new societies.

As we saw, Durkheim's individualism prevented him from drawing this conclusion from his analysis. Besides, moral authority was vested in society, not the State. Political power was intrusive and suspect. But the functionalists are really only giving a political twist to his basic equation of a *sui generis* society, normative integration and the sacred (religion). It is this assumption which gives meaning to a concept like 'political religion': only societies with moral cohesion are Societies, only societies with 'religion' are Societies; modernising societies persist, despite the immense centrifugal forces to which they are exposed; therefore they must have 'religion', and their manifest ideology conceals a latent religion. [28]

The argument is only tautological insofar as we accept the underlying equation of the religious, the social and the moral. But if we treat this assumption as an hypothesis, or an heuristic device, we are faced with the problem of the relationship of religion to ideology. In many ways, this forms the fundamental theoretical locus of this work. I would contend that ideology be treated as a subspecies of the wider category 'belief system' *alongside* religion, and ask: is it conceptually useful to ignore the conventional distinction between the two, simply because they produce some similar effects?

I think that to blur the distinction is to accept a *simpliste* and misleading view. It is one thing to demonstrate an analogy between religion and, say, communism and nationalism, even to use 'religion' as a partial model for understanding some aspects of 'ideology'; quite another to equate them, or subordinate one to the other logically. [29] Ideologies inspire rather different kinds of sentiments, organisations and activities—a greater optimism and activism, certain types of research and education and leadership, etc.; more important, their sanctions, goals and values diverge radically from those of the world's religions. The distinction between 'religion' and 'ideology' isn't 'between ultimate values and proposed ways in which these values may be put into effect' —even if the religious value-judgment could be extruded from that ambiguous word 'ultimate'. [30] The real criterion of the 'religious' is substantive: its goal and sanction is a *supra*-empirical referent, extrinsic to nature and society. [31] 'Ideology' isn't 'this-worldly'; since it knows only the goals and sanctions of human actions and their historical situations, this description misleads. A Ghanaian might cling (might have clung) to Nkrumaism, a Turk to Kemalism, with 'religious' fervour, as panaceas for the trans-formation of 'this' world; but such a superficial resemblance hardly suffices to bestow religious status on their beliefs. Metaphor and explanation should not be confused.

The use of the term 'political religion' to equate ideology with religion overlooks the great differences in their tone and assump-tions. It completely misses the profound transformation in a society which forsakes an Islamic or Buddhist outlook and ethic for a secular nationalist or socialist *Weltanschauung*. They express two worlds of thought and action. Even if they coexist uneasily, and even when they seem to combine for a time, their assumptions and activities are utterly unlike and comparison is more misleading than helpful, unless we are speaking figuratively. There is a twilight zone between them, where mutual comprehension seems within reach. A man may combine religion and nationalism or socialism, like Afghani perhaps, or the Buddhist socialism of U Nu and the Christian socialism of Nyerere. But such personal syn-theses cannot easily be replicated to provide a long-term founda-tion for a contemporary society. In times of rapid change, they are generally unstable, even at the individual level, and on examination tend to reveal a subordination of one outlook to the other.

Another argument which is sometimes used to show that nationalism is no more than a political extension of religion is based on the religious origins of many nationalist movements. It is true that religion may reinforce nationality, even 'preserve' it, as Arnakis argues in the case of Greece. It was the Byzantine Church which transmitted, not only the literature and culture, but even the idea of Greece, frozen under Turkish rule. Turkish-speaking, Vlach-speaking, Albanian-speaking Orthodox subjects of Turkey, even when they were settled in Anatolia, were loyal, or sympathetic, to Greek independence; while Bulgarian-speaking Muslim Pomaks, and Greek-speaking Cretan Muslims supported Turkey (the populations generally migrated, or were exchanged by the two countries after the First War; in the case of the Pomaks, the Second). Throughout the Balkans, Islamisation meant eventual Turkification. Yet this equation only became apparent when nationalism had already emerged; for before 1900 nobody thought in terms of 'Turkification' only of 'Ottomanisation'.[32] But what should we conclude from the fact that national self-definition was formed initially, at any rate, in terms of a deep religious allegiance? Can this be taken as support for the view that nationalism is simply the politicised expression of 'religion', arising under the tensions of modernisation?

I think not. Once again, the same distinction applies. To say that religion in the Near East and Eastern Europe was inseparable from politics and social affairs, and therefore that religion provided the basis for ethnic identification, and hence nationality, is one thing.[33] Assyrians, Greeks, Armenians, Druse, Jacobites, Maronites, might all possess the status of millets, and constitute potential nationalities like the Mormons, the Quebecois, even the Irish. But it is quite another thing to argue that Assyrian or Armenian nationalism is a derivative of their religion, in the simple sense of an extension of its outlook to the political sphere. Nothing is further from the truth. Orthodoxy may well have 'preserved' intact the sense of community as fertile ground for nationalism, when and if it arose. But its role ends there. It was the Enlightenment that acted as catalyst for the nationalist movement. In Rumania, for example, the Orthodox Church was subservient to the Bulgarian Patriarchate, whose ecumenical character was used as an instrument of Phanariot hellenisation of the upper classes in the eighteenth century. After its age-long crystallisation of Rumanian ethnicity the Church became an obstacle to a truly Rumanian nationalism; the origins of the latter are to be sought rather in the researches of enlightened but heretical Roman Catholic Uniate priests in eighteenth-century Transylvania.[34] Traditional religion does play a part in the rise and elaboration of nationalism, as I hope to show later. But it is a rather indirect, ambiguous and reactive role. Between traditional religion and nationalism there is a decisive break. The deductive quality of the concept of 'political religion' which, in the functionalist dialectic, provides the 'answer' to the 'question' of societal reintegration, only obscures and confuses this interesting, but complex, transformation. Religion often provides the sociological material for nationalism to work on, but it does not and cannot explain the latter's character or appearance.

In this area, as in others, the functionalist methodology is always prone to the danger that the empirical cases serve only to confirm the general thesis. Its virtue, in the study of nationalism, is its suggestion that the latter is closely linked to the seedbed of pre-existing religious beliefs and organisations. Its defect is that the reasons given for this relationship are *a priori* ones, which deflect from causal investigation and issue in misleading conclusions.

The 'mass society' model

'Disintegration' theories of modernisation do not all adhere to the functionalist perspective. Durkheim's classical analysis of integration has inspired an alternative approach, among those who are troubled by the apparent political consequences of large aggregates of men densely packed into new urban conglomerations, and available for political manipulation.

Halpern, writing about Middle Eastern urbanisation, sums up the prevalent type of nationalism as an expression of 'organised insecurity'. The analysis owes much to Mannheim's concern about the destruction of elites and elite culture under the impact of democratisation, mass education and political technology.[35] These new phenomena stem, in the Middle East, from the progressive uprooting of villagers from their rural setting. In Egypt, Algeria and Syria, old customs and beliefs are losing their meaning with the advance of urban culture. Family and village ties can no longer be restored. The old religious and communal groupings disintegrate. For the deruralised, 'the glass of Islam is shattered'.[36] City life presents a bewildering patchwork for the newcomers; under- or unemployment in factory and office, insalubrious bidonville conditions, the aimlessness of semi-literate crowds, the lure of entertainments which poverty denies. Repeated disappointment of expectations and the failure to find unambiguous norms bring inevitable feelings of anxiety and helpless frustration. Into this psychological crisis step the ideologically extremist religious and political movements with their promise of immediate rewards and messianic activism. The Ba'ath, the Moslem Brotherhood, the Communists, appeal to the confused and alienated masses, and channel and mobilise their resentments for revolution. The nationalist promise is the control of change, the organisation of insecurity, the ordering (and understanding) of modernisation. In the name of the citizenship ideal, it admits the excluded masses into the political community. Its end is power for the powerless, dignity for the self-despising; its means is the nation-state—powerful, efficient, pure, above sectionalism, fulfilment of the nation's destiny, embodiment of its true virtues and tradition.[37]

For Halpern, Berger and even Binder, nationalism is but one, though perhaps the most important, of the current responses of the new urban middle and lower-middle classes to the experience of physical disruption and cultural disorientation.[38] In the well-known pluralist thesis of Kornhauser, it is superseded by totalitarian Fascism and Communism.[39] Kornhauser concentrates on the European experiences, notably Weimar. From it he derives a model of a type of modern society particularly susceptible to totalitarian takeovers. As 'masses' differ from 'classes' and 'mass movements' from moderate 'class movements', so 'mass societies' are to be distinguished as an analytical type from 'pluralist', 'corporate' and 'totalitarian' societies. The peculiar features of 'mass societies' are:

1 Elites are permeable, they can be easily infiltrated by nonelite groups; likewise, nonelites or masses are manipulable by elites

2 The individual is no longer protected from centralised authority by a network of voluntary intermediate organisations

3 Value-standards are uniform but fluid, the individual is isolated, and the personality is alienated from self and others

4 Politically extremist and antidemocratic movements emerge to attract a variegated composition of adherents whose social ties are weak and who suffer under the strain of atomisation.

This social isolation springs from the disintegration of corporate, traditional societies, from 'major discontinuities in social process', particularly in community and authority. These discontinuities are 'those factors that weaken social arrangements intermediate between the individual and the State', [40] specifically:

1 Sudden democratisation unaccompanied by the growth of independent voluntary functional associations

2 Rapidity of urbanisation, in its early stages, uprooting and atomising large populations, especially where the social disparity between areas is great

3 Rapidity of industrialisation, in its early stages, particularly in large cities and factories if accompanied by prior repression or absence of workers' unions

4 Severity of national crises—especially defeat and depression.

The following of 'mass movements' consists of the 'available'—unattached intellectuals, marginal members of the middle class, students, the unemployed, isolated industrial and farm workers, and the politically apathetic. Pried loose from traditional groups and functions, they are ready to join messianic movements destructive of constitutional order and civil liberties.

People cannot be mobilised against the established order until they have first been divorced from prevailing codes and relations. Only then are they available for 'activist' modes of intervention in the political process. Thus it is that when large numbers of people are available, and when opportunities exist for the further creation of mass consciousness (as when pre-existing elites are inadequate to protect their institutions), Fascist and Communist movements alike gain support at the expense of political parties committed to the social order. [41]

Urban anomie and crowd extremism in the diffusion of nationalism
Despite the diffuse influence of Pareto's elite theory, Kornhauser's formulation owes most to Durkheim. At its heart is the relationship between the individual, the State and intermediate associations, to which Durkheim returned at the end of his life: individual

liberties are the product of a conflict (not just a combination) between the State and these secondary associations.[42] In the anomie of urban existence with its sectionalism and economic uncertainty, these functional groupings are undermined; desires become unregulated and far exceed the possibilities for their attainment, established norms lose their hold without replacement, and expectations are built up which can no longer be satisfied. It is a situation which, for Kornhauser, had already emerged in the late Middle Ages in north-western Europe, where rapid urbanisation was the prelude to outbursts of revolutionary chiliasm;[43] but it is also to be found in the countryside in recent times, as when rural depopulation in France atomised large numbers and drove them into reactionary Poujadism.[44]

This model of aimless individuals drifting in anonymous cities and naked before the power of the State has, despite its tautological elements and inconsistencies, a compelling attraction for the sociological imagination;[45] and particularly in the generation which experienced Fascism. The question is, how far can Weimar be generalised without distortion? First, as a model, I do not think it is applicable in the case of nationalist movements. It is largely irrelevant to an explanation of the *emergence* of nationalism. Where it is useful, is in its portrayal of those factors, notably urbanisation, which act as vehicles for the rapid *diffusion* of nationalist slogans among 'marginal' groups. But these suggestions need to be divorced from an otherwise misleading picture. Second, as a 'mass movement' nationalism does not always manifest the alleged characteristics: its objects are indeed 'remote' from personal life (independence, individuality, etc.); its mode of response to them tends to be direct (active intervention, passive resistance, riots, boycotts, etc); it lacks an internal structure of independent groups; it often mobilises 'uprooted and atomised sections of the population'.[46]

And yet not all nationalist movements are anti-democratic or 'extremist'—even if an unequivocal meaning could be given to these epithets. The Indian National Congress began as a liberal reformist movement, and under Gandhi it was explicitly controlled in its 'direct action' and not notably antidemocratic, owing much to the British parliamentary example so influential even among Hindus who asserted Indian spiritual superiority.[47] Zionism, too, though it fed an authoritarian wing in Revisionism, was generally a self-critical, democratic and constitutional movement.[48] In Persia, Argentina, Czechoslovakia and Nigeria and in French West Africa, nationalism, while attacking naturally the colonialist or imperial regimes, was a liberal, reformist and democratic force before the military interventions. Even where they curb civil liberties, no post-independence African movement aiming to integrate its population, would wish to subvert the established order—if only for fear of a rash of secessionist movements across the Continent. Political order and civil liberty do not always go together, and neither do extremism and a large-scale following (one need only contrast the Nasserist and Wafdist varieties of nationalism in Egypt for an equally common permutation).

Perhaps it is for these reasons that Kornhauser is relatively silent about nationalist movements. His model is, in any case, largely structural; it fails to differentiate Fascist and Communist *ideologies*, while recognising divergent class bases for the movements. Omitting cultural factors, the 'mass society' model could never generate an adequate theory of nationalism; the confrontation of opposing cultures in a single territory, the role of foreign domination, the cultural homogenisation policies of the modern state, are factors that powerfully modify the experience of alienation and atomisation in the city, and are highly relevant to the origins and appeal of nationalism.

Perhaps it is unfair to criticise a model for not achieving what it never intended, were it not for its great influence in the field, and the use to which it can (and has been) put. Besides, its very defects can provide illuminating suggestions about relevant factors in the study of the genesis of nationalism. Even if classic nationalism is typical of an earlier stage of education and commerce antedating that of 'mass society', the critique of the latter can give insights into the former.

There are two exaggerations in the model which yield insights. The first concerns the connection between urbanisation, anomie and extremism. Kornhauser is aware that there is no direct causal relationship; it depends whether secondary associations develop. But does it? In Africa, urban, tribal and other voluntary associations sprang up aiming to assist ex-tribesmen to adjust to the demands of urban industrialism. Now it is just these unions which trained them for political participation, and channelled their sense of disorientation into nationalist movements for which they provided a ready-made base.[49] Either, therefore, urbanisation doesn't produce 'anomie' always, or secondary groupings are irrelevant in accounting for the rise of ideological movements. In fact, I believe the role of both 'anomie' and 'secondary associations' has been overrated and over-generalised, rather like the part played by emotional insecurity in some psychological accounts. Nobody would wish to deny that migration and resettlement, especially in the very different conditions of city life, often cause personal disequilibrium and social disorganisation. But one should be careful not to infer from this that, unless social ties are retained, man will automatically join extremist groupings to shield himself against isolation, social and emotional.

The persuasiveness of this argument is due, in great measure, to the poetic power of images of crowd psychology and ephemeral collective behaviour, which lurk in the background.[50] Even the 'democratic critics' of mass society fear the inconstancy of purpose and loss of community among the intimidated masses, in contrast to the informed 'publics' of the eighteenth century.[51] 'Mass man' is 'crowd man', a helpless victim of some 'mental contagion' in a pure, involuntary aggregate of men momentarily stripped of their social attachments.[52] But either this involves us in suppositions about the workings of the unconscious, or we are forced to ignore intervening psychological factors. Is it not more realistic to posit some mechanisms of intermental exchange—propaganda, conversation, social conformity—to account for the undoubted collective frame of mind which precedes group action? This assumption fits the nationalist case much better. For it can be shown that it is particular pre-existing groups and institutions that are won over to the cause, in addition to 'marginal' individuals. In particular, the new educated and 'modernist' elites provide the firmest adherents. And their 'extremism', too, can be explained as much by the frustration of their goals, as by the fear of isolation and impotence, by hope deferred rather than involuntary anxiety. No atavistic impulses, no herd instinct to belong, need be invoked.

Mention of elites brings me to the second exaggeration. It is quite true that the intelligentsia, especially, have experienced some isolation. But this is not so much social as cultural, and less a product of urbanisation than of literary education. The contact and conflict of two types of culture and society places certain groups in a kind of cultural no-man's-land, even though they may retain their social ties. This is true as much of army officers as merchants and intellectuals. A certain detachment does occur, but its significant aspect is mental. Here, the image of the uncontrolled crowd combines with the lack of an historical framework and cultural context to ignore the intellectual and emotional alienation of groups during the early stages of modernisation. The matrix of nationalism is not a single, uniform, atomised society, but a profoundly disturbing and exciting clash of two worlds of perception, assumption and relation.

I said before that urbanisation (and the communication possibilities this allows) is an important background factor in the diffusion of nationalism, once it had emerged. I think one can go a bit further. Nationalist movements are all urban-based, though, as in China, they may fail to secure sufficient support and enlist the peasants. At the same time, they originate in the town. And yet their imagery is full of nostalgia and idealisation for the countryside and folk virtues. One would not wish to claim that this is the primary leitmotif, but it does provide a consistent spatial colouring for the nationalist dream of fraternity. It would indeed be remarkable if the recent experience of urbanisation were not reflected in this imagery.

But we should not insist on the connection too much. Ulam has shown how Marxism too reflects the nostalgia for the security and status of rural communities, despite its promise of abundance through full industrialisation.[53] Empirically, too, it is not easy to correlate any rate or degree of urbanisation with the inception of nationalism; it may be considerable, as in Western Europe, before the advent of nationalism, or negligible, as among the very small nationalities of Central Asia and the Far East—Oirots, Buryats, Tuvinians or Yakuts—who all developed 'primitive' nationalisms after 1900 under the pressure of Russian colonisation.[54] It is rather the sense of discontinuity, of violent and rapid change, which such processes as urbanisation manifest, that is relevant; for it makes difficult the re-establishment (and discovery) of shared values and beliefs, so necessary to sustain a complex industrial society, according to this perspective.

'Mass society' theory shares with evolutionary functionalism the preoccupations of Durkheim and Rousseau with what may be termed the 'missing factor' which will restore society's cohesion and viability. Both omit cultural factors, both seek structural solutions to their problem of order; for the functionalist 'political religion' is not Weber's 'religion surrogate', but a building-block in the edifice of the ordered modern society. Underlying the pessimism of both visions is a double regret—at the passing of traditional society, with its network of corporate meanings and solidarities, and at the failure of the modernising societies to opt for the Western pluralist combination of freedom with stability. Standing completely outside the nationalist experience, which they judge purely as an instrument for the attainment or obstruction of other ends, they fill out Kedourie's problem with sociological analysis describing the ways in which traditional communities have disintegrated, and the problems this has raised for reconstruction. But we have not been able to discover from them either, the connections between that process of disintegration and the birth of nationalism, nor the reasons behind the connections.

Chapter Four

ANTICOLONIALISM

Nationalism is really only anticolonialism: so runs the most popular explanation today.

Foreign conquest

At the simplest level, nationalism is seen as a natural response to foreign oppression, i.e. colonialism. Men have always lived in groups. Group loyalty is a constant. The unknown outsider is feared. The conquering outgroup is always hated and resisted. Domination by outsiders is 'unnatural'. Colonialism, the domination and annexation of vast tracts of land and strange peoples, has been the practice of European states since the sixteenth century— due to their early superiority in wealth and technology. This century, however, has witnessed the rise of educated native elites able to expel the foreigner, under the banner of 'nationalism'.

The theory is as simple as it is untenable. History is replete with conquests and periods of foreign domination, which provoked little or no opposition. Great, sprawling, polyethnic empires have been perhaps the historical norm. In the ancient world, only a few peoples—Egyptians, Persians, Greeks and Jews —possessed a sense of group consciousness sufficient to inspire resistance movements against 'alien' peoples. Most conflicts in the Middle Ages were dynastic or religious. Moreover, the 'theory' assumes what is to be explained, why one group comes to see another as 'alien'; and it further assumes that foreign domination is always perceived to be 'oppressive'. Yet the initial successes of Islam were, to a considerable extent, due to the perceived mildness of its rule, especially after the Byzantine empire's heavy taxation. To accept, moreover, the naturalness of groups is to accept in advance the nationalist framework, which is exactly what requires explanation. But nationalism is not logically necessary, and the love of freedom by no means universal.

Our objection to this very common 'theory' can be stated more precisely. To say that 'nationalism is really anticolonialism' is either an explanation or a stipulative definition. As an 'explanation' as we saw, the 'theory' is either circular, assuming what is to be explained—or false, since people don't always resist foreign intrusion or rule, and freedom as a widespread intrinsic value is a *modern* phenomenon coextensive with 'nationalism'. As a *definition* of nationalism, anticolonialism or a 'collective grievance against foreigners', as Minogue puts it, still leaves us with the further problem of defining 'foreignness', and is rather too broad to be of use in research. Resistance to foreigners can take place on behalf of the village, religious community or dynasty—as in the early 'primary revolts' and 'pacification wars' in Burma, Nigeria, Indonesia and North Africa.[1] Further, just what is it that is covered by the terms 'colonialism' and 'anticolonialism'? Does this include the Ottoman, Habsburg and Romanov empires, and the resistance to their rule in the nineteenth century? And if so, why? Can it not be but in terms of the already rejected 'explanation'?

There is a more serious objection to defining nationalism solely in terms of anticolonialism and resistance to outside rule. Men do not seek collective independence and build states simply because they react to a 'common enemy'. For that would mean that the colonised only become aware of themselves as a unity, a 'social self', a distinct identity, in contrast to the coloniser, the 'significant other', in Mead's terminology.[2] The former would derive their values and self-image dialectically in opposition to those of the colonisers, by a process of role and value dissociation and comparison.[3]

I think this seriously oversimplifies the situation, even in the case of nationalist movements where there is no pre-existent sense of unity of the group, or which lack a base of pre-existent cultural ties, as in sub-Saharan Africa. In these, as in the European nation-alisms, the inspiration was more *positive* than a collective self-assertion against an outgroup and a 'common enemy'. Their aim was not merely the rejection of standards imposed from 'outside', but also the creation of a new type of political and social entity, with arrangements well adapted to the local mores and environ-ment. The 'significant other' too is more complex; it consists not only in the superimposed colonial situation and foreign values but also in the *pre*-colonial traditional norms and activities of the area.

Nationalism therefore is inadequately defined as 'anticolonial-ism' (in the sense of 'foreign rule'). It is a narrower concept than 'resistance to foreign domination', and a more positive and crea-tive one. It is also directed as much to internal problems as to external threats.

The theory of capitalist imperialism

More sophisticated versions of 'anticolonialism' theories rely on the notions of 'underdevelopment' and 'exploitation'. At bottom, they are *'conflict'* theories, because they assume a perennial conflict between groups for scarce resources.

The best-known, the *'theory of capitalist imperialism'*, underlies the recent analysis by Peter Worsley.[4] Imperialism proper, he maintains, can be dated really from the post-1885 scramble for Africa by the Western European powers. The very brevity of imperialist rule results from its disturbing and revolutionary character. It was a relationship of power, of asymmetrical dependence:

> In so one-sided a relationship of power, the transformatory effects flowed largely one way: the nonEuropean had to make the adjust-ments; the coloniser was the agent of change, not the object.[5]

The original military conquest was bolstered by administrative coercion and a legitimating rationale of racial superiority. The personalities of the natives were, as Fanon and Mannoni showed, 'infantilised', made childlike, dependent creations of their pater-nalist white rulers. The colonialist's power was also reinforced by a 'refined etiquette of segregation', but it was based ultimately on force.

But to what end was this power wielded? Worsley has no doubts on this score:

It is no ideological assertion, but a simple generalisation rooted in empirical observation, that the prime content of colonial political rule was economic exploitation.[6]

The colonies, especially after 1885, were less important for national 'glory', settlement or strategic purposes than as outlets for investments, as markets and as sources of raw materials and cheap labour. 'Finance-imperialism married with "social" imperialism' constituted the underlying pattern; whatever the nature of the political institutions and traditions mediating the nexus of economic relations, the end was always identical:

> Underlying this diversity is one unifying characteristic: it is the imperialist power which dominates the situation, and seeks to solve its internal socio-economic problems ... by exploitation of colonial territories. ... For however important 'psychological' exploitation, the central raison d'être of imperialism is the extraction of profit from the labour of the indigenous people by Whites by virtue of their control over the political machinery of the state.[7]

The results of this exploitation were the uprooting of villagers, the creation of a network of communications, the spread of literacy, the massive influx into the towns and the creation of a new urban bourgeoisie and intelligentsia—all leading to 'that compound of nationalism and social revolution which was to be the hall-mark of the twentieth century. This new anti-Europeanism was not a final defiance. It was a new challenge which sought to redefine and re-order the world in a totally new way.'[8] It arose in two stages: first, an *elite* nationalism of the educated middle classes in the cities, then a *mass* nationalism of the middle classes, urban workers and even peasants in the countryside.

> At different rates and times in different countries, but usually in the same direction, modern mass nationalism took root, and drove out the older liberal nationalism.[9]

There is only one qualification to this general picture. One must, of course, distinguish between the older classic nationalism of Europe based on 'nations', i.e. groups with pre-existent cultural ties, on the one hand, and movements in, for example, Africa, on the other, which seek 'to establish independent states on the basis of common citizenship of entirely novel political and cultural entities', i.e. colonies whose sole bond is their common colonial fate.[10]

Worsley objects to Kedourie's intellectualist approach and his universal but unhelpful explanation in terms of a 'need to belong'. Nationalism, he finds, does serve needs, sociological ones,

> the real needs of the mass of the population: sometimes separate though parallel needs, sometimes needs common to all. The needs satisfied by contemporary Afro-Asian nationalism can be simply stated. They are:
> 1 Independence
> 2 Decolonisation
> 3 Development[11]

Sharing the experience of 'White, capitalist domination', 'people drew together and were forced together'. The emergence of the nation is thus a social process, not a 'self-enclosed logical operation'. It is the natural answer to the colonial experience.[12]

'Finance-capital'

This account owes much to the neo-Marxist theory of capitalist imperialism, popularised by Lenin.[13] Its roots stretch back into early economic theory, but it was given its present form by Hobson and Hilferding.[14] Hobson, writing in 1902 with special reference to South Africa, saw in underconsumption and oversupply of products at home the driving force behind the annexation of colonies. Surplus exports could be dumped in these territories, and they could also serve as new markets. But more important was the utility of colonies for investments, to offset oversaving at home, as well as for financial deals, which were largely in the hands of a small but powerful group of financiers.

Hilferding's account was more rigorous and operated within the Marxist framework. He defined finance capital as the banks' industrial capital, 'capital at the disposal of the banks and used by industrialists'. The advance of capitalism was marked by its concentration in ever fewer hands, and the creation of monopolies and cartels, utilising protective tariffs. The key to Hilferding's analysis lay in the inevitability of imperialism as the only solution to an advanced or 'mature' stage of 'rational' capitalism. For concentration of capital brought inevitable restrictions in the home market—higher prices and a loss in sales. Hence the need to compensate for this loss by increasing exports; this in turn created a worldwide competition of cartels and the internationalisation of capitalism.

Now colonies provided additional assets. Their mineral resources coupled with the injection of loan capital on a massive scale brought in a supply of raw materials for home industry, and, more important, higher consumption markets for exports. The only problems were the securing of an adequate labour force and the protection of monopoly interests. Here the military power of the State could be called upon. So, unlike its predecessor, free trade, 'finance capital' is necessarily violent and expansionist; that is part of its 'rationality'. Likewise State power now becomes the ideal of the finance bourgeoisie in contrast to the previous peaceful *laissez-faire* stage. This in turn means that the nation is exalted over other nations, leading to a world struggle for power —in contrast to the earlier limited nationalism. The final stage is an imperialist nationalism, tinged with racialism. In Hilferding's words:

> It (the world struggle of 'finance capital') is at root an economic phenomenon; but it is justified on ideological grounds through that peculiar transformation of the idea of the nation, which no longer recognises the right of every nation to political self-government and independence, and which no longer expresses the democratic principle of the equality of all human beings at the national level. On the contrary, the attitude characteristic of monopoly in the field of economics is again reflected in the superior status which is thought due to one's own nation. This status seems to be above all others. Because the subjugation of foreign nations is carried out by force (that means, in a very natural way), the ruling nation appears to owe this domination to its special natural characteristics—i.e. to the character of its race. Thus, in the ideology of race, there develops, disguised as natural science, the reality of finance capital's striving for power, which in this way can prove that its actions depend on and are made necessary by nature and science.[15]

Lenin added little to this account in his famous pamphlet; but he laid more emphasis on the advantages of colonies as sources of raw materials, and the consequent division of the world into spheres of economic exploitation. Monopoly control was in his eyes the distinguishing trait of modern, as opposed to Roman, imperialism.

The whole theory, of course, is based on Marx's assertion, in Volume III of *Capital*, of the tendency of a falling rate of profit with the advance of capitalism. The competition of capitalists coupled with a rise in working conditions leads to greater investment in the means of production and less in living labour. More labour-saving devices reduce the ratio of income to capital. If we supplement this analysis with the Marxist theory of class conflict, we can readily appreciate how the growing polarisation of conflict at home of a capitalist system 'in distress', must rationally be extended abroad, if the bourgeoisie are to retain their predominance.

The 'interest group' thesis

The other major 'conflict' theory of anticolonialism does not rely on the Marxist framework. At the same time, it makes considerable use of the concepts of 'class conflicts', 'exploitation' and 'underdevelopment'. It is therefore convenient, for purposes of analysis, to treat the two theses together, while noting their differences.

The 'interest group' framework is most explicitly utilised by J. H. Kautsky.[16] He starts by insisting that he limits his analysis to the impact of a single causal chain: the influence of industrialisation on the politics of underdeveloped societies—which differs greatly from its effects in Europe:

> The social tensions which modernisation and industrialisation produce everywhere and which in Europe were necessarily turned inward, resulting in conflicts dividing societies, are, in underdeveloped countries, largely turned outward. Instead of blaming each other for the difficulties growing out of modernisation, the various social strata all blame the colonial power, the result being, not internal conflict, but that internal unity of anticolonialism which is the basis of nationalism in underdeveloped countries.[17]

Nationalism is 'the drive of a relatively thin stratum of intellectuals who absorbed the skills and values of advanced countries, towards rapid modernisation in opposition to the aristocracy and independently of the colonial industrial powers'.[18] This is because they are now under-employed and culturally displaced in their traditional societies. So that nationalism in underdeveloped countries is the product of quite different forces than those which produced nationalism in Europe; it is really opposition to the colonial economic status and its native beneficiaries, and has nothing to do with language, as in Eastern Europe.

Kautsky agrees with Worsley that capitalist colonialism is its own gravedigger. Its aims are contradictory. It tries to preserve the political status quo so as to exploit the colonies' labour and resources more easily. But it simultaneously, by its modernising impetus, has to create new skilled groups to provide this labour force. In particular, three new groups emerge: a native bourgeoisie, a small urban working class, and most important, the intellectuals. These new groups challenge the old groupings typical of agrarian societies—aristocrats, peasants and an artisan middle class. The intellectuals especially attack capitalism for shoring up the traditional regimes and demand native industries and a redistribution of wealth. They see that colonial capitalism 'does not want industries in the colony to compete with its own industries for the colonial supply of raw materials or for the colonial market'.[19] The intellectuals' desire for rapid industrialisation produces their nationalism, just as their anticolonialism fits with their need for quick modernisation. The result is an ambivalent attitude to the West; they want what the West apparently denies them, and turn against it exactly because they admire it.

The material and cultural 'interests', then, of the intellectuals as the new elite, reacting against the depredations of colonial capitalism, create the socialistic nationalism of the developing countries. And their interests are reinforced by the parallel interests of the workers and native bourgeoisie, in conflict with outside exploitation of advanced economies.

The theory of 'historyless peoples'

The ultimate roots of all these 'anticolonialist' theories go back to Hegel. World history, he maintained, was a dialectic of the spirits of peoples contributing to the realisation of reason and freedom. But freedom and reason are embodied in the state. It follows then that the most progressive peoples are those capable of state-building—for the state expresses the people's will to survive. Conversely, peoples without states cannot contribute to the development of civilisation; and they would soon cease to be peoples. Finally, according to Hegel, if a people has proved itself incapable of building a state over the course of time, it will never be able to build one.

This last proposition is the cornerstone of the so-called 'theory of *historyless peoples*', adopted by Engels, and, to some extent, Marx, in their earlier years.[20] Neither, of course, furnished a complete theory of nationalism, but their writings are marked by a number of notions and suggestions towards one. [21]

The key to this embryonic theorising is (a) the identification of language and nationality, (b) the contrast drawn between the 'great' nation-states of Western Europe and the small nations of Eastern areas. Marx and Engels favoured large-scale, even multinational, political units, since only they could provide an adequate framework for effective industrial capitalist production and so generate a class-conscious proletariat. Small, underdeveloped peoples were a barrier to economic progress: Montenegrins were 'pious freebooters', Mexicans 'les derniers des hommes', and, as for the Chinese, Engels wrote:

> It would seem as though history had first to make this whole people drunk before it could rouse them out of their hereditary stupidity.

In *Po und Rhein* (1859), Engels sums up the 'great nation' thesis inherited from Hegel:

> All changes (in the map of Europe), if they are to last, must in general start from the effort to give the large and viable European nations more and more their true national boundaries, which are determined by language and sympathies, while at the same time the ruins of peoples, which are still found here and there and which are no longer capable of a national existence, are absorbed by the larger nations and either become a part of them or maintain themselves as ethnographic monuments without political significance. [22]

So, for example, Engels followed Hegel in thinking that the Slavs could never form a nation-state on the British or French model, unless it be under reactionary Tsarist Panslavism; better their absorption by Germany or Austria-Hungary. [23]

The linguistic spur to nationalism is assumed (as in the German Romantic version of nationalism which we examined). For example, the resistance of the Rumanian peasantry in Transylvania to Tsarism and the Ottomans was partly ascribed to their eighteenth-century literary movement: 'When the Rumanian language was suppressed in Wallachia and Moldavia, the Rumanians of Transylvania faithfully preserved the tongue of their ancestors.' [24]

Generally, nationalism is a weapon of the bourgeoisie and its intellectuals:

> It is of course true of every nation that insistence upon nationality is now to be found only among the bourgeoisie and their writers. [25]

At the same time, an ambivalent note is struck when we are directed to observe the contrast between the 'honourable national spirit' of the proletariat, and the 'antiquated national prejudices' of the English and French peasantry. [26] This fits with the picture of the proletariat as the 'national class', in the Communist Manifesto, constituting itself '*the* nation' [27] and with the idea of socialist *inter*nationalism.

The 'great nation' thesis examined

The link between the Marxist origins of 'conflict' theories of nationalism, and the modern 'anticolonialist' theories we outlined at the outset of this chapter is, of course, the *role of capitalism*. Nationalism everywhere is a product of the early stage of capitalism. But in Europe capitalism had different effects from those it generated elsewhere. In Europe, according to Karl Kautsky:

> In proportion as economic development has proceeded, there has grown the need for all who spoke the same language to be joined together in a common state. [28]

And yet, he ruefully acknowledged the other side of the coin: 'the railroads are the mightiest means of the modern period to arouse national hatred'. [29]

This statement should put us already on our guard against the Marxist tendency to simplify the rise and course of nationalism. If these writers distinguish so sharply between the 'nationalism' of Europe and that in underdeveloped countries, why assume that 'capitalism' is nevertheless the 'basic' cause of both varieties? Can we assign the rise of so complex a phenomenon as nationalism to any one cause? Might not different types of nationalism be more realistically explained by a variety of causal chains converging in several combinations?

The *critique* of the Marxian tradition of 'conflict' theories must start therefore with its '*great nation*' thesis, with its identification of nation and language. This thesis contains within itself a basic contradiction, besides making a false identification, as I shall argue, between language and nation. The contradiction is between the linguistic definition of the nation, on the one hand, and the need for economic centralisation expressed in the large 'productive state'. In Western Europe (the model's basis) there is no contradiction; but as Karl Kautsky and Rosa Luxemburg conceded, the contradiction was vividly exposed in Eastern Europe under the impact of advancing capitalism. Rosa Luxemburg unhesitatingly opted for the large productive state—the West European model—and castigated the nationalism of the intelligentsias of Eastern Europe, especially Poland.[30]

In so doing, she may have argued consistently according to Marxist tenets, but this only served to expose the inability of the Marxian framework to account for the phenomenon of nationalism in Eastern Europe. To inveigh against the intellectuals or workers in this area for resorting to nationalism casts serious doubt upon the utility of the 'great nation' thesis, and on the emphasis upon the productive state, the great leveller and creator. This is not to say that the State in its administrative and political aspects did not have a profound influence on the development of nationalism even in Eastern Europe. As will be seen, it played a vital role. But not solely for the reasons adduced by Marxists, i.e. as a tool of capitalism. Empirically, the 'state' or empire did not always play its allotted role in the Marxist drama; its rulers had often totally different goals which conflicted with the economic advancement of the population or any one of its classes. In particular, military goals were favoured. If these could be achieved by state bureaucratic means, proportionally less importance accrued to the role of private capital. Historically, also, we must observe that the rise of nationalist movements often antedated the arrival of capitalism or industrialisation in that area, for example, in Serbia or Transylvania. Movements here had little in common with nationalism in the Western nation-states, whose movements, as in France, appeared when language and territory and economy were perceived to be almost coextensive.

Capitalism, colonialism and imperialism

If the Marxian framework tends to straitjacket the European experience of nationalism in its attempt at explanation (as opposed to description), does it fare any better outside Europe?

The answer can only be a clear negative, and on the selfsame grounds. Once again, it is guilty of reductionist oversimplification because of the all-pervading role it assigns to 'capitalism'.

Basically, the neo-Marxist theory and its modern derivatives fail to distinguish clearly between capitalism, colonialism and imperialism. And the reason for this confusion is the curious way in which the 'great nation' thesis is extended outside Europe. What happens is that the great nation-state (of Western Europe) becomes the imperialist-capitalist nation-state hungry for colonial investments and markets. 'Anticolonialism' is therefore the 'great imperialist nation's' mirror-image, the counter-state, as it were, forced together by imperialism's modernising capitalism. Nationalism therefore is again the product of capitalism.

Before we can, however, consider whether the Marxian 'conflict' framework can supply an adequate account of the rise of nationalism in 'underdeveloped' countries, we must ask if it can explain the antecedent phenomenon of 'imperialism'. Now, if we simply *define* imperialism as capital investment-cum-rule in foreign territories, the need for an 'explanation' is eliminated. But is the definition historically useful? I doubt it. For example, France's conquest of the Maghreb was motivated by political and strategic considerations, together with the Christian missionary zeal of Charles X. Capitalists were loath to invest in this apparently barren area. When they did so, it was only under strong government pressure.

Of course it is always possible to argue that this conquest, like so many others, was the result of the pressure of 'potential' or 'anticipated' interests—as though to say there *must* be some capitalist interest or objective necessity as the ultimate cause. And it is always possible to back this preconceived faith by turning up some obscure financial benefit.

But if we reject this rather determinist line of argument, we are still left with the task of *explaining* imperialism. Schumpeter has convincingly argued that the heyday of imperialism, in the non-Marxist sense of that term, preceded the period of the 'decay of capitalism', in neo-Marxist terms. That means, at a stage when there was no pressure of accumulation on the rate of profit, of working class demands, as yet; but greater monopolies. Moreover, all classes cooperated and benefited from the conquest and annexation of colonies. So such conquests were uninfluenced by the conflict of classes at home. Thirdly, Hobson's emphasis on under-consumption at home holds only in the absence of social reform and redistribution of wealth; yet this very period saw the timid beginnings of such a trend.[31]

In fact, big business exerted little influence on foreign or colonial policy at this time—whatever the case with American military-industrial influence today. The point is that the capitalists before the Second War adapted to colonial policies, being interested mainly in short-run profits rather than expressing 'objective' class interests.

At most, then, we may observe a correlation between British overseas investment and her imperial expansion. Lenin's table (taken from Hobson) should not be interpreted as a *causal* statement. There is no evidence that British imperial expansion was the result of an increasing need for investments overseas—even in the private political papers of statesmen, we find that colonies were of interest for reasons of trade, emigration, strategy, even markets, but hardly ever for investments.[32]

What then lay behind the drive of imperialism? Mainly the desire to strengthen the position of the particular European state in Europe's power struggle—not the benefiting of City financiers. So, for example, the British Government, as the guardian of political power and order, replaced the East India Company when the latter got itself into difficulties.

It is interesting that originally the terms 'imperialism' and 'colonialism' were neutral in meaning. Imperialism only began to acquire a pejorative sense with the resuscitation of Napoleon's empire by his nephew, and Disraeli's use of unprincipled methods of acquiring territories overseas.[33] The same shift of meaning, this time to the Leninist usage, can be observed with 'colonialism', with its corollary 'nationalism', the reaction to an imported system of European economic and political domination.

The nub of my argument can now be approached. It is this: empirically as well as analytically, the three terms, 'imperialism', 'colonialism' and 'capitalism' should be kept separate. To confound them into one pejorative precludes the possibility of an explanation of nationalism in these areas which will do justice to its multifaceted character, and to the obvious differences between the political experience of these societies. We should note that, just as capitalism can operate without 'colonialism' (the Middle Eastern oil companies), so colonial domination can be exercised without resorting to a 'rational' capitalism, as in the case of the Portuguese possessions in Africa. It is 'predatory', rather than 'rational' capitalism, to use the neo-Marxist terminology, which requires colonial rule; yet the motor of 'predatory' capitalism (if indeed there be a single one) is the desire for power (imperialism, in an older sense).

If these concepts are kept distinct, then, historically, colonial rule was the result, not of a need for investments or economic exploitation, but of the need and desire of the great powers to acquire territory overseas, to bolster their prestige and power in the European competition. Political rather than economic interest was the motive force behind 'imperialism'; and the system of rule which Worsley so ably analyses as a kind of zero-sum 'parallel society' was the resulting colonial situation. And just as there were different degrees and types of 'imperialism', so we must be careful to distinguish between various degrees of 'colonial' oppression and kinds of colonial domination (direct and indirect, settler, slaving, etc.). What is true of nearly all colonial situations is the predominance of the administrative over the merchant or missionary elements. Political constraint is the basic feature of colonialism. And in the conflict between traders, missionaries and officials, it is the latter who usually have the final word. The frequency of such conflicts undermines completely the notion that they are all equally 'locked' in a structural situation determined by an economic causal chain of which they are the unwitting victims, and which allows little room for their varying purposes—an assumption that underlies the analyses of even the modern derivatives of Marxian 'conflict' theories.

The 'third world' model

We are now in a position to examine the 'conflict' theories (Worsley's Marxian and J. H. Kautsky's 'interest group') of nationalism itself.

Though these two types of 'conflict' theory differ in important respects,[34] they share a basic assumption: the underlying notion of a 'third', 'underdeveloped' world, apart from the committed, white, industrialised power blocs. The rich whites stand over against the coloured poor—a dichotomy that translates Marx's original polar classes from the *intra*societal to the *inter*societal plane. If it can be shown that 'objectively' the underdeveloped countries constitute a unity, a 'third world', then the conflict of global classes would turn 'colonialism' into a mere intervening variable, a tool of the white rich in the developed countries. 'Colonialism' would then become the analogue of the State's role under a capitalist system, according to Marx's analysis; the colonial state is nothing more than the 'executive committee' of the whole white bourgeoisie of the developed imperialist countries. The real conflict is then between white, capitalist imperialism and coloured, poor 'anti-imperialism', resisting foreign class exploitation.

Taken to this logical conclusion, the Marxian 'conflict' framework is revealed as a unilinear evolutionism. The difference between the European and non-European routes to industrial modernisation recedes into the background. The more rigorous the Marxist analysis employed, the less important appears the role of the colonial system of rule and the colonial situation. The less important too becomes the territorial unit of rule, the colony itself.

This last point is crucial. What marks out the nationalisms of Africa, and, to some extent, Asia and Latin America, is their reliance on the colonial *territory* as the basis for the embryonic 'nation'. Nationalist movements here are 'single-state' nationalisms. Their great fear is a separatist 'tribalism', and, one suspects, an engulfing Pan nationalism (the leaders' protestations to the contrary notwithstanding); witness the failure of Pan-Turkism, Pan-Negroism, Pan-Arabism (cf. the 1969 Rabat failure) and, to date, even Pan-Africanism. Ataturk's 'heartland' nation-state is the dominant model, with a self-limiting emphasis on internal development.[35]

If, *per contra*, one abandons the rigour of Marxist class conflict analysis, it becomes increasingly difficult to talk in terms of a class-united 'Third World'. And the variations of colonialism as a predominantly *political* system, or better set of systems, become proportionally more significant.

Is it then useful to think in terms of a united 'Third World'? I suppose that the most plausible meaning of that overemployed concept, the 'third world', is political in intent. It owes much to the euphoria of the Bandoeng era. But 'objectively', the divisions between Africa, Asia and Latin America are far greater than their unities, the differences far exceed the similarities—even in purely economic terms. Think of the contrasts between a fairly prosperous African state like Ivory Coast, and poverty-stricken Mali, or the relative modernity of large parts of Turkey and the feudal conditions of Saudi Arabia.

What these countries do share, of course (with the exception of China), is their relative *political* weakness in the Cold War situation. But again, this political weakness is not simply a reflection of their technological backwardness, or the predominance of agriculture over industry. It is also a matter of time (the early start of the West) and history, but, more important, of political factors, such as communal will and appropriate ideology, and social factors, such as lack of cohesion. Now these political and social factors vary from country to country, alongside the purely economic. As economic historians like Gerschenkron point out, 'backwardness' is a relative concept, with a series of graduated rungs from the case of England, the first to emerge into self-sustaining growth, to the later (European and Japanese) developers, to those who have not yet achieved this state of affairs, partly due to their poor assets and even more to the increasing 'exogeneity' of the growth process.[36] Likewise there is a continuum of political assets within the developing countries, which contributes to their internal divisions.

The political weakness of the 'uncommitted' nations is also a matter of people's subjective perceptions. And these are, of course, very relative. They vary, like prestige rankings, from country to country, and from group to group, within countries. Here too we may find a clue to the varieties of nationalist experience.

It is clear, then, that with the collapse of the 'third world' model as an analytic tool, we must abandon the Marxian 'conflict' framework if we are to explain the emergence and course of nationalist movements in these areas. It is no good for Marxians to distinguish European from non-European paths of 'development', and their correlative nationalisms, if they then go on to *explain* the latter in the same terms, or nearly, as they do the former, i.e. by using the 'great nation' thesis covertly to emphasise the ultimacy of the role of capitalism as primary determinant. The argument is reductionist and deterministic.[37] If we *must* have a monocausal theory of nationalism, then science and its technological applications remain a more acceptable candidate than 'capitalism'. In fact, the actual situation calls for a more sophisticated treatment of the problem.

Nationalism and social revolution

A further difficulty is posed by Worsley's analysis of nationalism in developing countries as ensuing from certain well-defined, if not always identical, needs of the mass of the population. Two of those needs—independence and decolonisation—read rather like a redescription or redefinition of nationalism itself. The third, 'development', raises doubts as to whether the needs are those perceived by the population or those imputed to their situation by the observer. It is difficult to imagine that fellahin and untouchables actually *perceive* this 'need for development'; even if their elites *see* the need, that is insufficient to explain their actions, or to assume that their nationalism 'satisfies' it—unless the observer imposes from outside his judgments drawn in turn from a particular socio-historical schema. Once again, we seem to be drawn towards that retrospective determinism, to which reductionist theories like neo-Marxism are so prone.

This doubt raises a more interesting question: in what sense, if any, is nationalism 'revolutionary'? What is the relation between nationalist movements and social revolutions? Does the greater part of the people come at a certain point to feel certain needs which they judge can only be satisfied by revolutionary activity, such as constituting themselves as a new political community?

It would require another treatise to answer this satisfactorily, since one would need to analyse the relationship between nationalism and each of the major social groupings across different varieties of movement. But a preliminary survey reveals, I think, significant variations in nationalist activity along a 'reformist-revolutionary' continuum; consider the obvious differences between Niger and Upper Volta, even Nigeria (if we accord all these 'nationalist' status) and, say, Algeria or Sudan. In the former, there was little in the way of structural change that could be labelled 'revolutionary', in the political sense of 'forcible interventions, either to replace governments, or to change the processes of government',[38] much less in the social sense of a 'sweeping, fundamental change not only in political organisation, but also in the social structure, economic property control, and the predominant myth of the social order'.[39] This is also true of many of the states of Latin America and the Middle East, though from time to time they may appear to pass through a more 'revolutionary' phase.

There are significant cases where the nationalist movement has started a social revolution (China, Cuba, France, Turkey, Mexico, Israel, Japan, to some extent India, Burma, Egypt, Iran, Indonesia, Yugoslavia, Czechoslovakia, Central Asia, Tartary); but the degree to which it has been the *prime* initiator of change, and the degree to which it has penetrated all groups, especially in the most backward areas, varies greatly. Moreover, there is the paradox that a nationalist movement can be revolutionary, as in Armenia and Greece, but fail to produce a social revolution among the population, or even its populistic variant.[40] One sector of the population may be unable to fit its material and ideal interests, or its cultural perceptions, to those of others, in a concerted action. Smelser's 'value-added' progression is distinguished by its rarity; the 'Great Revolutions'[41] and the Nazi revolution are perhaps the only cases where, at a *single* historical point, the key groups succumbed to a series of converging pressures to produce a convulsion in the social order, under the impact of a pervasive ideological movement.

But even in these cases, nationalism was but one element in the ideological compound that galvanised the movement into revolutionary action. It may have been predominant in the French and Chinese, perhaps the American and Cuban, cases; but religious, Marxist and racialist ideologies were the major elements in the English, Russian and Nazi revolutions, respectively.[42]

If the word 'revolution' connotes a primarily political reorganisation, we might well concede that nationalism is a revolutionary movement—though it is not always violent in its methods, it is always a set of demands, backed by a potential threat of violence, even if only by a kind of 'demonstration effect' from afar.[43] But if 'revolution' is taken to include sweeping socioeconomic and cultural changes, then of itself, for all its democratising potential, nationalism has not always constituted a revolutionary force. There are very few cases (Holland, England and its dominions) where nationalism has not played *some* part in a revolutionary process, but it has only rarely been a sufficient condition of revolution (Turkey, Japan, possibly China, Cuba, Mexico, Ghana, Tanzania and France).

The nationalist ideology is of course 'revolutionary'. It demands autodetermination of the whole community and popular sovereignty. The 'nation' is the source of law, authority, belief, identity. Other gods are banished or rendered impotent. Yet, despite all this, the Italian case remains typical. The Risorgimento was a revolution manqué. It stirred large parts of the populace; Garibaldi, Alfieri, Mazzini, Verdi, retain a hold on the affections and respect. It helped to accomplish the unification of the peninsula, even if Cavour proved more effective. But it also failed to homogenise the population—North and South, capitalists and labourers, city and countryside, Catholics and Socialists. The great changes that occurred in the mode of production, styles of life, ways of thought and relations between individuals, cannot be ascribed to the motive power of the Risorgimento. As Pareto and Mosca saw, its democratic impulse was stifled by the corruption of the ruling oligarchy. As in Greece, it failed to achieve the mission which men like Mazzini and Korais envisaged—to renovate, purify, remould the whole community, in the image of the idealised past and messianic future. Instead, its energies were displaced on to external objects (the Mediterranean and Byzantine mirages), or dissipated by internal dissensions and conflicting goals.

The role of the intelligentsia

There are, however, certain points in the analyses of Worsley and J. H. Kautsky, which merit attention and are not directly dependent on their Marxian framework.

In particular, their stress on the role of the intelligentsia—especially by Kautsky. Indeed, the 'interest group' approach is least affected by the dubious assumptions of the Marxian framework.

The intelligentsia do, indeed, play a definitive part in the rise of nationalist movements—everywhere. There is, of course, nothing new in highlighting the key role of this section of the population. Max Nomad put forward this idea at the turn of the century—in relation to socialist movements, and Mannheim's work on the *freischwebend* intelligentsia is a commonplace now. What I think is relatively new and valuable is Kautsky's analysis of the reasons for their involvement and leadership. Unlike Worsley, whose neo-Marxism tends to lead him towards a kind of retrospective historical determinism in his elite-mass nationalism sequence, Kautsky places more emphasis on the independent actions and desires of the intellectuals. It is not just their 'objective' position in a traditional society under the onslaught of capitalistic colonialism that counts; what matters even more is the fact that they, and they alone, *perceive* this situation and react to it in a number of ways, though within a basic pattern.

The merit of this approach lies in the possibility of its extension to other groups, and in the possibility that cultural motives may influence action as much as economic interests. This possibility breaks the determinist circle, which threatens to ossify even the more sophisticated Marxian analyses. It also adumbrates the important point that 'the intellectuals' divide under the impact of modernisation.

The other merit of 'interest group' theory is its stress on the 'displacement' and uprooting of key groups, particularly the intelligentsia. This is not again just a matter of economic loss; it is as much a loss of status and a problem of cultural alienation 'at home'. This breeds a nostalgia for an idealised past, which forms one element in the ideology of nationalist movements.

In the succeeding chapters I propose to focus more closely on the sentiments and activities of the 'intelligentsia'. But, before doing so, I should not wish to give the impression that the role of other groups is insignificant in the emergence, let alone the diffusion, of nationalism. 'Interest group' theory provides a useful antidote and background to exclusive concentration on any particular sector of the population, however important. Economic interests remain a strong motor of group activity, even where they cannot be invoked as a primary determinant. The rise of commerce and a wealthy bourgeoisie, if not a necessary condition, is often an important contributory condition, of the rise of nationalism. One has only to think of cases like the Tatars, the Greeks and Armenians, India and Indonesia, France and the United States, of the Gold Coast and Argentina, to name but a few.

Yet never, I would argue, has the rise of a middle class been a sufficient condition of nationalism; and one can think of cases (the Jews of Eastern Europe, the Transylvanian peasants, the Oirots and Tuvinians, the Polish aristocrats, Catholic agrarian Ireland, isolated Montenegro, the Magyar landowners, Chinese and Yugoslav peasants, or poor Negroes in the United States, among others) where the direct influence of even commercial

capitalism and its bourgeois bearers has been negligible—often
the movement antedated the rise of such classes. (Of course,
there have always been rich 'entrepreneurs' at all times, *some*
of whom were nearly always to be found among the supporters
of the nationalist movement.) The French model must not be
over-generalised. Even neighbouring Germany's movement was
not really led by the emergent 'middle classes', i.e. a commercial
bourgeoisie.

Factors other than commerce and a bourgeoisie, I would
contend, are more closely linked to the rise of nationalist movements. 'Conflict' theories which start from capitalism fail to reach
their explanatory goal, and oversimplify the complexity of the
causal mechanism.

Chapter Five

TRANSITIONAL MAN

So far, we have examined two types of sociological theory of nationalism: the 'disintegration' and 'conflict' varieties. We also considered a more historical theory, a kind of 'idealist' conservatism.

All these attempts to explain the complex phenomenon of nationalism, we concluded, broke down—mainly because they tried to straitjacket the phenomenon to fit the theory, and confused definitions with theories. Not to mention their recourse to tautology and oversimplification.

There was also, however, the suggestion that these models and theories contain some valuable insights, and raise problems of significance. Perhaps their chief merit is to sensitise us to the role of certain important factors which contributed to the rise and diffusion of nationalist movements: philosophical speculation, a sense of cohesion, capitalist exploitation, urban anomie, shared values, class conflicts, etc. The trouble with these theories was their one-sided accentuation of a single condition, or set of conditions, as necessary or sufficient for all or most cases of 'nationalism'. Whereas, it emerges from the foregoing analysis that a certain theoretical scepticism is a prophylactic for our problem; and that it is sensible to regard these 'factors' as 'contributory' conditions, until a more sophisticated methodology can provide a rigorous specification of the limits of their applicability.

The new education

There is, however, one factor which *does* appear to be a necessary condition of all nationalist movements. It is the factor glanced at last—the role of the intelligentsia—and it forms the point of departure for a third group of sociological theories of nationalism.

This rather diffuse group of theories seems to come closest to the central issues evoked by the problem of nationalism, and particularly of its origins and appeal. I shall term them 'modernisation' theories, simply to highlight their central focus of concern. The previously examined theories were all, in a sense, aware of the connection between modernisation and nationalism. But they tended to treat 'modernisation' as a prop in the background of the landscape, a general setting of various ideologies and movements. Or they reinterpreted 'modernisation', and subordinated it, like Marx, to another all-encompassing concept. The theories to be considered now, on the other hand, attempt to make a direct connection between nationalism and 'modernisation' as such, believing this link contains the decisive clue to the problem. One might equally well refer to this group of theories as 'communications' or 'westernisation' theories; but I have preferred a rather more inclusive term, because it brings out the main assumptions which lie behind the more specific subcategories. In this chapter I look at those 'modernisation' theories which stress the role of communications generally; in the next, those that link nationalism to the impact of processes emanating from the West.

The argument of both kinds of 'modernisation' theories, at the broadest level, can be summarised as follows: nationalism is the product of a new type of education, which first affects a small, disaffected minority within the traditional society, the 'intelligentsia', and then spreads to other groups, using the mass media and literacy to reach the masses. This novel type of education is radically opposed to the traditional elite or folk varieties. It stresses secular, utilitarian values, is linguistic in form, relates individuals through sets of shared symbols, and transmits memories and experiences to posterity. It overturns an hierarchical order and creates 'new men'. It opens up undreamt of vistas, subjects all ideas to the tests of reason and observation, and endows individuals with a new status and sense of identity. It replaces precedent and myth and custom by the habit of critical enquiry, technical efficiency and professional expertise. In turn, this education breeds a radical spirit of enterprise, innovation and achievement, and a sense of purpose and continual change which sums up that great revolution of 'modernisation' sweeping the world.[1]

The vanguard of 'modernisation' is the intelligentsia, and the modernising intellectual of the Western Enlightenment is the prototype. Historically, we can tell the story of the spread of the new education and its concomitants as that of the 'impact of the West' on non-Western societies. It is true that the most traditional of agrarian societies changed—and 'progressively' at that. But only in the West did the peculiar spirit of technological innovation take root, from inside—to be emulated and imposed on other lands.

The story of 'modernisation' is therefore an account of the varieties of selective adaptation or imposition of Western beliefs and institutions in alien settings. A good example of this process of 'borrowing' from Western models is furnished by the Middle East. Muhammad Ali and Mahmud II imported Western techniques and education into Egypt and the Ottoman Empire in the early nineteenth century, and unwittingly created new social groupings and a new consciousness, which gradually challenged the rule of the landowners, *ulama* and merchants.[2] Education replaced birth as the criterion for wielding authority, and abstract concepts ousted customary allegiances. In the Iraq of Nuri-es-Said, much later, to send deliberately thousands of students abroad to learn Western techniques was to graft a modern component on to the traditional economy and society. Roads, dams, factories, hygiene and other facilities entered the social consciousness; the engineer, entrepreneur and bureaucrat were elevated into key political positions.[3] They are now the vanguard of the politically effective and articulate citizenry, and are often to be found in military garb. In the post-1945 era, mass media have reached into every village, activating and uprooting and moulding new groups. Communications and education stir the local scene from afar, and villagers are 'mobilised' *in situ*. And so the cultural and social concomitants of industrialisation uproot the traditional ways well before industrialisation proper appears. Modern education, spreading from the West in waves, imposes a new social order on top of the ruins of the old.

The grocer of Balgat

Modernisation theorists who stress the crucial role of 'communications' and a 'communications revolution' have found in this approach a useful tool for analysing the political changes in societies newly exposed to the impact of the West. Modern Turkey provides a typical case-study of this 'communications revolution'.

In his well-known analysis of the transformation of Middle Eastern societies, Daniel Lerner presents a parable of the three stages of the modernisation process: tradition, transition, modernity.

Tosun, Lerner's Turkish informant, is the man from the modern city, Ankara, who in 1950 entered the now strange world of the little village of Balgat, a few miles away. There he encountered two opposed characters: the village Chief, contented, paternal, loyal, military-minded, fatalistic, the epitome of traditional Turkish values; and the Grocer, restless, heterodox, worldly, unsatisfied and alone:

> The Grocer is a very different style of man. Though born and bred in Balgat, he lives in a different world, an expansive world, populated more actively with imaginings and fantasies—hungering for whatever is different and unfamiliar. Where the Chief is contented, the Grocer is restless. To Tosun's probe, the Grocer replied staccato: 'I have told you I want better things. I would have liked to have a bigger grocery shop in the city, to have a nice house there, dress in nice civilian clothes.'[4]

The Grocer saw himself as different from the other villagers, indeed as locked in some sort of struggle with them. He alone knew of a better existence, other ways of life—and envied them. The other villagers were constricted in their vision. They gasped at the very idea of imagining themselves 'president of Turkey'. The Grocer, however, was not only quite prepared for this role in his self-image, but even had a clear idea of what he would do as president:

> I would make roads for the villagers to come to towns to see the world and would not let them stay in their holes all their life.[5]

The Grocer for Lerner is a man in mental transition. His psyche is turned towards the modern urban society. He is the paradigm of the 'transitional man'.

D

The chief characteristic of 'transitional' men is their dynamism. Outwardly, theirs is a febrile restlessness. Inwardly, they stand at the point of 'engagement', when they are just perceiving 'connections between its private dilemmas and public issues'.[6] The Transitionals exhibit the key traits of inconsistency and ambivalence over old and new values and life-styles. In Turkey, Lerner estimates, some 30% of the population in 1958 had left behind the constrictive personality and compulsive view of the traditional type, but had not yet acquired the self-assurance and cosmopolitan aspirations of the Moderns. The Transitionals are 'men-in-motion'. They are torn by the conflict between 'new aspirations and old traditions'. They are psychically mobile, and often physically, too. Lerner cites the social psychological findings of Mustafer Sherif to support his basic proposition that

> mobility tends to be systemic, i.e. physical, social and psychic mobility 'go together' in every village.[7]

Secularisation is another characteristic of the transitional type. Questions which were formerly answered within a religious framework are now increasingly seen as socio-economic in nature. Precedent and custom lose their hold; knowledge and economic gain become the touchstones of action. The Transitionals hold opinions on all matters, they become social and political activists, they acquire the desire to participate in public issues. They are the men of the future—like the workers of Egypt, or the deruralised peasants of Syria's nationalist Right. Such men are most powerfully moved by the symbols of 'nation' and 'class'. The ritual and symbols of religion have lost their meaning.

'Empathy' and the mass media

In Lerner's account, the three characters—the contented Chief, the restless and ambivalent Grocer, and the self-assured Tosun from the cosmopolitan city—represent three stages in an inevitable progression: namely, the global process of 'modernisation'. All societies, that is, must pass from a face-to-face, traditional stage through an ambivalent, uncertain 'transition' to reach finally the plateau of the modern, 'participant' and national society and culture.

The baseline of Lerner's theory of 'modernisation' is the

tension he perceives between the Western model and the aspirations of the people of other areas of the world.

He holds that:

> the sequence of current events in the Middle East can be understood as a deviation, in some measure a deliberate deformation, of the Western model.[8]

The Western model is an historical fact. But it does not possess merely an antiquarian relevance. If we study the components of the sequence by which Western society evolved over the centuries, we shall find that these elements have global relevance.

> Everywhere, for example, increasing urbanisation has tended to raise literacy; rising literacy has tended to increase media exposure; increasing media exposure has 'gone with' wider economic participation (*per capita* income) and political participation (voting).[9]

Lerner finds additional support for this contention in the 'tacit assumptions and proclaimed goals which prevail among Middle East spokesmen'. For, in their eyes (and Lerner's),

> . . . Western society still provides the most developed model of societal attributes (power, wealth, skill, rationality) which Middle East spokesmen continue to advocate as their own goal. . . . What the West is, in this sense, the Middle East seeks to become.[10]

There is, of course, a considerable difference between Western and non-Western 'modernisation'. But the difference is not one of kind; it is only one of *pace*. The evolution of Western society, from the age of the Renaissance, is to be telescoped into a few decades. And this is possible, because the knowledge and products of centuries of Western innovation are readily accessible to all, given the desire for these benefits and their accompanying 'spirit' of innovation.

But exactly at this point lies the rub. There will be no sustained modernisation, unless men arise who *desire* it. Desiring innovative change implies a new type of personality structure. Men must no longer see life as ordained and their status as ascribed; the future must now appear manipulable, their advancement as achieved. A pragmatic and purposive rationality must replace the older cyclical fatalism.

The personality structure which embraces this 'modernity' has a new set of inner mechanisms. 'Empathy' is the term which Lerner uses to describe these. He defines it as follows:

a high capacity for rearranging the self-system on short notice,

or more simply:

the capacity to see oneself in the other fellow's situation.[11]

The empathiser adapts easily to changes in his environment by identifying with new aspects of that environment; such identification being achieved by the two Freudian mechanisms of projection and introjection. So a man enlarges his identity; he incorporates new demands into the Self. His is a mobile sensibility.

Now empathy, Lerner maintains, is widely diffused in modern, national societies. Indeed, psychically mobile personalities are typical only of urban, industrial, literate and fully participant societies.

Transitional societies, on the other hand, exhibit a lower diffusion of empathy. It is a burgeoning characteristic of such societies. It must be, by definition. For the empathic capacity alone

enables newly mobile persons to *operate efficiently* in a changing world.

It alone constitutes

an indispensable skill for moving people out of traditional settings.[12]

Yet Lerner concedes that 'empathy', for all its motor and causal power, is itself a result of certain antecedent conditions, stated in the following complex proposition:

. . . the media spread psychic mobility most efficiently among peoples who have in some measure achieved the antecedent conditions of geographic and social mobility.[13]

Here again, Lerner looks back to his baseline, the Western model, which he insists

reappears in virtually all modernising societies on all continents of the world, regardless of variations in race, colour, creed.[14]

And the main features of this model are in turn derived from the final 'end-state', which are implicitly those of present-day Western, notably American, society. These features are: urbanisation, literacy, exposure to mass media, and political participation (voting). According to Lerner, these are closely correlated. The indices of modernisation tend to reinforce each other. They form a determinate sequence of phases, with an immanent logic of its own—governed by a spiralling of individual needs. It requires only the antecedent condition of geographical mobility into towns to set the whole sequence in motion.

The mass media is the supremely decisive feature for Lerner. Their function is that of an internal 'mobility multiplier'. That is, they greatly expand the range of situations in which a man can imagine himself. If they demand a pre-existing capacity for empathy, they in turn immeasurably increase its possibilities; for they open up an infinite *vicarious* universe. The media bring the 'opinions of mankind' to bear on the self-images of individuals and nations. They teach 'interior manipulation', portraying possible roles and situations and opinions, all of which may confront him.

> As a young bureaucrat in Iran put it: 'The movies are like a teacher to us, who tells us what to do and what not.'[15]

Ambivalence

What is the relevance of all this to the rise and spread of nationalism?

It is interesting that nationalism as a distinct phenomenon gets only a passing mention in Lerner's opening theoretical statement. Whereas the empirical surveys of the individual Middle Eastern countries are replete with observations on its role, indicating its differential, but strong, appeal for various social and cultural groups. The surveys leave a distinct impression that the 'nation' is the major political symbol for most political actors, and the claims of 'nationalism' something none can afford to underrate.

This apparent discrepancy can be explained by reference to the meanings Lerner gives to the term 'nationalism'. These meanings are admittedly implicit, but they have the force of a leitmotif. Nationalists are men who reject the West, are ethnocentric, and, above all, hold *ambivalent* feelings towards the advanced nations. They reject the West politically, but admire its spirit and institutions; they espouse its values, but hate its domination. They desire its benefits, they seek to imitate its ways, they clamour for the admission ticket—but on their own terms, in their 'own way'.

Nationalism in the Middle East is extreme. It is frenetic,

xenophobic and febrile. Its 'rejection' of the West is a surface phenomenon, an expression of aspirations outrunning the possibilities of fulfilment.

Obviously, we are back to the Grocer of Balgat. It is the 'transitional man', the man who has begun to empathise, who is reaching out for new worlds beyond attainment, whose discontent turns to ambivalent nationalism; he admires and rejects the West simultaneously, because the West possesses what he longs to have, but knows he cannot.

There is, therefore, no real contradiction between nationalism's fleeting appearance in Lerner's 'theory' and the emphasis assigned to it in the empirical sections. 'Nationalism' for Lerner really means the political ambivalence of Transitionals; so that he is implicitly talking about nationalism, even where he does not utilise the term. It becomes a natural part of the processes associated with the 'transition', an inexorable consequence.

But we can go further. As in other 'communications' theories, Lerner makes an implicit distinction between two processes: (1) the growth of nations and nation-states, and (2) the rise of 'nationalism' and the nationalist movement. It is a distinction which corresponds to that between the secular trend to a Western-type society identified with the state of 'modernity', on the one hand, and the 'deviations' and 'deliberate deformations' of that trend in non-Western settings. The growth of nations was a fundamental trait of the evolutionary sequence in the West; in a sense, it is just a redescription of that sequence. The rise of nationalism, by contrast, manifests the ethnocentrism of non-Western societies. Perhaps the key passage in this connection is the following:

> But these societies-in-a-hurry have little patience with the historical *pace* of Western development; what happened in the West over centuries, some Middle Easterners seek to accomplish in years. Moreover, they want to do it their 'own way'. A complication of Middle East modernization is its own ethnocentrism—expressed politically in extreme nationalism, psychologically in passionate xenophobia. The hatred sown by anticolonialism is harvested in the rejection of every appearance of foreign tutelage.

But, argues Lerner, in effect one cannot reject the 'behavioural and institutional compulsions' which he asserts underlay the variant ideological forms of modernisation in Europe, America and Russia. One cannot obviate these 'historical regularities' by trying 'new routes and risky by-passes'. Attempting to telescope and remould this sequence to fit the conditions of a particular area will only result in that frenetic and xenophobic nationalism which we are now witnessing in the Middle East. Of course, it is politically possible to denounce the West; and the importance of this 'manœuvre' should not be underrated. But it is merely a secondary diversion from the real problems. These problems are the 'hurdles' of modernisation; and the passing interest of the political 'manœuvre' cannot obscure the fundamental framework in which this kind of 'nationalism' operates—namely, the inexorable progress of the three-stage evolutionary pattern based on the Western model.[16]

The conclusion is clear. 'Nationalism' occupies for Lerner and other 'communications' theorists an ambiguous position. On the one hand, it is a kind of gateway through which all must pass during the transition to modernity. On the other, it is a somewhat regrettable, if secondary, diversion from the swiftest manner of surmounting the transitional phase. Deplorable, irritating, frustrating—but, it appears, inevitable.

Modernising and westernising

Lerner's account is perhaps the most explicit and arresting example of the theories of a whole school which sees the basic ingredients of the process of 'modernisation' as consisting in 'communications'. The argument is roughly this: to enter the political arena, to build national cultures, to arrive at a developed 'modernity', men must become mobile—physically, socially, psychically. The instruments and paths of this mobility are those of literacy, empathy and the mass media.

Some writers on 'nationality' (which is a rather different concept from 'nationalism') do also stress the discontinuities of commerce and trade, the growth of an integrating division of labour, and

> the complementarity of acquired social and economic preferences which involve the mobility of goods or persons.

Karl Deutsch has suggested that the rise of industrialism and the modern market economy 'offers economic and psychological rewards to tense and insecure individuals—to men and women uprooted by social and technological change, exposed to the risks of economic competition, and taught to hunger for success'. Taken together, these economic and psychological factors have led to the need to belong to a group—a need best fulfilled by 'putting their trust in their nation'.[17] At the same time, he thinks that 'mobilisation' does *not* refer primarily to the entrance of large numbers of people into the arena of social and economic competition; like other 'communications' theorists, he sees this crucial process as one of activating individuals for 'relatively more intensive communication'—especially mass communication, to create a 'public'.[18]

The basic assumptions behind all these 'communications' theories are threefold:

1 The process of 'modernisation', once set in motion, follows an inevitable progression with its own momentum, despite minor variations
2 This progression is basically modelled on the pattern of Western evolution
3 The key to the 'modernisation' process is the growth of mobile personalities possessing the capacity to transmit information in a meaningful manner between individuals and groups; and this creates national cultures and communities.[19]

It is most convenient to take assumptions (1) and (2) together in this section, and evaluate their tenability. The topic of 'modernisation' is vast, and clearly beyond the scope of this work. Since, however, assumptions about 'modernisation' underlie, as I shall argue, the most convincing theories of nationalism, the subject must be broached, however cursorily and inadequately.

The conception of 'modernisation' taken from the West is not only ethnocentric, but crudely determinist.

It conceives of 'modernity' as an 'end-state', and as an exclusive system of interdependent parts opposed to another homologous system called 'tradition'; the assumptions, practices, institutions, roles and values of these total orders are diametrically opposite and separate. And the chief empirically discernible trend in the contemporary social scene is the painful but inexorable exchange of the one system for the other—usually through a dislocating transitional epoch.

Critics of this approach have called in question both its

'systemic' models, and its analysis of empirical processes. Gusfield for instance has argued,

1 That traditional societies aren't homogeneous in every case—there are many conflicting or coexisting traditions in a particular society—Great and Little, urban and folk, etc.

2 That in practice traditional elements are often fused with modern ones—in syncretistic African cults, for example

3 That traditional elements sometimes favour innovative changes—one thinks of the capitalistic English landowners in Tudor and Stuart times, or the uses of Emperor-worship in Meiji Japan

4 That, conversely, modern elements may sometimes reinforce traditional ones—as when sanskritisation followed hard upon westernisation of the upper classes in India and spread Brahmin values among the masses.[20] 'Tradition' and 'modernity' are better apprehended as *interpenetrating*, rather than exclusive, systems of thought and action. They are really only ideal-typical clusters of perceived choices, which also serve as legitimations for action.

A slightly more relativistic definition of 'modernisation' is found in a set of lectures by W. C. Smith. He is concerned to distinguish 'modernisation' from its historical twin, 'westernisation'.[21] The latter is a time-and-place-bound process, and of much less use in describing contemporary developments in countries of Asia, such as India. After all there are now many alternatives within the West itself; this is in contrast to the couple of Western models offered in the last century. Besides there are now a fair number of non-Western models for developing nations—Russia, China, Japan, Cuba, etc.—whose experiences may make them rather more suitable as 'process models' for leaders of these countries. In fact, as Dore argues, the developmental recipes with greatest relevance for poor and backward areas are just those which are showing some success in their modernisation programmes in sociologically juxtaposed settings and contemporary conditions.[22] Smith's final argument is the familiar one that socio-cultural and economic differences in the starting-points for development of nations automatically entails differences in their 'routes' of modernisation, and in the stages through which they pass. Altogether, the concept of 'modernisation' really signifies an increase in the range of techniques and possibilities open to men, as well as in their awareness of alternatives and choices.

An explicit rejection of the idea of 'modernity' as an end-state is found in the essay by Nettl and Robertson on this issue.[23] 'Modernity' for them is only a kind of 'moving target', ever sought after, ever elusive. They define 'modernisation' as:

> the process whereby national elites seek successfully to reduce their atomic status and move towards equivalence with other 'well-placed' nations.

This is an outward-looking, internationalist and relativistic definition. 'Modernisation' is here no endogenous growth; it is heavily dependent on the subjective definitions of the situation and role-playing of the national elite actors. This would accord with the 'transitive' use of the verb, to modernise, for which Dore has forcefully argued; 'modernising' refers to sets of actions and policies of specific leaders looking to other nations whom they take as their models. The context of 'modernising' is therefore fluid and varies with the context:

> There are as many forms of modernisation as there are modernising leaders.[24]

We have here, then, two conflicting approaches to the concept and subject-matter of 'modernisation': an 'objectivist' version, stressing the structural constraints and regularities of sequence; and a relativistic and 'subjectivist' approach, stressing the multiplicity of perceptions and choices of actors in a broad situation.

Clearly space and relevance forbid me to enter into the objections to both of these rather crudely delineated approaches. Suffice it to point out that, while leaders of developing nations do obviously have some latitude for decision-making, they operate within specific historical and structural limits. One asks oneself how it would be possible for leaders consciously to shut out modernising influences, to stem all its ramifications. Not even the Latin American technocratic dictatorships, or the traditionalist monarchies of some Middle Eastern countries, can completely seal off their domains from those outside influences which would bring those areas close to the assumptions and practices of the so-called more advanced nations—though they can do much to impede the pace.[25]

The basic position, therefore, which underlies my own analysis can be stated summarily:

1 There is no 'upper limit' to modernisation processes, there is no end-state called 'modernity' at which one 'arrives'—in this I agree with the relativists and 'subjectivists', but
2 There *is* a 'lower limit' to the processes of modernisation, and it needs a special impetus to move assumptions and structures away from those which can usefully be labelled 'traditional'— here the 'objectivists' rightly insist on a distinctive structural process *within* the variegated processes of modernisation.

This fundamental structural process, I believe, is the reciprocal influence of the scientific and technological revolutions. The national elites (and others) have become modernisers to the extent that they have been touched by the assumptions and spirit of empirical science. A society can be said to have begun to modernise when a significant group within it base their actions on scientific assumptions, trying to apply the principles of technological organisation to other areas of social and political life, and to influence the policies of the rulers in that direction. The concept of 'modernisation' derives its meaning from its implementation of, and aspiration for, the norms of rationality, efficiency and innovative change, based on technology, and applied methodically and continuously. It has a uniform core, but multiple forms.

By definition, therefore, there are modernising, but no modern, societies. They share a few key features and aspirations, but realise them in different ways.

Communications and the birth of the cosmopolitan

For Lerner, Deutsch and other 'communications' theorists, the essence of 'modernisation' was the process of 'mobilisation' though empathy, information and the mass media. New horizons, new roles, strange experiences and imaginings, more intensive networks of memories and messages, were created by the mechanisms of 'communications'. And the mechanisms in question were those evolved in the West; their effects outside the West were held to be identical to the Western results—with a little local colouring, perhaps.

However, it is not the ethnocentrism of the 'communications' model of modernisation that offends *per se*; it is rather the deterministic use of the model itself, that must be challenged.

Put simply, there *is* no fixed model of 'empathy' or the 'mass media', and there is no single determinate process of 'modernisation'. Within certain limits, there are a variety of forms and overall frameworks of mass media; and again, within certain limits, there are different degrees and forms of 'empathy', insofar as any precise meaning can be attached to this concept.

Now it has yet to be shown that the degree and kind of 'empathy' or mass media are correlated with the permeation of society by scientific attitudes and techniques, i.e. of modernisation. People with differing assumptions and beliefs react after all quite differently to exposure to the same new 'sights', including those portrayed by the mass media. The 'communications' theorists operate with a one-dimensional view of the effects of the mass media. 'Modernisation' for them is a process whereby the mass media

1 bring new knowledge of the world,
2 induce expectations which outrun the possibilities of satisfying them,
3 create new statuses which provide arenas for nationalists.

Peacock has rightly characterised 'communications' theory as the American variety of the European sociology of knowledge; he argues that it lays too much stress on the information purveyed by the media, and ignores the media's form and total image system.[26] Systems of communications are not just conveyors of tidbits of information, or of discrete images of goods and experiences; they define broad types of action, they symbolically portray whole sets of ideals and beliefs.

This means that the (Western) media operate within certain *assumptions*. They may help to multiply 'modernisation', to diffuse its assumptions more rapidly. But of themselves, they cannot generate the desire for new knowledge or higher expectations or statuses. These new assumptions and aspirations of 'modernisation' must first take root locally, to allow the mass media to hold any meaning for its audience. The vision of new goods and knowledge will appear 'of another world', dream-like, unless those who do not possess them are already socially impelled and psychologically attuned to desiring them. The reason why the

Grocers of Balgat and many other villagers want the new goods and life-styles is not simply because they had 'seen' them, visited Ankara, been to the cinema, etc. Rather it was because they had already seen their advantages and accepted the assumptions underlying what they saw, that is, they had come to adopt the 'value' and *interpretation* which their possessors put upon them.

One can 'see' the new sights, and fail to desire them—either because one has not grasped the meaning attributed to them, or because one has understood only too well just what acceptance of these desires and goods entails, and rejects them out of an awareness that the price to be paid for their acquisition is, under a given belief-system or in terms of economic or political interests, too 'costly'. This is an attitude characteristic of the tradition*alist*, who consciously rejects innovation—as opposed to the so-called 'traditional' man, who *inter alia* doesn't know that he is upholding a given tradition. Secondly, it is possible to 'see' the new sights and goods, and as Lerner at one point suggests, desire them on a strictly selective basis. [27] Exposure to mass communications systems does not automatically carry with it the desire for 'modernity' and its benefits. It does not necessarily implant a 'mobile sensibility', or 'empathy', even where there has been physical mobility. In Uganda and West Africa, the seasonally migrant labourers come to town to increase their income for their meagre farms, or to earn enough to pay the bride-price, or to see the sights and benefit from the town's amenities. Yet many remain fixed in their traditional orientations and retain most of their previous roles and statuses, even when they settle in their ethnic slum quarters. [28] And among many uprooted and newly urbanised workers in Western Europe in the nineteenth century, could be found a similar desire to return to their rural order and traditional status, till industrialism finally prevailed. [29]

The crucial defect, then, of 'communications' theory is its omission of the particular context of beliefs and interpretations and interests within which the mass media operate. This affects considerably the degree to which people become 'empathisers', and the experiences and situations with which they tend to empathise. Further, if we accept the idea that the notions of rational efficiency and technological adaptability indicate a high degree of 'modernisation', then one might argue that the mechanisms of projection and introjection which define 'empathy' could serve equally well as a barrier as they could as an agent of innovative change. For empathic 'understanding' is no guarantee in itself of the capacity 'to operate efficiently in a changing world', as Lerner would have us believe. [30] This latter capacity may actually be hindered by too great an ability to see oneself in the other fellow's situation. It may paralyse the will to act decisively, substituting imagination for action, by the process of 'thinking too precisely on the event'.

'Empathy' then, is as relative a concept as 'modernity' (and a good deal more nebulous), and there would appear to be little causal connection between them. Is this also true of the Western-type mass media? A glance at the contemporary Middle Eastern scene gives us the answer. Importing large-scale radio transmitters, as in Egypt or Algeria, is not correlated with the expansion of scientific attitudes and technological and economic growth. [31] And Peacock's study of the Indonesian *ludruk*, the classical liturgical drama, shows that a *non*-Western type of communications system is the most politically and ideologically effective for the purpose of stimulating mass participation in nationally organised constructive labour enterprises. [32] Once again, it is difficult to find a direct connection between the introduction of Western-type 'communications systems' and the capacity and will to modernise societies.

We are now in a position to examine the alleged relationship between empathy, the mass media and 'nationalism'. Lerner, I contended, considered nationalism an inevitable, if somewhat regrettable, accretion of the 'transitional' phase. It is a kind of ambivalent and xenophobic political passion. Nationalists simultaneously desire westernisation, but reject the West. Now the incipient empathisers, the argument runs, those but recently exposed to the conjurings of the media, are exactly the people who are likely to be most prone to this frenetic, extremist nationalism. For are they not, by definition, the most restless and unsatisfied of men? . . .

The very neatness of the argument should make us pause, and ask: why should exposure to different ways of viewing the world and man of itself produce this frenetic reaction? Why should an increase in the capacity to put oneself in the other man's shoes cling to the symbol of the nation? Why stop there? The Grocer of Balgat said he wanted to go to America, after all. And millions of small traders, redundant artisans, bankrupt shop-keepers, village teachers and others, have done just that. Lerner's 'transitional man' is an emigrant in search of bread and safety, not a nationalist whose primary question is one of roots and esteem and justice. The Grocer is a would-be assimilationist into the technologically most advanced civilisations; he is an incipient cosmopolitan. And were not the first great modernisers, the men of the Enlightenment, and 'transitionals' to boot, citizens of the whole earth, self-proclaimed prophets of universalist rationalism, extolling the virtues of a cosmopolitan culture and deploring the national differences and divisions they so keenly understood?[33]

In fact, there is nothing in the form or content of mass communications systems or mobile sensibilities that lends itself to the rise of nationalism as an ideological movement. Factors such as geography, trade flows, defence and taxation systems, are, as Deutsch shows, just as likely to contribute to the formation of communal discontinuities or *nationalities* as the introduction of media systems, especially in their latest mass phase, which relies less on language than on audiovisual effects.[34] But nationalities, as we shall see, must be distinguished from national sentiment, and even more from the ideological movement called 'nationalism'; and the mass media and high empathy can constitute as great a barrier to the inculcation of national sentiment and to the appeal of the nationalist movement as it may help to diffuse its ideals. Once again, the operative norms, interests and beliefs governing the use and form of the media are all-important. For example, British radio news, concentrating on national events or on Britain's role in world affairs, can be said to strengthen the pre-existing tendency to insularity and exclusiveness; whereas, the French news, ranging over world events unrelated to France's role and reporting on distant areas by continent, could not by the same token be held to reinforce French patriotism, but rather reflects the elite's cosmopolitan aspirations.[35]

A close scrutiny of Lerner's empirical findings reveals the link between incipient cosmopolitanism and empathy and media exposure. The group which Lerner characterises as the most 'transitional' of all (all groups in the Middle East, with exceptions in some Turkish cities, were either 'traditional' or 'transitional') —the workers—were the least affected by the symbol of the 'nation'. The recently uprooted and urbanised Egyptian workers were more concerned with the need for socio-economic reform and the symbolism of 'class' than with the regime's nationalistic preoccupations.[36] Only four out of nineteen urban factory workers in Egypt in 1954 thought the achievement of nationalist goals to be the biggest problem facing Egypt. Lerner notes the readiness of workers to leave the country for economic betterment. He quotes one worker's response:

> I can't choose any exact country to live in. I am ready to go anywhere if there is work for me there. I am sure I can work in any country.[37]

Higher empathisers, like the white-collar workers, were activistically nationalist; whereas, the highest group of empathisers, those most exposed to the media (at least in cultural scope rather than frequency or intensity) were rather more ambivalent in their attitude to the enemy, the British in this case. Interestingly enough, the traditionals, the rural fellahin, were almost equally bitter about the British presence as the white-collar workers. One is reported as saying:

> The English are our enemies. People say they are the root of all the evils.[38]

This ambiguity in Lerner's typology and in the concept of 'empathy' is supported by a study of the Syrian Nationalist Right. The social composition of this group 'showed them to be mainly poor, illiterate farmers', relatively isolated from the city, devout and xenophobic Muslims.[39] They were of the Traditional rather than the Transitional group. The people most exposed to the media were members of the middle and conservative Right, and of the Reform and Revolutionary Left; these were also the most educated groups, and hence presumably 'transitional'.

What this suggests is (a) that, insofar as this kind of threefold typology can encompass the complexity of political attitudes in the Middle East, the incipient empathisers, the newly urbanised, the people most exposed to the mass media, tend to be just as 'cosmopolitan' as 'nationalist', on Lerner's definition of 'nationalism'—or not classifiable as either, (b) that there is something odd and vacuous about Lerner's definition of 'nationalism', if it can be attributed to so many varying social groupings covering such a range of perceptions and attitudes. Or rather, Lerner seems to be redefining 'nationalism' as a concept to fit each group's perspectives. But is the 'nationalism' of the fellah identical with that of the white-collar worker, or the Syrian effendi? Doesn't this blur the concept to the point where it is of no more analytical use? Nobody denies that many social groups may embrace nationalism; but for this statement to have significance, we must first carefully define the ostensive limits of 'nationalism', before we can analyse the processes of its 'adaptation' to the needs and situations of different groups.

The 'painful threshold' theory of nationalism

Though Lerner's definition of nationalism is too vague for his purposes, it nevertheless allows him to present a vivid analogy of its general role and effects, which simultaneously serves as his explanation of its appeal.

Nationalism can be likened to a gateway to modernity, which is full of stress and pain, but cannot be avoided. Its symptoms, the dissatisfaction and febrile passion and angry rejection of the Other, are the inevitable distortions of the transitional phase through which every individual and every area must pass to attain the benefits and satisfactions of the participant culture of the modernised West. Lerner's account is rather more dramatic, perhaps, than that of other 'communications' theorists. For him, nationalism is the authentic voice of this 'painful threshold' of modernity, an expression of a sudden wrenching of the individual from his patriarchal moorings and constricted world-images. The uprooting is as much a psychic disturbance as a physical event. Other writers like Deutsch see in nationalism also the expression of a gradual growth of identity and group cohesion through the transmission of common memories and experiences. Only in certain conditions, when the system of transmission is manipulated and blocked to new information by the use of stereotypes, does nationalism signify a closure of the 'national mind' and a hardening of national consciousness into 'national will', which leads ultimately to self-destruction as in Nazi Germany.[40] The *movement* of national*ism*, the commitment to its ideology, carries with it this frustrated and negative character. (This is a very common evaluation among writers in this school of social science, whose own explicit value-orientations proclaim a cosmopolitanism and neutrality, over and above the nationalist mêlée. But often, as I have shown, the Western, even American, bias is not completely overcome.)

I should like to take issue with both the analogy and the evaluation of the character of nationalism. The 'painful threshold' analogy is an attempt to capture the apparent Janus-nature of nationalism, by substituting the concept of 'ambivalence' for that of nationalism. It is then a simple step to showing how this 'ambivalence' distorts the vision and hampers the effectiveness of the nationalist intelligentsia, so highlighting the negative character of nationalism. This 'explanation' is clearly circular. The attitude of rejecting the West while admiring westernisation ('nationalism') is identical with the meaning given to the concept of 'ambivalence'. As such, this approach hardly advances the search for a causal explanation of the rise and appeal of nationalist movements It is simply a piece of tautological psychologism.

Another serious objection to the analogy and the evaluation is that both are superficial and one-sided. Nationalists aim to construct nations out of populations that lack, in varying degrees, a sense of identity and purpose, or are ethnically heterogeneous, economically backward and socially divided. They provide often elaborate and sophisticated analyses and programmes for communal regeneration and collective decision-making. They must often build up from nothing the whole apparatus of the sovereign state, and instil a sense of group dignity through the creation of an autonomous system of education and culture. These are the very real and pressing tasks of adapting populations to a 'modernising' environment with often meagre local resources and harshly unfavourable conditions. Turning a social grouping into a 'nation' exercising sovereignty in its own 'nation-state' is a taxing and agonising task; but it is also a positive and constructive one, a challenge to man's potential.

One reason for this superficial and one-sided evaluation of nationalism is its identification with 'rejection' *per se*. This confuses the 'nationalism' of the traditional peasant, for example, with the 'nationalism' of the urban intelligentsia. Whether we call it 'nationalism' or 'ethnocentrism', the sentiment of the peasant, his bitter enmity to the outsider, is really a kind of traditional solipsism; his 'nationalism' is monocentric and closed. The 'nationalism' of the educated civil servant, the teacher, the officer or the professional, is quite different. It is outward-looking, it accords value of a sort to the outsider, it is concerned with self-sufficient autonomy and sovereignty in a family of nations of equal status. We should not confuse the two attitudes, even where they feed into each other in specific situations. It is the outward-looking, 'modern' nationalism that has provided the fuel for nationalist movements all over the world since the French Revolution. The solipsist attitude rarely provides a sufficient basis for political movements.

There is another, deeper reason, however, for the negative evaluation of nationalism in 'communications' theory. It is the failure to appreciate the degree to which nationalism can furnish people with a satisfying, credible and meaningful faith and goal once the traditional religious images lose their hold. Nationalism can possess a double advantage: conferring dignity and solidarity, and providing an impetus for modernisation. Dissatisfactions may help to turn men towards nationalism, but the latter is not an expression of this discontent, but its opposite—the solution of those yearnings in a practical and realistic form. Nationalists are often serene men. They possess confidence in their work and their lives are bent to a goal. They have reached such security, mental and physical, as this era allows. They have succeeded in using the search for 'roots' to infuse the future with hope and purpose. They are engaged in a definite practical collective programme. And all this within an anthropocentric image of the world, which does not involve a leap of faith beyond the scientific-technological premisses of modernising societies. One can indeed claim that that nationalism is one of the most convincing collective realisations of the principles of the Enlightenment.

It is primarily for this 'positive' reason that the analogy of the 'painful threshold' breaks down. The real pain precedes the conversion to nationalism; the real threshold lies at an earlier phase than the nationalist one, the crises of authority, identity, scarcity and meaning. It is here that men grope for the answers to questions that the traditional conceptions and images ignored or belittled; *their* answers were addressed to outworn problems, or the new scientific perspectives made the traditional answers increasingly implausible and shallow and undynamic.

Adopting the nationalist solution goes some way to substituting more meaningful answers to contemporary problems. For, in the first place, its analysis relates directly to the new problems, especially those of development; and further, its answers, if not as all-embracing as those of the older world-images, make up for this lack of comprehensive sweep and profundity by an immediacy and potency which is admirably adapted to the this-worldly orientations and concerns of the present age.

For many people, perhaps an increasing majority of mankind, the nationalist appeal is synonymous with the aspirations of modernisation. The 'modern' world is a world of nation-states, jealously guarding their sovereignty. The symbol and apotheosis of this nationalist undergirding is, paradoxically, the 'internationalist' United Nations. Are we then justified in thinking that nationalism is simply an inevitable phenomenon of the modern 'transition'? Will it gradually subside?

This question forms the context of the next chapter.

Chapter Six

INDUSTRIALISATION AND THE CRISIS OF THE INTELLIGENTSIA

Emigrants do not generally make good nationalists. The children of the millions who streamed out of Eastern Europe in the late nineteenth and early twentieth centuries may have become good American patriots; but their fathers provided poor material for the nationalist movements in the homeland. Why, the nationalist leaders asked themselves, did these men not express their discontent by opting for national self-determination and a separate nation-state? Why was it that so many of the more talented and spirited among the dispossessed preferred the arduous and risky road of exile and adaptation to a completely new environment? And what was that quality which they themselves possessed, and the emigrant so conspicuously lacked? He lacked, I think, the new sense of history which lies at the root of so many nationalist movements.

Industry and science

The subtle tension of the emigrant and the nationalist provides, I think, the key to one of the most complex and original attempts to come to grips with the ubiquitous phenomenon of nationalism.[1] Ernest Gellner shares with other 'modernisation' theorists the underlying assumption that we should consider three significant contemporary processes as interdependent: the rise of nationalism, the pre-eminence of the intelligentsia, and 'modernisation'. He differs from the 'communications' school of thought, which I examined in the previous chapter, in his insistence that culture, language and communications generally, form the dependent variables in the causal chain accounting for the rise and appeal of nationalism. The concept of modernisation should not be equated with 'communications' *tout court*; culture and the new education are rather inevitable concomitants of modernisation. Strictly speaking, one can say that modernisation 'produces' literacy, culture, communications, and hence nationality; it does not denote these variables.

One can best visualise 'modernisation', argues Gellner, as a kind of tidal wave sweeping out from the West across the globe, and bringing in its train industry, science and their social and political consequences. Of its relationship to its companion concept, industrialisation, he writes:

> The two are to be distinguished only as the narrower and wider aspects of the same phenomenon. Industrialisation proper may be preceded—in certain odd cases followed—by the trappings, terminology, expectations, slogans of industrial society. A complex of anticipatory borrowings may have almost as much impact on a society as the thing itself. [2]

At first blush, this sounds rather reductionist; as though modernisation were a mere epiphenomenon of the real thing, industrialisation. There are a number of passages that support this conclusion, and I shall return to the issue later. For the moment, however, we need to set this in the context of Gellner's emphasis on the important function of the completely novel type of cognition characteristic of industrial society: I mean, science.

> Modern science is inconceivable outside an industrial society; but modern industrial society is equally inconceivable without modern science. Roughly, science is the mode of cognition of industrial society, and industry is the ecology of science. [3]

What is so new and interesting about this kind of knowledge? First, it is the only 'effective' kind of knowledge, where previous ideologies were merely putative beliefs. Secondly, it is a disturbing influence: it fails to guarantee intellectual stability, it fails to endow the world with any moral meaning, and it refuses to underwrite any system of social and political hierarchies—all in contrast to former belief systems. Its rise therefore is a watershed in human development.

This implicit identification of 'modernisation' with a revolution in economic techniques *and* a transformation of beliefs simultaneously, is not far from the position I adumbrated in the last chapter. There remains a difference to which I shall revert. One should note the possibility of having the transformation of beliefs without a simultaneous technological revolution, as in ancient Athens—a case of muted modernisation which Gellner seems to reject as irrelevant. [4] It can also be argued with some justification that scientific revolutions generally do and/or must precede an effective technological-industrial one, as occurred in England. [5] More important for contemporary conditions, industrialisation proper could be long delayed, although a considerable minority of the population had already imbibed the scientific temper and methodology—with shrill consequences. [6]

But these qualifications leave Gellner's position virtually intact. The revolution that is sweeping the world today is, by and large, a dual one, call it what you will: in men's consciousness and beliefs as much as in his environment and the 'material conditions of his existence'. And it gains this ascendancy, argues Gellner, in the minds and over the lives of men, because of the 'demonstration effect' of its capacity to control man's environment and gradually solve his problems. Science-cum-technology is the key to human advancement, as it was to the spectacular phenomenon of Europe's growth. [7] It is a plain empirical generalisation that,

> the most important thing at present happening to the majority of mankind (i.e. its 'underdeveloped' part) is the diffusion of industrialisation and all it implies. [8]

Man's essence today is defined by industrialisation:

> His essence resides in his capacity to contribute to, and to profit from, industrial society. [9]

It follows that the most significant cleavage in the world today is between those societies that have become fully industrialised, and those that are still industrialising and aware of the possibility of attaining their goal.

A theory

Within this setting, Gellner sets out to explore the mechanisms linking industrialisation with its universal concomitant, nationalism. I shall recapitulate the broad outlines of the theory, before examining some of its contentions in greater detail.

The starting-point is the doctrine of nationalism itself. This consists in three main propositions:

1 All men have a 'nationality' as they have 'a nose and two eyes'
2 They wish to live with those of the same nationality and dislike being ruled by someone else
3 This state of affairs is desirable.

Nationalists, of course, make a number of more exuberant additions, but this forms the essential 'core' of the doctrine. Since the first proposition is logically untenable, nationalism is not 'natural', as is commonly assumed. At the same time, Gellner holds against critics like Kedourie that nationalism is sociologically necessary, i.e. that there are very powerful factors in the 'contemporary and recent social conditions which do make these suppositions (sc. of nationalism), in those particular conditions, natural and probably irresistible'.[10]

Before the French Revolution (roughly), the chief political units were either smaller or larger than the nation-state. Men's loyalties were directed to tribe, village, lineage or city-state, or to sprawling dynastic empires and universal churches. They seldom coincided with the linguistic-cultural area, i.e. the nations. And in the great span before, 'foreign' rulers were a fairly frequent phenomenon. Why then the recent ubiquity of the 'nation-state' and the wide appeal of 'nationalism' in the modern world?

Gellner's answer is complex, as can be seen from the diagram of causal relationships overleaf (arrows indicate causal direction). The starter is the 'tidal wave of industrialisation', which has two main consequences: an integrating impetus and a divisive effect. Together these consequences dictate the size and nature of 'nation states', and also the social composition of nationalist movements.

Industrialisation and modernisation proceed in two ways. They erode traditional agrarian societies, upsetting their careful balance of roles and intricate network of relations. Second, they 'hit' different areas of the globe unevenly, affecting them at different times and rates, and with a differential impact. They are uneven in their destructive force, which means that each area makes its own transition to industrial modernity; no sequence in any one society is likely to resemble that of another, though certain elements are shared by all.

Industrialisation and modernisation uproots large numbers of people culturally and/or physically. This dual migration and mobility has two major consequences, or better sets of consequences. I take those in causal chain A of the diagram first.

The erosion of the traditional order of roles, with their system of rights and obligations, has the effect of increasing the importance of 'culture'. The latter Gellner defines as

> essentially, the manner in which one communicates, in the broadest sense.

In modern society, 'culture' replaces 'structure' (the system of role relationships):

> . . . communication, the symbols, language (in the literal or extended sense) that is employed, become crucial.[11]

Culture now comes to define 'belonging' in the affective sense, and, more important, citizenship with its associated rights and duties. So it is natural that loyalties will be expressed in terms of 'culture', and that men will define their identity in terms of culture. There follows a key sentence:

> And the classification of men by 'culture' is of course the classification by 'nationality'.[12]

Now, the argument continues, if culture and more particularly linguistic education are now so important, this is because it is now widely felt that

> the size and complexity of the social context required for the production of an acceptable specimen of humanity has changed radically of late.[13]

Villages are too small to produce 'fully life-sized human beings', i.e. effective citizens. Only a State-organised and financed educational system can do that. Only education makes a full man and citizen, and such education must be conducted in some language; hence the attachment to language, and the spate of linguistic nationalisms today—which in turn reinforces the trend towards 'culture' by way of feedback. The following passage gives the main drift of the argument:

TABLE I   MODERNISATION, NATIONALISM AND LANGUAGE*

Gellner's main model:

Industrialisation/Modernisation

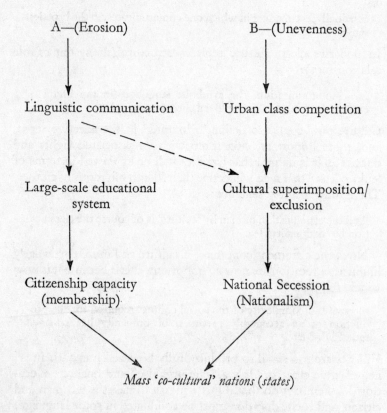

A—(Erosion)   B—(Unevenness)

Linguistic communication   Urban class competition

Large-scale educational   Cultural superimposition/
system   exclusion

Citizenship capacity   National Secession
(membership)   (Nationalism)

Mass 'co-cultural' nations (states)

* N.B. *'Modernisation' subsumes other structural factors but these have been
omitted for the sake of clarity (see Appendix C).*

TABLE 2   MODERNISATION, NATIONALISM AND LANGUAGE

A Modified Version:

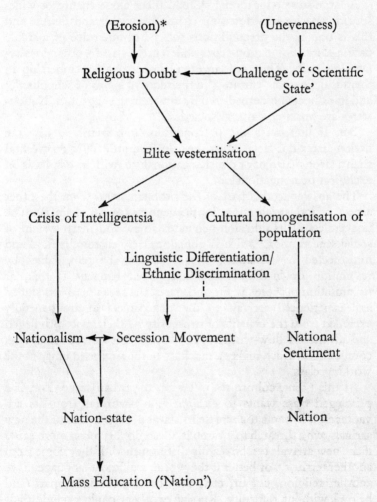

* *Sc. economic and physical uprooting.*

The minimal requirement for full citizenship, for effective moral membership of a modern community, is literacy. This is the minimum: a certain level of technological competence is probably also required. Only a person possessing these can really claim and exercise his rights, can attain a level of affluence and style of life compatible with *current notions of human dignity*, and so forth.[14] (my italics.)

A large-scale educational system, then, alone ensures a widespread capacity for exercising citizenship rights and duties; and this is one of the preconditions for the maintenance of a stable nation-state. For nation-states differ greatly from other loyalty-evoking units. They are large and impersonal; membership in them is defined by 'culture' ('in the sense of a *kind* of schooling'); and it is direct and unmediated by intervening subgroups. Nation-states are 'mass co-cultural societies'.[15]

But, if literacy is the precondition of citizenship, why are nation-states not larger than they, in fact, are? Why do we find such a strong current of divisive nationalism, with its emphasis on exclusion of nonnationals?

The answer to this part of the problem stems from the other aspect of industrialisation, its unevenness (causal chain B). The unevenness of its diffusion generates a new and sharp system of social stratification, which is unhallowed by custom, is fluid and unprotected by sanctions, and is seen to be remediable—by revolution or 'national' secession. What happens is that, as urbanisation proceeds in fits and starts, the recent and less skilled and experienced arrivals to the city proletariat are generally excluded from the benefits of prosperity by their more privileged and advanced fellow-workers. The net result is a fierce urban class competition, which makes a mockery of the supposed unity of the working class.

At this point, culture reappears on the urban scene. For, if a privileged class wants to exclude fellow-workers from its advantages, if it wants to increase its status at the expense of the new arrivals, who threaten to swamp it, it can do this much more easily if the new arrivals can be readily distinguished. If they come from another territory, or better if they speak a different language, have another religion, colour, etc., they can be classified apart (and below) without difficulty. Russian workers could exclude their Ukrainian or Polish co-workers, Azeris their Armenian counterparts in the Baku oil industry, Rhodesian and South African workers their coloured fellows; and English whites can create an objective and subjective subproletariat of their coloured Commonwealth co-citizens today.

It is hardly to be wondered at, then, if the excluded and detribalised now seek to make a virtue of necessity, and listen to the appeal of their culturally similar intelligentsias for a new nation-state to be formed to contain and protect them. Men become nationalists not out of sentiment, but out of

> genuine, objective, practical necessity, however obscurely recognised.[16]

Nationalism is the movement of national secession, led by the intelligentsias and backed by the excluded mass of less skilled workers. Both have been uprooted; both are culturally, often physically, mobile; both are exposed to the dislocating consequences of modernisation and industrialisation. The new emphasis on language makes the native clerks feel excluded, and often they *are* no longer substitutable, as before. The new competition for scarce resources pushes out the less skilled and experienced workers. So the 'two prongs' of the nationalist movement are the creation of modern conditions; they bear out Gellner's contention against Rostow's 'reactive nationalism' that

> it is the need for growth that generates nationalism, not vice versa.[17]

Gellner is explicit about the relationship between nationalism and the nation-state:

> Nationalism is not the awakening of nations to self-consciousness: it invents nations where they do not exist—but it does need some pre-existing differentiating marks to work on, even if, as indicated, these are purely negative (i.e. consist of disqualifying marks from entry to privilege, without any positive similarity between those who share the disqualification and who are destined to form a new 'nation').[18]

Nationalism is the desire for secession, for the formation of a nation: It is the

> yearning for it (sc. the nation) and the acceptance of it as a norm. . . .[19]

Spurred on by the need for economic and cultural development, it acts as a stimulus to both. Its advantages outweigh its excesses. For it helps to protect human dignity and increase cultural diversity. Above all, there is the fact that without nationalism, we might well have found that our planet came to resemble South Africa's present situation: an extremist white caste would barter their erstwhile liberalism for the short-run advantages flowing from the oppression of a vast majority which threatened to submerge them. That nationalism divides the world into a 'system of locks', where political boundaries separate areas of different levels of economic development, is a fillip to growth and some insurance against 'both tyranny and political folly'. Nationalism provides the ideological drive for mobilising underdeveloped areas into composite puritannical nations bent on rapid industrialisation in the teeth of outside competition.

Affinity and interest

The above summary and accompanying diagram represent an extremely cursory and schematised outline of Gellner's complex theory, and I shall shortly make up for some of these omissions when I examine certain key issues raised by his theory. Before doing so, however, it is necessary to appreciate what I take to be its chief aims and achievements, by considering its overall structure.

Unlike previous 'theories' (with the exception of Kedourie's and possibly Kautsky's), this is actually a *theory* of nationalism. First in the sense that it addresses itself to a problem of nationalism *per se*, requiring separate explanation, and explicitly recognises the need for such a treatment. Secondly, because its propositions are for the most part amenable to specification and disconfirmation.

In addition, Gellner insists strongly on the unevenness of the processes of modernisation, and hence the variety of possible 'transitions' to industrial modernity. Nationalism is tied in closely to this aspect of the matter, i.e. to certain concrete aspects of modernisation, rather than to 'modernisation-in-general', the vacuous, highly generalised notion which hampers neo-evolutionary functionalist theory. In short, it links nationalism to literary culture and industrial competition.

Thirdly, the theory avoids the circle of nationalist assumptions which dominate critics and adherents alike. The concepts of the nation and nationalism carry an inherent relativism, embedded as they so profoundly are in highly particularised socio-historical conditions. But they are in no sense 'artificial' inventions of illogical philosophers and starry-eyed poets.

Fourthly, as a result a much more balanced picture of the significance and advantages of nationalism emerges. As I see it, Gellner's evaluation of nationalism, ignoring its more florid accretions, provides a refreshing contrast to the portraits of Kedourie or Lerner. Gone are the worlds of sinister romantic conspiracies and pained, wearisome ambivalence. In their place, we are given the image of a bracing movement, a sort of latter-day Calvinism, but rather less gloomy and more colourful. The satisfaction of immediate, pressing needs gives this puritanism its appeal—not sentiment or revelation; and its validation derives not from its logical incongruities, but from its capacity to satisfy those needs, irrespective of short-run mishaps and 'excesses'.

Perhaps the chief merit of the theory concerns the balance in its central structure. I mean, of course, the balance between 'affinity' and 'interest'. No one could claim that Gellner does not give sufficient weight and attention to the intricate complexities of the novel cultural factors, especially language; at the same time, there is a strong undercurrent which insists on the importance of economic interests which the 'idealist' school of historians has tended to underestimate. Gellner is very conscious of this 'community of interests' which cultural affinities must themselves satisfy, of Voltaire's

> Quand ceux qui possèdent, comme moi, des champs et des maisons, s'assemblent pour leurs intérêts communs, j'ai ma voix dans cette assemblée; je suis une partie du tout, une partie de la communauté, une partie de la souveraineté: voilà ma patrie.[20]

And he would, I feel sure, agree with the converse:

> What attachment can a poor European immigrant have for a country where he had nothing? The knowledge of a language, the love of a few kindred as poor as himself, were the only cords that tied him: his country is now that which gives him land, bread, protection and consequence. *Ubi panis, ibi patria,* is the motto of all emigrants.[21]

If this is so, the problem, then, becomes one of explaining how it has come about that cultural affinity assumes such importance for so many, why more did not take the path of emigration, but staked their honour and welfare on making a success of the 'national' venture, why the collective route was taken with so little prospect of success. This explanation remains within the 'interest' framework, by extending the meaning of interest in the manner of Weber, i.e. beyond the normal economic orbit. Nationalism is not a sudden madness or malaise, but one of the very few practical alternatives for the majority of people, a serious answer to serious problems.

Finally, Gellner also stresses the prominent role of the intelligentsia as the leaders of nationalist movements. But the explanation is a good deal more subtle than Kautsky's simple equation of their own interests with those of anticolonial modernisation. It lies in the close connections between the rise of literary culture as the chief mode of interpersonal relations in modern society, and the uses of urban class competition. This is particularly important for our appreciation of their role after the achievement of independence, when full, effective citizenship use becomes increasingly dependent on level of educational attainment. I shall devote a good deal of attention to this explanation later.

Within this framework, the theory poses certain difficulties, whose resolution requires us to modify and extend certain of its hypotheses. These, I hope, will suggest new distinctions and lines of research, which will be taken up in the final chapter.

My criticisms concern four main propositions: that an uprooted proletariat tends to be one of the two main 'prongs' of the nationalist movement; that the divisions within the intelligentsia are spurious in the long term; that nationalism is really a phenomenon of the 'transition'; and finally that 'nationality' is really a matter of language, and hence, implicitly, that nationalism is basically a linguistic movement—which involves consideration of the problems of definition. This last area is undoubtedly the most important for our purposes, but I take the more empirical criticisms first.

Ethnic secession and the working classes

Why are nation-states smaller than the former polyethnic empires which they have replaced? Because they arise from the success of national secession movements, which are themselves the end-product of a process whereby the class struggle in the cities is superimposed upon cultural differentiae. If new arrivals to the city can be distinguished, not merely by a relative lack of skills, experience and status, but by linguistic, religious, ethnic, chromatic or even territorial differences, they can be much more easily excluded from the prosperity of their fellow-workers (what little is theirs); and so will readily listen to the nationalist appeal of their 'co-cultural' intelligentsias, which are also excluded from access to the best jobs by the new linguistic exclusiveness of their cultural counterparts. Hence the spate of secessionist nationalisms and 'successor states'.

Obviously this aspect of the theory is addressed to the particularly complex and bitter effects of industrialisation in an ethnically heterogeneous milieu—for example, Eastern Europe or the Middle East. Kedourie had argued that the nationalist ideology itself, by its emphasis on linguistic group identification (in the German Romantic version), inflames ethnic sentiment in such mixed areas.[22] By contrast, Akzin offers a more socio-historical account: ethnic groups whose expectations for access to political and economic facilities are frustrated, and which live in close proximity to other such groups, tend to become antagonistic to those neighbours and claim the same stretch of territory. Ceteris paribus, inter-ethnic tensions are the primary, but not the only cause, of nationalism's diffusion in such areas.[23]

Gellner goes further. He wants to get behind ethnicity itself, so as to lay bare the reasons why people should prefer, at a particular time and place, to identify themselves under an ethnic rubric—which is but one variant of the more general cultural, i.e. national, classification. And his answer is an amalgam of the new significance of culture and the equally new struggle for scarce resources among city workers and intelligentsias. This is the aspect of the theory that harks back most to the 'conflict' approaches discussed in Chapter 4.

Now for this part of the theory to hold, it would have to be demonstrated, (a) that all secession movements hitherto have been preceded by the confluence of these two factors, i.e. the novel role of culture and urban competition, (b) that where one of the factors was absent, national secession did not take place, or at least that the movement failed to get off the ground and

E

develop a popular base. I think the evidence on both counts is doubtful.

With regard to (*a*), many successful secession movements preceded altogether the coming of industrialisation and a proletariat. The Greek, Armenian, Serb, Czech, Italian, Hungarian, German, Turkish and Arab movements, generally led by the intelligentsia, comprised various combinations of other social groupings—officers, peasants, civil servants, small traders, the *haute bourgeoisie*, priests, artisans, gentry and even aristocrats (provided they are not landowners—one thinks of the aristocrats in nineteenth-century Poland). The peasants of Burma, the officers in Egypt and Turkey, the priests in Rumania, the pig-dealers in Serbia and the Philike Hetairia in Greece founded by wealthy merchants, are familiar examples of enthusiastic supporters of nationalist movements. It is only after industrialisation that we find some factory workers and industrialists (as among the Tatars), but rather more white-collar workers, swelling the ranks. But the rise of nationalism antedated their adherence, and its success did not depend primarily on their support. One looks in vain for a Kurdish, Naga, Burman or even Palestinian proletariat, playing a decisive role in these highly developed secessionist movements.[24]

Turning to (*b*) the absence of one (or even both) of these factors —distinct culture (especially language) and urban class competition—does not prevent the development of nationalist secession movements. This is shown by the four cases I have just mentioned—despite arguments that three of them are still in the balance and might require the mobilisation of a radical proletariat for success.[25] Other cases of culturally distinct groups which lacked uprooted workers, yet developed incipient nationalisms, are furnished by the Welsh, Corsicans, Dagestanis under Shamil, BaKongo, Turkmen, Bashkirs, Zulu, Ashanti and Ganda, and Achinese in Sumatra. There are also the nationalist movements of liberation from Spain in early nineteenth-century Latin America, as well as the cases of the United States and Ireland, where not only was a proletariat or industry absent, but the population was actually similar in culture to their Spanish or English masters.

A negative kind of support for Gellner's thesis is, however, provided by a host of cases which possessed cultural distinctiveness, yet were economically underdeveloped and lacking in urbanised workers—such groups as the Vlachs, Frisians, Wends, Sorbs, Savoyards, Udmurts, Mari, the many Caucasian tribes like the Rutuls, Laks, Tats, Nogays, Cherkessians, etc., the Iban, Baluchis, Pathans, Druse, Assyrians, Galla, Mandingo, Masai and Puerto Ricans, to name only the larger and more obvious cases. Such groups failed to develop any kind of nationalism. It is not clear, however, whether the failure to possess a deruralised proletariat was the key factor which led to the absence of nationalism. [26]

One might advance a further argument. If secession results from the economic exclusion of the culturally dissimilar members of the proletariat, we should expect groups and areas with *less* resources and skills to produce the most intense cases of nationalism, as with the Basques, Bretons, Flemish and Ukrainians. Yet a no less intense nationalism prevailed among the diaspora communities of the Greeks, Armenians and Jews, who were as advanced, or even more so, than their immediate neighbours, both culturally and economically. Gellner probably has these cases in mind when, in a note, he alludes to this possibility producing a scapegoat situation and hence a 'reactive' nationalism. [27]

But these are by no means the sole examples. One need only recall the diaspora Ibo, the Serbs of the Banat and Novi Sad, the Crimean Tatars of southern Russia, middle class Bengalis, the Ewe in Togoland, the Chinese in Singapore, Indonesia or Malaysia—not to mention the Boers and North Americans on the frontier. [28] Were all these nationalisms the result of a scapegoat situation? The case of the more educated and advanced minority, and the conditions which prompt it to turn to nationalism, merits greater attention.

The social composition of nationalist movements

We shall be able to get a better picture of the modifications required for this part of Gellner's theory if we take a closer look at the social composition of some nationalist movements, with special regard to the role of the workers. I say *some* movements, since this is a vast and virtually virgin territory. A cursory inspection must therefore suffice.

My argument concerning the social composition of nationalism, and its relation to industrial proletarisation, can be stated as follows: first, nationalist movements may overlap with the onset of industrialisation, or precede it altogether. In the latter case, the main adherents of the movement are various sections of the middle classes and/or the peasantry, or sections of it, or even tribesmen. In the former type of movement, the middle classes are still dominant in the nationalist cause, but *some* of the up-rooted workers may join them.

Secondly, one must distinguish, as Worsley does, the elite from the mass phase of nationalism. There is no necessary transition from the former to the latter, but we find a number of cases where nationalism started as the preserve of a small educated and quite wealthy elite, as in Ghana, and then spread to other groups in society, finally reaching the peasants and workers. On the other hand, we have several cases where nationalism remained a pre-dominantly middle-class affair.

Thirdly, the detailed composition of the nationalist movement varies considerably. The intelligentsia always contributes representatives out of proportion to its numbers, if by 'intelligentsia' is meant lawyers, journalists, academics, doctors and teachers, and all who possess higher education qualifications. So do clerks and civil servants, and officers, especially in this century. But we also find considerable numbers of the bourgeoisie, both wealthy capitalists and small traders and shopkeepers. Dispossessed aristo-crats tend to be less conspicuous, but priests quite often join the movement, especially the lower clergy, in the steps of the Zealot ancestor. Finally the peasantry retain a kind of solipsist hatred of the alien, which can often be raised by messianic hopes into support for the nationalist cause, as has happened in a number of Far Eastern countries. The workers are the least important sector for nationalist support, except in a few instances, since it affects them least.

We may start our empirical survey by recalling Lerner's findings that, at any rate in the period 1950–4, the workers who had recently flocked to the cities of Syria and Egypt were relatively indifferent to the nationalistic goals of their leaders. Hard-pressed in their economic condition, they wanted economic reform and found the symbolism of class more meaningful. Nationalism had more to offer the white-collar worker, the professionals, the officers, and previously the liberal merchants.

The Indian case adds a historical perspective. Initially, the nationalist Congress party, founded in 1885, served the interests of both the traditional landowners who resented the undermining of their authority by British policies, and the newly westernising Hindu middle classes, who suffered discrimination in taxation and in recruitment to Civil Service positions. Native industrialists and entrepreneurs also joined the party to ameliorate their position in the face of British industrial competition.[29] The result was a Congress that fought for political representation for these classes, and opposed British economic and military imperialism.

It was only in 1908 that the impact of the rising working class made itself felt, with the general strike of textile workers in Bombay; but only after the wave of strikes in 1920–1 did the nationalist leaders consider the workers as a possible base for mass support and include a social policy in their independence platform, under the influence of Gandhi.[30] Yet even then, Congress made no special appeal to the working class *per se*, though Nehru's Congress Socialist Party favoured this approach. For peasant violence was an equally effective weapon for mass mobilisation and civil disobedience—and numerically far more impressive. Further, it was apparent that too exclusive a preoccupation with the rather specific demands of the workers tended to deflect attention from the main nationalist goal of Swaraj, and also alienate support among the industrialists and *haute bourgeoisie*. We conclude from this that the early nationalism of the wealthy and newly educated was only gradually supplemented by the mass nationalism of the more radical members of the intelligentsia, appealing to the landless peasantry as well as the workers; and that the extent of social 'penetration' of nationalism (into the majority of the population) was correlated with the degree of British repression and length of rule.

Africa exhibits a roughly similar overall historical pattern. In British West Africa, for example, the small African working classes, never exceeding 5 % of the population in 1956, were only sporadically drawn into the nationalist vortex. Strikes were infrequent in the inter-war years, and unionisation on a regular basis was delayed till the end of the thirties—in French Africa till 1946, after a brief period during the Popular Front of 1936–40. After 1945, African trade unions did become bastions of militant nationalism in the Sudan and Ghana, to a lesser extent Nigeria; this was partly because of their all-purpose functions, contrasting with their more specialised role in Europe, partly because of their insistence on the rights of *African* workers (as opposed to the *equality with* European workers in wages, conditions, etc., characteristic of French African unions), partly also because the nationalist leadership was stronger in these territories and ready to subject rival organisations to its purposes.[31] And yet only in Kenya and Tunisia do

> the unions appear to have acted for some time as the basis of the nationalist movement and to have acted as substitutes for political organisations when these were forced underground.[32]

Davies, who includes for his purposes the rather different countries of Muslim North Africa, lists only Guinea, Ghana, Tanganyika, Algeria, Mali and the Ivory Coast (in addition to Kenya and Tunisia) as cases where the unions early allied themselves to the leading nationalist parties right up to independence. He adds that in Nigeria, Morocco and the Cameroons, the unions

> at one time appeared in the vanguard of the nationalist campaign, only later to move into an opposition role.[33]

Nationalism, generally, in West Africa, can, however, be dated to the latter third of the last century, if not earlier.[34] It made its appearance somewhat later in North Africa, and did not appear in East and Southern Africa till the earlier third of this century.[35] Again, the earlier nationalist parties of the petty bourgeoisie or professional elites were generally uninterested in the possibilities afforded by workers' organisations in strengthening the nationalist campaign; this holds also of the early parties in Tunisia, Kenya and the Gold Coast, not to mention the elite leaderships in French Equatorial Africa, Nigeria and Sierra Leone, which survived to form the first independence governments.

Some further evidence of the relative lack of importance of the workers (and peasants) in African nationalism is afforded by Hunter's table of the previous occupations of members of parliament in selected African countries.[36] Only Tanganyika and the Congo reveal a significant percentage of working class representation (25% and *c*. 15·5%); the most heavily represented categories are the professionals, especially teachers, the lawyers, the civil servants and the 'trader businessman'. This is supported by the Smythes' detailed study of the Nigerian elite, where 'skilled labour' is listed as zero in their 1958 sample of 156 'elite' members and as 1·2% in the Nigerian *Who's Who* of 1956. Once again, the professions, civil servants and teachers, and to a lesser extent, businessmen, preponderate.[37]

Is this type of social composition of nationalism peculiar to India, Africa and the Near East? In Europe, the position is rather more complex. As we saw, early nineteenth-century nationalisms preceded industrialisation altogether, and their programmes and goals were entrenched by the time the social-democratic and communist parties became an active force at the end of the century. But the further east we travel, the more ambiguous the role of the worker becomes. The gradual erosion of German social-democracy by nationalism, culminating in the voting of war credits in 1914, is all too familiar. But the important thing to note for our purposes is that it takes place too late to constitute a test case for Gellner's hypothesis; you could hardly call this erosion a national secession movement.

The Polish case is rather more instructive. Nationalism started as a half-hearted desire by a few aristocrats and urban followers to regain rights lost in the Partitions. Later it evolved into a full-fledged movement of the gentry and romantic intellectuals like Mickiewicz, Krasinski and Hoene-Wronski; this was the time of the ineffective rebellions of 1830, 1846 and 1863 when the dispossessed sons of aristocrats turned against their Russian masters who dominated the administration.[38] However, the emancipation of the Polish serfs by Alexander II in 1864 made the Polish nobles rather less interested in political independence, and Polish industry became increasingly tied into the Russian economy in the period of 'organic work'. Only the petty bourgeoisie and the intelligentsia clung to nationalism—aided by the peasants in the Prussian sector, who resented Bismarck's clumsy attempt to attack their religion. The Russian sector of Poland was the most industrialised part of the whole Russian empire; and the gradual growth of Pilsudski's Polish Socialist Party in the teeth of Luxemburg's vehement denunciations, is eloquent testimony to the incipient appeal of nationalism among the Polish workers at the turn of the century.[39] Here it does seem that the workers added considerable weight to the already long-established demand for secession on religious, linguistic and historical grounds.

Jewish nationalism presents a rather more involved picture. Both Dubnow's 'Diaspora nationalism' and the Zionism of

Smolenskin, Hess, Pinsker and Achad Ha'am were originally middle-class movements, both in Germany and Eastern Europe. [40] Industrialisation, however, led to the rapid proletarisation of the Jewish masses in the Pale cities like Lodz from the 1870's on. In 1897, a Jewish working-class organisation, the Bund, was founded to spread socialism among the Jewish masses, much to Lenin's chagrin. For the Bund had come to the conclusion that, to reach the Jewish workers, they would have to employ Yiddish, the language of the *shtetl*. Lenin suspected that this tactical concession masked a deep-seated betrayal to the traditional ethnocentric sentiment of these recent arrivals from the *shtetl*—a sentiment that, while originating in messianic religious ideals, was reinforced by the Jewish worker's experience of exclusion by his non-Jewish counterpart who betrayed historic feelings of anti-Semitism. Martov at this juncture thought socialism insufficient and wrote that

> a working class, which is content with the lot of an inferior nation, will not rise up against the lot of an inferior class. . . .

And the Zionist Marxist Borochov, denouncing the admission by non-Jewish weavers in Bialystock of a few Jewish comrades 'out of socialist pity' as a 'numerus clausus in the factories', concluded that:

> We Socialist-Zionists are convinced that our freedom depends primarily on the national self-help of the Jewish masses. [41]

Another example, it appears, of nationalism converting the proletariat—especially in view of the contribution made by labour-Zionists in colonising Palestine after 1905. Yet the latter were a trickle compared to the mass exodus to America, or the mass who remained to reap the benefits of the minority clauses in the Versailles Treaty. [42] The bulk of the Jewish proletariat did not opt for Zionism, even under Hitler's threat; they clung instead to their small-town semi-religious ethnocentrism.

Rather less support for Gellner's hypothesis can be derived from a consideration of the third advanced group in the Russian empire. One cannot even discern a clear divide here between an elite preindustrial phase of nationalism, and a mass industrialising period; for the Tatar case of nationalism was dominated by its vigorous bourgeoisie. Till 1905, the great merchants and intellectual reformers led the way. The small Ishahist movement of this period was really only a radicalisation of the parent Jadidism, and originated suitably among pupils of the bourgeois Kazan 'Muhammadyah' school. The majority of the leaders of the 1917 Kazan Socialist Committee were Ishahists, including Vahitov and Sultan Galiev, for whom their Marxist-Leninism but thinly veiled an Asian socialist nationalism.[43]

The predominantly bourgeois character of even this late phase of radical nationalism is not difficult to understand. In 1926, there were in all some 85,000 workers of Tatar origin, scattered in and around Tartary; most Tatars were 'semi-peasants', leaving their villages for seasonal labour, and this lack of size and concentration of the Tatar working class made it a politically ineffective force, except in a few factories. It was the radical bourgeoisie in its *industrial* phase, who, with the intelligentsia, formed the backbone of the nationalist movement—together with the Jadidist clergy.[44]

The Tatars were a fairly literate people with considerable economic resources; yet, even after industrialisation had replaced their commercial by an industrial bourgeoisie, the workers were an insignificant element in the intensive nationalist movement. It would seem that Gellner's thesis requires further specification, to take into account the ecological distribution of the proletariat, in the attempt to link the latter to the secessionist demand. The other factor we need to consider is the conscious policy of the (Russian) government—more particularly the relative weighting of its 'integrationist' and 'rejectionist' policy strands in dealing with ethnic minorities.[45]

If the modified Worsleyan hypothesis about the stages of the diffusion of nationalism does not work in the Tatar case, even under conditions of relative industrialisation, what can we expect of the less 'advanced' nationalities, especially in the eastern half of the Soviet Union? Industrialisation here was an imposed phenomenon. The Bolsheviks, at a loss to find anything resembling an uprooted proletariat in Central Asia, had to follow its Tsarist predecessors in importing Russian colonists into the area and finally try to invent a native working class by unveiling the women and drafting them into the factories.[46] Uzbeks, Kazakhs, Tadjiks, Turkmen to some extent—even Oirots, Tuvinians, Buryats and Yakuts—developed fairly strong local nationalisms; but, as we saw, the low rate of urbanisation there prevented the development of a *mass* movement in Kornhauser's sense, and we can now add that the urban intelligentsia tended to operate within the framework of a fragmented, local peasant or tribal ethnocentrism, which undermined their pan-Turkic aspirations. In any case, their nationalism had no chance of turning to a native proletariat, since this role was pre-empted by the Russifying colonists (at first christianising, then communising).

A good example is provided by Yakut experience. Some 288,000 people were scattered across the vast expanse of this largest Soviet Republic in 1926, of whom 82·3% were Yakuts and 10·4% were Russian colonists, the rest being made up of small tribes. A continuous native-grown nationalism in response to Tsarist colonisation had emerged from 1906; yet even in 1936, despite the gold rush of the early 1920's, and the growth of timber, fishing, furs and coal industries, the Yakut working class numbered a mere 1,845 (miners and industrial workers), some 4·2% of the total population of workers—as against the 15% Koreans and Chinese, and the over 70% Russians. Despite overt Russian concessions to the nationalities, the *korenisatzia* policy of giving a certain proportion of administrative posts to different language groups in a given area (in ratio to their numerical strength) did not prevent the re-emergence of Great Russian nationalism in 1936 from preying on the absence of local proletariats, to the detriment of *mestnichestvo* (local 'subnational', 'tribal' nationalism of the minor nationalities) manifestations.[47]

One last example, this time from the Caucasus, underlines the need for caution in assigning too great a role to the proletariat in nationalism, even in conditions of relatively intensive industrialisation. From about 1870–83, the oil industry was greatly expanded in Baku; output rose from a meagre 250,000 puds a year in the 1840's to some 115,000,000 per annum in 1885, and 377,000,000 per annum in 1897. Industrialisation was speeded by linking the Batum to Baku railway to the Russian heartlands, to Western Europe and to Constantinople. Russian and Armenian workers streamed into the Azeri-occupied industrial zone, bringing a rise in interethnic hostilities. Azeri nationalism, a kind of incipient Muslim pan-Turkism, had already emerged in the 1860's, in response to the unenlightened Shi'ite clergy, who spoke Persian. Even in the 1890's, men like Agaev, Hussein Zadeh and Topchibashev the lawyer were concerned with social reform in the face of clerical opposition; their Muslim nationalism was only secondarily directed at the Russian and Armenian intelligentsias.

Stalin's call for a general strike in late 1904 opens a new phase. Yet the creation of the Social Democrat Azeri Muslim Hemmet party under Narimanov among the Baku oil workers did not revolutionise them nor turn them against their Russian rulers; instead it led to mutual massacres between Azeris and the Armenian Dashnaks. The fairly pro-Russian and non-nationalist Hemmet party remained popular among the Azeri workers even after the creation of the more bourgeois Musavat (Equality) party by Resul Zadeh in 1911. The latter's pro-Turkish orientation, its rather lukewarm espousal of pan-Islamism and its vague pan-Turkic programme held more appeal for Azeri intellectuals and merchants than for the workers (or landowners and peasants and mullahs). In the end, it was only the political alliance of Russian and Armenian forces against Enver and Talat Pashas' pan-Turkist aggression in the Great War that could persuade the Azeri workers to espouse the nationalist cause at all. [48]

These examples merely scratch the surface of the topic of the social composition of the nationalist movements, and of the role of workers in providing a mass base for secession. But this preliminary review of a number of cases does permit us to draw a few tentative conclusions.

1 The timing of industrialisation is crucial. We can distinguish between nationalist movements which achieve their goals (mainly independence and unity) altogether before the onset of industrialisation, and those which overlap with its arrival (we shall consider later the possibility of nationalism in industrialised societies). Only the latter cases are eligible for inclusion in Gellner's secession-of-the-proletariat category. Hence one must immediately distinguish two types of nationalism, a preindustrial and an industrialising variety.

2 A second and closely related, but different, variable is the phase of social penetration of the movement. The Indian case was a clear example of an elite origin of nationalism among the wealthy and educated which led gradually into a mass phase, pulling in the workers, artisans and peasantry. Not surprisingly perhaps,

farmers are particularly attracted to the protectionist aspects of economic nationalism, and white-collar workers are the chief beneficiaries of the personnel nationalisation policies, which are a marked feature of integrationist nationalism, in the new states of Africa and Asia.[49] Often, however, the mass phase is absent, because urbanisation lags and industrialisation remains a distant promise; the degree of social penetration achieved by the nationalist movement into the majority of the population and outlying groups is severely curtailed. Or it may be elite policy to restrict the movement's scope and programme, in the manner of the Girondins or some of the African and Middle Eastern parties (e.g. Lebanon, Northern Nigeria, Gabon, etc.).

On the other hand, the mobilisation of the masses need not correlate with the extent of urbanisation or industrialisation. War, or social revolution, may 'compensate' for the omission of these factors, and produce the mass phase which penetrates into the countryside—as in Algeria, Mexico, Vietnam and Kurdistan.[50]

3 The social composition of nationalist movements is highly variegated—both over time, and space. It is impossible to tie nationalism to the aspirations of any social groups *in a consistent manner*—be it workers or petty bourgeoisie or bureaucrats or officers. Recently officers have been increasingly prominent, but there is a case for including them in the category of the intelligentsia, since they are increasingly recruited from those who possess Western educational qualifications of an above average standard.[51] The only exception to this dictum is the intelligentsia itself, which, alone among social and cultural groups, has consistently supplied personnel (usually the leaders, too) to the movement; but not even all of them have joined. And even where other groups do contribute a disproportionate share of adherents, they rarely alter the structure of the movement's aims and ideology on a permanent footing.

4 In ethnically heterogeneous milieux hit by the uneven impact of industrialisation, there is some force in the argument that would explain national secession movements by an economic-cum-cultural rejection of recent arrivals to the urban factory scene. But, as both the Azeri and the Jewish cases demonstrated, this is only one of a number of probable courses inherent in the logic of the situation—the others being involvement in socialist revolution, physical emigration, and often an uneasy oscillation

between traditional ethnocentric collectivism and anonymous attempts at individual advancement by 'breaking into' the privileged caste, or assimilation. In a number of cases, the emigration option has come a close second to national secession in numerical importance; this holds especially for the ethnic groups of Eastern Europe which sent so many of their members to America. Akzin's point about industrialisation reinforcing the sense of ethnicity, only where there have been *previous historic* antagonisms between two groups, one of whom is now denied comparable facilities, is an important factor in this area, as it is in North Africa. But this only places the onus of explanation one stage back; it provides no account of why the denial of access should lead to ethnic secessionist demands and the formation of a nation-state on its own.

5 In colonial territories, industrialisation may canalise the workers' frustrations on to the regime of the outside power and its capitalist backers. But: (*a*) this will depend once again on the degree of progress of industrialisation proper, (*b*) other groups can equally well serve as a mass base for a middle-class movement's goals. The latter in turn is heavily influenced by the perception of the cultural policies and *political* relationship between the regime and the group's self-appointed spokesmen, since this may well decide the felt need of the original nationalists for a broader base. Not industrialisation *per se*, but the repressive and culture-bounded nature of British rule in Burma, for example, dictated the G.C.B.A.'s radicalisation and its alliance with the political *pongyis* like U Ottama and U Thilasara in the 1920's, at a time when industry tended to be foreign-owned.[52]

The crisis of the intelligentsia

Gellner is quite clear about the overriding importance of the intelligentsia in nationalist movements. Really, nationalism's primary function is the resolution of the crisis of the intelligentsia. The broad character of the ideology is largely a reflection of the problems and concerns of its original adherents or 'bearers', to use Weber's term.[53] Theirs are the interests and attitudes which set the identifying seal on all the varieties of this ideological movement. We should avoid simplification here. These interests and problems are not a simple function of exposure to westernisation. We must also take into consideration their *local* settings at a given historical moment, since the reception of the enlightenment is dependent on the 'ripeness' of conditions 'at home'. The new education stirs only such as are 'ready' for it, i.e. structurally available and culturally attuned. It nurtures a class of 'outward-looking' nationalists, only after the Copernican revolution of ideas, interests and status perceptions. And this revolution necessarily involves a primarily *internal* conflict—against the fathers and, more important, the tradition and its defenders, against all those with a vested interest in the *status quo*.

There is nothing elitist about this methodology. Nobody is arguing that nationalism is *simply* a movement of the intelligentsia. It is manifestly not. After all, it is an urban movement, which may on occasion be transported, actually or figuratively, into the countryside of peasants or tribesmen. The growth of communications and mobility obviously helps to spread nationalism, as it does every other ideology, to outlying groups. This is abetted by the generalising power inhering in some of the nationalist propositions (as extensions of democratic ideas), attracting groups with varied 'material' and 'ideal' interests. Nevertheless, if we are interested in the explanation of the *recurrent origins* of nationalism, rather than its subsequent diffusion to other groups, we shall do well to stick to the crisis of the intelligentsia.

How shall we conceive of this group? 'Intelligentsias' must not be equated with 'intellectuals'. The latter have existed in all ages. Ossowski holds that they are often lumped together with the 'leisured' classes in the popular consciousness; they are literary 'drones' in opposition to the manual workers. In traditional societies, they formed a compact stratum of magicians, scribes, priests, orators, etc. In 'open' industrial societies, they are elusive. Neither a class, nor a stratum, they live in the interstices of the economy, a socially and educationally heterogeneous grouping.[54]

For Gellner, 'intelligentsia' is an historically specific term. It defines 'a class which is alienated from its own society by the very fact of its education', a species of 'internal graduate', you might say—and often similarly jobless. Second, whereas previous clerkly castes sustained the norms and structures of their societies, the skills and beliefs of intelligentsias entail a rejection of their societies' norms, etc., as no longer subjectively and objectively viable under the impact of Western modernity. Third, intelligentsias are a 'phenomenon essentially connected with *the* transition' (sc. to industrial society); and, starting with the eighteenth-century *lumières*, they have 'followed the wave of modernisation on its outward movement'. Last and most crucially, the typical dilemma of the intelligentsia is a choice between a rationalist, westernising tendency and a romantic, *narodnik* posture; yet the dilemma was really 'quite spurious', since

> ultimately the movements invariably contain both elements, a genuine modernism and a more or less spurious concern for local culture, or rather the re-employment of what had been a traditional culture for the enrichment and the trappings of a new education-rooted way of life, and for the provision of the defining differentiae of a new political unit. By the twentieth century, the dilemma hardly bothers anyone: the philosopher-kings of the 'underdeveloped' world all act as westernisers, and all talk like *narodniks*.[55]

With the first two features of intelligentsias, many would concur. 'Intelligentsia' does not denote a class in the usual sense; it draws its membership from all social groups.[56] University education or certain types of employment—the 'professions'—are often taken as rough 'external' criteria; but they too raise thorny problems. No attempt will be made here to examine the various definitions which have been given of the concept of the 'intelligentsia'. For our purpose, the concept refers not just to the educational qualifications and occupational structure of individuals, but more vitally to a set of problems and concerns which are known to agitate the members of this socially heterogeneous category. A certain circularity appears to be unavoidable; there is no firm line of demarcation in this instance. All we can say is that a given type of situation, the confrontation between modernising currents and the traditional order, unfailingly produces a category which is particularly exposed to certain problems, issues and dilemmas, by virtue of its cultural contact and educational exposure.

Is the 'intelligentsia' a phenomenon of the 'transition'? In the last chapter, I expressed serious reservations about the idea of any 'transition' to an end-state; and it seems to me that the continued existence and influence of 'intelligentsias' in America, France and Russia, in the above sense of the term, support my view that modernisation is a recurrent and possibly never-finished process away from a traditional state of affairs, but not towards a set goal. But the argument is partly circular, unless we grant my previous contention that industrialisation must be distinguished from modernisation (in the sense of a continuous application of science-cum-technology to every sphere of society). But all this takes us far from nationalism and into the debate about the 'convergence thesis' of industrial society.

Gellner's last point about the spurious nature of the dilemma of the 'intelligentsia' is, however, directly germane to the rise of nationalism. Indeed, you might say that it constitutes the matrix of the problem. The argument so far is that (a) using the external (educational and occupational) criteria of the concept of the 'intelligentsia', this category is unfailingly over-represented in nationalist movements, and especially in their leadership, (b) that they are the most relevant group in exploring the *emergence* of nationalism, rather than its subsequent diffusion. The ideology of nationalism is born of their situation and problems.

Of course, not all the members of this category become nationalists. Far from it. We can distinguish three broad currents of response to the impact of modernisation among those exposed to its influence. The first stream of action is the 'assimilationist', the mental and often physical immigrant. He desires to strip himself of all his particularistic 'accretions', so as to enter, as it were, into a common humanity. (Till recently, this was tantamount to Gellner's westernising tendency.) His is a global cosmopolitanism, which denies the significance of ethnic and national divisions and identities. The second movement, the romantic *narodnik*, is really a kind of retreat into a modified version of the traditional religious outlook. These are the 'traditionalists' who consciously and deliberately reject, not just the West in all its 'materialist splendour', but the whole spirit of modernisation, whose challenge and benefits they have intuited. 'Western arts, Eastern morality' is the motto of all those sufficiently troubled by this challenge, but unwilling to barter their heritage for it; while recognising simultaneously the need to adopt secondary, 'technical' innovations for 'self-strengthening' against the 'crafty foreigners'.[57] The pages of Dostoevski are replete with expressions of this basic attitude: Russia is seen as an exemplary, purified, holy monastery, sole witness to the uncorrupted faith—a profound expression of the urge to 'return to religious roots', which is one factor in the growth of nationalist ideology.[58]

The third current of thought and action I shall call 'reformist'. This is not to be equated with simple religious reform, which has existed at all times—witness the Cluniac reform, the Mut'azilites and Karaites. These internal protestant movements were very limited challenges to traditional beliefs and hierarchies, since they insisted on basing themselves on precedent and various aspects of the tradition. 'Reformism' is a much more thoroughgoing affair, because it is essentially a response to the impact of modernisation. Its main aim is the achievement of a workable and theoretically viable 'higher synthesis' of all that appears most valuable in the outlooks and spirit of the traditional world-images and the modernising ones. 'Reformists' see their situation as the classical confrontation of tradition with modernity, of the meeting of two apparently opposed, but secretly complementary, worlds—if only one could find the key to their higher union. It is this underlying conviction of a 'higher harmony' that gives their activity the appearance of selectively convenient adaptation and eclectic reinterpretation. Theirs, however, is a powerful, if only barely visible, influence. For they desire a complete renovation of, not merely the theology and ritual, but the customs, superstitions and above all educational systems of their religious heritage. They wish to strip away all 'inessential accretions', all 'impurities' that have for centuries overlaid the wellsprings of their religion. This true religion must be removed from the ossifying husk of 'tradition' and from the influence of its traditional exponents. They see their task as a never-ending one of revision, reinterpretation, rationalisation and enrichment, in an upward spiral, based on some overarching theoretical vision, the 'essence' of the religion.[59]

These three currents of thought testify to the inherent *disunity* of the intelligentsia. In concrete cases, of course, we often find a cross-fertilisation and a blurring of the boundaries between them. But a closer examination may reveal that a given instance of nationalism can only be understood by reference to the relative weighting of each of these three currents among the intelligentsia, just prior to the emergence of the movement. There is also the possibility of correlating distinct types of movement with these currents.

In the very long run, Gellner may well be right that the various currents of thought appear in every case of nationalism—but in the medium- and short-range, the dilemma is painfully real and deep, and has had far-reaching consequences. The secular evolution of Turkey differs profoundly from the traditionalist nationalism of, say, Pakistan; and China's latest brand of nationalism is far removed in spirit and action from its earlier phase, or from the religious nationalism of U Nu's Burma or Obrenovic's Serbia. For the people involved, the character of a given nationalist movement, and hence of the independence regime, is vitally influenced by the orientations of its leadership, which springs from one of these three sections of the intelligentsia (or sometimes a combination of two of them). It is therefore important to combine an analysis of the structure of the intelligentsia's overall situation with an appreciation of the various courses of action open to them, within the constraints of that situation. For it is a situation of widespread crisis and disorientation: an assault on authority, on identity, on belief; a decline in solidarity; a denigration of established status; an imbalance of power, sometimes violent; and an often rapacious exploitation of scarce resources and labour, all against the background of unprecedented rises in the level of communications and expectations. To all these storms, the intelligentsia is first exposed and least protected. And, since power accrues primarily to them, it is no accident—and no ideological quirk—that their reactions to this situation are so important, not just as a harbinger of things to come, but as a decisive element in their society's evolution.

Economism and the transition

Gellner thinks that nationalism, like the intelligentsia, is a phenomenon of the 'transition'. This has led to the accusation that he is indulging in a form of economism. It is pointed out that he utilises a step-like theory of history, in which plateaux of stability alternate with a radical transformation of conditions, as in the Neolithic revolution, which leads to a new and materially and culturally 'higher' plateau. Industrialisation, which generates nationalism, is one such steep step. When it is globally complete, nationalism will wither away (though not, it appears, nation-states). *The* transition is industrialisation.

We need to separate out two assertions here, (*a*) that there is a once-for-all transition, (b) that this is basically an industrial one. I think that Gellner can be defended against the 'economism' of (b), but that there is considerable doubt about the transition (a), and especially nationalism's course.

With regard to the charge of 'economism', we already noted the high place assigned to science in the transition. Gellner's polemic against Rostow's 'reactive nationalism' is really the sociologist's reply to the trap which economists often fail to avoid—the invocation of a one-sided 'idealist' interpretation, when economic explanations are felt to be inadequate. More positively, the Neolithic parallel is not intended to convey the message of an equally one-sided 'economism' (why then all the detailed analysis of the role of language and citizenship, etc.?), but that industrialisation is a *total*, civilisational revolution affecting every sphere of man's thought and action. Again, the sentence 'development requires, above all, education' could for Gellner equally be reversed. His polemic is directed at the 'idealists', both nationalists and antinationalists, both historians and economists; but the core of the theory concerns the role of culture, its quite novel significance, and its reciprocal influence *on* the process of industrialisation. Without this novel role, there could be no 'national' classification, no 'nationalist' secession, no consensus about the rights and duties inhering in citizenship, etc. For culture today is the great leveller and homogeniser; yet it is also the crucial divisor of populations, because it has so many different forms and expressions. The longer the exposure to culture, the greater the likelihood of attraction to nationalism.

This goes some way to explaining the relationship between the nationalist and the emigrant. The man who is but lightly touched by this culture, and is excluded from the privileges of the advanced urban classes, has few 'roots' and little to lose; such a man is most prone to the option of emigration. Uprooted morally as well as physically, he has not yet found new roots at a different level and through different bonds. His old solidarities are in ruins, and he can see no new solidarities to take their place. He stands in the interim. A lingering sense of the old solidarities may persist in the new world; diaspora communities may succour the homeland effort, morally and financially. But, unless the conditions in the new haven prove unfavourable, a new sense of solidarity and identity is gradually built on the cultural base of the new country rather than the old. In effect, the emigrant exchanges one potential nationalism for another, but usually over generations, and without a clear perception of the process.

Migration may in some deeper sense form a kind of attribute of the present historical epoch, but that does not eliminate the lasting tension between the emigrant lacking in a sense of history and solidarity, and the nationalist who possesses both. Both started on the same journey—away from the local ties and habitual certainties—and both set their face against local inclusion and traditional allegiances. But, in the unfamiliar city, their paths diverged. The excluded and the uprooted chose different solutions to common problems. We are not yet in a position to determine the forces that have led to this crucial bifurcation.

Are migration and its cultural counterpart, nationalism (which is a kind of cultural journey, and hence not a once-for-all solution), destined to pass with the full industrialisation of the less advanced societies? Deutsch, associating nationalism with the 'mass mobilisation of precommercial, preindustrial peasant peoples', agrees with Gellner in thinking that

> nationalism has drawn much of its strength from the successively lower levels of material civilisation—the *Kulturgefaelle*, as the Germans called it—met in each country by many travellers journeying eastward from America to China, or going southward from the temperate zone to the equator. Everywhere on this ladder of economic inequality, nationalists found richer neighbours to resent and envy; poorer neighbours to despise and fear; but few, if any, equals to respect.[60]

Once this inequality is reduced by nationalism's

> convulsions and inescapably centralised efforts to lift oneself by one's own shoe-laces, economically . . .[61]

education may be sufficiently diffused at a high level to allow us to tolerate linguistic pluralism, as do the Swiss, and to scale down nationalist demands (Gellner seems to envisage the continuation of the present system of nation-states, which he considers a long-run boon, since it insures to some extent against tyranny and political folly, through cultural-political pluralism).

But is this sufficient to enable us to consider nationalism a phenomenon which will soon pass? Seton-Watson cites the American Negro, Quebecois and Nazi examples as an argument against the view that nationalism will pass with full industrialisation. Actually, his first two examples conform to Gellner's theory, since both are cases of 'new arrivals' to the urban economy and culture. The Nazi case is peculiar; but there are strong arguments for excluding it from the definition of nationalism, and treating it partly as an example of Interwar Fascism, partly as a unique combination of elements. Seton-Watson is on stronger ground when he argues that a second condition—apart from modernisation—must be satisfied before nationalism can cease to exist: the nation must attain 'independence and unity'.[62]

Gellner could easily accommodate this demand within his framework. The real difficulty for a view that considers nationalism 'transitional' is the empirical evidence furnished by post-1945 Europe and America. A recent survey of contemporary Western trends shows that nationalism is still the dominant political and cultural force in Europe; despite a short period of disenchantment, there is a growing disassociation of democratic nationalism from Fascism, and the difficulties of European unity (itself partly but another updated nationalism) demonstrate, not just France's 'anachronistic' neo-nationalism, but the continued psychological orientation which treats economics and defence as matters of the 'national interest' primarily. If national*ism* as an ideological movement no longer dictates defence and economic policies, it is still 'available' as a source for such policies, because there has been no corresponding decline in *national sentiment*. For most people, the nation-state is still the 'home', from which the individual derives his self-respect and identity. It is indeed rare to come upon indifference about nationality; doubt perhaps one may find, pride often, but indifference hardly.[63]

This is supported by psychological evidence drawn from European children's national imagery, which showed that distinctions about 'foreignness' are imbibed at the age of six to eight.[64] Snyder presents other political and cultural examples of the resurgence of nationalism in Europe—the success of Strauss in Germany, the new Rumanian nationalism, the anti-Russian sentiment in Czechoslovakia and the continuing hostility of the Polish population to Germany and Russia.[65]

It is just possible to view these manifestations of nationalism as a function of the failure to achieve complete modernisation: once completed, there will be no need for this expression of discontent. But, if that is the case, how do we account for the strength of the Gaullist following in France and the national sentiment among many white Americans, which will not tolerate a humiliation in, say, Vietnam? Is this, too, evidence of incomplete modernisation? But these examples raise a suspicion that we are in fact dealing with a mirage in postulating an empirical state of full modernisation (modernity); and that this fallacy arises from a tacit equation of 'modernisation' with industrialisation only, a position which many, including, I have argued, Gellner, would wish to avoid. If highly industrialised America (the white sector) evinces strong nationalist sentiment, as did the French bourgeoisie in 1968, we are forced to the conclusion that there is no strong and necessary connection between nationalism's course and the trajectory of industrialisation; and that other aspects of a continuing process or processes of 'modernisation' (the wider phenomenon) are more directly linked to the expression of discontent in terms of nationalism.

These aspects of modernisation will be touched on in the last chapter, after a more detailed consideration of the problem of defining nationalism, which Gellner's theory highlighted, and of the various types of nationalist movement.

The linguistic criterion of nationhood

The argument so far has concentrated on three issues. We have found that (*a*) the social composition of nationalist movements is extremely heterogeneous, and that the role of the working-class must not be overestimated therein, (*b*) although the intelligentsia always furnishes key personnel to such movements disproportionately, their internal cultural disunity must be stressed, if we are to get at the origins and special character of a given case of nationalism, (*c*) it is very doubtful if we are justified in talking of a once-for-all transition, and that all the available evidence suggests that nationalism will be with us as a recurrent phenomenon for a long time. At the same time, there is no substance in the charge of 'economism' levelled at Gellner; the merit of his theory, it seems to me, lies exactly in the balance it maintains between 'ideal' and 'material' factors, i.e. between culture and the social consequences of economic change.

We can now turn to what I think is Gellner's major contention, that 'nationality' classifications are 'cultural' ones, and that these are (or rather must be) linguistic classifications; and hence that we can interpret nationalism as a basically linguistic movement. In fact, for Gellner, 'culture' and 'language' are more or less interchangeable terms in modern conditions. The criterion of nationhood is language.

I should like to scrutinise the argument that lands us in this linguistic reductionism.

Gellner holds that the precondition for full, effective citizenship is literacy. As industrialisation proceeds, it disrupts on a vast scale. It makes people 'structureless', without clear-cut roles, rights and rules. The former individuals, occupying each his allotted social niche in the traditional order by ties of kinship and immemorial custom, now become 'masses'; they are, as Kornhauser would say, 'available'. But, in modern society, man is man, and no longer identifiable with his role(s). He can divest himself of his roles, just as he can choose and change his organisations on a contractual basis, with a fair amount of liberty. Bureaucracy, though it may circumscribe closely personal freedom within the organisation, though it can be described as the 'kinship of modern man', still allows considerable leeway for the individual and his idiosyncrasies. It does not define a man's identity or encompass his personality, and it is not coextensive with his thoughts and activities—besides we have organisational pluralism (in this respect it resembles the relations between the individual and the global system of nation-states).

Gellner now makes an all-important assertion: 'culture' replaces 'structure' as the distinctively modern mode of interpersonal relationships, as a consequence of this erosion of 'structure', and because

> ... a very large proportion of one's relationships and encounters—
> in fact, they *are* more frequently encounters than relationships—
> are ephemeral, non-repetitive, and optional.[66]

The connection between this empirical assertion and the idea that culture is a 'replacement' is further elucidated by the following passage:

> when interlocutors and contexts are all unfamiliar, the message itself *must* become intelligible—it is no longer understood, as was the case in traditional societies, before it was even articulated—and

those who communicate *must* speak the same language, *in some sense or other*.[67] (my italics)

There are two grounds for criticism here. The first is that we have here what looks like an implicit assumption about a universal need to belong, which is shared by Kedourie and others. The argument is not a simple one of probability, a factual observation that 'culture' does, empirically, replace 'structure' in modern society. The italicised 'musts' in the above passage read as though they contain a teleological assumption, based on the idea of a universal need to belong to some community. It is to fulfil this need that 'culture' *must* become the new cement of solidarity, the bond of society. It must do so by virtue of the need for some social tie, following the decline of ascribed role-structures.

There are two possible interpretations of this universal 'need to belong'—as the need of individuals, or of societies. With regard to the first, why, one wonders, *must* the message become intelligible? Why the imperative of understanding at all? Such an assumption about individual psychology precludes any discrimination in the matter of differential human understanding. How is it that some individuals 'understand' more than others, or interpret the same message in very different ways? How can we explain breakdowns in 'intelligibility', if we operate with this generalised assumption? We might escape these difficulties if we talked in terms of individual desires and habits, rather than the elastic concept of 'need'. Human beings, after all, do very often feel a strong desire to return to some cosy security with a routine of habits and activities, when such a pattern has been suddenly overturned. But even here it would be rash to generalise. Some may actually feel liberated from the routine, others may fluctuate in their attitudes to it. Not all will feel the urge to return to the womb, or crave for a substitute. In other words, this question of individuals' needs, desires and habits requires empirical investigation in each case. It cannot be settled from such *a priori* assumptions.

But suppose that we read the above passages in terms of *societal* needs, and say that the survival of societies requires a minimum of effective communication. There can be no quarrel here, since it is true by definition—communication is part of the meaning of the term, 'society'.

Gellner obviously means something rather more specific in

his use of the term 'culture'—as is clear from his contention that small-scale societies *could* do without it, since role-relationships serve to bind them together. What Gellner appears to be asserting is that if societies are to survive or be renewed under modern conditions, they must be based upon the tie of language, in the broadest sense. Now, since we see that societies have survived or been renewed as nations, we must conclude that this is due to the role of this type of culture in satisfying the society's needs.

There is little doubt that culture, and especially linguistic education, has assumed tremendous importance in the modern epoch. But this empirical *trend* should not be converted into a necessary social concomitant of industrialisation; for that would imply a retrospective argument from the fact that societies have survived under modern conditions. It strains the evidence, and involves us in teleological assertions. In fact, language is by no means the only binding force in modern societies.

This brings up my second criticism. I would contend that (*a*) 'culture' is a much broader category than language, (*b*) the classification by 'nationality' is not to be equated with the classification by language, and (*c*) nationalism is not a linguistic movement. Over and beyond this, Gellner's assertion that literacy is the precondition of effective citizenship, i.e. of nationhood, needs to be amended and specified.

This last point is taken first, by referring to my emendation to Gellner's model of causal relations between modernisation, education and nationalism, as rendered in the second diagram.

Only 'a nation-size educational system can produce such full citizens', argues Gellner; *hence* something the size of a 'nation' is the minimal political unit in the modern world.[68] This presupposes that the majority want citizenship and its benefits, which they perceive, and therefore desire education, to enjoy it. But you can only have citizenship in a 'nation', whether this is a linguistically homogeneous unit or not. This means that our would-be citizens are in effect converts to nationalism; they want to live in a nation-state, they desire to be members of a culturally homogeneous nation. But that would invert Gellner's causal chain: nationalism now becomes the precondition of mass literacy, not vice versa. The italicised 'hence' is misleading.

In fact, neither of these opposed positions correspond to the usual empirical sequences. To begin with, we need to make a sharp distinction between the exposure of the traditional elite and the 'new men' to Western education—which affects a tiny group only —and the imposition, indoctrination and cultural homogenisation of the mass of the population in a state-wide educational system. Historically, there are two main types of causal sequence relating the 'nation' to the latter type of educational system or 'mass education'. Both sequences start from the westernisation of a small elite. In the first case, the absolutist rulers (who are usually themselves 'westernised', be they Emperor, Czar, Sultan or colonial governor) impose a uniform system of education in a particular language for the purpose of efficiency in taxation, administration, justice, etc.—and, beyond this, to make 'their' populations more homogeneous and (hopefully) loyal. Such a 'mercantilist' protonationalism tended to treat the subject as a kind of personal resource, and the territory and State as a private estate of the ruler.[69] Here the state and the rulers were the starters in the causal chain leading through mass literacy to the growth of a common national sentiment based on territory and language being coextensive, and resulting over centuries in the formation of 'nations', as in Western Europe.

The second type of historical sequence is exemplified by the French revolutionaries and Meiji or Kemalist reformers. The exposure of the elite to western education leads to that crisis of the intelligentsia, which we already described; and thence, by mechanisms yet to be explored, to the birth of nationalist movements aiming at independence and self-government for the group, often through secession from a much larger unit. (Such a movement is often aided by the presence of linguistic differentiae plus a certain amount of discrimination against the speakers of this language—as Gellner argues.) The nationalist movement then gains independence for the group and power for itself. In the new state, the nationalists often find that their population is insufficiently welded together and too heterogeneous for the various taks of regeneration and development which the leaders envisage. A mass system of education is therefore installed to mould the population into a real 'nation', to give them the requisite skills for effective participation in social, political and economic life, and instil in them a patriotic spirit. The nationalists continue the work of the absolutist rulers, only more self-consciously, with greater sense of purpose, and as a corollary of their ideological beliefs. It is the nationalists who have decided what is to count as an 'effective citizen'. *Their* goals dictate who will be 'an acceptable human specimen'—not some mysterious tacit consensus emanating from the consequences of the industrialisation process.

The key to my whole argument against these teleological overtones in Gellner's argument is contained in the reference he makes to the 'current notions of human dignity', in the sentence I italicised (see page 116). Gellner gives us no clue as to their origins—although conceding they have undergone remarkable changes recently. This is curious. Human dignity is a concept much stressed by nationalists, and one could forcefully argue that the 'need' for linguistic culture and for educated citizens are best viewed as minority perceptions of elites who are much influenced by the recent prominence accorded to the idea of 'human dignity'. So that it is this idea which, in many concrete cases, can be seen as one root of the drive for mass literacy, education and the stress on language. The *claim* to the vote, by virtue of belonging to a common 'humanity', has historically often preceded the growth of linguistic co-culturality—irrespective of educational qualifications, as the debate over A and B voter rolls in Africa proves. (This should not, of course, be construed as some kind of covert monocausal 'idealist' rebuttal of an apparently 'materialist' argument. We have yet to explore the roots of this change in valuation set on membership of the human race, and no claim is made for the preponderance or primacy of value changes. All that is intended is an historical emendation to Gellner's argument, and an extension to distinguish the earlier elite phase of nationalism to the later State-induced mass one.) [But see Appendix C.]

The distinction between elite and mass nationalism, and this outline of the two common historical sequences leading to nationhood and mass education, highlights the role of language in the formation of 'nations'—as opposed to the emergence of 'nationalism'. Roughly, linguistic differentiae can play an important part in the growth of *nations*, as nationalists themselves recognise; *but*, language is a rather insignificant factor in the rise of the nationalist *movement*. Now this paradoxical contrast is only obscured if 'nationality' ('nation') is equated with 'language group'; for then we are left with the task of explaining the success of nationalist movements in linguistically heterogeneous areas, like Ghana, Tanzania or Zambia. Gellner, it seems to me, places too much weight on the role of language as the source of nationalist movements, and this results from his equation of language group and nation. Actually, such an *identification* only minimises the role of language in the formation of nations.

The upshot of all this is the need to keep the task of definition analytically quite distinct from that of explanation. Actually, we have four problems on our hands:

1 to define the 'nation'
2 to define 'nationalism' (the ideological movement)
3 to explain the formation of 'nations'
4 to explain the emergence of nationalist movements.

Empirically, these tasks will naturally overlap. But methodological clarity is best served by concentrating on each of these problems in turn, at least initially.

In fact, Gellner himself has distinguished five senses of the term 'nationalism':

1 a type of social organisation, with large-scale, unmediated membership, cultural homogeneity, etc.
2 a theory, formulated by the critics of nationalism, to the effect that a state's rulers and boundaries should correlate with 'nationality'. This is a theory of government, shorn of
3 accretions amounting to florid theories, formulated by the nationalists themselves, stressing race, folk, community, etc.
4 a sentiment corresponding to nationality—an epiphenomenon
5 a generic concept of loyalty, or patriotism, which holds that a society is good because it is 'mine'—an attitude which is common to all ages, and needs to be distinguished from its subspecies, nationalism proper.[70]

Clearly (1) corresponds to our use of the term 'nation', while (2)—and (3)—are identical with our 'core doctrine' of 'nationalism' and its various embellished versions, respectively; (4), national sentiment, I feel, needs some elaboration, since it can exist independently of the nationalist ideology or movement; while (5), we argued, is a different problem altogether.

If these distinctions were firmly adhered to, the role of language in both the definition and the explanation of nationalism and the nation would fall into place. The inflation of language as the criterion of nationhood results from two factors, the failure to separate the four tasks above, and the acceptance of the German romantic ('organic') version of nationalist ideology as the only genuine version. In the first chapter, I tried to demonstrate why this identification of nationalist doctrine with the Fichtean theory was untenable; and the next chapter attempts to show why we should not equate the concept of the 'nation' with that of the language group. For the present, the argument is confined to two points.

The first is that 'culture' is a far broader concept than 'language'. Indeed, the italicised passage 'in some sense or other' (see page 144) underscores this appreciation. Culture includes customs, the ancestry myth, institutions, history, law, and particularly religion. The latter has, in fact, been the main mark of differentiation for a number of nationalist movements—the Boer, Ibo, Pakistani, Jewish, Ewe, Burmese, Greek, Serb, Croat, as well as the Muslim nationalisms in the Soviet Union. Possession of a unique language was a secondary 'sub-differentiating' characteristic. The emphasis on possession of a common language, which leads to the so-called 'language problem' in multilingual nation-states like India or some African states, comes at a rather later stage of social evolution; and it is really more a *product* of nationalism and its ideal of the homogeneous nation, than its cause or defining mark.[71] There is therefore little empirical support for the slide from defining nationhood by common culture to the linguistic criterion which Gellner assumes.

The second point concerns the relationship of language development to the nationalist movement. Many nationalists have, it is true, been addicted to philological studies. There is also a strong correlation between literary renascences and language modernisation, and the rise of *some* nationalist movements. But the point here is surely that these linguistic activities reflect the growing national sentiment of their practitioners. Linguistic reformers do not discover their nationalism through their intellectual labours. The vernacular is glorified, and elevated to become *the* popular language (but not in every case even in Europe), only *after* its students have become nationalistically inclined, and *because* they have already made this self-discovery. Linguistic studies, like historical, become an often unselfconscious means of justifying their prior nationalist conviction

—to themselves as well as others. Language reform, as the cases of the Balkans and the Ottoman Empire amply demonstrate, is the work of those who are imbued with the desire to renovate their community and make it self-sufficient and culturally independent —as in the days of an idealised age of grandeur.[72] (The preference for the demotic is an added populist element, which requires separate explanation.)

Nationalist movements, therefore, even in Europe, are not linguistic movements—any more than they are historical or ethnic or religious or territorial movements. All these attempts to 'reduce' nationalism to some kind of more readily intelligible variable end up by defeating themselves on empirical grounds— or become tautologies. Nationalists have not spilt their blood, or others', they have not expended their energy and lives, to forward the cause of a language, or even a culture. The struggle for independence may include the banner of language separatism; but the roots of that endeavour lie deeper than a desire to communicate adequately. The ideal of nationhood, which has stirred these men and women, is more complex, less earthy, yet more compelling and powerful. It is an ideal of a different order altogether.

The definition of this ideal, and of the movement which strives to realise it, is the next task.

Part Two

VARIETIES OF NATIONALISM

Chapter Seven

DEFINITIONS

In A.D. 6, Caesar Augustus placed Judaea and Samaria under direct Roman rule. As a consequence, he ordered the taking of a population census as well as an inventory of the annexed territories for the assessment of tribute.

Josephus tell us that thereupon a rabbi, 'a Galilean, named Judas, incited his countrymen to revolt, upbraiding them as cowards for consenting to pay tribute to Rome and tolerating mortal masters, after having God for their lord'.[1] His plea for sedition was backed by Saddok, the Pharisee:

> They maintained that this census would lead to nothing less than complete slavery, and they called upon the people to vindicate their liberty. They argued that, if they succeeded, they would enjoy the consequences of their good fortune, and, if they failed, they would at least have the honour and glory of having shown greatness of spirit. Moreover, God would surely assist them in their undertaking, if, inspired by such ideals, they spared no effort to realise them.[2]

Zealots and pan-Hellenes

So began the ill-fated Zealot movement. From this moment, the ideals and conceptions of this strange guerrilla uprising, recently illuminated by the excavations at Masada and the discovery of the Dead Sea Scrolls, gained a growing hold on the oppressed people, till it burst forth in the tragic revolt of 66–73. Our main witness,

F

however, is hostile to these ideals. Josephus, a well-born priest and Pharisee, deserted to the Romans, and his *Jewish War* and *Antiquities* are filled with an ambivalent apologetic on behalf of his people. Wishing to enlist non-Jewish sympathies for the mass of the 'peaceful' Jews, who on his account were driven into revolt by the fanatical Zealots, and needing also to justify his national secession in the final War, he tends in both works to underplay not only the impact and magnitude of the Zealot movement, but more important, its ethical character and the mainstream religious nature of its ideals.[3]

But it is just this religious grounding of Zealot conceptions— like that of its successor, the Bar-Kochba revolt of 132–5, and its predecessor, the Hasmonean struggle of 165–42 B.C.—which Josephus himself reveals so strikingly in the final appeal which he puts into the mouth of the Zealot commander on Masada in 73, when he persuades the doomed defenders to kill themselves rather than fall into Roman hands. To Eliezer ben Yair, the Zealots had long ago resolved

> never to be servants to the Romans, nor to any other than to God himself, who alone is the true and just Lord of mankind. . . . We were the very first that revolted from them, and we are the last that fight against them; and I cannot but esteem it as a favour that God hath granted us, that it is still in our power to die bravely, and in a state of freedom, which hath not been the case with others who were conquered unexpectedly . . . it is by the will of God, and by necessity, that we are to die: for it now appears that God hath made such a decree against the whole Jewish nation, that we are to be deprived of the life which (he knew) we would not make a due use of. . . .[4]

As a strict Jew, Eliezer was convinced that 'the same God who had of old taken the Jewish nation into his favour, had now condemned them to destruction'—as the destruction of His holy city, Jerusalem, proved. We see here the underlying religious basis of the Jewish martyr-ideal. God alone is the absolute sovereign of the Jewish people; his covenant with them is exclusive and binding, and implies a 'theocracy' as its only political counterpart (a word coined by Josephus in this very context). Only a godly high-priest could rule the Jews, as God's vicegerent on earth; hence it was not just cowardly, but an outright blasphemy, to pay tribute to Caesar. Further, Judaea was regarded as Yahweh's holy land, his sovereign possession; it followed that to use its resources

for tribute to a heathen and mortal lord was an act of apostasy to
Yahweh.[5]

This selfsame ancient doctrine was invoked by Mattathias in
Modi'in at the inception of the Maccabean revolt of 165 B.C. We
read that Antiochus Epiphanes of Syria

> wrote to his whole kingdom, *that all should be one people*, and that
> everyone should leave his *laws*: so all the heathen agreed according
> to the commandment of the king. Yea, many also of the Israelites
> consented to his *religion,* and sacrificed unto idols, and profaned the
> sabbath (my italics).

Mattathias refused to sacrifice and killed the collaborators in
Modi'in.

> Thus dealt he zealously for the law of God, like as Phinees did unto
> Zambri the son of Salom. And Mattathias cried throughout the
> city with a loud voice, saying, Whosoever is zealous of the law,
> and maintaineth the covenant, let him follow me.[6]

The roots of this attitude stem from the prophetic tradition, from
Elijah's example of fiery faith, and from the prototype, Phinehas,
whom Yahweh praises for killing a Jew and his non Jewish
paramour 'in that he (Phinehas) was zealous for my zeal'.[7] This
faith had, however, been developed by the time of Jesus through
the addition of two new elements. The first was the peculiar
Pharisaic doctrine of 'synergism', the notion that man was God's
co-worker in his redemptive plan, and that if man chose to help
Yahweh in this work, He would bless and aid him. The other
element was, of course, the growth of messianic expectations, the
belief in the coming of the Lord's Anointed, who would deliver
his people and restore the kingdom to Israel. Hence the rash of
Messiahs, bloodily suppressed by the Romans.[8]

One looks in vain for a similar intensity of expression in the
attempts at unification and resistance to foreign rule, which mark
the other usually-cited example of ancient nationalism—that of
classical Greece.[9] The fierce sentiments of loyalty which ruined
Greece during the great Peloponnesian war were directed wholly
to the individual city-states. Rarely did the body of Hellenes put
aside their internecine differences to resist foreign invasion; even
during Xerxes' threat, only Attica and the Peloponnesian League
combined, and the Athenians quickly withdrew their ships from
the Ionian revolt.[10] Persian gold was a precondition of Sparta's

final victory over Athens, and even the offensive Peace of Antal-
cidas—the Great King's *diktat*, if ever there was one—could not
rouse the city-states to take effective steps, when Philip posed the
ultimate threat to their freedom. The words of Pericles' funeral
speech refer to the inhabitants of Attica, not to the Greeks:

> In this *land* of ours there have always been the same people living
> from generation to generation up till now, and they, by their
> courage and their virtues, have handed it on to us, a free *country*
> (tēn gar chōran [land, country] hoi autoi aei oikountes).[11]

It is the city (*polis*) on which the Athenians should daily fix their
eyes, wondering at her greatness, until they fell in love with her
(*erastas gignomenous autēs*). Thucydides uses similar concepts when
he makes the Plataean allies of the Athenians remonstrate with the
Spartans who in 431 have invaded their independent territory.
Reminding them of Pausanias' promise, the Plataeans claim that

> After he (Pausanias) had liberated *Hellas* from the Persians with
> the help of all the *Hellenes* who came forward to share the risk in the
> battle that was fought near our city, he made a sacrifice to Zeus the
> Liberator in the market-place of Plataea, and calling together all
> the allies, he gave back to the people of Plataea their *land* and their
> *city* (gen kai polin) to be held by them as an *independent state* (tēn
> spheteran echontas autonomous oikein) guaranteed for ever
> against unprovoked attack and against foreign domination . . .[12]
> (my italics)

The city and its rural hinterland, with its ideals of the rule of law
and self-government of the citizenry, remains the focal point of
attachment.[13]

But there is another side to this conventional picture. Levi has
argued that a broader perspective (in time as well as space)
reveals that

> the Hellenic 'state' was not the Polis, but a community with the
> character of a federal State with a religious basis, in which the
> Greeks preserved, less effectively, the unity of the Homeric-
> Mycenaean monarchy.

By contrast,

> The Greek city, in fact, was simply the common home of a group
> of Greeks who were agreed to organise their own lives by laws
> which were not contradictory to the general principles of their
> religion, and so of the morality of the pattern of life that the
> religion imposed.

The Polis

was not a 'sovereign state' in our sense of the word, but more like a 'canton', autonomous within the political code of an ethnic community.[14]

Levi's argument is controversial. He looks on the internecine strife of Greek city-states as expressions of bids for unification of Hellas by one regional or socio-economic 'party' over another, using the religious legitimation of the oracular cults as foci of pan-Hellenic organisations. Thessaly's Anthelian league bid petered out, when the Delphic Amphictyonic and Peloponnesian Olympic 'oracular states' began to vie for supremacy over all Greeks in the sixth century, only to be challenged by the Athenian Delian League in the fifth. The failure of these unification attempts was largely due to the differential pace and degree of political and socio-economic development in various regions of Greece, which led to cantonal loyalties in rivalry with pan-Hellenic ones; but this did not obliterate the religious unity of Greece transmitted by the oracles, which furnished a common pattern of traditions, customs, beliefs and ethical practices, based on the transcendence of certain common deities. This unity was also expressed in the criteria for entry to the various aristocratic Games, in the rules for founding colonies, and in the quasi-sacred canon of Homeric poems. All of which stressed the idea of a common Greek citizenship—and citizenship laws the Greeks considered the most important of all.[15]

There is little doubt about the religio-ethnic unity of the Hellenes, even if the above argument is not acceptable *in toto*. This homogeneity was reinforced by linguistic unity. The dialects were readily intelligible to Greeks of the period; and they were clearly marked off from the nearest set of dialects in the general Indo-European group of languages. For Andrewes, 'in general, language was an effective criterion to distinguish Greek from foreigner'. In addition, the performance of certain 'customs' was crucial for Greeks; they made large collections of 'barbarian customs'. (There is, however, one crucial reservation. As Forrest points out, the incidence of conflict and differences between Ionians and Dorians, in particular, is too great to allow us to ignore this *intra*-Hellenic ethnic sentiment, which perhaps weakened attempts at Greek unification.)[16]

Greeks were extremely conscious of their differences in culture, and especially political institutions, from the Persians and other 'barbarians'. Herodotus' political debates involving Darius' accession and the account of Spartan freedom, as well as the theme of the metopes on the Parthenon, indicate the strength of the Greek distinction between 'civilisation' and 'barbarism'. The clearest expression of pan-Hellenism is to be found in the appeals of Isocrates, for whom anyone who had partaken of Greek education was a Greek. More generally, the accusations of 'Medism', and the appeal to services rendered to the Greek cause, show that this sentiment of unity—however much it was utilised for sectional purposes—had some resonance and meaning for the population.

Ethnocentric versus polycentric nationalism

Zealotism and pan-Hellenism exhibit important differences, from the standpoint of closer definition of 'nationalism'. For the present, however, I want to underline a basic common feature: both are examples of what can be termed 'ethnocentric' nationalism. 'Ethnocentric' nationalism must be distinguished from 'polycentric' nationalism; and this contrast forms an essential preliminary to the task of defining nationalism.

For an 'ethnocentric' nationalist, both 'power' and 'value' inhere in his cultural group. Indeed, these dimensions are inseparable. My group is the vessel of wisdom, beauty, holiness, culture; hence power automatically belongs as an attribute to my group. Whatever the factual distribution of power at a given time, real strength, being God-given, is not to the mighty of the earth, but to those who stand in a special relationship with the divine. So much the better, of course, if the facts correspond to this belief; but the reverse, my group's suffering, is to be construed as evidence of nothing except divine displeasure for human folly or sin. In the Greek context, the hubris of a Xerxes, not Greek prowess, brings about the Great King's debacle. It is Zeus, who in Aeschylus' *Persae* overthrows Xerxes—the Greeks being mere intermediaries of his will. Likewise, the Assyrians and Babylonians are God's instrument for visiting God's wrath on the people who broke his covenant.

'Polycentric' nationalism, by contrast, resembles the dialogue of many actors on a common stage. As the term implies, this kind of nationalism starts from the premiss that there are many centres of *real* power; other groups do have valuable and genuinely noble ideas and institutions which we would do well to borrow, or adapt. 'Polycentric' nationalism is of course no less concerned with the collective self; but it conceives its role in very different terms. It seeks to join the 'family of nations', the international drama of status equals, to find its appropriate identity and part. 'Polycentric' nationalists are often self-critical and eclectic; they can even fall into a kind of derivative, self-denying position at the national level. But, on the whole, this outward-looking, multi-centred nationalism clings to the spirit of the Meiji reformers, and to Ataturk's dictum that there is one civilisation, but many nations, and Turkey wishes to join the mainstream on this basis. 'Normalisation', the idea of becoming a 'nation' like all others, in a condition of dignified equality, has also been a major source of Zionist aspirations—in contrast to the solipsist ethnocentrism of the older Judaic ideals which we saw were fundamental to the outlook of most Jews from the Maccabees to the Pale *shtetl*.[17]

An analogy may clarify the distinction. At the Great Dionysia festival instituted by Pisistratus beneath the Acropolis, it was customary for the choirs of satyrs, the god's attendants, to dance and sing their 'goat song'; their leader (who was also the composer of the song) came forward and, assuming the role of some character related to the events, engaged in speech with them. This was the common practice before the innovation of Thespis, who introduced an answerer to engage in dialogue with the chorus-leader—so beginning the movement towards the full tragic drama of the fifth century.[18]

This development from primitive agrarian village ritual to highly articulated city dramatic dialogue illustrates the distinction between the two types of nationalism. Some of the confusion over the question of the antiquity of 'nationalism' is the result of this failure to distinguish these types. The first or 'ethnocentric' kind of nationalism, which characterised the ancient (and medieval) world, was typically 'protagonistic' in the sense indicated above: that is, the 'nation' was assumed to be the centre of the world, and alone significant—while round about the 'nations of the world', heathen and barbarian, formed the undifferentiated chorus in the background. In this traditional, exclusive and solipsist conception, there was but one actor. The rest were mute instruments of God or fate. For Greek and Jew alike, their 'natio', their culture and religion, was the indisputable truth; hence only what their nation did or suffered had any meaning. Other peoples simply 'wandered in darkness'—in varying degrees, perhaps.

This distinction between the two types of nationalism is purely analytic and ideal-typical. I have, it is true, not found an example of 'polycentric' nationalism in the ancient world, or before the French Revolution, except in scattered writings.[19] But we find many examples of 'ethnocentric' nationalism in the modern world: for example, Russian Panslavism and Polish messianism or the 'primary resistance' movements against Western intrusion in Nigeria or Ghana in the nineteenth century, and perhaps Abd-el-Kader's resistance to the French invasion of Algeria.[20] If the many 'messianic' and 'millennial' movements in Africa, Asia and Latin America are treated as cases of incipient nationalisms, they naturally fall into this 'ethnocentric' category.[21]

There is a sense in which it is correct to say that the 'ethnocentric' nationalisms form a kind of outer circle of 'weak' cases of the movement. This weakness, however, has nothing to do with the movement's intensity, as the Zealot example demonstrates. What we are pointing out by calling them 'weak' is the 'submergence' of the idea of the 'nation' and its 'independence' under that of the religious culture and the divinity. Zionism, in the 'normalisation' sense, would have been inconceivable to the Zealot. On the other hand, the modern Greek war of independence is still largely permeated by the Byzantine Orthodox religious ideals; here we see the moment of bifurcation between the idea of a war of resistance to foreign unbelievers to preserve the group's culture, and the idea of a war for the creation of a new nation-state on mainly secular lines.[22] An interesting and important part of the analysis of nationalism in the modern era concerns the relative weighting of these two conceptions—the self-preserving and the self-renewing ideals.

Nationalism in the ancient world

Of course, the main intent of this analysis of theories and typologies is concerned with the 'polycentric' type of nationalism, which has sprung up with such force in all continents since the French Revolution. But, since in practice we cannot entirely separate the two types even in 'modern' movements, and since the topic of 'ethnocentric' nationalism is interesting and important in its own right, we need to devote a little more space to ancient nationalisms. Closer definition of the one will help in the more difficult task of defining the 'polycentric' form.

It is often said that we distort the history of the ancient Near East, if we read back into it the vertical and horizontal cleavages of the modern era. Reading through the Egyptian and Mesopotamian inscriptions and texts, one is struck by the paucity of references to anything resembling our concept of 'peoples' or 'nations' as such. The Assyrian kings refer to the objects of their warlike expeditions by such phrases as 'the inhabitants of Tyre and Sidon', 'the tribute of Jehu, son of Omri', 'the house of Omri', 'the towns . . . of the Upper Sea', 'Midas king of Mushku', 'the country of the Medians', 'the country of the Hittites, Amurru-country in its full extent . . . Israel, Edom, Palestine . . .'—these are the descriptions of the enemies whom Adad-Nirari III, Tiglath-Pileser III and Sargon II 'smash like pots'.[23] Egyptian inscriptions from the New Kingdom likewise tend to refer to the names of lands, towns and kings—'the Prince of Rehob', 'Hamath', 'Megiddo', 'them of Pahel'; 'No land could stand before their arms, from Hatti, Kode, Carchemish, Arzawa, and Alashiya on, being cut off at (one time).'[24]

Closer inspection, however, reveals that the writers were conscious of the fact that the Near East was a kaleidoscope of peoples of diverse cultures, in perpetual coalition or conflict. When we read that the 'foreign countries made a conspiracy in their islands. . . . Their confederation was the Philistines, Tjeker, Shekelesh, Denye(n), and Weshesh, lands united', we see that the author differentiates clearly between the territorial and ethnic units. These peoples of the Sea, whom Ramses III (c. 1188 B.C.) caused to 'turn back from (even) mentioning Egypt . . .' and would not 'let foreign countries behold the frontier of Egypt' are designated as 'their princes and their tribespeople'.[25] In the Assyrian inscriptions there is mention of a certain Zabibe, 'Queen of the Arabs'; and Sargon is depicted as catching 'the Greeks who (live on the islands) in the sea, like fish', settling in rebuilt Samaria 'people from countries which I myself had conquered', and imposing on them tribute as is customary for 'Assyrian citizens'. The Hyksos are referred to as Asiatics, Hezekiah is called a Jew, and Ia'ubidi of Hamath is 'a commoner without claim to the throne, a cursed Hittite'. [26]

The modern practice, therefore, of presenting ancient history as that of 'peoples'—Hittites, Hurrians, Assyrians, Persians, Medes, Phoenicians, Scythians, Urartians, Arameans, Elamites, Kassites, Sogdians, Khwarezmians, Mannaeans, Sumerians, Egyptians, Nubians, Canaanites, Turanians, Parthians, Edomites, Amorites, Phrygians, etc.—is not unjustified, provided we hold to the distinction between the two types of 'nationalism' above. For each of these groups had their own gods, rituals, practices, and often languages; and the larger, sedentary groups tended to consolidate their position through the institutions of a kingdom.

All the above-named groups share two features: cultural distinctiveness and territorial contiguity. And these are just those features by which some anthropologists define African 'tribes'. The French word 'ethnie' has no English equivalent; but it denotes exactly this mixture of cultural-regional criteria. [27] This definition, however, would cover not only the better-known ancient 'ethnie' in the above list, but also the rather less familiar 'tribes'—Lullubi, Guti, the Brahuis of the Hindu Kush, the nomadic Cimmerians who invaded Anatolia in the seventh century, the Saka of Turkestan, the Parni of East Persia, the southern Russian Sarmatians, the Ellipi north of Elam, not to mention many smaller tribes. [28]

To class the Assyrians together with the Brahuis and Parni does not seem to advance our task; it immediately raises the question of subdividing the rather loose and all-encompassing concept of 'ethnie'. Can we say that the Assyrians and the Urartians have reached the further stage of 'nationhood'? And, if so, by what criteria? And in what sense of the term, can we call their conflicts 'nationalist', their wars 'national' ones?

To the founder of the third and greatest Assyrian Empire, Adad-Nirari II (911–891 B.C.), his campaign against Assyria's enemies was, in his own view, a war of 'national liberation'. His aims, and those of his more famous successors, were to protect 'the land of the god Assur', to increase its strength by booty taken in razzias, and to crusade on behalf of the supreme god, Assur, and punish the king's enemies as 'wicked devils'—enemies of his god. The religious purpose was paramount in the cruel policy of deportations and extortions, and we never glimpse any sense of self-doubt, of moral scruples in relation to this policy, in their kings' inscriptions. [29]

> To the city of Suru of Bit Halupe I drew near, and the terror of the splendour of Ashur, my lord, overwhelmed them.

This record of Ashurnasirpal II (884–59 B.C.) is typical, and it reveals the essential religious basis of political power in the ancient world. The great king of Assyria and its empire, and the ensi of a small Sumerian city-state, like Gudea of Lagash, were alike in resting their authority in the principle of divine election. To lose one's sacred city, as Rusas I of Urartu lost Musasir in 714 to Sargon II, was the source of such overwhelming shame to Rusas that

> with his own dagger he stabbed himself through the heart like a pig and ended his life. [30]

The Urartians, like the Assyrians, had their own ('Vannic' Hurrian-type) language, a compact territory near Lake Van in Armenia, their own economic system based on vast royal estates worked by slaves and prisoners, their own metallurgical industries, a peculiar art and massive architecture, and above all its pantheon of deities in Musasir, headed by the national god, Khaldia. [31]

We are clearly face to face here with something rather more advanced than the 'tribe', and we find a correspondingly developed political group ('ethnocentric') consciousness, based on the sense of divine mission. In this sense, Persians, Carthaginians, Romans, Egyptians, Hittites, Mittanians, and Babylonians are on a par with the Greeks and the Jews. All of these large social groups were not based primarily on kinship ties like 'tribes'; but they were, at one point or another, 'resisting foreign rule' to preserve their religio-cultural heritage—or extending their own rule (that of their gods) over other similar groups (ethnie), as well as over 'tribes'.

In this weaker sense of nationalism, then—a sentiment for the preservation of collective (ethnic) solidarity and cultural and political autarchy—the ancient world, from the time of Tuthmosis III and Suppiluliumas to the revolts of the Jews and the Sassanid revival, was the scene of 'international' strife and alliance. [32]

In all this time, however, we never meet the international*ist* sentiment, which is closer to 'polycentric' nationalism. Only in some of the prophets and in the hymn to Aton of Akhnaton, do we sense a new and different conception, allowing a measure of 'value' to other peoples:

> The countries of Syria and Nubia, the land of Egypt,
> Thou settest every man in his place,
> Thou suppliest their necessities:
> Everyone has his food, and his time of life reckoned.
> Their tongues are separate in speech,
> And their natures as well;
> Their skins are distinguished,
> As thou distinguishest the foreign peoples.
> . . . .
> The lord of all of them, wearying himself for them,
> The lord of every land, rising for them,
> The Aton of the day, great of majesty.
> All distant foreign countries, thou makest their life (also),
> For thou has set a Nile in heaven,
> . . . .
> The Nile in heaven, it is for the foreign peoples
> And for the beasts of every desert that go upon (their) feet.[33]

The desirability and possibility of definition

The foregoing discussion deliberately operated with loose and comprehensive concepts of the nation and nationalism—roughly defining 'nation' as the ethnic-cultural group or 'people', and 'nationalism' as self-centred collective resistance to foreign rule to preserve the group and its culture. But the differences between the 'nationalisms' of Greece and Judaea, and those between such 'peoples' as Urartians and the Lullubi, by themselves call out for an attempt at rather more precise definitions of these concepts. When we add to these differences those that characterise the attributes of large modern groups, the argument for greater precision becomes compelling. The danger of reification of these concepts, which has wrought such havoc politically, is, I feel, sufficiently recognised now, for it not to prevent us insisting on the *desirability* of defining nationalism closely. Surely, if nothing else, our review of previous theories and approaches to nationalism demonstrated the indispensability of separating the task of definition from that of explanation to avoid tautology.

But how far is definition possible and fruitful? Weber, one recalls, was characteristically cautious:

To define 'religion', to say what it is, is not possible at the start of a presentation such as this. Definition can be attempted if at all, only at the conclusion of the study.[34]

Two objections can be made to the utility and possibility of definition of nationalism. The first is logical, and as such, pertains to all definitions. Popper, for example, has argued that definitions cannot capture the 'essence' of phenomena. To attempt to enclose the phenomenon, as it were, within arbitrary walls, only ends in an infinite regress: the definiens must be further defined, since it will always contain more definienda, especially in the social sciences. This does not, of course, preclude us from making *ad hoc* distinctions in meaning within a term, if this serves to clarify the problem under discussion. But this is a mere operational demand.[35]

The other objection is methodological. As Coleman points out, the variables with which the social sciences usually operate are mainly qualitative, and their combinations are too complex for clear and consistent definitions. Nowhere is this more apparent than in the field of nationalism, where the best we can hope for is an approximation to a clear and relatively consistent description in practice.[36]

I do not think these arguments are sufficiently weighty to override the need for definitions in this field. The task of defining nationalism is certainly very difficult, and the methodological objection must be treated seriously as a prophylactic. Earlier writers, it is true, did seek to pursue the chimera of universally valid, once-for-all definitions of nationalism, and ended up with more or less partial, more or less clear, descriptions of the phenomena. But few imagined that they were pinning down some elusive 'essence'. What most scholars found necessary for the later tasks of classification and explanation of nationalisms, was a more adequate conceptualisation of the main features of the phenomenon, under which they might subsume particular behavioural instances. In short, what they needed was an ostensive, substantive definition, which would demonstrate the limits of the field. Only an ostensive definition would help us to designate 'nationalist' phenomena, and give the term jurisdictional limits. It is this kind of 'working definition', stripped of essentialist notions, that is the only possible and fruitful one in the empirically indistinct field of nationalism. This is the type of definition which I am in search of here.[37]

While this makes Popper's objection largely irrelevant, in that this sort of definition is really just a kind of shorthand term of the 'naming' type common in the natural sciences, it still leaves us with the practical methodological problem of procedure in arriving at a suitable definition. There are two alternatives, it appears. Either we simply stipulate a definition of nationalism, and admit concrete instances only insofar as they conform to the definition. Or we adopt the empirical approach: taking all the movements or groups which are conventionally labelled 'nationalist' and 'nations', we try to find the elements common to all these cases, if there are any.

Both procedures have their disadvantages. The stipulative tends to narrow down the field in a highly arbitrary manner, while the empirical approach usually fails to come up with sufficiently distinctive common denominators, which can mark off the phenomenon from other related ones.

A compromise course between these two extremes seems to me to offer the only hope (a rather slender one, it must be admitted) of avoiding these disadvantages—which are so damaging in our field. My method has been to take all the instances of *nationalism* in the widest sense in which the term has been conventionally used (i.e. 'collective resistance to foreign rule'), and then go on to ask if there are additional common elements. Empirically, this led to the distinction between the outer 'ethnocentric' and inner 'polycentric' circles of nationalisms, as well as other distinctions shortly to be elaborated. Within the two types of nationalisms, certain additional elements recurred continually, in more or less intense form in specific cases. These common elements could, in the subsequent stage, provide the defining features whose presence indicated a concrete instance of nationalism. Hence, there is an element of stipulative arbitrariness in this method, but only *after* a careful empirical review of as many concrete instances of 'nationalism' in the broadest sense as was possible. Only then was it possible to arrive at an ideal-typical definition of that key concept, the *'nation'*, which provides a touchstone for the 'deviations' of concrete instances.[38]

But it should be stressed that there is no once-for-all unique definition of 'nationalism' or the 'nation'. We are simply singling out clusters of recurrent features only, and 'nationalism' refers to these.

Nationalism and national sentiment

The origins of the term 'national*ism*' are obscure. The first reference to it appears at Leipzig University, which was founded in 1409 after a religious and scholastic dispute at Prague involving Bohemian and non-Bohemian '*nationes*'. The sense in which the term was used was restricted: a union to defend the common interests of the compatriots of one of the four '*nationes*' among the Leipzig professors! According to Hubner's Staats-Lexicon of 1704, the term was forbidden in the seventeenth century. (Of course, the organisation of medieval universities into '*nationes*' was widespread: but there is, as far as I can see, no reference before this to 'national*ism*'.)

The next reference appears in a passage of Herder, distinguishing between advantageous and 'excessive' national borrowings:

Mann nennts Vorurtheil! Pöbelei! Eingeschränkten Nationalism![39]

In France, nationalism seems to have been used first by Abbé Barnel in 1798;[40] but in the early nineteenth century it is rarely found. It does not appear in the Brockhaus or Meyer Lexicons. In England, its first use is theological; the 1836 *Oxford English Dictionary* gives for nationalism the doctrine that certain nations are objects of divine election.[41] In 1844, it is equated with collective egotism, but on the whole the terms 'nationality' and 'nationalness', with the meanings of (*a*) national fervour, (*b*) a sense of national individuality, are carried over from the nineteenth century.

The principal current difference between the English and the Continental meanings of the term is normative. On the whole, the English senses of the term are fairly neutral. French and German uses, however, equate it with chauvinism and exaggerated xenophobia—'*Ueberwertung der eigenen Nation*', as one dictionary puts it.[42]

Apart from this difference, the term, as currently used, has a number of referents. Its uses have included:

1 national character or 'nationality'
2 an idiom, phrase or trait peculiar to the 'nation'

3 a sentiment of devotion to one's nation and advocacy of its
interests
4 a set of aspirations for the independence and unity of the nation
5 a political programme embodying such aspirations in organisational form
6 a form of socialism, based on the nationalisation of industry
7 the doctrine of divine election of nations
8 the whole process of the formation of nations in history.

This variety of usages is perplexing, at first sight. But, if we
simply drop (1) and (8) as either irrelevant to the definition of
'national*ism*' (as opposed to that of the 'nation') or vacuous, we
are left with two fairly clear groups of meanings: those numbered
(2)–(4), and (5)–(7). The former group refers to sentiments, consciousness, attitudes, aspirations, loyalties, more or less clearly
articulated. The second group refers to doctrines, ideologies, programmes, activities of organisations, movements. The important
distinction between the two groups of meaning is roughly summarised by the entry under 'nationalisme' in Robert's *Dictionnaire
Alphabétique*:

'Nationalisme': 1 = Exaltation du sentiment national; attachement
passionné à ce qui constitue le caractère
singulier, les traditions de la nation à laquelle
on appartient, accompagné parfois de xéno-
phobie et d'une certaine volonté d'isolement.
2 = Doctrine, mouvement politique qui reven-
dique pour une nationalité le droit de former
une nation plus ou moins autonome.

I propose to reserve the term 'nationalism' for the doctrine and
the movement of (2), i.e. the second group of meanings. (1), the
first set of meanings, seems to me to require an altogether different
term, 'national sentiment'. 43

You could say that in ancient Greece, there was considerable
'national sentiment', but little 'nationalism'; a strong and widely
diffused consciousness of belonging to the Hellenes and aspirations for the maintenance of its independence from outside control, but very little in the way of a doctrine or movement to
express these attitudes in beliefs and action. Whereas the Jews
seem to have possessed both a strong sense of 'national sentiment'
and well articulated and active 'nationalist' movements and
doctrines. 44

'Nationalism' and 'national sentiment' need to be distinguished for analytic purposes, though empirically they are often closely related. But a moment's consideration will convince the reader that, in Africa for example, there have been strong, active, highly articulated, durable 'nationalist' movements, but hardly any 'national sentiment' outside the adherents of the nationalist movement itself. Nationalists in Africa have had an even harder task to convince the members of 'their' culturally heterogeneous populations that they ought to think of themselves as members of the Ghanaian, Kenyan, Tanzanian 'nations' first, and give these entities their primary loyalty, than did their counterparts in Central and Eastern Europe. To argue, as many do, that these movements are not *genuine* nationalisms, presupposes a stipulative definition of nationalism which is Europo-centric. The elegance of these definitions is achieved at the cost of ignoring common elements between the 'nation-based' and the non-'nation-based' nationalist movements, which it can be shown are more important than their admitted differences.

'Nationalism' and 'national sentiment' form an analytically distinct pair of concepts. Likewise with the concepts of the 'nation' and the 'nation-state'. You can have a 'nation' (say, Poland in the nineteenth century) without a nation-state', and you can have an embryonic or potential 'nation' with its own state (as in the 'state-nations' of Black Africa), but you cannot logically have a 'nation-state' without the prior 'nation'.

It will be necessary to return later to the distinction between 'nations' and 'nation-states', when we come to the question of defining the term 'nation'. For the present, we need to be clear about the distinctions between four key terms which require separate definition:

(1) nationalism; —national sentiment; (2) nation; —nation-state. [45] The first task is the definition of the first pair of terms; and from now on I am concerned particularly with 'polycentric' nationalism.

The ideal of independence

Perusal of the writings of modern nationalists reveals a bewildering variety of concerns. These recurrent themes usually include: the ideal of communal fraternity, the desire for popular sovereignty, the need for communal regeneration and self-help, the notion of finding one's identity through self-purification, the search for 'roots', the need to belong, a new sense of human dignity realisable only in a national state, the ideals of participation and of building the 'new man', the idea that every nation should have a state for its self-expression, and every individual attach himself to the nation-state for self-realisation, the return to the communal Golden Age, the identification with nature and 'natural man', etc.

In this welter of hopes and ideals, which one could extend at will, three notions stand out continually. They form the *sine qua non* of modern 'polycentric' nationalism. These are the ideas of (collective) autonomy, individuality and pluralism. Together they make up the modern 'ideal of independence'.

The doctrine of autonomy of the individual is, of course, associated with Kant. In its collective form, it owes, however, far more to Rousseau and Fichte. Because of its communal individuality, the group should be free from external interference and internal divisiveness to frame its own rules and set up its own institutions, in accordance with its needs and 'character'. The group is self-determining, because its individuality gives it laws which are peculiar to itself. Only the assembly of all the citizens of the community, acting in concert, can make laws for the community; no section, no individual, and no outsider can legislate. The ideal of the *volonté générale* is the anthropocentric version of the 'ethnocentric' ideal of the deity as the sole lawgiver for the community, entailing resistance to externally-imposed rules—as Maccabees and Zealots showed.

The idea of collective individuality is older than Rousseau, but the extension of this, viz., that 'nations' are 'personalities' with the concomitant rights and duties, that each nation possesses a certain character, and that the world's principal division is the one into 'nations', does not seem to have been held by many before the eighteenth century. 'Ethnocentric' nationalists of course, assumed that there were other nations, which had their barbaric laws, but, so concerned were they with the preservation of their own culture, that there was no attempt at conceiving of the world as naturally divided into the primary groupings of 'nations'. Besides, the 'nation' as such was not yet freed from the more significant idea of the collective religion, the community of believers and performers.

The third idea, pluralism, refers to the conception that world order and liberty depend on the realisation of a system of nation-states, each of which contributes to the common fund of humanity by expressing its own cultural character in a state of its own. World recognition of dignity implies the idea of an international order of status equals, the 'family of nations'. It is hard to find more than hints of this third ideal of 'polycentric' nationalism before the French Revolution. [46]

These three highly idealised motifs are the most fundamental themes in modern 'polycentric' nationalism. On their basis, we may now define *'nationalism'* as *an ideological movement, for the attainment and maintenance of self-government and independence on behalf of a group, some of whose members conceive it to constitute an actual or potential 'nation' like others.*

The logical corollaries of such attempts to attain and maintain 'national' independence are:

1 securing fraternity and equality among co-nationals or citizens, by integrating them into a homogeneous unit
2 unification in a single nation-state of extra-territorial co-nationals
3 stressing cultural individuality through accentuation of 'national' differentiae
4 the drive for economic autarchy and self-sustaining growth
5 attempts to expand the nation-state to maintain international power and status
6 renewing the cultural and social fabric of the nation through sweeping institutional changes, to maintain international parity.

Logically, the ideal of independence entails this syndrome of activities by nationalists, and a case could be made for including them in the definition itself. On the other hand, economy and simplicity are prized attributes of definitions, and the phrases 'attain and maintain' and 'like others' are intended to convey the understanding that we must include these corollaries. In concrete instances, nationalist movements will select their goals from these corollaries, depending on the circumstances. The most important of these circumstances is naturally whether political sovereignty has been already attained, or is likely ever to be.

Discussion of these corollaries will be left to a later chapter, when we consider the types of nationalist movement. For the moment, we should merely grasp the complex nature of the independence ideal, which must be broken down into the motifs of autonomy, individuality and pluralism. It is from these motifs that the propositions of the 'core doctrine' of nationalism, listed in the first chapter, are reached; and they too supply the momentum for the varied and radical activity of nationalist movements in different circumstances.

The 'independence ideal' designates a rather wider field of referents than political sovereignty. The attainment of the latter does not end the activity or impetus of nationalism. Political independence is typically perceived to be insufficient without economic autarchy and, if possible, cultural self-expression. There may be even more pressing problems of cultural and social integration. In any case, we often witness a painful process of reorientation by the nationalists on taking power; and the 'post-independence' phase of nationalism, if less politically dramatic, is often the most significant for the society's later development. The 'independence ideal' may also affect men in societies which never experienced the lack of political sovereignty—as in the French Revolution, the Japanese Meiji reformers and the Persian revolution of 1905–6.[47]

Nationalists reject the often-repeated distinction between 'cultural' and 'political' nationalism. Prudence may dictate the temporary playing down of the overt political implications of the 'independence ideal' in favour of a limited cultural autonomy, such as was favoured by the 'personalist' schemes of the Austro-Marxists, Otto Bauer and Karl Renner.[48] But, as Lenin and Stalin, as well as the Habsburg rulers, were quick to realise, the 'right' to have one's own language taught in one's own schools, courts manned by one's own judges, newspapers produced by one's co-nationals and for them, an indigenous literature and art, one's own local institutions such as churches, and one's own customs, has immediate political consequences. For they only made sense within the overall context of a doctrine that links politics intimately to culture, in the widest sense, that bases political obligation and activity on the autonomy of a body of citizens who are or will be culturally distinctive and homogeneous. Besides, there are no limits to the doctrine of 'rights', which, however limited the concessions may be in practice, constitute a precedent, which can be used to diminish further the power of the State and undermine its stability. Sociologically, too, the concession of minority

cultural rights, as at Versailles, by curtailing the national sovereignty of the majority in the State, serves of itself to strengthen
the rights of the minority through the appeal to legal safeguards;
in effect, the cultural concessions become a grant of limited
political autonomy, a 'state within a state', as happened in Mandate
Palestine. [49]

The definition of nationalism above is designed to be as comprehensive as possible, while enabling us to distinguish the
doctrine from relatives such as Fascism, imperialism, racism and
populism. Besides its implicit political goals, it has two other
features. The first is that it can refer to movements which arise in
areas, whose populations do not constitute a 'nation'. Among
peoples scattered around the world, such as Greeks, Chinese,
Armenians and Jews, or among a conglomeration of 'ethnie' in a
colony, we find movements arising which utilise the three notions
inherent in the 'independence ideal' with no modifications, apart
from the assertion that their individuality is at present latent, and
that time and continual interaction of the population sharing
common institutions will gradually generate it. This position is
strictly Rousseauan, as we saw; and only the domination of the
'organic' version of nationalism in nineteenth-century Europe
has obscured the doctrinal possibility of nationalism inventing
nations. [50]

The second feature of my definition of nationalism is its so-
called 'subjectivist' bias. Unlike the definition of the 'nation',
'nationalism', it is often argued, ought to be defined by subjective
attributes—will, sentiment, aspiration, etc. I agree with Rustow
that the distinction between 'objective' characteristics, like
economy, geography or history, and 'subjective' ones, is at best
dubious. But I differ from him in thinking that definitions must
contain elements all along the so-called 'subjective-objective'
continuum (and so must explanations). Simplicity must not be
bought at the cost of precision, as is the case with his own definition of the 'nation'. [51] That is why, as the reader will have noticed,
the term 'nation' could not be left out of the definition of 'nationalism'; it would be most odd if it were. What is true is that
'nationalism' (and to some extent 'nation') is defined in terms of
individual perceptions—usually those of a tiny minority of the
given unit of population. At the same time, those perceptions do
refer to independently verifiable characteristics or processes.

Considerable space has been devoted to the definition of 'nationalism', since that is the object of my labours. By contrast, the concept of *'national sentiment'*, while not quite so epiphenomenal as Gellner suggests, can be dealt with rapidly. It can be defined as a sentiment of supreme loyalty to the 'nation', aspiring to its unity, purity, autonomy and strength. This corresponds, in fact, to most definitions of 'nationalism', which fail to distinguish the doctrine or movement. Take, for example, the R.I.I.A. report on nationalism, which defines the latter as

> a consciousness, on the part of individuals or groups, of membership in a nation, or of a desire to forward the strength, liberty or prosperity of a nation, whether one's own or another.[52]

Hans Kohn, too, defines nationalism in terms which I would reserve for national sentiment:

> a state of mind, permeating the large majority of a people, and claiming to permeate all its members; it recognises the nation-state as the ideal form of political organisation and the nationality as the source of all creative cultural energy and economic well-being. The supreme loyalty of man is therefore due to his nationality, as his own life is supposedly rooted in and made possible by its welfare.[53]

Renan stresses *'le sentiment des sacrifices'* and *'le consentiment, le désir clairement exprimé de continuer la vie commune'*;[54] even Weber treats nationalism as an activating sentiment only: for him it is

> a common bond of sentiment whose adequate expression would be a state of its own, and which therefore normally tends to give birth to such a state.[55]

The only point I want to make about the concept of 'national sentiment' is that it is, like 'nationalism', variable in both intensity and diffusion. Individuals may give their primary loyalty to the nation grudgingly or enthusiastically; and the loyalty with its accompanying aspirations is typically uneven across a given population. 'National sentiment', in fact, is even more relative than 'nationalism'. At least, in the case of the latter, one can be pretty sure of the intensity of the adherents' conviction.

Statists and ethnicists

If the definition of 'nationalism' is partly dependent on that of the 'nation', the latter is equally dependent on that of 'nationalism'.

We can only arrive at a more useful definition of the nation by examining the 'individuality' component of the nationalists' 'independence ideal'. What meaning, if any, do nationalists typically give to this component? Is there a constant pattern or image?

At a sufficiently abstract level, such an image can be discovered. Despite local variations, which stress varying differentiae, there is a remarkable similarity in the concept of the nation in its general features in most nationalist thinking. Of course, there is an inherent circularity in this approach; but this logical disadvantage is counterbalanced by the comprehensiveness of its empirical method, whose aim is to produce an abstracted ideal-type of the nationalist ideal of the nation.[56]

The following definition of the nation is reached by such an enquiry into the chief common elements of this ideal: *The nation is a large, vertically integrated and territorially mobile group featuring common citizenship rights and collective sentiment together with one (or more) common characteristic(s) which differentiate its members from those of similar groups with whom they stand in relations of alliance or conflict.* This definition is only intended to convey the essentials of the many images of the ideal nation held by nationalists everywhere. But it can also be used ostensively. Any group which does not possess one or more of these features is not (yet) a complete nation. For example, diaspora groups lacking a territory and often subject to residential restrictions cannot qualify for the status of nationhood; they deviate in one significant respect from the ideal-type. Pre-independence Americans lacked important cultural differentiating marks from their English masters and still do; so, like their creole counterparts in Latin America, their nationalism was not founded upon the basis of a pre-existent nation. Their bids for independence are no less nationalist for that; but, unlike their Eastern European counterparts, they had no 'nation' to fall back on yet.

For, just as there are many nations without nationalisms, so there are as many nationalisms without nations.

The terms, 'nation' and 'nationalism' are analytically and empirically distinct. And where nationalism arises without a pre-existent nation, the 'nation' for which it strives is only an embryo, a project, a 'nation of intent'.[57]

This definition is what we may call an 'ethnicist' one. By

contrast, my definition of 'nationalism' is nearer to the spirit of the 'statist' viewpoint. There have been many controversies over the question of definition of the concepts 'nation' and 'nationalism'; but none so prolonged and confusing as that between 'statists' and 'ethnicists'. It needs to be examined in some detail, since it is crucial to the subsequent tasks of classification and explanation.

Roughly, '*statists*' define the nation as a territorial-political unit. Nationalism becomes 'the aspiration of the colonised population for self-government of the new political community whose boundaries were established by the coloniser'.[58] '*Ethnicists*', *per contra,* see the nation as a large, politicised ethnic group, defined by common culture and alleged descent. Nationalism accordingly turns into a cultural movement.[59] I argue here for an 'ethnicist' definition of the nation, while refusing to see national*ism* as a cultural rather than political movement. The main point must be to retain the crucial conceptual distinction between 'state' and 'nation'.

A recent tragic example will clarify this dispute. Which shall we call the 'nation', Nigeria or Ibo Biafra? Undeniably, there have been two historical nationalisms, both as genuine as any other movement, one a pan-Nigerian, the other an Ibo one. We cannot deny the title of 'nationalism' to the Nigerian one, simply because 'Nigeria' was only a 'nation of intent'.[60]

The 'statist' would argue that the Nigerian movement was the genuine one because Nigeria was (or would be before independence) the only 'nation', defined as the society 'in which the state is the social institution in which ultimate individual and group loyalty is invested'. For the most consistent 'statist', Silvert,

Nationalism is the acceptance of the state as the impersonal and ultimate arbiter of human affairs.[61]

Nationalism is defined functionally, and its primary function is the ultimate settlement of dispute, through the institutionalised mechanism of State power. Movements therefore which fail to accept the State for the settlement of disputes, as the Ibos failed to accept Nigeria after 1966, cannot be nationalist, but 'communalist' or 'separatist'. Geertz is even more explicit about this. We should, he argues, distinguish the fundamentally different desires for an efficient state and for better living standards, on the one hand, and for the assertion of personal and communal identity during eras of painful disorientation, on the other. 'Nationalist' movements are State-oriented and State-grounded ones: anti-State movements are merely communalist or separatist secessions, based on the 'primordial sentiments' of race, language, religion, etc.[62]

This quasi-Hegelian view of nations and nationalism would, if carried through consistently, make nonsense of most standard histories of the subject. All the East European and Middle Eastern movements would be denied the title of 'nationalist', and the stateless Poles, Czechs, Magyars, Bulgarians, etc. would not constitute 'nations', because in the early nineteenth century, they were not the societies in which the State was the institution invested with ultimate individual or group loyalty. 'Statists' accepted the view of Kossuth in 1848:

> 'What do you understand by "nation"?' inquired Kossuth.
> 'A race which possesses its own language, customs and culture,' was the Serb reply, 'and enough self-consciousness to preserve them.'
> 'A nation must also have its own government,' objected Kossuth.
> 'We do not go so far,' Kostic explained; 'one nation can live under several different governments, and again several nations can form a single state.'[63]

In Europe, the logic of this position would force one to deny the title of nationalism to all the secessionist movements of the nineteenth century. Only Russia, Ottoman Turkey and Austro-Hungary would qualify as 'nations', and even the Italian and German movements would fail this test. (You could only have Prussian, Bavarian, Saxon, Neapolitan, Piedmontese, etc., nationalisms.) Outside Europe, the Pakistani, Boer, Naga, Karen, Ewe, Ba-Kongo, Zionist, Kurdish, Achinese, Quebecois, Buryat Mongol and Uzbek movements would be separatist, but not nationalist, movements, and not eligible for the status of nationhood—and presumably never eligible!

This curious argument stems from the circumstances of what one may call the 'western' standpoint. Roughly, this equates nationality with citizenship, the legal concept. But languages other than English have separate terms for legal citizenship and nationality. German, for example, distinguishes *Staatsangehörigkeit* from *Nationalität*, citizenship from ethnic nationality. So does Turkish: the term *tabiiyet*, citizenship of the State, was opposed to *milliyet*, the ethnic or religious community.[64] The same distinction is made in East European languages. It occurs in French, but historically *patrie* and nation were not opposed; the supporters of the concept of *la nation* and its sovereignty were called (and called themselves) patriots during the Revolution.[65] Nevertheless, the equation of State and nation, of legal citizenship with ethnic nationality, has arisen out of the peculiar circumstances of the formation of England and France as nation-states. In these cases, and these almost alone, the cultural homogeneity of the population in these territories developed conjointly with the progress to political sovereignty of the 'nation'. As Akzin remarks:

> Britain and France neither are nor were in the past mono-ethnic in the strict sense of the word, and they certainly don't live in isolation from other States and nations. But in both cases convergence between the two circles of the total State population and of the total membership of the predominant ethnic group is sufficiently close to leave most observers in these countries with the impression that the two are, broadly speaking, identical.[66]

But this impression is misleading. The object of nationalist devotion is the 'nation', not the State—even when the two happen to coincide after independence in a mono-ethnic state. If we follow Weber in defining the State as

> a human community which successfully claims within a given territory the monopoly of the legitimate use of physical force,[67]

we can appreciate that such an object would not quite measure up to nationalist requirements. The nationalist demands allegiance to the whole collectivity and defines identity in terms of that group. This is rather different from the demand for loyalty to the machinery and personnel of an impersonal State. For the nationalist, the State is, as it were, the protective shell for their nation, and a *sine qua non* of its political self-realisation, especially in the modern world. He therefore aims at communal self-government and native political institutions. But he does so in the interests of another, higher entity—the potential or existent 'nation'.

There is another, empirical objection to equating the 'nation' with the 'state'. States vary immensely in size, complexity and structure. Consider the following:

1 Sumerian city-states ruled by the assembly of elders or by a lord (*ensi* or *lugal*) or by temple priests, e.g. Eridu, Kish, Nippur.

2 Greek city-states: confederations of them as in Thessaly or Arcadia, plutocracies as at Corinth or Corcyra, democracies as at Samothrace, Megara and Athens, mixed constitutions founded on Helotry as at Sparta—and the tyrannies, of course.

3 Renaissance states, whether Republics like Venice, family-centred oligarchies like Florence, tyrannies like Urbino, Milan, etc.

4 Feudal principalities like those of Hanover, Württemberg, and their modern survivals—Liechtenstein, Andorra, Monaco.[68]

5 Provinces like the States of the United States, India or the Soviet Union Republics and Yugoslavian provinces, cantons like the Engadin, Vaud, Uri, Appenzell, Zurich, etc.—each with their own religious, linguistic, socio-economic and political structures.[69]

6 Nation-states like France, Poland, Bulgaria, Somalia, Tibet and Norway—which are, to all intents, mono-ethnic.

7 Polyethnic states such as Burma, Yugoslavia, Kenya, the Soviet Union (and the United States?), Belgium, Indonesia, Congo, etc.

8 Empires (centralised bureaucratic despotisms!)—the Habsburg, Ottoman and Tsarist, the Mongol Khanates, the Achaemenid Persian, the Chaldean and Assyrian, Hellenistic and Roman and Chinese, the Caliphates and Ashokan and Carolingian, etc.

9 Kingdoms confined to a single ethnie and territory—the Urartu, Croesus' Lydia, Prussia, Burgundy, the Kandyan, Ptole-maic, the ancient Hindu kingdoms, the Sassanids, modern Thailand, the Sultanates of Sarawak and Oman, etc.

10 Polyethnic kingdoms like Ethiopia and Afghanistan, where the politically dominant majority is reinforced by the monarchy.

All these were political formations with enough resources, stability, legitimacy and effectiveness to endure and operate over their territory without external interference as '*societates quae superiorem non recognoscunt*', in Bodin's phrase (though this must be modified in the case of small principalities and provinces).

To equate the 'nation', whose forms are variegated enough in any case, with such a motley of political structures hardly con-duces to definitional clarity. One can also appreciate the difficul-ties of a movement which tried to 'take over' a Mongol Khanate or even the Habsburg Empire. When a movement did take over the Ottoman Empire, it was significantly dubbed the 'Young

Turk' movement, and its ideology was increasingly pan-Turanian or pan-Turk; and its attempts at Turkification of the remainder of the Ottoman Empire proved a dismal failure.[70]

The 'statist' definition of the nation is therefore rather misleading. It obscures what should remain as a fundamental distinction —between 'nation' and 'state'. It makes nonsense of most so-called nationalist movements, removing a major part of their contentions. The ideological bias of such a fruitless equation will be apparent from Kossuth's attitude.[71]

Herder's legacy

If the nation cannot be defined by the 'statist' criterion, the way is clear for the 'ethnicist' alternative. Unfortunately, the latter criterion is itself ambiguous and the subject of disputes 'within the camp'. There are those who want to assign a rather broad connotation to the term 'ethnic'; while others insist on a more precise criterion. I have opted for the wider meaning, where 'ethnic' is identical with the term 'cultural', without further specification. This follows from an argument by elimination.

Strictly speaking, I suppose, ethnicity refers to common descent. Coleman insists on this usage in his definition of the 'tribe':

> a relatively small group of people who share a common culture and who are *descended from a common ancestor*. The tribe is the largest social group defined *primarily in terms of kinship*, and is normally an aggregate of clans, intermediate to nationality.[72]

The classical etymology supports this meaning. In the Iliad, ethnos is used in two senses: that of a 'band' or company of friends (*ethnos hetairōn*) and then a 'tribe' (*ethnos Lukiōn, Achaiōn*)—of the Lycians, or Achaeans. In later Attic, it refers to a larger grouping, the 'people'.

It is hard to take this position seriously. Commonly accepted 'nations' like the Poles, Hungarians, Burmese, Greeks, Persians and Tatars may have a mythical founder (usually of their State), but do not invoke a common ancestor; in many cases, they would be hard put to it to find a suitable candidate, since Abrahams and Oguz Khans are the exception. Besides, 'pure' descent groups simply wouldn't be large enough for political efficacy. Even the Medes and Jews and Hellenes traced their history back to tribal confederations. And, in any case, just how far back is the ancestor to be placed? Most accepted 'nations', in fact, have a considerable documented history of intermarriage: the Khazars converted to Judaism, the House of Osman Islamised and hence Turkified Balkan Christian boys, even the English had some French admixture in the Norman period and the Germans did not hesitate to Germanise Posen, whose inhabitants were anything but 'German' till then.[73] Of course, imputed common descent is always a useful argument to bolster nationalist assertions, but it is usually a minor claim even with them.

Philology is safer. It is far more open to verification; even if one runs the risk of some disconfirmation, there is usually enough positive evidence at hand to convince politicians who want to be convinced. In fact, language has provided one of the main criteria for defining ethnicity and nationhood. In ethnically heterogeneous areas, the national census is really the linguistic one, and 'mother-tongue' in the Soviet Union today remains the main criterion of nationality on one's identity card.[74]

The most potent single factor, sociological ones apart, in the identification of nations with language groups has been the influence of Herder. This is curious. It is true that he regarded language as the key to the self, since words are the 'companions of the dawn of life'.[75] A nation may lose its independence, but will survive if it preserves its linguistic traditions; a precept which was not lost on his Polish, Czech, Serb and Ukrainian followers. Herder's theory of language was experiential: language was born as men tried to express to themselves their feelings aroused by events and things which surrounded their lives. Yet he does not seem to have drawn the conclusion that language is the only, or even the most important, criterion for distinguishing a nation; or that the classification by nationality, which is that by culture, is *ipso facto* the classification by language.[76]

'What nature separated by language, customs, character, let no man artificially join together by chemistry.'[77] Herder was still deeply influenced by Hamann's mystical pietism, and his thought is too diffuse and comprehensive to be satisfied with any single criterion of diversity. Fichte and Schleiermacher may have insisted on this identification, because it so aptly suited the German cause. But the humanitarian thought of the Enlightenment, which permeates Herder's attitudes, was as interested in

anthropology as language for providing a key to social understanding. For Herder, the focal point of diversity in the universe
is its manifestation of God's will, which for men means that we
must 'learn not to think in other people's thoughts', if we are to
renew ourselves in accordance with His will.[78] Herder's cultural
'polycentrism', his search for roots, fastens equally on folklore,
ritual and customs, myths, and folksongs, as language. All are
clues to a people's collective 'personality' and sense of identity;
for all together constitute parts of the total process of societal
Bildung, the augmentation of societal values.[79]

It remains the case, however, that the notion that nations are
really language groups, and therefore that nationalism is a linguistic movement, derives from Herder's influence, modified by
the simplifications introduced by Fichte and other German
Romantics. This equation has been reinforced by the success of
movements where it was difficult to distinguish the two—especially for the foreigner. The Greek independence movement, like
the Serb, had strong religious motivations; but to the contemporary western outsider the contest of Orthodoxy and Islam
appeared secondary, since religious disputes had receded in the
West. The linguistic criterion even dominates Marxist analysis,
Lenin's as much as Bauer's. And, as we have seen, this Herderian
current has entered into contemporary sociological explanations
of nationalism—which simply assume the linguistic criterion of
nationhood.

The arguments against identifying nations with language
groups can be summarised as follows:
1 The possession of a common language by two populations
located in different states is no proof that they belong to the same
nation. French is spoken in Haiti, France, French-speaking
Switzerland, among the Belgian Walloons and Quebecois, not to
mention the elites of many sub-Saharan African states. English,
likewise, is spoken throughout Great Britain (itself polyethnic),
the United States, Canada, Ireland, Australia, English-speaking
South Africans and Indians, elites in other sub-Saharan African
states, the West Indies, New Zealand and Liberia. The fashionable
appellation 'English-speaking peoples' simply underlines the
dichotomy between nation and language. The equation would
make of the Portuguese-speakers of Portugal and Brazil one
nation, and unite Spain and the Philippines to Puerto Rico and

most Latin American republics. Such far-flung nations may appeal to pan-Turkists or pan-Arabists or pan-Germanists, but few scholars would allow this single factor to override all the other divisive influences, even in the matter of definition. Simplicity, they may well feel, can be bought too dearly.

2 It is also doubtful how far we could automatically concede the title 'nation' to all those who spoke the same language within the same State. English-speaking Irishmen or Negroes were not thought of as part of the same national unit by themselves or even by most of the English. The same would hold for all the elites; one wonders how far the idea of 'black Frenchmen' permeated the social consciousness.[80] To insist that they nevertheless were part of the 'objective' nation, linguistically defined, is possible, but sociologically flies in the face of the facts. The Jews and Armenians of many a country spoke fluent French, German, Arabic, Russian, Polish, etc., yet even the 'assimilationists' on both sides admitted the magnitude of the task of integrating them.[81]

3 Language groupings are as ambiguous and imprecise as ethnic groups. There appears to be no objective criterion for fixing the minimum linguistic difference to distinguish a language from a dialect or a patois. Einar Haugen has shown how the development of a vernacular literary language is a continuous cycle of formation and dissolution, which depends on social attitudes and values, and on politics and geography.[82] Within certain structural limits, the distinctions between these three 'grades' are functional. The dialect is a non-prestigious and 'underdeveloped' language, i.e. it is not employed in all the situations and for all the uses for which it might be; and a patois is an unwritten, unofficial and degenerate dialect. In France, the patois were used for spoken languages, till they were superseded by the regional literary dialects and ultimately by the Parisian elite language; just as Piedmontese was superseded by Tuscan Italian. Likewise the Attic *koine* superseded the other written dialects of Greece, each with its specialised function.[83] Languages emerge through two processes, the standardisation of form and functional variation in writing; and they are gradually transformed from local vernaculars into nationally accepted, official and multipurpose languages. Sometimes this process is undertaken by the nationalist movement with varying success; contrast the progress made by the attempts in France, Finland, the Ukraine, Indonesia and Israel, with the

failure of the Norwegian, Irish and Hindi movements, despite their political success.

So that we are unable to locate the structural degree of *linguistic* difference which determines success or failure in language-creation, or dictates the emergence and success of some national groups and not others. Brabant and Provençal French, Piedmontese and Calabrese Italian, Plattdeutsch and Bavarian German, and the English dialects, are as distinct in phonology and philology as Czech and Slovak, Latvian and Lithuanian, Serbian, Croat and Slovenian, Bulgarian and Macedonian, Dutch and Frisian, Swedish and Norwegian, or Russian and Ukrainian, but while the former pairs are regarded as colourful folk dialects, the latter are accorded the status [*sic*] of distinct languages, which could afford one of several bases for the claim to separate nationhood.

4 The degree of language difference bears little relation to linguistic strife or nationalism. First, not all language differences are noticed, let alone made the subject of ideological dispute and emotive symbolisation. In Scandinavia, the Congo and West Africa, the 'language gap' does not hinder mutual intelligibility; the latter appears to be a function of intergroup attitudes rather than differences in linguistic structure.[84] I mean by this that groups may speak structurally distinct, even unrelated, languages, but ignore the differences, reciprocally or unilaterally. The language differences do not become a barrier to social intercourse or lead to hostility. Secondly, conscious and emotively symbolic language differences need not be divisive. This is true above all of Switzerland and Alsace, but we find it to some extent among immigrant Jews in Israel, and it holds with regard to the provinces of China; and not all linguistic differences in India or Nigeria with its 250 languages or Indonesia with its *circa* 35, have led to linguistic strife. One is aware of the many countercases here—Belgium, Canada, Iraq, Burma, etc.—and it would be, I think, correct to designate these movements as nationalisms. But the point is simply (*a*) that not all language differences lead to language disputes, (*b*) that not all language disputes are cases of nationalism (consider the fierce battle in 1913 in the Palestinian Jewish schools over their language of instruction between German and Hebrew and the present desire of many who feel themselves primarily Belgian to limit the current linguistic strife).[85] If we are to main-

tain the language-nation equation, both these subpoints should correlate; and it must also be shown that all nationalist movements are cases of linguistic strife, which we saw was not the case (preceding chapter).

All this applies to cases of bilingualism. But Fishman points out that horizontal divisions of diglossia in functionally exclusive domains need not be divisive. Elites have often been characterised by distinct languages, as Tolstoy describes for the early nineteenth-century French-speaking Russian aristocracy.[86] Danish was an elite language, so was Spanish in Guarani-speaking Paraguay. Then there are the well-known cases of medieval Latin, classical Arabic in Egypt and Syria, and Sanskrit in parts of India. There is also the example of triglossia in the Hausa area; in northern Nigeria, Hausa and Arabic, as opposed to the tribal languages, were combined with English—or French in the Hausa part of Niger.[87] English and Russian appear to have become the elite languages now, and to have followed the advance of science and technology, which creates a tendency to uniformity away from the belletristic national unitary languages. Indeed, linguistic strife appears to be largely passé in Europe, but I do not think this will lead to a reduction of movements for collective independence and autarchy, as I have defined 'nationalism'.

Finally we should note the familiar cases where linguistic differences were structurally minimal, yet strong nationalist strife arose—as between Serbs and Croats, Russians and Byelorussians, Czechs and Slovaks and Hindi- and Urdu-speakers. The differences between Danish, Swedish, Dano-Norwegian, New Norwegian, Faroese and Icelandic are rather slighter than their political strife in the past would lead one to suppose, if one were to adopt the linguistic criterion of nationhood.

Summarising, there is no doubt that linguistic homogeneity and distinctiveness is an invaluable vehicle and symbol of nationhood and nation-formation; but it would be misleading to consider it either a sufficient or a necessary mark of the ethnic nation. The role of language and its close connection with the new education should rather be reserved for the task of explanation, and even here it should not be exaggerated—as the experience of many a westernising intelligentsia in the new states testifies.

G

Ethnos, natio and populus

It would, I feel, be tedious to go through all the favoured criteria for defining the 'nation' in the 'ethnicist' sense. It can be shown that all the attempts to reduce the ethnic rubric to a single criterion—religion, history, customs, institutions, mythology, folklore, race, etc.—are inadequate. None of these could *by themselves* cover the conventionally-accepted lists of nations; and to use one of them as an *a priori* definiens will not only exclude commonly accepted cases of 'nations' and 'nationalisms', but require us to invent a new terminology to designate the related phenomena. It will also require us to justify the benefits of this arbitrary definition in the face of a theoretical charge of reductionism and infinite regress. 'How choose one criterion rather than the others?' would be a question without easy solution. Let us take then as given, the definition of 'nation' in the broad 'ethnicist' sense. 'Ethnic' here signifies 'cultural' generally, and nations, whatever else they may be, are species of cultural units. The problem now is to spell out the main features of this species.

As defined above, the nation was a group with seven features:

1 cultural differentiae (i.e. the 'similarity-dissimilarity' pattern, members are alike in the respects in which they differ from non-members)
2 territorial contiguity with free mobility throughout
3 a relatively large scale (and population)
4 external political relations of conflict and alliance with similar groups
5 considerable group sentiment and loyalty
6 direct membership with equal citizenship rights
7 vertical economic integration around a common system of labour.

These seven characteristics fall into three groups. If you take the first two features and add in a common kinship network, you have a working definition of the *'tribe'*, of which there are some six thousand in Africa, and many more in Siberia, India, the Caucasus and Indonesia—not to mention the Lullubi and Parni whom we met in the ancient world, and the individual Median and Israelite tribes *before* their union in a centralised state.

Feature 4 implies *some* degree of centralisation (not necessarily political, however). If we add all the first five characteristics together, but drop the kinship basis, we get the sociopolitical formation, typical in the ancient world, the large politicised '*ethnie*'. The Swiss Confederation after 1291, the Israelites from Saul onwards, the Medes under Phraortes, the Canaanites and Assyrians, the Ashanti and Bugandans, the medieval kingdoms of Serbs and Bulgars, Burma of the Pagan dynasty—are all cases of large cultural-territorial groups, with common external political relations and a fair level of group sentiment. The typical 'ethnocentric' nationalism belongs here.

Finally, we come to '*nations*' proper. Nations are 'ethnie' which are economically integrated around a common system of labour with complementarity of roles, and whose members possess equal rights as citizens of the unmediated political community.[88]

I have already discussed the first two features, and the fourth is straightforward enough. I confine the following brief remarks to the others.

Akzin holds that 'nations' are simply large, delocalised and politicised ethnic groups. The Assyrians are a nation by this criterion, the Lullubi are not; the Yakuts would be included, but not the Evenki. His nation corresponds, in fact, to our 'ethnie'. We have subdivided this category which produced such unease earlier to accommodate the different formations of the Swiss cantons before and after their alliance against the Habsburgs and the Dukes of Savoy.[89]

This triple evolutionary division corresponds, I believe, with the change in meaning of the term 'natio' from its original tribal-ethnic sense in classical Latin to the enlarged sense of the whole community of citizens which it seems to have acquired first in the French Revolution.

I think this etymological development convinces us of the need to extend Akzin's oversimple dichotomy between tribal-ethnic groups and nations. We need *three* terms: tribe, ethnie, nation. For modern 'polycentric' nationalism would not be satisfied with the features of size, territoriality and politicisation, which are enough for Akzin to define the nation. The modern nationalist would insist in addition on internal homogeneity and economic autarchy. Members of the group, in his vision of the ideal nation, would work a common economic system which is self-sustaining and not dependent on some other larger system. Members would also have the same rights and duties, for any other arrangement would smack of sectionalism. It would reintroduce that element of personal dependence in feudalism which Rousseau so detested.

These additional economic and political features are largely absent from the ancient world—if we can rely on our scanty sources. Cross-class economic integration and isonomic political rights were non-existent. The exception is Athens, of course; but, the question of size apart, she does not seem to have possessed sufficient cultural dissimilarity from her opponents to constitute an ethnie, let alone a nation.[90]

Group sentiment, as we saw, is often taken to serve as the sole definiens of the nation. This would leave us in no position to differentiate *national* sentiment from any other group feeling—village, district, clan, class, congregational, etc. On the other hand, it should not be treated as a mere epiphenomenon. Nationalists cannot envisage an ideal nation without a high level of group sentiment, and its presence or absence helps us to measure the proximity of a given group to the status of nationhood. It serves to link national solidarity to other forms of solidarity, describes the degree of group cohesion in certain respects, and warns us of the relative nature of actual examples of the concept 'nation'.[91]

The problem of optimum size is a vexed question. Scale and numbers seem to be integral to the nationalist vision; the Geneva of Rousseau appears politically ineffective and economically unviable under modern conditions. To make 'independence' meaningful, you need collective power, and hence statehood which only makes sense in a sufficiently large territory. This excludes Anguilla, for example, from the status of 'nation', though its national*ism* is as intense as any. Besides, it is difficult to see what autarchy could mean here.[92]

But if this excludes very small and localised groupings, it leaves the striking range of 'nations' untouched. Contrast the 80 million Germans with the *c.* 600,000 Basques and 1,150,000 Ests and the scale of their areas. Size and scale are shaky criteria. All we can say here is that the dimension of size is unhelpful over the half million mark.[93]

We can now sum up this discussion of the nation's features. If we list out the seven features, we find that some pertain to small 'tribes' (some of them already quite large in comparison with

clans), some more to ethnic groups or 'ethnie', and all to the third
and widest circle, 'nations'. They can be set out as follows:

Group		Features	Examples
Tribe	(Kinship +)	Cultural differentiae	Lullubi, Parni,
		Territorial mobility	Evenki, Kru, Saho.
Ethnie		Large size	Assyria, Urartu,
		In-group sentiment	Greeks, Jews,
		External relations	Pagan Burma, Arabs,
		Cultural differentiae	Bulgars, Magyars,
		Territorial mobility	Sassanid Persia.
Nation		Citizenship rights	Jacobin France,
		Economic integration	Turkey, Bulgaria,
		Large size	Poland, Hungary,
		In-group sentiment	Somalia, Israel,
		External relations	Norway, Tatars,
		Cultural differentiae	Armenians, Swiss,
		Territorial mobility	Belgium, Quebecois.

Two other categories are necessary to complete the analysis.
The first is the 'nation-state'. This poses no problems. We may
define it as a 'nation' with *de facto* territorial sovereignty. The
examples in the above list include France, Turkey, Poland,
Bulgaria, Switzerland, Somalia, Belgium, Hungary, Israel and
Norway. The other three nations listed—the Tatars, Armenians
and Quebecois—do not possess *de facto* sovereignty either in
Bodin's sense, or in Weber's. (The 'satellite' states of e.g. Eastern
Europe stand on the borderline, but are legally recognised, and
sometimes assert their sovereignty.)

The second category which is required is that of the 'state-
nation'. These are political formations with *de facto* sovereignty,
i.e. states, which do not (yet) possess two out of the above seven
features—cultural differentiae and in-group sentiment. Nigeria
and Ghana are obvious cases; to a much lesser extent, Tanzania
and Zambia fall into this category, though lack of distinguishing
cultural marks throughout their ethnically heterogeneous populations is being systematically offset by the nationalist integration
policies of Nyerere and Kaunda. The deliberate fostering of a
nation-oriented in-group sentiment will, it is hoped, produce that
sense of community and common history, which played so large a
part in producing the individuality of the older nations. The
same hope informs Congress India and Tito's Yugoslavia.

The introduction of the concept of the 'state-nation' breaks the otherwise unilinear evolutionary pattern of the ascending sequence, tribe—ethnie—nation—nation-state. The 'state-nation' in Africa arose from the colonial unit, which was imposed arbitrarily upon the tribes and ethnie of the precolonial era. Typically, then, a modern African state is a collection of tribes and/or ethnie, accorded the status of collective political sovereignty. The fundamental task of the nationalist here is not so much the maintenance of that sovereignty, but the realisation of the 'independence ideal' by endowing the populations with a sense of collective individuality, so that their autonomy will be a meaningful unity.

I think this hierarchy of increasingly large and complex units helps to get round the difficult problem of nationhood in the ancient world. I would contend that the chief political actors in the ancient Near East and Mediterranean were city-states, tribes, ethnie and empires. The Greeks, it is true, did show some sense of common Hellenic citizenship rights, but they lacked any system of economic integration around a common division of labour. The same, I think, applies to the Jews, though it seems that by the time of the Roman occupation there was a greater degree of economic integration. On the other hand, their common citizenship rights were inseparable from the Mosaic code, that is, from religious injunctions and rituals, as revised by Ezra and his successors. This is very far from the Athenian (post-462) concept of isonomic rights in virtue of secular membership of the demes, and even further from the ideal of the *citoyen* as patriot in the thinking of the French revolutionaries. As for Rome, 'Italia' did at one point possess a certain resonance and special status, as the aftermath of the *bellum sociale* and Virgil attest. But there was no economic integration or autarchy, and citizenship rights were soon extended outside Italy.

So that in dealing with the Assyrians, Medes, Hittites, Egyptians and Philistines, we are confronted, not by 'nations' in any sense of the term, but by the simpler and commoner formation of the 'ethnie'. The 'ethnie' may be a decentralised military aristocracy, as with the Canaanites or Medes, or a highly centralised bureaucratic monarchy, as in Egypt, Assyria or Sassanid Persia. The important point is that the 'ethnie' has no sense of membership with citizenship rights for the majority of the population, and little organic solidarity in the economic sphere. The common situation is that an aristocracy or upper class of some kind lives in the cities or off estates, while the mass of the population are peasants whose economic relations are bounded by the village and kinship networks, and who do not partake of the privileges and rights of the aristocracy and priesthood. This ancient pattern lasts right up to the Revolution in France, where Montesquieu still refers to the nation as *les évêques et les seigneurs* who control the Estates-General.[94] And the same is true of Rumania in the eighteenth century, where the concept of the nation included only the upper stratum as opposed to the folk or plebs; the aristocrats contest Micu's plea for the rights of a Wallachian 'nation', while conceding the existence of a Wallachian 'people' speaking one tongue.[95]

It was only after the French Revolution that the *populus*, the *peuple* (in fact, the third estate, but theoretically and by precedent the whole body of citizens) was recognised as the sovereign 'nation'. The total population, and not just the aristocrats and clergy, now constituted the 'nation', the sole fount of legitimacy and authority. As such, this new 'people's nation' can only have dealings with other similarly constituted nations; else the single 'people's nation' appears as an aberration in a world of ethnie. The concept of 'natio' has finally been shorn of its kinship origins, and its purely external definition; it now increasingly shifts its centre of attention to the problem of securing internal homogeneity and distinctiveness, so as to qualify for the society of true nations. It is in this sense that democratic republicanism has been the first ally and agent of the 'polycentric' nationalism of the modern state-nations, and nation-states. And where it has been discarded, it is because it has been recognised as a less swift method of securing the internal conditions of international status equality.[96]

Chapter Eight

TYPOLOGIES

The position so far is this: We have found certain activities, attitudes and assumptions recurring in many parts of the world with sufficient similarities to merit inclusion in a single category, which, after careful definition, we have labelled 'polycentric nationalism'. Everywhere the elements of this category exhibit almost identical features, almost identical aspirations—first, for the attainment of self-rule and independence; second, for its maintenance through the corollaries of integration, unity, individuality, autarchy, prestige and power. These particular aspirations are all expressions of one overall striving—to be part of a recognised political and cultural unit, a 'nation'; if necessary, to invent one, for the protection and sustenance of a threatened identity. The nationalist is one who harbours these particular aspirations so ardently, because they are necessary stepping-stones to 'nationhood', the supreme postulate of his political ethics. To him, men are not 'realised', humanity is 'unfulfilled' and hence 'underdeveloped', until the world is constituted into nation-states, which give political recognition to the aspirations to nationhood latent in every individual, whether he recognises it or not.

Polycentric nationalism, then, is a unity. It reveals the same basic pattern in Africa as in Europe, in the twentieth century as in the nineteenth, over large and small territories, among numerous or tiny groups.

The preceding chapter attempted to establish this unity: the next chapters aim to reveal the diversity of 'polycentric' nationalism. There is no paradox: our position is that nationalism is most fruitfully conceptualised as a single category containing subvarieties, genus and species, a diversity within a unity. That is, all nationalisms show certain basic features which mark the elements of the category, but various additional features are present in some cases, and other features in other cases, leading to a convenient grouping of cases in subtypes. Because the aspiration to nationhood is a double abstraction, finding its expression only in the lower-level particular aspirations listed above, we should expect it to vary considerably according to phase and situation of the movement's members. And this is just what happens.

It is this considerable variation and range of the expression of the basic nationalist striving that helps to explain why theories which try to give an overall account of the whole range of nationalisms run into difficulties. Either they explained too much, and failed to see the significance of differences between movements and groups of movements. Or they were forced to exclude in arbitrary fashion cases which failed to fit the explanation, and amend the definition accordingly. In this way comprehensiveness was sacrificed to greater precision. But if, as we saw, all-embracing generality is both unhelpful and misleading, over-precision in this field is inappropriate and of dubious legitimacy. As we noted, the result is tautology; the distinction between the chosen definition of the 'nation' and 'nationalism' is blurred with the subsequent explanation of the rise of nationalist movements and ideologies. Certain cases of nationalism are called 'genuine', and an unknown number of other cases conventionally labelled nationalist, are relegated or excluded, without any explanation of their basic similarities to the 'genuine' cases.

But the issue of 'genuineness' cannot be settled on *a priori* grounds alone. There would be no end of such narrow and conflicting 'stipulative' definitions.[1] The main question is: does the definition help in the solution of the original problem? We therefore need a more empirical elucidatory approach before we can decide the question of 'genuine' movements. The whole range of nationalist movements has first to be classified into serviceable analytic categories, so as to provide a clear view of the range of variation in the object of our study, before we embark on an anlysis of causes and consequences of nationalism.

Historical taxonomies

Historians have been the first to admit the diversity of national-ism within an implicit overall unity. Despite their traditional concern with the uniqueness of each nation's experiences, they have attempted to chart the emergence of nationalism as an ideological force by constructing spatial, chronological and analytic typologies, to accommodate major departures of dis-tinct groups of cases from a chosen historical model.

Historical taxonomies appear to have been mainly the products of historians of ideas; their primary referent has been, not the movement or group, but the ideology in its various historical and geographical garbs. The simplest type of scheme is the straight chronological. A common example is the four-stage evaluative parabola:

1815–1871 'integrative' phase, especially in Central Europe,
1871–1900 'disruptive' phase, i.e. of the old political units,
1900–1945 'aggressive' phase, culminating in the Nazi orgy,
1945– ? 'contemporary' phase, world-wide diffusion.

The story is one of a long decline from a pristine reasonableness into an inflammation and thence into a madness, from which we are beginning to recover, since contemporary nationalists couch their demands in more moderate terms. [2]

Moralistic tales like this one no longer have much meaning. Even in its own terms it is unhistorical; the Serbian, Greek and Belgian movements are both early (i.e. in the 'integrative' phase) and of major importance: all three were thoroughly 'disruptive' of the existing political set-up, which expressed Metternich's neo-traditionalism. Conversely, by any standard, the Japanese and Indian cases were 'integrative', though they appeared in the 'disruptive' period. And so on. Moreover, the dates chosen are quite arbitrary, being based on the German model. There is no clear division between the periods, only an uneven flow of ideological elements. One may also question whether 'contem-porary' nationalism is so moderate and whether its diffusion is so neatly recent as the scheme suggests. Indeed one could dismiss such chronological taxonomies out of hand, were it not for the persistent use of Fascism and Nazism as the crucial evaluative and historical reference-point. While this is understandable, I believe that this conception is erroneous, and that the latter are related but different ideologies, movements and sentiments, though they quite often appear together. To equate them is not only to introduce completely new elements into our definitions, but to make the moralistic 'inflammation' picture seem almost irresistible, with all the consequent distortions in our perspectives on nationalism.

A more complex chronological scheme is revealed in Trevor-Roper's distinction between the 'historic' German, Italian and Hungarian movements, and the 'secondary' Czech, Polish and Zionist examples.[3] There is a shift of emphasis from the ideology to the movement, but it is limited. For it is not so much the chronological succession that concerns Trevor-Roper, but the diffusion of the ideology from one group to a neighbouring one, which makes the latter nationalisms ideological derivations, at once emulative and reactive to the primary cultural models. Such diffusion theses suffer from an over-neat mechanistic and retrospectively determinist bias. Why, one wonders, was it that these groups, and not others, were so receptive to nationalism, and why so rapidly? Surely the mechanics are more complex than indicated. But can we even make such distinctions? Again, historically, we have examples of nationalism (U.S., Argentine, France, Serbia), which pre-date, or are contemporaneous with, the 'historic' cases. Doesn't this fact of itself suggest the need for a sociological taxonomy (and explanation)? But then it is claimed that the 'historic' cases are the 'originals'—at least, of linguistic nationalisms. At this point we can see clearly the European ethnocentrism of all historical schemes, and the need to dismiss all extra-European cases as 'borrowings', which results from paying too much attention to the *ideology* at the expense of the *movement*. The tracing of ideological pedigrees on a world-wide scale reveals the inherent implausibility of the whole undertaking, even if concentration on Europe conceals it. What are the ideological links between German and Venezuelan, or Italian and Japanese nationalisms, in historical terms? Historically it would be better to look to the French Revolution as a common intellectual ancestor, if ancestors *must* be sought.

Better still is to forsake the quest for neat periodizing and ideological lineages. Carlton Hayes' six ideological strands of nationalism still show traces of these formulations. He recognises the approximate contemporaneity of four types, which he calls the 'Humanitarian' (evinced in the writings of Bolingbroke, Rousseau and Herder), 'Jacobin' (Robespierre, etc.), 'Liberal' (the English school, particularly Bentham) and 'Traditional' (e.g. Burke, Schlegel and Ambroise). Later these were supplemented by 'Economic' protectionist nationalism (which seems to mix socio-logical elements with ideological), and finally by 'Integral' totalitarianism (Maurras, etc.), the forerunner of Fascism.[4] Again there is a strong regional bias (Franco-English), and some of the categories shade easily into each other, e.g. Traditionals and Humanitarians. But the main trouble is with the formulation of the typology in terms of purely *ideological* distinctions. A typo-logy of this kind is not easily amenable to sociological analysis, for different strands of the ideology may be found within a single movement, e.g. Traditional, Jacobin and Integral elements in Syrian Ba'athism.[5] Moreover, it is as parts of a cultural system, or programme of ideal ends, that the particular emphases exert an influence in the world of political action, or in society at large.

Perhaps the best-known example of a complex ideological typology encompassing spatial, chronological and purely in-tellectual elements, is Hans Kohn's distinction between 'Eastern' and 'Western' nationalisms. In the seventeenth and eighteenth centuries in the 'West' (i.e. England, U.S., France, Holland, Switzerland), nationalism was predominantly a political expression of the rising middle classes and harked back to Renaissance cultural models. It was a rationalist, optimistic and pluralist kind of nationalism. It was couched in the language of the social contract and stressed the communal realisation of the Enlighten-ment's ideal of progress. In the socially more backward 'East' (Central and Eastern Europe, and Asia) in the nineteenth century, nationalism was a cultural movement of the lower aristocracy and the masses. Ideologically, it was characterised by two inter-twined elements: an emotional but authoritarian consciousness of the inferiority of the ancient organic Volk *vis-à-vis* the advanced West, and a messianic sense of chosenness for a mission to man-kind. Both elements converged on the one sure support of nationalist aspirations in such settings, namely, tradition, which derived from the Holy Roman or Tsarist Orthodox empires.[6]

This scheme highlights a crucial distinction: between the rationalist and instrumental 'voluntarist' and 'subjectivist' version of nationalist ideology, and an evolutionary and expressive 'organic' and 'objectivist' version, to which we shall shortly return. It becomes less acceptable when it goes on to use these versions to provide the basis for a typology of causes. It assumes a necessary correlation between types of social structure and philosophical distinctions, whereas the evidence points to a far more complex relationship. For example, the formulation of the 'organic' version of the theory was the work of politically frustrated sons of clergymen and minor officials, mainly in early nineteenth-century Germany.[7] But in other settings army officers, intelligentsias, small shopkeepers, technicians, deruralised peasants and civil servants are some of the many groups most attracted to this form of the nationalist doctrine. We must investigate in each case why various combinations of social groups in different settings embrace one or other of these cultural formulations, often changing from one to the other—for example, the adoption of Negritude in West Africa or Satyagraha in India after an initial phase of 'voluntarist' liberal nationalism; or why in the *same* setting we can find both versions (the 'voluntarist' and the 'organic') in conflict, as happened in France during the Dreyfus Affair.[8] To do this, we must separate our descriptive classification from the subsequent explanation, and formulate both independently.

The other objections to this scheme are: (1) its silence about Latin American and African developments and experiences; (2) its spatial aspect—'West' and 'East' cannot be concrete referents, since on Kohn's admission, Spain, Ireland and Belgium belong to the 'Eastern' camp, being at the time socially 'backward'; (3) the remnants of chronological periodising—one thinks of early Indian rationalist nationalism, or the instrumental developmentalism of Turkish or Tanzanian attempts at integration, which blend 'voluntarist' and 'organic' elements in a single movement; (4) the unwieldiness of the two categories, which are made to do too many jobs, and cover too many levels of development, types of structure and cultural situations within each category. For example, using his criteria, we should distinguish between the different developmental stages at the inception of the nationalist movements, in Central Europe, in agrarian Eastern Europe, and in Islamic feudal areas like the Middle East. If the ideological criterion is chosen, we might well wish to subdivide the 'voluntarist' category into the 'individualist' (Anglo-Saxon) and 'collectivist' (French) formulations.[9]

All this adds up to a charge of mixing too many and too diverse elements together in the fashioning of the categories. But if we drop the concrete accretions, and retain only the 'voluntarist' and 'organic' versions of the ideology as ideal-types, we are left with an important distinction concerning the affirmation or denial of individual rights in relation to the group.

The distinction can be put as follows: both versions affirm the desirability of a world system of nation-states, and the inability of the individual to opt out of this system. One *must* be a citizen somewhere, of some unit. In the 'voluntarist' version, it doesn't inherently matter where you are a citizen; you are free to enter into and opt out of any national unit, provided always you observe the rules of that unit, and fulfil your obligations in return for the enjoyment of national rights. The nation-state is conceived in the image of a civil association founded by a (primordial or recent) contract; it has unmediated membership and a rational-conventional basis. Nationality is mainly a question of subjective consciousness.[10]

There is no question of entering into, or opting out of, any particular national unit, except at birth or death (in some visions, not even then), according to the 'organic' version.[11] The individual has no meaning apart from the community of birth. Individuality is predicated of the group. The individual can realise himself through it alone. It has a life history, it is self-generating and self-sufficient, a seamless, mystic entity, ascertainable through objective characteristics—of history, religion, language and customs. Nations are 'natural' wholes, they constitute the sole historical realities. Therefore the individual is primarily distinguishable in terms of his nationality, and only secondarily by social and personal traits. To opt out of the community is to risk the loss of a man's individuality.

Both these ideological versions assume the existence of entities with ascribed characteristics, civil associations or historical organisms, to which the individual is related. A third version, which I shall term 'activist' or 'creative', does not make such an assumption. Its nation is a product of achievement. (This is not the same as Fichtean striving and will. Fichte assumed that the 'nation' existed; it was only necessary to add the political dimension, the sovereign state, by an effort of will.) This version is well illustrated by Herminio Martin's description of Brazilian 'developmental nationalism', where 'the "nation" was defined, not as a given ascriptive solidarity, but as realised in and through the "project" of transcending its own backward situation in the effort of development'.[12] True, the State framework sets the boundaries of the task, but the nation is not a condition to be attained. It is not a state, but a process, a dynamic flow of structured activity, and development is like an endless slope rather than a once-for-all plateau. It is the creativity of the plan and the energy of the effort of self-transcendence that marks off a nationality.

Sociological taxonomies

In contrast to the historical schemes which focus on the ideological formulations, sociological taxonomies take the national group, or the nationalist movement, as the unit of analysis.

One of the earliest sociological taxonomies is that of the political scientist, Handman. His scheme is in terms of groups.[13] He distinguishes four types of nationalisms; 'irredentism', 'oppression', 'precaution', and 'prestige'. 'Irredentism' seeks the unification of an independent state with conationals under foreign domination; 'oppression' signifies the reaction of the small ethnic (mainly East European and Irish) nationalities to their discriminatory conditions. The cited examples, however, tend to blur this distinction; no differentiation is made between the explicitly cultural basis of, say, Serbian or Ruthenian nationalism, the more politically oriented Irish movement, the irredentism of the oppressed Poles and the diaspora elements in the Armenian movement. It is not so much a case of opposition between the 'irredentism' and the 'oppression' of ethnic groups, since the irredentist Italians and Germans could, and did, cite oppressive conditions; and Rumanians, Greeks, Poles and Bulgarians were violent in their irredentism, the moment a significant section of the group had freed itself from oppression. This in itself would prove nothing, since it is clear that a given case of nationalism will have to be placed under more than one rubric. But it does point up the lack of clarity in this particular distinction. All nationalisms can claim some measure of oppression, and none more so than small groups. It is what they try to do about their condition that interests a sociological taxonomy of nationalisms. 'Irredentism' is one such attempted solution; its converse and counterpart is surely 'secession' from the oppressive political unit.

The other pair of distinctions is more helpful. 'Precaution' nationalism is the identification of commercial interests with naitonal security and prosperity under the stimulus of competitively organised states, and it leads to imperialism. 'Prestige' nationalism is a cultural sentiment of inferiority, which springs from a perceived lack of esteem for past achievements and un-realised potentialities—Handman's examples are Action Française, Corradini's Fascism and pre-1921 Germany. The distinction here is between an economic State nationalism and Fascism. We argued that it is unhelpful to call Fascism a type of nationalism, and perhaps Handman is really drawing attention to the exclusive and messianic elements in Pan movements, when he cites a special 'prestige' category of nationalisms. On the other hand, 'precaution' nationalism is particularly valuable in pointing up the economic role of the State in promoting nationalism in conditions of independence.

One of the better-known sociological schemes is that of Louis Wirth. His typology of 'hegemony', 'particularist' (secession), 'marginal' (frontier) and 'minority' nationalities defines them as conflict groups.[14] It is not clear whether 'hegemony' includes irredentist as well as State-directed expansionist movements; nor how such irredentisms relate to the 'frontier' type; nor whether the latter arise indigenously, or in the 'homeland', or both. The 'secession' category, on the other hand, is clear. But Wirth's 'minority' type, which includes Negroes (in U.S.) and Jews, who cling to their own culture—unlike the border groups (e.g. Alsatians, Silesians) of the 'marginal' category—is odd. After all, many minorities have held to their traditions for centuries, like Copts, Kurds and Tajiks, but only recently have they been touched by the wind of nationalism. As for the U.S. Negroes and Jews, should we not distinguish the nationalists among them? They are not far to seek.

This is an example of the broader criticism of the group approach in dealing with some of the problems of nationalism.

It is suitable for questions such as the growth of nations, which are Deutsch's chief concern.[15] In considering problems of nationalist aspirations and activity, and their causes and consequences, a group approach suffers from a tendency to presuppose group unity, as in Wirth's 'minority' category. If in addition we wish to estimate the 'intensity' and 'achievement' of a particular case of nationalism, the group focus will only provide partial indicators. The members of a group may have a vivid sense of their group identity, and this is of undoubted importance in helping to spread the nationalist cause. But, as we saw, it is a necessary constituent only of a nation; it is neither a necessary nor a sufficient condition of nationalism. To get at the latter, we need to go to the movement and its membership.

I shall therefore pass over the taxonomies of causal factors in the formation of nations which Ginsberg and Seton-Watson present in their recent lectures—at least for the present. Not only does it properly belong to the subsequent causal analysis, but both are concerned with a parallel but different issue, the growth of national communities.[16]

But Seton-Watson does also present a brief taxonomy of nationalist *movements*, which reflect the growing trend away from European ethnocentrism, characteristic of the earlier 'group' and 'ideology' typologies. He separates 'independence', 'irredentist' and 'nation-building' movements; and he suggests that 'Nations which are independent, territorially satisfied and deeply nationally conscious have no need to be nationalist any more'. This classification provides us with a good starting-point, using the movement as the referent. But Seton-Watson fails to differentiate the main ways in which the State can 'build' the nation, and to subdivide the large 'independence' group according to the situation of the movement. The merit of this scheme, however, is that it gets away from the usual area approach to arrive at a purely analytic classification.[17]

This last feature is less marked in Worsley's equally brief taxonomy.[18] He has three categories: 'unitary', 'heterogeneous' (my terminology) and 'Pan' movements. The latter type denotes movements which 'transcend established state boundaries: they are built upon much wider cultural affiliations . . .'—religious, linguistic, physical, continental (e.g. Pan-Islamism, Slavophilism, Negritude, Pan-Africanism). The other two types are modelled on the contrast between the 'orthodox' national movements of nineteenth-century Europe based on an homogeneous ancient state, and the 'new state' movements of sub-Saharan twentieth-century Africa (there are a few 'orthodox' cases here too—Somalia, the Ewe and BaKongo). Put like this, the distinction is slightly misleading; after all, some East European movements could not fall back convincingly on the memory of an ancient former state (Slovaks, Ukrainians, Rumanians, Germans, Yugoslavs). One should not minimise the power exerted by such memories in certain conditions, provided that the group has preserved its cultural distinctiveness. But it isn't a simple political criterion we are looking for; what matters is the degree of coextensiveness between polity and culture, for that provides one key to the aspirations of nationalist movements.

The essential point in Worsley's scheme is that the 'European' movements aimed to found states 'on the basis of pre-existing cultural ties—of religion, language, "race", etc.—by fostering enhanced consciousness of these ties'. The 'African' movements, by contrast, had no such ties co-extensive with the colonial polity, to fall back on to as a psychological, social and political support for their contention. The 'national group' did not exist, it had to be created out of the culturally heterogeneous small groups and 'tribes' which peopled the arbitrarily drawn colonial units.

We shall elaborate this important distinction later. It needs to be broken down further. It does seem a better basis for a classification than to contrast the 'ethnic' European with a vague category of 'underdeveloped' cases, spanning Africa and Asia as Minogue does.[19] The concern with 'development' tends towards spatial typologising based on a hemispheric industrialised/industrialising dichotomy. This is to overlook distinctions within and across the North–South division, which reduce its importance for our purposes. (It also involves difficult theoretical assumptions about a 'convergence thesis'.) Minogue also seems to assume a similar level of development between the ancient cultures of Asia and the small-scale lineage structures of Africa. By contrast, his other categories, 'Pan' and 'Diaspora' (where members of an ethnic group are scattered across the globe and desire to return to their alleged or historical 'homeland'), are far clearer.

It is possible, however, to rephrase Minogue's distinction as the contrast between an 'anti-colonial' and a 'linguistic' nationalism, as Kautsky recommends.[20] 'Anti-colonialism' is a movement of intellectuals desiring rapid industrialisation for 'their' colonial units. Kautsky is careful to except Latin American experiences from this category, and to recognise its similarities with Ireland. The nub here is that the colonial power must be far more developed, i.e. industrialised, than the colonised. The Middle East under Turkish rule must therefore be excluded; thereafter, in the twentieth century, it becomes a case of 'anti-colonial' nationalism, because of Franco-British industrial superiority. Central Asia under Tsarism, Indonesia under the Dutch, Africa under Britain and France, French Indochina, Belgian Congo, Portuguese Angola and Mozambique, and the British possessions in South-East Asia, all fall under this heading. In all these cases, what counts is the relative positions of coloniser and colonised in *economic and technological* terms.

This is certainly an important, indeed crucial, factor. But in Chapter 4 I tried to demonstrate that the colonial relationship was more consequential for the rise of nationalism in its *political and cultural* aspects than in its economic and technological. We may now add that the undoubted 'anti-colonialist' animus of the intellectuals is not the only feature of the nationalism of some of the countries in this group, just as language is not the only cultural differentiating mark of the Central-East European group (e.g. Serbs and Croats, Jews, Greeks). There is an 'ethnic' element in those ex-colonies which have large or 'strategic' dominant groups, e.g. Kenya or Burma; and the movement may derive as much from *their* sense of cultural identity as from the colony-wide exploitation. It is the forming of effective boundaries that dictates the types of nationalisms. And these boundaries are cultural or political.

There are more empirical objections to the distinction. For one thing, it ignores the 'Pan' and 'Diaspora' groups. For another, it is sometimes difficult to apply. Were the small East European nationalities in a 'colonial' relationship to Russian Tsarism? Is Portuguese colonialism that modernising agent which is such an essential element in Kautsky's model? What about the Czechs, as contrasted with, say, the Bosnians or Ruthenes in Galicia, under Habsburg domination? Moreover, does the degree of cultural complexity of a group not affect the nature of the colonial relationship?

For these reasons we shall have to exercise care in the formulation of a 'colonial' category, and concentrate attention on the political will and form behind economic manipulation rather than the effects of the latter alone.

The most comprehensive recent typology of nationalist movements is that put forward by Symmons-Symonolewicz. [21] He starts by criticising Kohn and Hayes for the moral and ideological overtones of their typologies, for ignoring the social movement, and for the vagueness of their categories. Instead, he insists on an unequivocal and ethically neutral definition of nationalism, drawn from Znaniecki and MacIver:

> the active solidarity of a group claiming to be a nation and aspiring to be a state.

His own typology draws on Coleman's distinction between a modernist nationalism of the westernised elite and a traditional and xenophobic one of the archaic early resistance movements in Africa. The second source of his classification is Wirth's conflict group categories.

One must distinguish, says Symmons-Symonolewicz, between the nationalism of majorities, usually represented by the State and political parties and a consequences of international relations or minority claims—and the nationalism of minorities striving for political and cultural emancipation and reacting against their inferior status. Only the latter minority cases are genuine nationalist movements, he claims, i.e. social movements aiming at national liberation.

Symmons-Symonolewicz's basic division is between Minority movements for self-preservation, and Liberation movements for independence. These major categories then are broken down into more precise subtypes (as in the diagram opposite).

The *Minority* category is, of course, an elaboration of Wirth's type. Only here the irredentist 'frontier' nationalisms of the Sudetens, the Alsatians and the Swabians are included, along with two other kinds of Minority movements. The 'segregative' nationalisms seek to perpetuate themselves by means of a separate but autonomous status, aiming for 'minority rights'; whereas the 'pluralist' nationalisms want to preserve their cultural autonomy through civic equality. Symmons-Symonolewicz cites as examples of the latter the ghettoes and *millets*, which seems somewhat

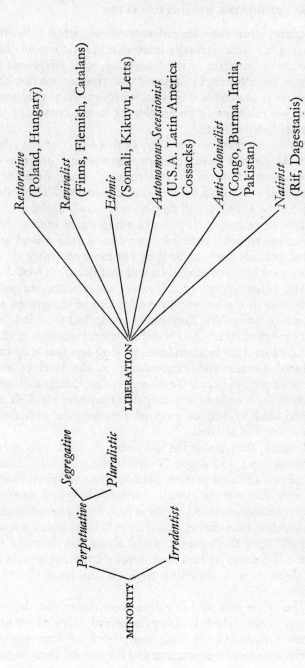

TABLE 3   TYPOLOGY AND MINORITY MOVEMENTS

MINORITY

Perpetuative — Irredentist

Segregative — Pluralistic

LIBERATION

Restorative (Poland, Hungary)

Revivalist (Finns, Flemish, Catalans)

Ethnic (Somali, Kikuyu, Letts)

Autonomous-Secessionist (U.S.A. Latin America Cossacks)

Anti-Colonialist (Congo, Burma, India, Pakistan)

Nativist (Rif, Dagestanis)

puzzling, since they desired segregation, while minority rights movements were generally interested in civic equality and entry into the mainstream of the State's life, with safeguards for their culture, etc. Nor am I convinced that 'frontier' irredentisms merit separate treatment as a distinct category, since they are usually offshoots of the expansionist aims of their co-nationals who now possess independence.

My main criticism, however, of this aspect of the typology is that, as defined here, Minority movements are not cases of nationalism at all, in the 'polycentric' sense, or in Symmons-Symonolewicz's own definition of nationalism. They often don't claim to be a nation, and they certainly don't aspire to statehood. In fact, of course, their claim to autonomy is merely the tactical first stage towards their ultimate aim of nationhood and state-hood, but this needs to be spelt out more explicitly. So does the distinction between modernist and traditionalist types.

The other group of *Liberation* movements are subdivided according to the historical development of the groups and their degree of unity. The Restorative group lost their independence, but preserved intact their social structure; whereas the Revivalist groups lost their independence so long ago that they have been reduced socially and intellectually to the level of the lower strata of a population. Third comes the Ethnic nationalisms of communities without any historical tradition, yet their solidarity is activated by various external pressures, as with the Somali, Estonians and Kikuyu.

I think the distinction between the first two subtypes is valuable and sociologically important, but the third raises problems. Cultural groups which possess sufficient sentiment to provide fuel for nationalist movements would surely possess some consciousness of a common past, some memories and totems on which to base their claims. This is the case with the Kikuyu and Somali. And this raises a doubt about the threefold division: is the difference in historical development not simply a matter of degree? Is it sufficient to form the basis of a *sociological* taxonomy?

The other axis of Liberation movements, the degree of the group's unity, which Worsley underlines, seems to me to provide a better basis. At the same time, some of Symmons-Symono-lewicz's categories are curious and they do not hang together. For example, he describes his 'Autonomist-Secessionist' type as consisting in regional entities with ties to the mother group, which later developed distinctiveness and hence a demand for autonomy, which when rejected, led to secession. He cites the U.S.A. and Latin American and Siberian examples. But the evidence does not point to any degree of distinctiveness in these cases at the inception of their independence movements; consider the rivalries between the thirteen colonies of America. These movements were the handiwork of small elites who envisaged nations-to-be, rather like the African nationalists. Symmons-Symonolewicz does recognise a category of 'nationalisms without nations', as in the Congo and Indonesia (do India and Pakistan, even Burma, fit this category?), but does not link this 'Anti-colonialist' type with the U.S.A. and Latin America. Finally, the 'Nativist' or xenophobic tribalist variety is quite out of place in this company. It obviously fits the far older 'ethnocentric' kind of nationalism outlined in the previous chapter.

Generally, the typology seems to hesitate between using the group or the movement as the ultimate referent of nationalism; its bias, on the whole, is towards the group, like Wirth's, and this is probably responsible for its flaws. The aims of the movements are decisive, in my view, for a classification of nationalisms; whereas the determinants of their opportunities to achieve these aims form the backcloth and lead towards causal explanation, a subsequent stage of the analysis.

Some taxonomic prerequisites

Apart from the particular shortcomings, certain general criticisms can be made of the previous schemes. These can be summarised in the form of three conditions of the utility of taxonomy in the solution of the problems of nationalism. These are the needs for:

1 comprehensiveness of empirical range
2 constancy in the use of referents
3 possibilities for using the types in subsequent research.

1 Previous taxonomies have been one-sided. They have in fact pointed up a few types, and then generalised from them to the whole field of 'nationalism'. Heightened one-sidedness is legitimate only if the types are then used as tools for the investigation of the selected distinction or subarea. But if our interest is in

'nationalism' as a whole (which it is, in all the previous taxonomies —at least, in intention), then we must avoid compressing diverse types under a single rubric, without subclassification, and we must at least try to systematise the whole range of types. To start from a single model, or work in a single area, and then note differences from other types, leads to imbalance and omissions. Only an empirical survey of as many cases as can be discovered, using as broad a definition initially as is justifiable, can hope to avoid the biases and crudenesses of a single-model or areal approach.

2 There is a tendency in the previous taxonomies to shift during the discussion from one referent or unit of analysis to another, or to predicate the types of some vague 'process' of nationalism. It seems necessary, however, both for the sake of clarity in terminology and for ensuring maximum utility for the taxonomy, to select one referent to serve as the sole unit throughout. Comparative analysis demands the greatest degree of similarity in the initial units and of sharp delineation of the types.[22]

The choice of referent depends on the needs of the problem. We have already seen that the social group referent is less appropriate than the movement or ideology in dealing with a topic like nationalism. Even if we confine the meaning of the latter term and describe it solely as a sentiment or consciousness, we are forced to acknowledge the uneven distribution, the variability and the instability of the latter in any given collectivity. If, as is argued here, we must include the other sense of the term, that of an ideological movement, then we are compelled to realise the implausibility of imputing a doctrine of the will to a whole group, or worse, of attributing will and activity to the total community without empirical evidence.

The ideology, on the other hand, suffers from being too remote from the sphere of action, if it is chosen as the sole unit of analysis in isolation from the movement which is its expression and vehicle. We have already noted the vagueness and slippery nature of attempts to draw up taxonomies in terms of strands and emphases in the ideology. But the main argument against isolating the ideology and taking it as the main referent, is that to do so risks attaching too much weight to the statements and declarations of a tiny minority of intellectuals in the generation of that enthusiasm for nationalism in far wider circles that forms the focus of our concern. It also entails operating in the confined conceptual framework which aims to establish causal priority for ideal or material factors. [23]

The movement, by contrast, is free of these methodological defects. Its manifestations can be operationally defined and fruitfully compared. Movements show sufficient initial similarities and subsequent internal differentiation to invite classification. They are defined in terms of both activities and beliefs, and hence dispense with the need for a *prior* theory of the relation of thought and change in the estimation of their sources and influence in social life. They are the foci of nationalist aspirations and enthusiasm, and their activities and demands provide the best indicators and richest source of material for a study of nationalism.

3 None of the sociological taxonomies known to me have been put to any research use (most have appeared in articles or lectures).

In this respect historians have done better. Hayes and Kohn, in particular, have related their taxonomies of the ideology to politics and the social structure, in a descriptive manner. No doubt simply to draw attention to the varieties of nationalism by the delineation of significant types, is an advance on a non-analytic approach. But it remains an academic exercise, if it serves no heuristic function.

By firmly embracing the nationalist movement as the unit of analysis, we have taken the first step in filling this gap. That is, provided we can form a clear idea of the lower limit of the 'movement'. We shall define it as 'an organised collection of individuals putting forward demands and pursuing activities designed to promote self-rule, integration (or the other corollaries) for the group which they conceive to constitute the "nation"'. (For my purposes, they must have a clear notion of the meaning of these goals—i.e. I am concentrating on the 'polycentric' nationalist movements.) A single propagandist does not constitute a movement, nor does a literary or antiquarian society, however much their researches and activities may deepen awareness of national roots and aspirations. It is only when a political demand for the reorganisation of the political set-up is formulated by a group which includes 'nationals' of the existent or projected 'nation', that we can begin to talk of a nationalist movement. Later the movement may embrace more than one organisation, and retain its analytic unity, provided that the aims of the organisation show a basic similarity of goal, whatever the divergencies in the methods employed. 'Movement' is therefore a concept broader than 'party' or 'organisation', but more precise and useful for our concerns than either 'ideology' or 'group'.

A final problem remains. My aim in presenting other typologies before attempting a more comprehensive version, was to build upon distinctions which, being recurrent, seemed to possess clarity and force. But, if we assimilate the types predicated of the group and ideology referents, will we not risk losing some valuable distinctions? Many of the types, 'irredentism' and 'secession', 'unity' and 'heterogeneous', 'state' and 'independence', are predicated of the nationalist movement. But the 'ascriptive' and 'activist', and 'organic' and 'voluntarist' distinctions refer to the ideology *per se*. I shall try to show that certain types of movements do have a built-in disposition to one or other ideological version; but the conjunction is not strict, not only because of the many accretions resulting from diffusion of ideas in this century, but mainly because the basic logic of nationalism makes intellectual movement from one version to the other an easy task, given the appropriate *social* conditions.

Take, for example, the 'organic/voluntarist' distinction. If applied fully, the difference in the social consequences of the two versions is as great as that between the contexts in which they first appeared. And yet, as the French Revolution progressed, what began as a doctrine of the revolutionary choice of the individual in relation to the government of the civil community, was rapidly transformed into an authoritarian ideology of enforced freedom, of the subordination of the individual to the organically conceived and constraining General Will. [24] Given the right social environment, it was a small step from this conception of a pure holistic Will to its identification with folk customs and vernaculars. It is therefore to the social differences rather than the intellectual strands and emphases that we must look in refining a taxonomy. Nationalism at no period in its development possessed the logical consistency and alleged imperviousness to social changes that was characteristic of Marxism. And even the latter has responded to the social exigencies in the situations of its bearers. [25]

Chapter Nine

THE VARIETIES OF
NATIONALISM

From the preceding review, we can see that nationalist movements can be distinguished in many ways—according to the interests and problems of the analyst. I am interested in their sociological differences, which form the most useful introduction to the problems of causal explanation.

Nationalist movements can be classified according to two divergent sets of criteria: (1) *Formal*, or 'external' criteria, (2) *Substantive*, or 'internal' ones.

The first set is concerned with the degree of intensity of the aims of nationalist movements, and their relative achievement in attaining their goals. The second set of criteria seeks to distinguish the kinds of situations and assumptions which generate those goals; it is therefore both more important and more complex.

Some preliminary distinctions

If we take these two variables, 'intensity' and 'achievement', and cross-tabulate them, four types of movement emerge.

(*a*) Classification of movements according to the *'intensity'* of their nationalism reveals a continuum ranging from very *'primitive'* to highly *'developed'* cases. This is a difficult criterion to apply, and any cut-off point must be somewhat arbitrary. Yet there is an undoubted gap between the 'primitivism' of the primary resistance of, say, the Ouagadougou Mossi to the French invasion of the 1890's[1] or of the Achinese to the Dutch in the 1870's,[2] and the complex and organised resistance of the Risorgimento or the Armenian Dashnaks. Or contrast the incipient separatism of the Chagga or Burmese Chin with the persistent, diffused and organised separatism of the Basques, Letts or Ibo.

It is possible to argue that such 'primitives' ought to be excluded from the category of 'nationalism'. This is Coleman's argument in the case of the pacification of the Nigerian kingdoms by the British.[3] His position contrasts with the omnibus concept of nationalism used by Hodgkin; any attack by an organised group on European domination in Africa is evidence for Hodgkin of 'nationalism'.[4] My compromise position of 'ethnocentric' and 'polycentric' kinds of nationalism accepts both the differences between the two kinds of movement, which Coleman underlines, and the similarities in their main aims, which I contend is the decisive test of inclusion in the 'nationalist' category. One should distinguish an 'inner circle' of persistent, well organised and articulated, dedicated and widely supported movements, from the 'outer circle' of fleeting, intermittent, incipient, barely self-conscious, esoteric or submerged movements.

If this argument is accepted, two problems arise. First, at which point should we place the line between 'primitive' and 'developed' nationalisms? Clearly there is no natural division. If we scored movements along such dimensions as the degree of their activity, the complexity of their organisation, the diffusion of their ideology in the group, the clarity of their aims, the persistence of the organisation(s), and the importance of the nationalist issue to the members, and hence their dedication, we might well find some 'inconsistent' results. Perhaps the nearest we can come to an operational line of demarcation is to ask if the movement openly espouses the ideal of 'nationhood' in a 'world of nations' and works persistently towards the goal of self-rule, or integration, etc., if independence has already been attained. In the case of the 'primitive' nationalisms, this ideal is only dimly perceived and half-heartedly embraced; hence the activity is often correspondingly reduced. Other ideals and considerations, e.g. religious, clan or dynastic, weigh more heavily than the element of a demand for the recognition of group identity and autonomy. The sixteenth-century Dutch group feeling and demands are a good example of this initial 'submergence' of nationalist sentiment and aspirations to religious, political and dynastic issues.[5] So is the initial subordination of specifically nationalist aspirations in the early Bolshevik movement.

The other problem concerns the main kinds of movements which make up the somewhat hybrid 'primitive' category. We should include.

1 'Primary resistance' movements, for example, Achinese, Zulus, Iroquois[6]

2 Incipient separatism, for example, Chagga, Chin, Lapps

3 Anticolonial 'messianic' revivalisms, for example, the Indonesian Padri movement, the Congolese Kitawala, the 'Burkhanist' Oirot 1904 faith, etc.

4 Provincial separations, e.g. Ecuador, Honduras, Niger, Chad.

The last type of movement, in particular, is a dubious inclusion. It is difficult to estimate the degree of group aspiration among the politically conscious minority of the backward, ex-colonial, territories, which were handed a separate independence (in Africa), or which separated themselves off from more advanced movements after independence, because of insufficient integration, poorly developed communications and the like (in Latin America). The other kinds of movements, particularly 'messianic' movements, appear to fall under the 'ethnocentric' rubric; but only investigation can determine the degree of their 'primitivism'.[7]

(b) 'Developed' and 'Primitive' nationalisms can be subdivided in terms of the second variable, *'achievement'*, into *'failed'* and *'successful'* cases.[8] The operational test is: did the movement gain and maintain (over a considerable period) 'independence', i.e. *de facto* sovereignty, for the chosen group? By this criterion Serbia and Latvia stand at the apex of the 'failure' category, which would include Armenians, Basques, Uzbeks and Ukrainians among the 'developed' cases, and Tajiks, Mari, Araucanians and Copts among the 'primitive' nationalisms. By contrast, the Poles, Burmese, Albanians, Argentinians and Ghanaians, who achieved sovereign statehood to a considerable extent through the exertions of their nationalist movements, are examples of 'successes'.

The distinction poses two problems, relating to what may be

termed the 'autonomous' and 'current' movements. The former are those which failed in their bid for sovereignty, but were accorded a measure of recognition, usually in the form of cultural and territorial autonomy, e.g. the Soviet Republics, the Yugoslav provinces, the minority national groups in the United Kingdom, and perhaps the Indian linguistic states. Contrast these with the total 'failure' (to date) of the Basques, Catalans, Bretons, Ewe, BaKongo, Corsicans, and Druse to win *any* form of recognition. In practice, however, the distinction is less impressive than it at first sight appears. As the fairly recent fracas between Serbian and Croatian professors showed, the autonomy of the Yugoslav provinces is necessarily tightly circumscribed.[9] In the Soviet Union, even the linguistic rights are under constant threat at the hands of the dominant Russian-speaking colonists.[10] Welsh is likewise threatened, in a political system from which the repressive apparatus of Communist countries is absent.[11] Only in the Indian context is cultural nationalism flourishing; but its very success must undermine the State and strain towards secession, as Nehru feared.[12] It would therefore seem to confirm the unreality of an absolute distinction between 'autonomous' and 'failed' movements.

Finally there are the '*Current*' movements whose outcome is hard to predict, because at a given point in time they are engaged in the struggle for 'liberation' or 'integration', etc., as in India today, or with the Kurds, Pan-Arabists, Austrian Tyrolese, Quebecois, Nagas and Palestinians. The difficulty in prediction which results from the multiplicity of external and contingent factors, highlights the dependent nature of the 'achievement' criterion, from the sociological point of view. One can say that the 'formal' criterion of achievement of independence is the province of the historian.

The relationship between the 'achievement' and 'intensity' criteria can be presented thus.

		Achievement		
		Failure	*Success*	*Current*
	Primitive	Tajiks	Holland	Portuguese
		Tigre	Chad	Guinea
Intensity				
	Developed	Letts	Kenya	Naga
		Ewe	Poland	Palestinians
		Croats		

A typology of nationalist movements

This substantive set of criteria attempts to get closer to the aspirations of the nationalist movements than the purely external judgments of the formal criteria. It tries to isolate the significant sociological elements in the situations in which the movements find themselves at various stages of their development. The very variety of the situations, however, makes the substantive typology far more complex than the formal. This is even more the case insofar as we define 'situation' in both subjective and objective terms. That is, we are as interested in the way in which that situation appears to the members of the nationalist movement, as in the light in which it presents itself to the sociological observer. The features to be isolated must accordingly be those which can be seen to be relevant to a nationalist in that situation.

The nationalist, we said, aims to gain and maintain 'nationhood' for 'his' chosen group. We should then expect him to raise two questions about the situation of the group for which he advocates 'nationhood'. The first is relatively simple: Is 'my' group already independent, and if so, what must I do to maintain this state of affairs? This gives us the first main criterion of nationalist movements. Do they operate on behalf of a group that is 'independent', or not? This is the criterion of 'independence'.

The second question the nationalist is likely to put runs: What are the characteristics in my chosen group to which I can point, to convince others that 'my' group is in fact a 'nation', and therefore a fit object of independence? The nationalist, in his mental initiation ceremony, has already convinced *himself* that 'his' group is morally and conceptually self-sufficient: it constitutes a mental 'nation'. To convince *others* of this truth, however, he must provide some persuasive sociological evidence, for this is the only kind of evidence that is likely to appeal to the uninitiated. The sort of evidence which is most appropriate would be one or more elements of social cohesion in the postulated group, say, a common set of customs, a differentiating language or religion, natural frontiers or a separate political history. In other words, he is concerned to establish whether the group already 'exists' or not, by determining the degree of its 'distinctiveness'. This provides us with our second criterion of differentiation—'distinctiveness'.

Since the question about 'distinctiveness' is logically prior to that of 'independence', I shall first classify movements in terms of the answers to that question.

(a) '*Distinctiveness.*' Suppose that our imaginary nationalist received an affirmative reply to his question: 'His' group did indeed constitute a 'nation' (on the 'ethnicist' definition). That is, it was a large horizontally mobile but relatively well integrated group with common citizenship rights and one or more unique cultural features which marked it off from other groups to which it stood in relations of alliance or conflict. We could call his movement a case of 'nationalism *with* nations', or '*ethnic*' nationalism (in the broad cultural sense of that term). Then, if this 'nation' was not yet independent, his aim would be to superimpose a state on to the nation's boundaries.

But suppose the chosen group could not be called a sociological 'nation'. Suppose it was composed of a number of smaller groups, or that it lacked one of the other criteria of 'nationhood'. For example, it was not vertically integrated or culturally dissimilar to a sufficient degree to possess a common identity to an observer, or a group self-consciousness. The first of these alternatives is common in Africa and Asia, the second in Latin America. These sociological conditions have not prevented the emergence of nationalist movements. These nationalisms are not just manifestations of anti-European sentiment, though that element has often given them their violent edge.[13] They too aspire to 'nationhood', to self-rule and individuality, integration and prestige, autarchy and power and unity—with all the familiar European consequences. If this is so, we must acknowledge a category of 'nationalisms *without* nations', or '*territorial*' nationalisms, for such nationalisms only emerge under the stimulus of the colonial state and its administration. More important, they are termed 'territorial', because their aspirations are fixed by the boundaries of the province or colonial territory. Its limits are theirs.

They possess no other boundaries, no cultural edges, only geographical-cum-political ones. In these cases, the task of the nationalist is to draw the envisaged 'nation' out of the skeletal framework of the territorial state.

We may take the distinction further. '*Ethnic*' nationalisms start from a pre-existent homogeneous entity, a recognisable cultural unit; all that is necessary is to protect and nurture it. The primary concern, therefore, of 'ethnic' nationalists is to ensure the survival of the group's *cultural* identity. That entails ensuring the *political* survival of the group and the physical protection of its members. The only insurance of political survival under modern conditions is protection from interference by hostile outsiders in a separate political organisation, or State. Hence, for this type of nationalism, independence is more of a means for cultural ends.[14]

'*Territorial*' nationalisms start from an imposed political entity, and possess no common and distinctive cultural identity to protect. But that does not make them social-class or coalition-type movements, against alien oppressors. The rub lies in the perception of the rulers as 'aliens'. The main aim is to take over the alien's political machinery and adopt his administrative unit as the basis of the projected 'nation'. The best way of demonstrating one's 'nationhood' to a sceptical world is to wrest as rapidly as possible its political prerequisite, sovereignty, from the hand of the unwilling colonialist. Independence, then, for 'colonial' cases, has a direct political function, and the movement has a primarily political tone.[15]

There is one other answer which could be given to the nationalist's question about the 'distinctiveness' of 'his' group. It is a compromise answer from his point of view: only a part of 'his' group can be convincingly called a 'nation' (still employing the 'ethnicist' definition). That is, 'his' group is the colonial unit, but the latter contains one large or 'strategic cultural' group and several small or peripheral groups. It is this large or strategic group which gives the movement its initial impetus, but for various reasons (chiefly the feasibility of the attempt) the movement aims to gain self-rule in terms, not of the identity of its dominant group, but of that of the whole colonial unit. An example is Indonesia, where the initial driving force for independence from Dutch rule was supplied by the Javanese 'ethnie'; yet the state they aimed at, and which ultimately emerged, was an all-Indonesian one (sometimes in the teeth of secessionist opposition).[16]

Of course, there is the converse case of threatened groups opting for a separatist counter-nationalism, as with the Karen or Ibo; but these 'secessionist' ethnic movements are sociologically assimilable to the main 'secession' category. There is also the case of a smaller, more peripheral group taking over the leadership of the anti-colonial movement—for example, Nkrumah's Coast 'tribes' versus the Ashanti or Obote's Nilotic versus Buganda. We should therefore define 'dominance' in the colonial unit in terms of other criteria than mere size. But its exact definition in each case is less important than the 'mixture' between the initial 'ethnic' impetus and the 'colonial' orientation. We shall therefore designate this residual type '*Mixed*', for want of a better term, to denote the peculiar amalgam of elements of the other two categories found in these situations.

The '*distinctiveness*' criterion

All nationalist movements, then, can be placed along a continuum. At one end, we have the '*Ethnic*' movements with a high degree of cultural distinctiveness; at the other, the '*Territorial*' movements bound only by aspirations and a common territorial-cum-political base. In between, lie the '*Mixed*' movements.

This fundamental 'Ethnic/Mixed/Territorial' division contains significant subvarieties. This is because the situation of the 'chosen' group contains so many variations relevant to the aspirations of nationalists.

The main recurrent kinds of situations appear to be the following:

1 The projected 'group' has no pre-existent cultural ties (Worsley's African 'heterogeneous' category); it is composed of a multiplicity of small ethnic groups—for instance, Tanzania, Senegal, Congo.

2 The projected 'group' is culturally homogeneous, but it shares that culture, or much of it, with its oppressors, unlike the previous case. The Latin American and British colonial states are examples.

3 The projected 'group' is composed of one, or more, 'strategic' cultural groups, and some minority groups, as in the cases of Guyana, Kenya, Burma, India, Ghana, Nigeria, Upper Volta.

4 The projected 'group' is culturally homogeneous, but is incorporated in a political unit which seeks to destroy its identity through absorption—for example, Norway, Belgium, Georgia, Kazakhstan, Lithuania.

5 The projected 'group' is again culturally homogeneous, but both incorporated and divided up between different 'oppressive' units, as with Poland, Somalia and Italy.

6 The projected 'group' is a culturally defined entity which is far larger in scale than the existing political units, which it 'contains'. The existing states comprise a patchwork dividing up the cultural unity. Examples are the Arabic and Turkic speaking areas, the African and Latin American cultural and continental areas, the Negro and Slavic descent areas, and the pan-Islamic religious area.

7 The projected 'group' presents sufficient common cultural features to entitle it to the status of a 'nation', but its membership is scattered over a number of political units in varying degree and proportions, as with the Greeks, Armenians and Jews. Its developed cultural consciousness, coupled with the demands of the rulers of the respective polities, make large-scale assimilation to the 'host' community difficult.[17]

I shall analyse each of seven varieties of nationalist movement in turn, which are based on these seven kinds of group situation —in terms of the main criterion of cultural 'distinctiveness'.[18]

1 *'Territorial' movements.* This broad category can be subdivided into the 'heterogeneous' and 'cross-cultural' types.

The *'Heterogeneous'* group are movements which aim to take over the colonialists' unit in the name of a new identity, which is wider than any of the existing group identities. Although it may be legitimised in terms of ancient historical precedent, the projected identity is really a total innovation.[19] It is a politically fashioned and politically oriented identity. It turns its back resolutely on the small-scale cultural identities of the traditional social order for one which promises greater possibilities of group development. From the standpoint of an 'ethnic' nationalist, the movement looks like a (temporary) coalition of ethnic groups to eject a common enemy; and the element of colour bar in the situation and the dependency psychology of the colonised gives this interpretation plausibility.[20] But if such movements were purely negative in their aims (contrary to all their pronouncements), we should be witnessing the break-up of all the ex-colonial units, and the inability of any ethnic group to work with, or compromise with, any other. Whereas this is only one trend among many. Nor does a subsequent case of secession on the part of an ethnic group, like the Ibo, *ipso facto* invalidate the description of the *pre-independence* movement as 'heterogeneous territorial', i.e. oriented to the whole territory of the colonial unit. Subsequent developments may well have brought out 'latent' ethnic conflict, but these were in fact often novel in kind.

The '*Cross-cultural*' cases correspond to situation (2) above, as the 'heterogeneous' to (1). In these movements, the aspiration for independence from the colonial power lays stress on the geographical and political differences. This is because the culture, or much of it, spans the political boundary between the colony and mother-country, as the (English) language united Ireland, the United States and the Dominions with Britain, Haiti with France, Brazil with Portugal and the other Latin American states with Spain. 'Culture', from the standpoint of the nationalist, acts in these cases as a 'fifth column' externally, while constituting no internal barrier (as in the 'heterogeneous' cases). The obvious solution is to build a counter-culture. But this takes time, and in any case must be politically induced by an act of will. Hence the fashioning of a 'political culture' is contingent on the success of the main nationalist aspiration for political self-rule, without which there would in any case be no opportunity to 'individualise' the group's culture.

2 '*Mixed*' *movements*. This category corresponds to situation (3) above. It contains many variants, 'single-group', 'dual-group', 'multi-group', etc., subtypes—as in Burma, Guyana and Kenya, Nigeria and India, respectively. While it is possible to elaborate complicated taxonomies in respect of these varieties of political ethnography, their complexity and transcience make the result less profitable than expected. More important, the crucial sociological factor for a delineation of the directions of nationalist activities is the *fact* of dual orientation in the movement to the colonial unit and to the 'strategic' group, or groups; and not the particular *form* assumed by that ambivalence. It is the tension between the group of origination and the group of orientation, which is decisive and consequential.

3 '*Ethnic*' *movements*. Situations (4)–(7) above comprise the main ways in which cultural distinctiveness can be combined with political discontinuity. The typical nationalist solutions to this 'discrepant' situation take the following forms:

(*a*) '*Secession*'. The most common course for a movement that claims to speak for a culturally homogeneous group within a larger political unit, is to break away and form a state of its own.

The situation of 'incorporation' in an empire, etc., is interpreted by nationalists as contrary to 'nature'. Unlike the 'territorial' types, which base their claim to independence on the factual or alleged wish of the colonised population to choose its own rulers and rules, the 'ethnic' types interpret the democratic 'right of self-determination' in terms of the practical conclusion of a syllogism. The right becomes a duty to 'realise' the major premiss that the sole historical reality is the culturally defined 'nation'. In 'secession' cases, the 'nation' is not only homogeneous, but culturally unique, as in Norway, Latvia, Pakistan, Ukraine and Serbia, or with the Czechs, Tatars, Nagas, Shan, Assyrians and Bretons. The commonest referent of 'uniqueness' is language (and custom), but religion (Jews, Armenians, Ethiopians) may set a group apart from all others. Or a combination of cultural traits may bring about the same result. In such cases, the urge to be left to work out one's own destiny is particularly strong in the nationalist movement, and it is often coupled with a sense of 'mission' to a humanity that is felt to be 'incomplete' without the group's peculiar contribution.[21]

There are also homogeneous groups, who share one or more elements of their culture with their neighbours. In that sense, they approach the Latin American 'colonial cross-cultural' type. But there is a crucial difference. A state like Argentina or Venezuela shared some significant elements of its culture, not only with its neighbours, but with its rulers; whereas the states of, say, North Africa shared with their neighbours exactly those cultural elements which divided them so markedly from their French overlords. (They also possessed some unique traits, like an ancient separate political existence.) We may notice at this point that the secessionist urge in these groups may go hand in hand with a wider 'Pan' cultural affiliation, provided the latter acts as a reinforcement for the separatist drive. That is, the primary line of demarcation is that with the ruling power, and the differences with neighbours tend, at least in the preindependence phase, to be secondary, unless deliberately exploited by the rulers. The need for a sub-division of the 'secession' category for 'sharers' of culture with neighbours is unconvincing in view of the 'Pan' functions in this regard, which we explain below.[22]

(b) 'Diaspora.' By contrast, this group of nationalisms is as rare as the former was common. It is similar to the 'secession' type in solving a problem of 'incorporation' through division and separation, amounting to total withdrawal. But here the dilemma is far graver from the nationalist standpoint. Therefore the solution is commensurately more radical. For, whereas the 'secession' type groups formed a territorially compact unit within a larger hostile area, an oasis in a vast desert, the 'diaspora' type is composed of a series of small communities scattered across many large units and receiving differential treatment, like beads of many shapes and colours on a thread. In one or more of these communities there arises a desire for self-rule, but none of them is compact or strong enough to form the nucleus of a separate state in the former hostile area. The only mode of ensuring the survival of the culture and its bearers is through evacuation of the communities to a territory outside the hostile areas—preferably to one able to attract a zeal for self-regeneration. Both conditions are best fulfilled by an 'ancestral homeland', with its memories, its promise of security through an historic right, and the historical delimitation of its identity. But above all, it enables the persecuted communities to 'return' for shelter and collective redemption. The classic cases are Garveyism, Zionism, Lebanese, Liberians, Greeks and Armenians. [23]

(c) *'Irredentism.'* Both division and 'incorporation' characterise the situation (5) of this important category. Many movements have, in addition to their separatist aims, the opposite drive to unification of all co-nationals in one state. Members of the projected 'group' live within the boundaries of other political units than that in which the main body of the 'nationals' reside. But 'irredentist' movements do not stop at advocating the in-gathering of co-nationals into the main area, in the manner of 'diaspora' nationalisms; they also desire to add the territory on which their severed kinsmen reside, especially since it is usually adjacent to the 'base' area, e.g. Epirus to Greece, Alsace to France and Germany. Not only are sections of the human composition of the group to be absorbed, but also the mutilated parts of its allegedly historic configuration. The territorial patchwork must be rectified. Poland and Bulgaria are good examples of this territorial 'irredentismo', which reinforced their original separatism. The movement may develop this aspiration before and after independence. The separation of sections of the 'group' is looked on as an obstacle to free self-development, but soon it becomes an axiom of this type of nationalism, an end in itself. 'Incompleteness' is not merely an insult, it is a negation of the 'nation'.[24]

(d) 'Pan'. The difference between this type and the previous one is that, while both aspire to cultural unity, the situation (6) confronting the 'Pan' nationalist demands the unification of *separate* political units contained within the larger culture area. This does not mean that it operates only after the attainment of independence by the constituent units; it may direct its attention to the separate provinces of an empire (or more than one), or to adjacent but separately ruled colonies, or to a network of separate principalities, as in Germany or Italy. The line between 'Pan' and 'Irredentist' movements is not always strict in a given case, e.g. the Mongols, Italians. But its peculiar characteristic is opposition to the '*balkanisation*' of an area deemed to constitute a unity, and the corresponding vision of a cultural super-state, usually on a large scale with a huge population.

Should a separate category be given to movements along the frontiers of political units, which aim to unite 'their' population and territory to some larger group with which it shares some common traits? Are these cases of a separate 'marginal' or '*frontier*' type, as Wirth suggested? Certainly they differ from the main 'irredentist' category in the greater intensity of their nationalism, but this is not surprising, given their aims and situation. But the main reason for not classifying them separately is that they aspire, not to a separate group existence, but to an absorption into the 'mother-culture'. They are not cases at all, on our definition, only inflamed appendages of the main 'irredentist' movement, even where they are the historical originators.[25]

The 'independence' criterion

In the preceding discussion we could not avoid reference to the stage of the nationalist movement. Here the great divide is the attainment of independence, i.e. *de facto* sovereignty, which creates two categories, pre- and post-independence movements, according to whether the 'group' for which the movement is striving is independent or not.

All the types of movement we have considered so far can be classified as '*Pre-Independence*' movements; the first consideration for the nationalist was freedom from control by 'hostile others' and the rapid achievement of self-rule. But suppose now that the answer to his first question about independence is: 'My' group has for long been sovereign, or has just attained independence; I must strengthen it and maintain this state, by preserving the *status quo*, or reviving its group will and identity, by expanding or unifying the group, or by increasing its self-reliance. All movements which return this kind of reply to the 'independence' question we shall call '*Post-Independence*' movements.

Strictly speaking, this latter term is slightly misleading. Two main kinds of answer were in fact given to the question: that where the 'group' (whether homogeneous or not) had been long free from 'alien' control, e.g. Siam, Ethiopia, and that of cases of recent attainment of sovereignty, e.g. Gabon, Burma. This bifurcation in historic conditions leads to correspondingly different emphases in the aims of the nationalist movements.

The main types of 'Post-Independence' movements closely follow the answers to the perceived need to maintain independence. In long sovereign states, there are two main varieties, '*Preservation*' and '*Renewal*' nationalisms. In the former, a ruling culturally demarcated group aims by a mixture of discriminatory and homogenising measures to perpetuate its caste-like rule, while posing as the champions of the whole unit in opposition to the outside world. The Ethiopian Amhara and the Afghan Pushtu aim to create an Ethiopian and Afghan national identity in all their subject ethnic peoples, while preserving their cultural and political supremacy. Their culture becomes that of the projected larger group. The main method is to absorb the most talented Galla or Tajiks, etc., into the dominant culture and hierarchy.[26]

'Renewal' nationalisms occur, by contrast, in culturally homogeneous groups. They usually start, again in opposition to the 'Preservation' type, outside the main centres of power, and if allied to social discontents, are directed against the incumbent ruler or regime, as in the Puritan, French, Chinese (Sun Yat-Sen), Persian, Swiss (eighteenth century), and Turkish (Kemalist) revolutions. All these movements operate in settings of, at least nominal, independence from ancient times, and in ethnically (almost) homogeneous groups. What then is the nationalist complaint? Simply that both the 'homogeneity' and the 'independence' of the group are endangered. The social dislocations produced by the onset of capitalism, and later industrialism, combined with the rulers' policies of concessions and privileges for foreigners, have brought a paralysis of the collective will and a loss of communal purpose and integrity. This can only be remedied by the infusion of a new spirit and moral purpose into the 'body politic' and the society, involving its modernisation and reintegration through sweeping changes. The ensuing revolution is as much a nationalist as a class-motivated phenomenon. In varying degrees, innovations felt to be necessary by nationalists are legitimated in terms of an ideal pristine Golden Age, or ancient model (Sparta), and the latter serves as a standard and goad against the lamentable present social divisions and political lethargy. [27]

In groups that have but recently attained independence, three kinds of nationalism appear. As would be expected, they tend to be the continuation of the 'pre-independence' phase of the movement. The first type is the '*Integration*' movement, the 'post-independence' successor to the 'territorial heterogeneous' variety. The aim is to weld a 'nation' out of the disparate cultural groups that make up the ex-colonial unit. There is no question here of rejuvenating an ancient and declined society, but the founding of a new and modern culture and society through political action. Of course, 'ethnic' nationalisms, after attaining independence, are eager to integrate co-nationals, or gather them in, but 'secession' and 'diaspora' movements are more concerned with cultural and economic individuality and survival, while 'Pan' and 'irredentist' movements are more interested in power and status through expansion. It is the 'territorial heterogeneous' type that is primarily concerned with cohesion and fraternity as an antidote to social disintegration. [28]

The second kind of nationalism, '*Protectionism*', often appears among 'Territorial cross-culture' movements. Unable to lay claim to cultural individuality, but fervently desirous of maintaining a hard-won independence, such movements stress the need for economic self-sufficiency against the competition of the more powerful foreigner. In this way, 'protection' nationalists, as in some of the Latin American states today, sharpen the boundaries and identity of the group, by making nationals conscious of the desirability of self-reliance, as well as the sacrifices entailed. [29]

Finally, there are '*Expansion*' nationalisms, which appear mainly as continuations of 'Ethnic irredentist/Pan' movements. The drive to satisfy power and status aspirations attributed to the group underlies the aim of incorporating the territory, as well as its co-national inhabitants, into the group's new state. These are the cases of frustrated aggression on which the Fascist ideology and tactics feeds best, as in Italy and Germany after independence. They are hardly a separate caregory, unless we include 'imperialism' under this heading. The Moroccan-Algerian or Kashmiri disputes are, from one standpoint, cases of 'expansion' nationalisms.

It will be clear by now that the correspondence between 'pre-' and 'post-independence' movements is only rough, and in given cases there is a mixing of elements of the various types, which is more marked after than before independence. There is, however, considerable overlap between the two groups of movement and we can tabulate the rough correspondence as follows:

		INDEPENDENCE	
		Pre-independence	*Post-independence*
DISTINCTIVENESS	*Territorial*	Heterogeneous————————Integration	
		Cross-Cultural ————————Protection	
	Mixed	....	Preservation*
	Ethnic	Secession/Diaspora	Renewal*
		Irredentism/Pan————————Expansion	

* The nationalisms take place in States that have long been sovereign.

The dotted lines indicate the lack of complete correspondence. At the same time, after independence the 'Mixed' cases come to resemble the 'Preservation' type sociologically, despite the fact that the latter refer to polities that have been long independent, whereas the former occur in the new states and colonies. The same ambivalence marks the correspondence between 'Ethnic secession' and 'Renewal' categories. But, as Bernard Lewis has argued in the case of Kemalist nationalism, 'Renewal' movements have strong secessionist tendencies. The culturally 'native' rulers are considered effete and hostile to the interests of the national group —just as the Tokugawa Shogun was thought of by the Meiji restoration movement, or Farouk and the Wafd by the Free Officers. By extension, these are cases of the formation of a new polity out of the womb of the old, oppressive and discriminatory one. We may perhaps expect 'Renewal' movements to occur from time to time in ethnically homogeneous milieux, when the impetus of the first 'secession/diaspora' movement has dried up.[30]

To bring the formal and substantive criteria together, I append two tables of types of nationalisms, with examples. But I should stress that a given case of nationalism may well be classified under more than one heading—given the complexity of most group situations.

TABLE 4   A TYPOLOGY OF NATIONALISMS

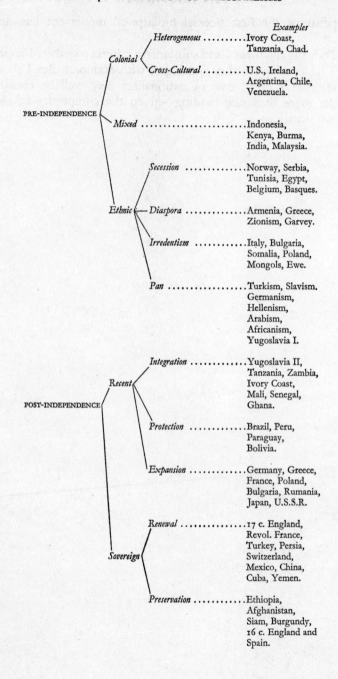

Examples

PRE-INDEPENDENCE

Colonial

Heterogeneous .... Ivory Coast, Tanzania, Chad.

Cross-Cultural .... U.S., Ireland, Argentina, Chile, Venezuela.

Mixed .... Indonesia, Kenya, Burma, India, Malaysia.

Ethnic

Secession .... Norway, Serbia, Tunisia, Egypt, Belgium, Basques.

Diaspora .... Armenia, Greece, Zionism, Garvey.

Irredentism .... Italy, Bulgaria, Somalia, Poland, Mongols, Ewe.

Pan .... Turkism, Slavism. Germanism, Hellenism, Arabism, Africanism, Yugoslavia I.

POST-INDEPENDENCE

Recent

Integration .... Yugoslavia II, Tanzania, Zambia, Ivory Coast, Mali, Senegal, Ghana.

Protection .... Brazil, Peru, Paraguay, Bolivia.

Expansion .... Germany, Greece, France, Poland, Bulgaria, Rumania, Japan, U.S.S.R.

Sovereign

Renewal .... 17 c. England, Revol. France, Turkey, Persia, Switzerland, Mexico, China, Cuba, Yemen.

Preservation .... Ethiopia, Afghanistan, Siam, Burgundy, 16 c. England and Spain.

TABLE 5 TYPES OF NATIONALIST MOVEMENT

FORMAL (Intensity and Achievement) by SUBSTANTIVE (Distinctiveness and Independence) CRITERIA

	TERRITORIAL				MIXED	ETHNIC					
	Pre-Independence Hetero-geneous	Post-Independence Inte-gration	Pre-Independence Cross-Cultural	Post-Independence Pro-tection	Mixed and Pre-servation*	Secession	Pre-Independence Diaspora	Irre-dentism	Pan	Post-Independence Renewal*	Expansion
PRIMITIVE — FAILED	Congo, Brazil, Gabon, Sierra Leone		South U.S.		Persia	Zealots, Arauca-nians, Tibetans, Achinese, Konzo, Kikuyu, Chagga, Copts, Corsicans, Oirots, Uigurs	Druse		Latin Americanism	Denmark	Egypt, Philistines, Elamites, Canaan-ites, Arameans
PRIMITIVE — SUCCESSFUL		Prussia, Burgundy	Australia, New Zealand, Canada, Brazil, Ecuador, Colombia	Brazil, Peru, Venezuela, Chile, Argentina	Ethiopia, Afghani-stan, 16 c. England, Sweden (17 c.), Lebanon	Holland, S. Arabia, Ecuador, Yemen, Scots, Swaziland				Sassanid Persia, Pagan Burma, Burma, Bulgars, T'ang China	Assyria, Hittites, Egypt, Rome (Italy), Lydia, Carthage
DEVELOPED — FAILED					Yugoslavia (pre-1945), Tsarism, Hungary	Ukrainians, Serbs, Croats, Tatars, Kazakhs, Uzbeks, Karen, Georgians, Biafrans	Armenians, Garveyism	Italy, Poland, Somalia, Bulgaria, Ewe, Mongols, BaKongo	Turkism, Hellenism, Negroism, Slavism	Peru, Dominican Republic	Germany, Greece, France, Poland, Italy, Japan
DEVELOPED — SUCCESSFUL	Tanzania, Zambia, Ivory Coast, Guinea, Mali	Yugoslavia (post 1945), Ghana, Tanzania, Mali, Zambia, Kenya, Uganda, Albania, India	U.S., Ireland, Argentina, Venezuela, Chile, Haiti		Burma, Indonesia, Malaysia, South Africa, Rhodesia	Norway, Czechs, Pakistan, Belgium, Tunisia, Finland, Egypt (1922), (South) Yemen, Boers	Zionism, Greece, Liberia		Germany, Yugoslavia, Mongolia	17 c. England Rev., France, Turkey, Mexico, Persia, China, Switzerland, Cuba, Egypt (1952), Japan	
CURRENT	Mozambique, Angola	South Vietnam				Welsh, Naga, Quebecois, Bretons, Basques, Anguillans	Palestinians	Kurds, Somalis, Tyrolese	Africanism, Arabism, Europe-anism	Cambodia	

These are types of 'Sovereign' Nationalisms, where the entity has enjoyed a long history of de facto independence (pre-independence Mixed types are very rare, e.g. Upper Volta).

Chapter Ten

'DUAL LEGITIMATION': THE MATRIX OF ETHNIC NATIONALISM

One of the most interesting of the types of nationalism, which were reviewed in the last chapter, was the 'ethnic' variety—particularly in its 'pre-independence' phase. Now that the tasks of critical evaluation of theories, of definition and of classification of nationalism have been completed, as far as was possible, an attempt must be made to tackle that most difficult task—the provision of a theory. In the belief that it is more profitable to investigate the rise of one variety of nationalist movement and compare cases falling under that rubric, I have chosen the 'ethnic' type, because there are a number of well-documented nationalisms in this group. At the same time, I know of no attempt to compare and explain their emergence—unless Gellner's and Kedourie's theories are meant to cover this type solely, and not all nationalist movements, as they seem to imply. The second reason for choosing the pre-independence 'ethnic' category is the desire to adumbrate an alternative model, and build on factors which these writers neglect to some extent. This ties in with my conviction that political and religious conflicts and problems are of greater importance in the rise of nationalism—particularly among the intelligentsia on whom this chapter concentrates—than language and class conflict.

The 'Scientific State'

The starting-point is the distinction drawn earlier between two kinds of nationalism, ethnocentric and polycentric. The former or 'weaker' kind was a movement of resistance to foreign rule in order to preserve the group's culture and freedom. The outsider was the 'barbarian', the 'heathen'; and value pertained only to one's own group and its gods. The 'polycentric' kind of nationalism sees the world as divided into nations, or collective individualities, each with its own 'value', each requiring a state of its own to realise its communal potential and sovereign autonomy, and each seeking to join the 'family of nations' by contributing its peculiar experiences to the common fund of humanity.

The question then becomes: how does the transition from the ethnocentric to the polycentric kind of nationalism come about? How does the monocentric and solipsist nationalism give way—if it does—to the pluralist vision of group autonomy and popular sovereignty? This is particularly interesting and significant in the 'ethnic' type of nationalism, where the transition, as one might expect, is hardest to make.[1]

Two historical sequences form the essential background for my model of the rise of ethnic nationalism. They are:

Empire ────────────⟶ 'Scientific State' ───⟶ Nation-State
'Possessive State' ───⟶ 'Scientific State' ───⟶ Nation-State

These two progressions are, of course, ideal-types; there are many deviations from them, and there is no inexorability about these sequences. For all its trappings, the Soviet Union could still be called an 'empire', for example.

The key to my analysis is the concept of the *'scientific state'*. The latter is a polity which seeks to homogenise the population within its boundaries for administrative purposes by utilising the latest scientific techniques and methods for the sake of 'efficiency'. The rulers use the bureaucratic machine and the fruits of scientific research and technological application to harness resources and mobilise the people in their territory. We are not dealing here simply with a centralising tendency, though that too is important. What matters is the new 'interventionist' role of the State—on the grounds that it alone can raise the living standards of the population, educate them, unify them, give them a sense of pride and well-being, and administer public affairs in a 'rational' and calculative manner.

This ideal-typical kind of State arose historically from two main types of political unit—empires and 'possessive states', or a certain type of patrimonialism. The following is a necessarily brief review of selected features of these polities.

The features bequeathed by empires to the 'scientific state' are of two sorts. First, there is the element of *'conquest'*. The first stage of many empires is a 'conquest' one, where the new conquerors form a dominant caste and monopolise all the high status positions in the empire. The Egyptian New Kingdom seems to have done this in Palestine and Syria; and the Mongol Khanates in the thirteenth and fourteenth centuries in Central Asia and Russia, as well as the Achaemenid Persian empire with its satrap administration, kept the governmental and high status positions for their own conquering ethnic group.[2]

But this state of affairs soon proves unstable. Even where the conquerors leave the mores and structures of the dominated intact, as did even the Assyrians on occasion or the later Mongol dynasties, such as the Persian Il-khans, a situation based solely on coercion and the isolation of the upper caste proves increasingly unfeasible. The conquest stage then yields to a *'cosmopolitan'* one. High status positions are thrown open to ever wider circles of people on the basis of merit or wealth, and the culture and religion of the conquerors become syncretistic. At Rome all gods were welcome.

The theoretical position of this 'cosmopolitan' type of imperium is admirably summarised in the famous speech of Claudius on the admission of the Gauls to the Senate, in which he makes it his policy to 'bring excellence to Rome from whatever source'. What proved fatal, he says, to Sparta and Athens, 'for all their military strength, was their segregation of conquered subjects as aliens'. Speaking of the conquered Gauls, he adds:

> Now that they have assimilated our customs and culture and married into our families, let them bring in their gold and wealth rather than keep it to themselves.[3]

This policy of enlightened self-interest paid off in the second century A.D.!

The two elements of 'conquest' segregation and 'cosmopolitan' assimilation are ingredients of the typical policies of what I have called the 'scientific state'. But there is a third source of its character: I mean the 'personalist' levelling and homogenising features of the European patrimonial states.

An illuminating account of the evolution of the Western type of *'possessive state'*, from its inception in the Norman experiments in eleventh-century Sicily to the great Tudor and Bourbon dynastic states of the early modern era, is presented by Adda Bozeman. [4] Such states are typically viewed as the personal possession of their rulers, client polities of individuals, whose resources and populations could be harnessed for personal-political ends. They are generally based on secular law, divorced from any theoretic notions; they are unified under a strong central government, whether of a monarch or an oligarchy of powerful families; their aim is to weld together into a compact solidary unit diverse cultures and religious groups; and they insist on their absolute sovereignty over their territory, which they look on as their personal resource. This was the ideal of the Normans and Frederick II in Sicily, of Philip the Fair and his Legalists *c.* 1300 in his dispute with Papal authority in France, and of the Tudor and Bourbon monarchs in England and France. [5] These personal-political ends of the rulers were increasingly conditioned by the system of European rivalries and alliances in the seventeenth and eighteenth centuries, when Prussia entered the 'balance of power' concert of absolutist states. Their ultimate effect was to encroach upon and pare down the independence of local and occupational or religious institutions.

These legacies of discrimination, assimilation, and levelling homogenisation of the population gradually spread to the East; and the contradictions, when applied to polyethnic empires such as the Tsarist, the Habsburg and to a lesser extent, the Ottoman, became insuperable.

But why did the rulers of these empires, Peter and Catherine, Maria Theresa and Joseph III, Selim II and Mahmud II, try to apply these principles? Why try to imitate the West?

Because by the eighteenth and nineteenth centuries, the impact of the scientific and technological revolutions of the West was too great to resist. For historical reasons, these revolutions appeared in fairly compact and homogeneous territories whose population possessed a relatively high sense of ethnic solidarity and esprit. That Holland, and more especially England, happened to be fairly liberal by this time, and in the throes of shaking off their authoritarian governments, appeared from the outside to be of little consequence—at any rate, for the time being. The Age of the Enlightenment is the age of increasing reform from above outside England, of increasing intervention by the state in the affairs of the individual, of a definite tendency to level down all intermediate structures between State and individual and tie the influential elites to the State's bureaucratic structure.

The 'possessive state' in the West turned into the 'scientific state'; and the polyethnic empires in the East tried to select from the successful models of the West those features most suited to their environment. In both cases, four elements were combined in varying degrees: assimilation of the population, discrimination against some of its subgroups, a levelling interventionism and centralisation, and finally, and most important, the attempt to apply the latest scientific methods and techniques to the problems of government.

The scientific-technological revolution, then, was mediated primarily through the agency of the increasingly powerful 'scientific state'. And this model was also applied in the nineteenth and twentieth centuries to the Western colonies of Asia and Africa. As Kautsky has stressed, the bureaucratic colonial governments in the underdeveloped areas were not merely conservative, but dynamic modernising agents of social change on a massive scale.

This is why the new type of state appeared so mechanical and lifeless to Schiller and Tagore, why the latter sees it as a kind of 'hydraulic press'—'an applied science and therefore more or less similar in its principles wherever it is used'.[6] The 'scientific state' was both impersonal and effective. It disrupted the old patterns, but constructed new ones. And all in the interests of the power and prestige of the ruling group. Efficiency became the criterion of power and status; and efficiency was increasingly measured by the extent of territory and size of population ruled, and by thorough utilisation of all the resources at the disposal of the rulers.[7]

One such resource was linguistic homogeneity. Obviously, one could administer a territory more effectively if public affairs were conducted in a single language. Hence the importance of the linguistic factor. If some groups within one's domains did not speak the language of the dominant group, the needs of the rulers for efficiency to match their rivals compelled them to homogenise and assimilate ethnic groups speaking other languages, or at least those among them who aspired to high status positions, especially in the government. But the legacy of discriminatory practices inherited from the 'conquest' phase of the empire's past now combined with the spiralling educational standards which resulted from the impact of science on organisation. The result was a fatal contradiction. The tests of admission to the ruling group grew ever higher and more difficult; the rulers were still swayed by this discriminatory legacy, yet simultaneously espoused an integrationist and universalist ethic, which, as we saw, also had its imperial precedents; but, to cap all this, there was the strong elite desire to turn their sprawling empires into compact 'possessive states' on the Anglo-French model, and utilise their scientific techniques which seemed to be so successful in the economic, military and political fields.

Language is important, then, as one of the modes of homogenising a population. Yet it is a dependent variable. It is also only one of the methods of integration. The Russification policy of Nicholas I, for example, was a religious policy of conversion—to remove hitherto unassimilable groups, such as the Jews; much as Catherine II's predecessors had tried with the Tatars.[8]

The second point is that language homogenisation, and other types of integration policies in polyethnic settings, produce what one may call *'sociological minorities'*. These are groups, with a distinctive culture within a large political unit, who, as a result of these policies of integration, become permanently oppressed. They are excluded from the privileges of the new scientific society; but the novelty in their situation is that they are made to become conscious of the fact—particularly if the rulers favour some groups and not others. Moreover, their exclusion *en masse* (a few educated and wealthy individuals, perhaps, pass the admission tests) is the more intolerable, as Gellner says, exactly because the usual legitimations for inequality are absent. One can go further. The proclaimed intention of these rulers is the welfare and progress of their subjects. It is, after all, for the first time in history a feasible proposition that the mass of the people can leave behind their age-long poverty and ignorance. The new 'scientific states' are based on an ethic of collective welfare and progress, whatever the actual practice. And the rulers' justification for intervention and innovation on this scale is the promise of man-made salvation.

Particularly in a polyethnic setting, therefore, the 'scientific state' is a powerful solvent of the traditional order. It is an intervening stage, unstable but dynamic, between the old order and the new.

'Dual legitimation'

But why does the 'scientific state' erode traditional societies? There are a number of reasons, some of which have been already discussed in evaluating other theories. The reason, however, which I wish to emphasise, and which has been rather neglected, is the central attack which is now made upon traditional religion.

The greatest danger to traditional societies of the advent of the 'scientific state' is its challenge to the *cosmic image* of the religious *Weltanschauung*.

Every society has to face the familiar 'problem of meaning' in its various aspects. For this end, if for no other, an image of the total order of the universe is built up. And the religious idea of a divine 'cosmos' over and above what men experienced in their daily existence helped to explain and justify, intellectually and emotionally, the 'imperfections of the world' and man's suffering.[9] Before the scientific revolution, 'nature' and 'society', those modern abstractions, were but rarely conceived of as separable spheres within a supraempirical order. Whereas, for us, they may seem to balance, reflect, or compensate for, the structural organisation and values of this world, for 'traditional man' they form an indivisible whole. The idea of the cosmos impregnates 'nature' and 'society'—or validates both as the true reality behind the 'smokescreen' of appearances of this world.[10] Of course, the details of these cosmic images varied greatly; but they can all be seen as so many 'salvation dramas' of a trans-historical kind leading to an ultimate 'higher harmony' beyond the comprehension of finite minds and partial visions—the kind of higher harmony against which Ivan Karamazov so bitterly inveighs.[11]

These cosmic images contained what Weber means by '*theodicies*'—resolutions of social psychological needs to explain human suffering and evil, which arise from men's experience of the discrepancy between destiny and merit.[12] Man was viewed as sinful, but capable of redemption. 'Power' and 'value' were attributes of the cosmos, not of man nor society nor history. Authority belonged to the cosmic order, since only it had a plan and purpose, however inscrutable.

This aspect of the model has been deliberately oversimplified, since it forms a backcloth to the analysis. Of course, there has been a vast range of religious attitudes to the 'Welt' in so-called traditional societies, almost as great as the historical and social variation in the structure of those societies.[13] This range of cultural attitudes is paralleled by an equally great variety of relationships between Church and State, which have been the subject of a typology arousing considerable controversy.[14] All I want to say here is that, with few exceptions, before the scientific revolution, religion has provided the basic assumptions upon which social and political institutions have been founded; and that religious organisations or groups have legitimated the activities of all public and private enterprises. Even in that most secular of ancient societies, Greece, religious sanctions and pretexts had to be invoked before the Peloponnesian and other wars.[15]

This was the kind of world from which the rising intelligentsia were now exiled under the pressure of the 'scientific state'. For the latter challenged, objectively and subjectively, both the validity and the utility of these traditional cosmic images and their corresponding ethic.

The nature of the 'intelligentsia' has already been examined in chapter 6. Its members come from all ranks of society. Their differentiating characteristic is exposure to higher education in some form. They usually aspire to professional positions in society or to public affairs. But initially, at any rate, they tend to be drawn from the sons of the traditional elites—often from the ranks of traditional scholars. Subsequently, they are exposed to the influence of 'western ideas' through travel or study, or both. And so, in this well-documented fashion, they become *doubly socialised*. For—and this is where the analysis departs from the simpliste diffusionism of the 'imitation mechanism'—they remain, for all their cultural alienation from the traditional society into which they were born, part of that society. Their first inspiration, their first exposure, if you like, is to their ancient tradition. I speak here, it must be recalled, of people who belong to groups with pre-existent cultural ties, i.e. with a fairly strong sense of cohesion and cultural distinctiveness—since it is the roots of *ethnic* nationalism that are in question.

These men who come to feel the impact of the 'scientific state', who see its material and psychological benefits—these men have already been impregnated with the sentiment of loyalty to the values of their group, and have been impressed with the power of the traditional cosmic image which expresses the outlook of the group. The revelation to Moses or Muhammad, the incarnation of Christ, the Enlightenment of Buddha, the invocation of Krishna or Kali, are the deepest cognitive and experiential roots of a whole communal order and set of loyalties into which these men have been socialised.

It is this prior socialisation into the traditional image and ethic, and into the whole network of social relations which have been gradually built up around these convictions and prescriptions, that makes the confrontation between the modern 'scientific state' and the old cosmic outlook so serious. It is a total dilemma —in the mind and in daily action a difficult and painful choice is continually posed.

The dilemma can be elaborated in the following manner. Basically, it was a 'crisis of authority'. The efficacy of the 'scientific state' challenged that of the traditional cosmic image. Physically, this modern type of state made inroads into the ethnic community. Culturally and psychologically, it undermined the assumptions and norms on which the group's activities were premissed.

There are two ways in which the 'scientific state' makes its power felt. The first is direct. Avineri has recently collected Marx's writings on colonialism and modernisation in Asia especially; and Marx is only one of the first of a long line of thinkers who have emphasised the exploitative, dislocating and yet productive and 'progressive' role of such colonialism, especially when it is imposed directly, as in India. The trouble with this line of theorising, as I already said, is that:

> Marx's sole criteria for judging the social revolution imposed on Asia are those of European, bourgeois society itself. Since Marx's socialism is a dialectical outcome of the *Aufhebung*, transcendence, of European bourgeois civilisation, he sees little reason to look for autochthonous roots of socialism in non-European society.[16]

For socialism, read 'nationalism'; and the identical criticism applies. At the same time, one cannot doubt the immense impact of the European-originating 'scientific state' in its direct economic and political modernising activities.

The other way in which the modern state makes itself felt is 'from afar', i.e. through the demonstration effect. This was especially true of Ottoman Turkey, where many of the rising intelligentsia looked to France, its power, order, rationality, progress and esprit. Especially to its freedom to innovate and to institute planned change. [17]

Here, however, interest is centred more on the direct impact of the 'scientific state'—not only in Eastern Europe, but also in those parts of Asia and Africa, *where* there were compact and culturally distinctive ethnic groups—for example, the Ibo and Yoruba, the Ashanti and Baganda, the Ewe and BaKongo, the Arabs, the Tatars and Uzbeks, the Hindus and Muslims of India, the Burmese and Khmers. [18]

For these groups, the dilemma posed by the 'scientific state' was acute. The fundamental and inescapable fact was this: this new homogenising and levelling state, based on scientific innovation, completely undermined the beliefs, practices, precepts and organisation of the traditional religion.

In every sector—war, administration, taxation, communications, trade, education, security, law and morals, even aesthetic taste and fashions—the scientific, homogenising state became the supreme regulative organ, the apex and coordinator of endeavours in hitherto unrelated fields. Gradually it provided the framework by which all activities could be compared and evaluated. The state was no longer a fairly static political structure, making periodic incursions in haphazard fashion into the lives of the ordinary villagers. [19] It was now seen in an entirely new light: as the dynamic agent for realising long-shelved projects, as a machine for harnessing untapped resources of all kinds, as a tool for creating uniformity, and for converting diverse social and cultural allegiances into a single political loyalty. The 'scientific state' took on the appearance, not only of a levelling 'hydraulic press', but of an active, unfolding principle, forcing an entry for the collective good into inaccessible areas of social life.

The basis for the claim to authority by the 'scientific state' was not simply superior force. Its claim lay in its possession of rational, effective knowledge; and further, in its ability and resources to use that knowledge for alleviating misery and injustice. It was, in the consciousness of the rising intelligentsia, the agent as well as the product of scientific knowledge. To them, it appeared to fuse '*power*' with '*value*'. That is, it seemed *capable* of 'delivering the goods', of eradicating poverty, ignorance, disease, even inequality and injustice—all the problems that the old theodicies had tried to 'transcend' and relativise;[20] and it also seemed to be a *beneficial* instrument for the salvation of man, to offer a new vision of man as able to redeem himself, to eliminate all the injustices and deprivations that had been his lot.

But there was a price for all this. Till now, God had been endowed with the attributes of 'power' and 'value'. The divine order had seemed omnipotent and perfect—compensating for the imperfections of the world. God had been the '*maker of history*'. Or, as in some Eastern religious conceptions, history and the world had been viewed as illusory, and reality lay elsewhere. In either case, another order had relativised and transcended the empirical world.

Now there was an alternative set of assumptions and values to hand. Worse still, for the believer, the 'scientific state', by its own inner logic, compelled men to choose between it and the old cosmic image. The crux of the matter was that the 'scientific state' demanded a heavy price for its benefits: it demanded ineluctably the 'privatisation' of religion. The writ of religion must no longer run in the affairs of state or in social relationships. The greater part of a man's actions must be based on the scientific assumptions and methods of the new type of authority.

So it was that the manifest power of the 'scientific state' challenged the authority of the religious world-image, of the divine order, and of the Deity. It was the state, and no longer God, which 'made history'. The shaking of trust in divine authority underlies the crisis of faith among the intelligentsia, and the clash between reason and revelation, science and tradition, sons and fathers, which so agitates them.

For belief and faith are founded on authority. Concerning the supraempirical, we tend to accept cosmic images on trust. If the confidence in their intramundane efficacy is shaken, the belief itself is endangered. Not intellectual arguments, but demonstrations of effectiveness in the world, uphold conviction. The belief in a history-making providence was shattered by the potency of that engine of science, the interventionist state, and its repeated and repeatable successes. Besides the latter, the ancient prophetic miracles which lay at the root of the validation of all religious traditions, paled into antiquarian irrelevance.

This crisis of authority which shatters ancient convictions is the situation of *'dual legitimation'*. The intelligentsia, and after them all other groups, enter into a split heritage. They are confronted with two sources of 'authority' which demand unconditional allegiance. The challenge of the 'scientific state' to the cosmic images is all-pervading. The historical lot of the intelligentsia, the 'logic of their situation', imposes a far-reaching decision.

The reactions of the intelligentsia

The contradiction at the heart of the situation of 'dual legitimation' has, I think, three logical resolutions. And it is along these three paths that the intelligentsia painfully divides.

1 The 'scientific state' was, historically, a peculiarly 'western' and alien instrument. As the essential motor of all major innovation, it would naturally evoke a double fear in the minds of conservatives and traditionalists. It diminished their authority and it removed the entire basis for their *raison d'être*. For even where the rulers tried to keep the religious structures and customs intact, and not offend their subjects' sensitivities, the 'scientific state' posed a grave threat to religious tradition and authority. In Malaya, for example, the British tried hard not to interfere with the indigenous beliefs and religious customs; yet their levelling and centralising policies inevitably encroached on the authority of the religious leaders, who were reorganised into a central administrative system, and this made them increasingly appendages of British advisers in all matters. [21] To a lesser extent, the same process of centralising efficiency undermined the position of the Patriarchate in Ottoman Constantinople, though at first it seemed to enhance it. [22]

The reaction of the orthodox to the challenge of the 'scientific state' was to deny its 'value' and 'power'. To the *'traditionalist'*, science and modernisation are, by and large, sinful and so really 'powerless'. For authority must be legitimate, grounded on revealed truth, not man-made pragmatic success. And science could not solve the 'real', i.e. religious, problems. Religion and science were incompatible. They spoke different languages. Hence to attempt a dialogue or synthesis between them could only bring moral and intellectual confusion.

The 'traditionalist', then, is the man who has understood the costs and implications of accepting modernisation, and found them too high for the benefits offered by the new 'devil'—the 'scientific state'. His choice is quite rational, given his premisses. And in practice, he is usually quite consistent in opting for a theocracy to safeguard the value of his tradition and its cosmic image. Curiously, his attitude can sometimes become transformed into a kind of Zealot 'ethnocentric' nationalism. Perhaps this was Afghani's real attitude, when he espoused a politicised pan-Islamism. [23] It is certainly the basis of the Muslim Brotherhood (often dubbed 'neo-traditionalist') and of Mau Mau or some of the Panslavists and the French clerical monarchists like Maurras and Barrès. [24]

2 The second position is that of the *assimilationist*. His attitude is equally decisive. The 'scientific state' has rendered the gods impotent. Allegiance must therefore be transferred to the only *effective* 'authority'. Only the State can 'deliver the goods', notably the material ones so long denied to the toiling peasantry or the rootless and underemployed urban worker, but also the cultural needs which centre on the old 'problem of meaning'. The 'scientific state' can now solve in a radically new manner the age-long problems of contingency, scarcity and impotence. [25] The new solution was not cognitive and emotional, but social and practical. Science, abundance and equality were the respective solutions to the old problems; and the agent of all this was the 'scientific state'. The price therefore was eminently worthwhile, and allegiance must be given to its demands. A set of problems conceived in supramundane terms were transformed by the power of the 'scientific state' into terrestrial ones soluble by the active effort of a common humanity. Man, stripped of his traditional dependency on the divine and his embeddedness in his particularist settings, could lift himself up to procure his own salvation by rational planning and a pooling of all his resources. It is to this type of a common humanity that the so-called westerniser with messianic expectations wishes to 'assimilate'. To become a citizen of the world is, in his view, the price that is required by the 'scientific state'; and he is only too glad to pay it.

3 The third, and for my purposes most important, way out of the impasse of 'dual legitimation' is the *reformist*.

The 'reformist' acknowledges the twin sources of authority, the divine order and the 'scientific state'; but, instead of opting for either, tries to combine them in a new synthesis which, he hopes, will transcend their tension. At worst, this solution is sheer eclecticism, a superficial reconciling of opposites which are irreconcilable. At best, it is a profound attempt to combine and harmonise in a new synthesis the genuine elements within the religious tradition and the true principles of modernisation which the 'scientific state' embodies.

'Reformists' must be clearly distinguished from the religious reformers of previous ages. Very briefly, past reformers were only concerned with necessary amendments to the tradition to prevent its ossification and decay. Theirs was a *limited reform*; a struggle of the socially aspirant to bring ritual and precept into line with communal change and new conditions—against the old interpretation of the tradition and its exponents. This goes some way to accounting for the fact that tradition is never completely static. All societies seek 'progress' *in their own terms*, and movements of 'progress', 'reform', schisms, etc., generally alternate with periods of stabilisation and petrifaction. Buddhism and Jainism can be seen as reform movements within the Hindu tradition; the Cluniac reform, the Karaites and Mu'tazilah represented attempts to amend and augment the received tradition within Catholicism, Judaism and Islam; and the Orphic and Dionysiac movements of ancient Greece were looked upon as filling out and making more meaningful the traditional aristocratic Olympian religion in the changing conditions of the sixth and fifth centuries. [26] Yet, for all this change, the earlier reform movements never stepped outside the tradition. They never questioned the basic cosmic image, even where they amended the ethic. They could never conceive of existence outside such a supra-empirical and transcendental order.

'Reformists', on the other hand, *do* step outside this basic conceptual framework. They look back at it, as it were, from the outside to discover what is of essential value in the ancient tradition. Theirs are movements of *continual reform*, which questions the cosmic base as well as the social ethic and the ritual and organisation. The 'reformist' movement may perhaps start as another minor movement of 'limited reform' against some meaningless custom, some irksome precept; but soon it appeals to the rationale of the 'scientific state', to the principles which it embodies. This is what happened among the Hadramis of Singapore, when a dispute between the Sayyids and the Irshadi over the marriage of a Sadah (the upper stratum) to an Indian Muslim led to an appeal to Rashid Rida's 'reformist' paper, *Manar*; and he in turn pronounced against the traditional descent criterion in favour of the modernist one of 'achievement'.[27] So the Irshadi Reform and Guidance Association of 1914 became the agent of unintended changes far broader than the original issue and calling into question the total social and political ranking system and assumptions of the Hadramaut.

The central point about 'reformist' movements is that, whatever their origins, they legitimise themselves in terms of the modernist principles of the 'scientific state'; and they then find themselves caught up in the tide of a current, as it were, which leads them far further than they intended. For example, the Jewish reform movement of the early nineteenth century in Germany started from changes in aesthetic modes of synagogal services and liturgy; but its appeal to external criteria outside the tradition, i.e. criteria of 'science' which appeared so potent in the political and economic spheres in Prussia and some other German principalities, led the reformers into a process of continual revision which came to embrace every sphere affected by the traditional religion—that is, most of life for the Jews of the period.[28]

'Reformists', in short, come to question the basic cosmic image of the traditional religion. They see it for the first time 'from the outside'. It becomes one among many such images. It can be compared (with other like images), analysed, sifted, reinterpreted, evaluated. It is suddenly 'over there', at a distance. It is no longer all-encompassing, unquestioned, unself-consciously 'mine' and 'right'. However noble and rich, it becomes one 'world' among 'many'; and one is free to step into other worlds of meaning and value. *The* world is no longer an interwoven unity. It is a patchwork of fragments, like the compartmentalisation of activities which often, or so it appears, accompanies modernisation. And these fragments we are free to barter—at a cost. The sole world of Othello made of 'one entire and perfect chrysolite' has now become a confederation of many chrysolites, each with its own virtue.[29]

In this way the situation of 'dual legitimation' weighs most heavily with the 'reformist'. He internalises those principles of the 'scientific state'—its 'urge' for continual change, and its application to every sector of life. But at the same time he holds to the traditional cosmic image of his forefathers into which he was socialised. He recognises two sources of authority; he can deny neither, and identify with neither. The protective circle of his cosmic identity is broken; but he cannot follow the 'assimilationist' and find a replacement in a purely social identity. He holds to God and the State, cosmos and society, believer and citizen, as his ground of thought and action.[30]

But this state of suspended animation cannot serve long as a basis for action. The question of reconciling them on a 'higher' plane becomes inescapable. The two sources of authority must somehow be fused.

This is achieved through the idea of *'providential deism'*. Put simply, this holds that God works in the world *through* the 'scientific state'. Against the messianic 'assimilationist', the 'reformist' argues that God does make history and that it is His plan that man is fulfilling through the agency of the 'scientific state'. The power still rests with God; only His intention is that man be His co-worker, that man intervene in history, control his environment, master nature, strive towards self-perfection. Only then, through man's efforts, will the age of social justice and freedom reign on earth.

'God helps all those who help themselves' is the motto of all 'reformists', all those who understand by religion a confessional, naturalistic, civic, universalist and above all ethical gospel of tolerant brotherhood. God is indeed in history; for He is commanding man to use his faculties of reason continuously for progress. God's providential foresight will bring man to the realisation of the design inhering in the universe, and the upward spiral of history. Man's duty is to hasten the time when the course of history will bring society into line with a divine order conceived on the model of Paley's Watch.

The main precondition, however, of this golden age to come and of man's agency is the total *reformation* of the religious culture and tradition of the community. It must be adapted to man's continually changing 'needs', and to society's 'spirit of the age'. Theology, ritual, organisation, above all, education, must be overhauled and 'rationalised'. Meaningless accretions, superstitions, archaic formalisms, literalist interpretations, constricted horizons, must be swept away; and only those features of the tradition which can pass the 'test of reason' should remain. For the rest, the general ethical principles of 'civilised society' must inform faith in the heart of the 'reasonable man'. Natural religion becomes ethical religion, the 'religion of virtue'.[31]

The 'revivalist' heresy

The 'reformist', however, is now beset by new problems, social and intellectual. It can be asked: what is left of the religion, when all that fails the 'test of reason' is thrown out? Can we avoid crossing over into messianic 'assimilationism'? Does the cosmic image retain any hold still? Which of our decisions and social arrangements depend for their sanction on the religious image and tradition? Can we avoid secularism?

But the failure to find concrete expression for a rationalist religion of such optimism is only one difficulty. Equally serious for 'reformists' was their failure to agree on any criteria for modernising their religion and adapting it to present needs. These needs are in a continual state of flux, the 'spirit of the age' is an ephemeral will-of-the-wisp. Can one construct a religious community on this fragile basis? Must there not be some cohesive and durable elements in a religion to replace the admittedly outworn tradition, but yet enable one to reconstruct the basic outlook and ethic of the community? An uninstitutionalised religion, based on mere enthusiasm, cannot suffice; for the respect and awe in which religion is held derives in part from this element of social continuity and self-maintenance.[32]

One might call this problem of finding the *constant* elements in a religious tradition and image the problem of its '*essence*'. The criterion then for 'drawing the line' in religio-educational reform is turned into the question of discovering an agreed 'essence' of religious belief and practice.

It might at this point be objected: why are the 'reformists' dissatisfied with a set of abstract rational principles as the essence of their religion? The answer is that such principles, if discoverable, would be too general. They would be pitched at too high a level to serve the needs of any concrete community, and would be generalisable to all cultures and societies. The purely universal implications of each religious tradition could only serve as the basis for a kind of eclectic 'religion-in-general', a world religion on the Bahai model. The motto of this type of religion is the saying of Baha'ullah:

> Everything is permissible that does not conflict with the common-sense of humanity.

And it is germane to my argument to note another of his precepts:

> It is no merit to love your fatherland, but to love the world.

The eclectic universalism of pure rationalist reformism leads to a cosmopolitan and non-nationalist outlook.[33]

But to return to the argument. A rationalist 'religion-in-general' is unable to serve as a guide for society as opposed to the individual. It cannot have anything useful to say about the problems of social order and change—as the old religious traditions once did. It is composed of a few rather vacuous, high-level principles, which cannot help man in his social existence. The 'reformist', therefore, is developing solely the *ethical* content of religion, has conceded too much to the 'assimilationist' attack. Total 'ethicisation' radicalises religion to the point of dissolving it.

The failures of religious reformists, in the cultural and social spheres, lead some among their number to seek for this elusive 'essence' of religion, which will serve as a social guide, in another place altogether: in the idea of the '*historical renovation*'.

I propose to call such people who break away from pure 'reformist' rationalism '*revivalists*'. But since this word has been used in another and simpler sense, my use of this term requires some explanation.

Religious revivalism usually means a fundamentalist return to uncorrupted Scripture coupled with pietistic inspiration and detailed fulfilment of the statutes of the tradition; a desire for a restoration of the primitive religious community and its religious relationship with the divine.[34]

The sense in which this term is utilised here is quite different. 'Revivalists' in my sense have a more complex vision. They hold that communities as a whole *re*discover God after a period of decline in faith, and they search for the constant 'essence' of religion in an idealised pristine age of religious faith which will serve them as a model for the task of future collective regeneration. (Other terms—'regenerationist', 'renovationist', etc.— would serve the purpose equally well, were these neologisms not so barbarous.) The nub, however, lies in the *interest* of this type of heretical reformist: his purpose is to conserve and salvage as much as possible from the communal tradition in order to regenerate his people spiritually. He believes that a moral revolution must precede a social and political one. He stands in the ancient Prophetic tradition, except that he is determined to come to terms with external political and social realities as he sees them, i.e. with scientific modernisation.

For the 'revivalist' the golden age of faith is also the golden age of communal splendour. He 'discovers' it in some period of the group's history—the Davidic kingdom, the Age of Companions, the Vedic ethos, the primitive Christian sectaries, etc. (there are usually a number of candidates for this honour, and some disagreements); but the point, of course, is that he can thereby hold up to his fellow men the purity of the past as a mirror for their 'glorious' future and an indictment of their 'shameful' present. That is his real purpose, and not disinterested historical research. He finds the 'essence' of his religion in the faith of an idealised past age, into which he reads all his aspirations for a future which will embody prized and 'unique' communal virtues. The blueprint for rebuilding the community's future so as to cope with present problems is provided by the glowing vision of the past.

This is the beginning of a gradual, often unperceived and unintended, *secularisation* of the 'reformist' position. The instability of the 'reformist' position leads apparently backwards to a new conservatism based on the religious tradition. But the appearance is often deceptive; what really happens is that the religious tradition is '*historicized*', it is fixed firmly to the concrete world of historical events (however selectively utilised). History is no longer the quarry for didactic illustration of religious doctrine; it is the anchor of the faith, and through its medium, using its precedent as legitimation for innovation, a subtle transformation is gradually worked.

The task of reforming a religious tradition requires knowledge of that tradition, and of the way in which it evolved. To distinguish 'essence' from 'accretion', substance beneath form, one must find an acceptable norm. The debate inevitably shifts its focus from the need for reform to the historical criterion for its implementation. Not only does this give great impetus to the study of the community's history; it involves the ideologue and researcher immediately in the task of invidious comparison.

These *comparisons* are twofold: between ages of the history of the community, and between the tradition of 'my' community at various times, and that of other communities. The periods of religious 'greatness' are increasingly measured by the secular criterion of worldly success. For example, the Age of Companions or the era of the great Popes become the high points, the golden ages, from which the religion and the religious community has declined.

At this juncture, a crucial step is taken. So far, 'value' accrued to the community which is the 'bearer' of the religious tradition, only insofar as it was the carrier. The collectivity derives its 'value' solely from its role as the bearer of a precious heritage. Now, under the conditions and problems which lead to the search for an agreed criterion of the 'essence' of the religion and historical comparisons, 'value' is transferred to the community *per se*. The glorious religion is now seen as an expression of the creative genius of the people, an expression of its inherent, but at present moribund, nobility and native energy. The collectivity now is not just the carrier and vessel of virtue; it is its source. It is identified with all value and hence power. The *'primary bearer'* of the religious tradition is now accorded recognition in its own right. The concept of the 'chosen people' is secularised and democratised unwittingly.

But, the 'revivalist' continues, who constitutes the 'primary bearer', the *'chosen people'*? His answer is that it is the ethnic group, the real 'subject' of history; for it alone experienced both the glorious splendour of the past, and the spiritual decline of the present. To the intelligentsia, suffering from the impact of the 'scientific state' and its demonstrable superiority, what was required to rectify the course of history and set the community on its feet, was a total *'status reversal'* for the ethnic community. The present position of the community is one of dejection because it is a 'sociological minority'. As numerous and potentially great as it may be, it is crushed beneath the weight and helpless before

I

the incursions of the 'scientific state' brought from afar. Only a thorough spiritual purification will enable the community to throw off both its own degenerate tradition and the western material superiority. The threat from outside cannot be countered until the weight of the generations inside is thrown overboard, until the community is renovated.[35]

If one examines the writings of 'revivalists' of this stamp—men like Blyden and Johnson in West Africa, Gasprinski and Akchurin among the Tatars, Korais, Obradovic and Karadzic in the Balkans, Abduh, al-Kawakibi, Rida and Rabbath among the Arabs, Krochmal, Smolenskin and Fraenkel among the Jews, and Sen, Dayananda and Aurobindo in India—we find a recurring concern with communal identity and purity. The basic idea seems to be that group self-respect can only be achieved by redemption through self-purification. This synthesises in an historical, intra-mundane fashion two notions that are central to the traditional salvation dramas or theodicies, and to the scientific temper of modernisation, respectively: namely, the religious idea that 'we are unclean' and sinful and impure, and the anthropocentric, modern concept of self-help and self-perfectibility through application of scientific thinking to the collective self.

The *ethnicity solution* of the 'revivalists' is concerned with dignity. For men who are doubly socialised, and so doubly alienated—from their own culture and from that of the alien state—the concern with the history of the community seen now as an independent 'ethnie' is the most appropriate 'definition of the situation'. It is here that Weber's concept of 'elective affinity' helps. The intelligentsia is sociologically determined by their overall situation of 'dual legitimation'. This provides it with structural constraints. It also leaves a certain measure of choice. One may in fact find individual members of the intelligentsia oscillating between the three logical 'solutions' which I have outlined. But interest here is centred on those who for reasons of socialisation and class position choose the 'reformist' path, and are gradually pulled by its internal logic towards the 'ethnicity solution'. Imperceptibly, they forsake the religious world-image for a secular one, which nevertheless retains within it certain ideas from the older world-view. For members of an upper-middle class stratum, with this double education, a solution of such a type serves their status needs; their needs for a spiritual 'status reversal', which would make them ideologues of their 'chosen people', define their situation, and attract them towards the ideal of the ethnic distinctiveness and autonomy of 'their' people.[36]

This is one major source of the nationalist idea.

In schematic fashion and without illustration, such is the process by which the loyalty to the religious community and its cosmic salvation drama gets gradually transformed and replaced, by allegiance to the ethnic community and its historical, anthropocentric world-image. The community is no longer valued simply as the elected bearer of the divine word or wisdom. It is prized for itself, and *its* discovery of the precious word of God, its production of great prophets and reformers in the past, is construed as but another, and signal, proof of its intrinsic worth. This is a silent internal revolution, but nonetheless significant for that. For it springs from the contradictions within the cosmic images of the religious traditions which can no longer cope with the new, utterly strange conditions. An alternative for dealing with the 'problem of meaning' is at hand, at the very moment when the traditional answers fail through their own radicalisation and extension. The great external challenge of the 'scientific state' drives the traditional solutions down the road to their final dissolution. Religion is sundered from tradition. All that remains are the fragments of a once all-embracing system, so many 'free-floating' resources for the construction of immanentist doctrines.

The rejection of the world-citizen

All 'reformists', whether of the rationalist or historicist wings, are essentially '*defensive*'. I mean by this that they are intent on conserving and protecting a core of values within the old heritage intact from outside, corroding influences. Their ultimate secularisation is unintentional. To defend the *true* part of the heritage, they must not only use the tools of the modernising West; they must adopt in large measure its basic spirit and attitude, its scientific outlook and techniques. Unseen, this adoption of alien values pushes them relentlessly on to the road of secular liberalism. Yet they see themselves as guardians of the genuine tradition, of the essential spark of moral nobility in their heritage. Their aim is to reconcile in a higher synthesis all that is most precious in their respective legacies with all that is most desirable in the offerings of the 'scientific state'. The 'reformist' is innocently optimistic; he seeks to embrace the modern world while reserving to himself and his fellows a 'chosen island' of sacred values, a plateau of calm from which to survey and interpret and blend the perceived opposition of science and tradition. Often this island of serenity is found by a special rereading of the original sources of the tradition—deliberately shorn of the preconceptions resulting from the additions and constant interpretations of subsequent commentators. Abduh in Egypt, Namik Kemal in Turkey, Dayananda Saraswati and Chatterjee in India, Iqbal in Pakistan, Lakhshmi Narasu in Burma, al-Kursavi and Marjani among the Tatars, the New Text School and K'ang Yu-wei in Imperial China, are among the many who have had recourse to this haven.

Contrast this position with that of the 'assimilationist'. His attitude is unreserved. It is founded on a *'messianic'* belief in the advent of a cosmopolitan world, free of oppression and injustice, because of the triumph of reason and science. The 'assimilationist' sees only a common human race, into which he wishes to acculturate: the differences and cultural traits of groups within humanity are purely secondary and destined to pass as so many 'ethnographic monuments'. The freedom to which he aspires is a corollary of a single status, that of *citizen of the world*. The rights and duties of citizenship in a particular state are merely devices of administrative convenience. Tiresome as they appear, their real function is to ensure a stable and harmonious political order in which essential benefits are distributed impartially and on the basis of merit. These benefits can only be realised when society has been rationalised to the point where movement from one 'society' to another entails no change of status or opportunities, i.e. when 'societies' have been replaced by a single world Society, constituted of equals in virtue of the identity of reason and moral worth inhering in their common humanity.

It is easy now to denigrate the naïvete of this optimistic assessment of the situation, its failure to comprehend the social realities beneath the philosophers' ideals. But the 'assimilationist', like the 'reformist', is putting a question which has, if anything, gained in importance over the last two centuries. The 'reformist' is troubled by the problem of continuity in the face of continual change sparked off by the scientific revolution, and his question to us remains: what, in this continual state of flux, is sufficiently permanent and valid to serve us as a guide for action and living? The 'assimilationist' puts an equally vital question: how real are the differences that divide humanity at present? Where, and how, do we draw the line between unity and diversity in social life? How can we realise the humanity of the human species without loss of freedom and self-expression?

There are, clearly, no easy answers to either question. Both the 'reformist' and the 'assimilationist' were convinced, nevertheless, that their solutions were transparently self-evident. The 'reformist' was, I think, slightly more realistic; but, even here, the relative failure of movements of religious reform provided a strong incentive to look elsewhere for an answer to the 'reformist' problem. That elsewhere turned out to be nationalism. But not before the 'assimilationist' too joined hands with the 'reformist'.

The trouble with the 'assimilationist' was his assumption of a common humanity. Instead of treating this as a hypothesis, a project to be realised by arduous effort, he tended to see all differences as so many regrettable, but minor, obstacles and deviations from the true underlying state of affairs.

In his apocalyptic haste, he failed to notice how 'western' the attributes of his 'humanity' were—indeed, how French and English. The subsequent disappointment of this error has been often analysed and it is widely assumed that the inegalitarian treatment meted out by a West that proclaimed its adherence to the principles of Christian brotherhood and democratic equality, to the many students who visited it with such high hopes, is the principal cause of nationalism. Their passionate adherence to nationalism is also traced to the subsequent failure by colonial governments to admit members of the native intelligentsia on their return from the West to high status positions in the colonial bureaucracy.[38]

I have no wish to deny that these factors contributed to the vehemence with which nationalism was often subsequently espoused. Certainly, the discrepancy between treatment in Western countries and subsequent rejection at home adds a tinge of bitterness to an already heavily charged situation. But insults in London or Paris, and denial of merit by shortsighted colonial bureaucracies in Delhi, Djakarta or Dakar, are not sufficient causes in themselves of large-scale movements aiming at self-government of a group which is conceived to be an actual or potential nation. The discontents of a tiny minority of students, if confined to these matters, would not have created nationalism, or the idea of the nation.[39]

The *'rejection'* of the 'assimilationist' is not only psychological or occupational. The underlying differences dividing humanity relate to the status of the 'sociological minority' in the grip of a world of 'scientific states'. Decision-making, on all key issues, is revealed to be the perquisite of minorities; and far from levelling down this horizontal domination, scientific modernisation increases it by destroying all irrelevant and inefficient intermediate powers. The 'scientific state' is not merely the executive committee of the ruling caste; it has brought that caste to its overwhelming position of strength, and by its 'inner logic' of 'efficiency' continually reinforces that position. The domination of society by the 'scientific state' is indeed relatively recent. It is a regular, 'mechanised', planned intervention. Its effect is to 'territorialise' the planners and agents of modernisation.

It is this state of affairs that the rejected 'assimilationist' slowly comprehends. The espoused world-citizenship, like the old cosmic images, is bypassed by the progress of the 'scientific state'. Those who cling to the notion project it increasingly into a future age of world *government*; they, too, realise that the cosmopolitan dream is nugatory in the presence of polycentric decision-making.

And with this political realisation goes a deeper cultural perception: the differences between religio-cultural traditions are actually reinforced by the trend of the 'scientific state', beneath a veneer of scientific cultural uniformity. The utopian world dream is consigned to arid sterility, and replaced by the more modest single-state messianism. Assimilationism is still-born.

Conclusion

The conclusion that emerges from this study can be put like this. The preconditions of the emergence of ethnic nationalism among the intelligentsia, the upper stratum initially, are the failures of the 'reformist' and 'assimilationist' solutions to the situation of 'dual legitimation'. In the case of ethnic nationalism, the former failure is rather more important, because of the vital part that religious tradition plays in the life and activities of members of the group. If the tradition cannot be adequately reformed, and the intelligentsia can neither return to orthodoxy nor enter into an assimilationist common humanity, the only practical solutions are a kind of continual emigration on an individual level, or an attempt at modernising the ethnic community on a secular, political basis.

Very roughly, then, we can state the following proposition about the *birth* of ethnic nationalism:

> *Nationalism is born among the intelligentsia, when the messianic 'assimilationists' try to realise their former vision by adopting the ethnicity solution of the defensive reforming 'revivalists'.*

What is vital is the convergence of the defensive reformists and the messianic assimilationists in a situation of 'dual legitimation'. Only this fusion produces the ideological spark of the nationalist movement. The degree to which this fusion takes place, and the particular structural conditions which govern that degree, require detailed empirical investigation which are beyond the scope of this preliminary exploration. I am all too conscious of the abstraction and the schematic nature of this model; but limitations of space forbid me to take this further at present. All that was intended in this concluding chapter was a theoretical exploration of one of the main types of nationalism, as it affected one major grouping in modern society.

Further research needs especially to be focused on the reformists, and the whole question of the relation of religious change and modernisation to the rise of nationalism. It would be especially interesting to test the model presented here against a case of ancient ethnic nationalism—to discover if the situation of 'dual legitimation' and the reform of religion correlate with the intensity and content of nationalist movements. [40]

What I think the model helps to explain is the Janus-faced posture of so many *ethnic* nationalisms. Nationalism is both integrative and divisive, because the 'assimilationist' stresses the vision of fraternity among equals, but the elitist-minded 'revivalist' underlines the cultural differentiae so necessary to the *renovation* of the community and the restoration of dignity through secession. Nationalism is ultimately both traditionalist and modernist; for it arises out of the historical concerns of the 'reformist' who defects, and the aspirations of the rejected 'assimilationist' for 'normalisation'—to be like all other nations.

Appendix A

NATIONALISM AND
SOCIOLOGICAL RESEARCH

Scholarly interest in nationalism has been largely the preserve of historians and, whatever the reasons, sociologists enter the argument late and at a disadvantage. Three periods of research can be discerned. Up to 1914, very little systematic work was undertaken. Interest was largely ethical and philosophical, and the critiques of Mill, Renan, Acton and others were concerned with the merits and defects of the doctrine.

The other main pre-1914 school of interest was the Marxist. Though Marx and Engels did not formulate a theory of nationalism, the increasing importance of the movement in Eastern Europe led their successors to devote considerable attention to the phenomenon. Kautsky, Luxemburg, Bauer and Renner, Lenin and Stalin all wrote tracts on the subject, mainly for tactical ends, but necessarily drawing on basic theoretical assumptions. In fact these were the most consistently sociological of the attempts to explain nationalism till the present decade.

A more neutral and detached attitude began to prevail after the First World War. Historians like the elder Seton-Watson, Hans Kohn, Carlton Hayes, Alfred Cobban and Louis Snyder were particularly active, and their approach was increasingly oriented to sociological factors, despite its European bias and its narrative and chronological format. Psychologists like Pillsbury and McDougall also became concerned with the problems raised by group action and sentiments, and the rise of Fascism stimulated further research in the general field.[1]

The rise of the new states to independence in Africa and Asia after the Second War ushers in the third and most intensive phase of research. The most important development has been the incursion of American political scientists, concerned with overall problems of 'political development'. [2] Apter, Coleman, Binder, Halpern, Pye, Geertz and Emerson are among the many who have increased our understanding of the peculiar problems of African and Asian political systems, and thereby helped to shift the study of the causes and consequences of nationalism away from its parochial European setting on to a broader, global plane. The political scientists have been rather more interested in the effects of nationalism and the functions of ideology for 'nation-building'. [3] This is a formulation which has appealed also to economists and linguists who have considered economic growth and language modernisation in the developing countries. [4] In addition, the rise of 'national communism' in Vietnam, Cuba and China has stimulated sociological development of the neo-Marxist arguments; [5] and the growth of mass media in these areas has drawn the attention of the cybernetic school of 'communication theorists' to the formation of national symbols. [6] Finally, one ought not to forget the prolific output of area specialists committed to a more traditional historical approach.

The burgeoning of interdisciplinary interest in nationalism indicates the key position of the field and phenomenon, in relation to other topics. One cannot, of cours divorcee, it from larger problems about the growth of nations and nation-states, and that means it is central to any consideration of modernisation and economic development. In addition, nationality and nationalism play an important role in social perception and identification, and in the standardisation and development of language. [7] Nationalism also stands at the junction, as it were, of diverse research areas— into race relations, international conflict, communication systems, values in economic development, romanticism and enlightenment, the evolution of political ideas, geopolitical strategies, the study of social movements and revolution, and many other topics. It is only in the 1960's that mainstream sociologists interested in the problems of developing countries have discovered the significance of nationalism as a subject in itself and as a testing-ground for current sociological theory.

Appendix B

SOME IDEOLOGICAL
RELATIVES OF NATIONALISM

The plasticity of ideological movements is nowhere better observed than in the relationship of nationalism to other ideologies and to the social situations of its variegated adherents. Weber's notion of the 'distortion' of ideologies from the original message of the primary bearers, through the adherence of successive social strata, is strikingly confirmed by nationalist development.[1] I think, however, that we can distinguish in a rough and ready way between nationalism and its closest ideological relatives.

Perhaps the doctrine with the nearest affinities to nationalism is *imperialism*. In nearly every historical instance, this ideology is carried by an ethnie or a nation, which believes it has a mission to endow other ethnie or nations with the blessings of its civilisation. Often we are dealing with a case of simple conquest empires, as in the Assyrian or Mongol cases, but the more subtle combination of a conquest empire with a cosmopolitan ethic usually has its origins in a belief in the conquering nation's overall superiority. The right to rule, *'parcere subjectis et debellare superbos'*, of the *pax Romana* or *pax Achaemenica,* is paralleled by the modern colonialist doctrines of the white civilising mission of French culture and British administration.[2] It is an easy step from the assertion that one's ethnie is the sole possessor of truth, virtue, strength, etc., a bulwark of culture in the face of anarchic barbarism, to the assertion of the right to prolonged tutelage and intervention. At the same time, while it fits perfectly with the sense of superiority inhering in 'ethnocentric' nationalism, imperialism is essentially a derogation, even a contradiction, of the main tenet of 'polycentric' nationalism—the right of each nation to realise itself in perfect autonomy, so as to be able to contribute to mankind.

Fascism is a further development away from nationalism. Its mainsprings are worship of the State as a corporate entity, belief in the Leader and the elite whose will is infallible, and a sense of what is often described as vitalistic nihilism. That is, the return to the worship of the primeval force or energy proceeds from the exhaustion of all efforts to construct a rationalist philosophy. This is ideologically a far cry from Fichte's subjectivist idealism, and even further from the democratic populism of Herder and Rousseau. One looks in vain for *étatisme*, the *Fuehrerprinzip* or nihilistic vitalism in Mazzini or Burke, Jefferson or Herzl, Gandhi or Sun Yat-Sen, Nkrumah or Bolivar, Nyerere or even Nasser. I do not see any of these elements in the writings of East and Central European nationalists, from Korais and Obradovic to Mickiewicz and Masaryk.

The first sign of these new elements can be found in Maurras' and Barrès' integral nationalism, and I would not wish to deny the ideological, much less the sociological, connection between the two doctrines. Nationalism is one element, as I argued in the Introduction, within the Fascist 'family'.[3] Nevertheless, I think it is analytically more useful to treat nationalism and Fascism as separate doctrines and sociological phenomena. There is, after all, a world of difference for adherents and spectators alike between the ruthless suppression of opposition and mobilisation for conquest in the name of the corporate State and Leader, of Mussolini's or Antonescu's Fascist movement regimes, and the suppression and mobilisation which characterises the nationalisms of Nyerere's Tanzania or Masaryk's Czechoslovakia or even Jacobin France fighting for its revolutionary existence. Whether we can simply say that the latter cases are examples of the 'polycentrism' of the weak, while Fascism is the 'ethnocentric' denouement of the powerful, I would question. There is certainly a similarity between Fascism and earlier 'ethnocentric' nationalism, but are we then to call Assyrian, Greek and Jewish collective sentiments and actions 'Fascist'? It is one thing to say, as I do, that Fascism is a *reversal* of the trend to 'polycentric' nationalism, with an ethnocentric undercurrent, quite another to equate it with the earlier form of nationalism.[4] This is to overlook the sociological peculiarities of modern inter-war Europe—not to mention the additional elements introduced by Fascism, which in themselves contradict 'polycentric' tenets, and substitute the State for the Nation, as the prime object of collective allegiance and identification.[5]

Racism, the doctrine that the world is divided into races, some superior physically and intellectually to others, and therefore endowed with the right to dominate, stands rather closer to nationalism. In this respect, one can contrast the position of South Africa with the doctrine of Negritude. The former is undoubtedly an extreme development of Afrikaner nationalism, the Broederbond providing the typical Fascist elite component (but without too much stress on the will of the Leader) and the Dutch Reformed Church providing the ideological legitimation of the right to rule. In a sense, the racist element is purely sociological, even contingent. One could easily envisage a kind of Fascist *cultural* imperialism, if the Afrikaner had been confronted by a vast majority of uneducated speakers of a different language or adherents of a different religion. The peculiarity, however, of the racist position is its biological premiss. Whereas, Orthodox Serbs and Greeks could be Islamised, and Czechs and Poles Germanised, the appeal to biological characteristics of differentiation automatically excludes the inferior from all possibility of salvation. The physically doomed can only be turned into helots, expelled or exterminated; else they will defile the racial purity of the superior race.[6]

Negritude merely inverts this position—against the white man. Its aim, of course, is quite different: to serve as a rebuttal against French depreciation of African *culture*. Ironically, its peculiar tinge of populism gives it its racist flavour. Whereas, for Blyden, the Negro race was *also* a repository of virtue, etc. (which all men should recognise)—a curious mixture of 'ethnocentric' and 'polycentric' nationalism—for the poets of Negritude, the 'ethnocentric' element has gained the upper hand in such a manner as to preclude the materialistic West from ever partaking of virtue, *because* they are of the white race.[7]

Racism has again reversed the 'polycentric' trend. But, without the additional Fascist elements, one can regard it as a peculiar development of 'ethnocentric' nationalism of a post-Darwinian kind. The notion of struggle for survival antedates Darwin, of course; one can find it notably in Fichte and Herder. This is the element that so easily leads towards expansionist imperialism. The importance of social Darwinism resides in its appeal to 'science' to justify a doctrine of immutable biological characteristics (and hence moral and intellectual traits), locked in perpetual group struggle for domination. There is little trace of this determinism of collective make-up in the original nationalist writings, and nothing in the core doctrine to point in that direction.

The purest contradiction of nationalism *in toto* is *Nazism*. At first sight, it appears to be an extreme development of 'ethnocentric' nationalism—a sentiment that Hitler knew only too well how to exploit. But this revolutionary combination of Fascist, imperialist and racist elements is founded on an altogether different principle. Here I refer not just to the many additions to 'ethnocentric' nationalism: the worship of force *per se,* the *Fuehrerprinzip*, the devotion to the State, elitism, militarism, Party loyalty, *Gleichschaltung*, etc. Nazism, the Nazism of the envisaged SS State and New Order, divides the world *horizontally* according to a principle of racial stratification—from the pure Aryan German overlords (Germans who did not fit this visionary 'new man' were to be excluded, even killed off), through the various racial castes, to the Slavic helots (Jews and Gypsies having been exterminated as too defiling and heretical).[8]

You can see the way in which the original vertical division of the world, envisaged by even 'ethnocentric' nationalism, gets gradually subverted by racial imperialism into this diametrically opposed racial casteism on a global scale, using pseudo-scientific 'Darwinian' notions of domination through struggle. But that doesn't lessen the contradiction with nationalism—either in logic or reality. Hitler's world is utterly alien in structure and purpose to those of Ataturk, Sukarno, Nkrumah and even Pilsudski; and I choose the nationalist dictatorships deliberately. The difference between Hitlerism and the early German nationalists, or the democratic Czech movement, the Wafd regime or the early Congress movement, is even greater. There is as much connection between nationalism and Nazism, as between nationalism and communism; the convergence between both pairs of ideologies is to be sought in the particular social contexts, not in ideological affinity or structural similarity.

These ideologies are generally considered doctrines of the 'right', whereas populism and communism are usually located to the 'left' of nationalism. I agree with Kedourie that the diversity of nationalism, when considered from this class standpoint, should warn us against the danger of analysing one doctrine through the use of categories drawn from the tenets and experiences of a totally different ideology.[9] *Populism*, in particular, is so heterogeneous a set of beliefs that it is difficult to place on any continuum.[10] But let us assume that its core is a kind of agrarian primitivism, a desire to restore the virtues and simplicities of a participatory, consensual farmers' republic, where men will be free of the burden of alienation consequent upon the advent of industrial capitalism. In his stress on the need for cultural roots, Herder is a populist of sorts; yet, like Rousseau, he values innovation and the virtues of every society. The step that populism takes away from nationalism, however, is its equation of the 'nation' with the 'people'. Again, one can argue that populism is just another form of nationalism, and this time the suggestion is more plausible insofar as populism is perhaps more of a mood or set of aspirations than a definite ideology. We met it in Worsley's characterisation of the mass phase of many nationalist movements.

Nationalist parties in Africa especially, have tied their political programmes of homogenisation and independence to a social one in which

> the small peasant and the virtues of village society were enshrined as the kernel of national identity,

with co-operative and small-scale farming.[11]

In these programmes, there are assumptions on the part of intellectuals to the effect that the rural population is fairly homogeneous (and constitutes the mass of the society's population, which is largely correct) and that 'citizens' are really peasants. The direct identification of the masses with the Party-State follows from these beliefs, in cases where these are the independence regimes (unlike, say, Russian populism). These assumptions also help to explain the emphasis placed on communitarian experiments under the rubric of 'African Socialism'.

There seem to be two uses of the term 'populism'. One is fairly strict and conforms to the delineation of its ideology above; its social base (intellectuals apart) is the small-farmer producer. A rather wider use views populism as an ideological myth which appeals to the small man, the *menu peuple*, everywhere; so there are populist elements in Nazism, McCarthyism, Peronism, etc. If it means the elevation of the uneducated, whose will to rule directly (in their own persons) as against the established order is the nub of the matter, then populism is a logical extension of one element in nationalist doctrine, the supremacy of the nation. (It is also a dimension of democratic doctrine, the participational one.) But if we adhere to the agrarian primitivist notion, then the two ideologies overlap, but belong to rather different traditions of thought. Their recent fusion is uneasy; and the more coherent and politically powerful ideology of nationalism usually wins out after a period.

The other major ideologies—democracy, liberalism, socialism, communism—have all combined with nationalism from the Revolutionary prototype onwards, and have been frequently discussed. In no case of symbiosis, except perhaps the initial years of the Bolshevik regime, did nationalism come second. The subordination of Marxist communism is doubly remarkable in view of its far more coherent ideology and structures. I suggest that the major reason has to do with the role of the State in the era of modernisation, which gives it an ambiguous image in the social consciousness, most happily resolved by nationalism's ability to harness the scientific agency of the state to the will of the community. *For this purpose*, nationalism identifies the community in a manner which is superior to the class analysis of Marxism, after independence is achieved. The much-commented-on 'polycentrism' of communism is the manifestation of this superiority, or of Marxism's self-inflicted handicap after the national revolution.

The role of the 'scientific state' forms the point of departure for the analysis of the rise of nationalism in the last chapter.

Appendix C

ADDENDUM TO GELLNER'S THEORY

In a personal communication, Gellner disputes certain aspects of my interpretation of his theory.

1 He thinks that my diagram give his theory a 'much more intellectualist' (or 'idealist') slant, and underplays the structural factors,

> such as the emergence of an uprooted lower class as a result of population growth, inadequate rural resources, some but inadequate opportunities in the towns and so forth or the emergence of a military and administrative modernised class as the result of centralising and defensive activities on the part of the Central Government.

The reader, however, will note that the titles of the diagrams stress that we are only dealing with *certain* factors—mainly relating to education and language—and not the wider range of variables that would probably need to be invoked for a full-scale theory. My modification of Gellner's model was equally one-sided.

The assumptions about rural pressures are clearly in the background of Gellner's theory. The last-named factor, however, about activities of the Central Government, seems to be underplayed in his exposition of the theory in *Thought and Change*. Its inclusion seems to me an important and necessary modification of the structure of the theory, since it allows more scope for historical variation and conscious choice. My own modification stressed the role of the centralising state as an independent causal factor (cf. further on this in Chapter 10).

2 Gellner feels he is not committed to a doctrine about a 'universal need to belong', while conceding the strength of such a sentiment. He also thinks it is not essential to his theory. Instead, he posits 'more basic sociological premisses':

> Given occupational and geographical mobility, a fairly high level of technical training as a prerequisite of most jobs, and the way in which the various aspects of life are inevitably compartmentalised (earning one's living, family life, local associations and so forth), it follows that anyone not accepted as a member of the culture or not equipped for such acceptance, will constantly find himself hampered, disadvantaged, humiliated and so forth. At the same time, no legitimation is available for such inequality. To elaborate such an ideology which would justify such inequality is almost impossible (at least to elaborate one which would also persuade those who suffer from its application), precisely because of those factors of occupational and other mobility. It is very difficult to pick out the class of those who suffer from disadvantages and make it a stable and permanent one, so that they could get used to it and internalise their condition.

This impossibility of discovering a persuasive legitimation for inequality is also at the roots of the recent emphasis on human dignity, according to Gellner.

This seems to me to constitute a new theory altogether. Gellner might reply that he is only making explicit what is implicit in the book; but I think that we have here a clear shift in emphasis. What seems to be stressed in the book is literacy (and communication generally). We are not told that it is the demands of the industrial system that determine (ultimately) what is or is not going to pass as an 'acceptable specimen of humanity', a full citizen and so on, unless, of course, the catch-all term 'development' is intended to convey this (I refer to the sentence on page 172 of *Thought and Change*).

If this is the case, then the charge of 'economism' becomes more serious. It is one thing, I think, to say that the tide of industrialisation (or better, modernisation) starts a causal chain leading via literacy, etc., to nationalism; quite another to claim that the 'needs' of the (already existent) industrial system *require* nationalism, which becomes an inevitable consequence thereby. The teleological overtone of the argument here becomes a mask for a theory that comes close to economic determinism, which is only avoided by the rural and administrative factors which were mentioned in para. (1) above.

One might also take issue with the rendering of the 'sociological premisses' themselves. It is by no means clear that modern life demands a fairly high level of technical training as prerequisite for most jobs (though that is the official ideology); the early industrial system (which most affects the argument, presumably) was content with armies of organised, but not highly skilled, assembly-line workers. Nor is it clear, in an era of intrusive bureaucracy, how inevitable the process of compartmentalisation of life-spheres is. What *does* appear to be the case is that the higher level of physical and cultural communication gives rise to increased mobility, which makes inequalities seem much less acceptable (though here again the needs of rulers of the State have played an important historical role in the process of democratisation). This aspect of the sociological background needs to be stressed. Its counterpart in the cultural sphere is what we usually call 'westernisation'. Not only can one go elsewhere where one is more acceptable; one can also import alien items, even cultural complexes, by adapting them to the local setting, to counter the rigidities and weaknesses in the local structures and assumptions.

By making this particular sociological background explicit, the psychologistic interpretation in the text can be avoided, without a commitment to an equally dubious economism.

Appendix D

NATIONALISM AND THE CLASSICAL REVIVAL IN RENAISSANCE ITALY

The secular *historical* 'revivalist' vision can in certain cases originate by a kind of 'demonstration effect' over time, and with it a lyric patriotism. Petrarch's visit to Rome in 1337 produced a theory of history completely at variance with the Christian purposive development of humanity from heathen darkness to Christian light. Instead, history was divided into two ages for Petrarch: the classical *historiae antiquae*, and the 'recent' (Christian post-imperial) *historiae novae*, and he hoped that his 'grandsons will be able to walk back into the pure radiance of the past' (*Poterunt discussis forte tenebris Ad purum priscumque iubar remeare nepotes, Africa,* IX, 453 ff.). The comparison here is between the pagan Romans who walk in light and the Christians who walk in darkness; the rejuvenating hope is for a 'revival under the influence of classical models', after the 'deplorable' and barbaric (Gothic) present (Gothic being equated by Italians of the period with 'German', 'Tedeschi' and 'modern', 'moderni').

According to Panofsky, the revival in question was not only a return to classical antiquity. It also involved a return to nature, together with '*self-realisation*' (in the double sense of 'becoming aware' and 'becoming real'). This constellation was accompanied by a continuous 'ethnocentric' undercurrent of Italian contempt for the people beyond the Alps (*tramontani*), as so many *nazioni barbare e straniere* (Vandals, Huns, Goths, French, Germans, Lombards), which preserves the original Latin attitude and idiom —*exterae nationes et gentes* (Cicero) and *nationes ferae* (Sallust).

For both Petrarch and Vasari (and Goethe), the rebirth (*rinascita*) of art and culture generally is identical with the *revival* of classical antiquity (even if in the early fifteenth century they appeared to diverge). It seems that external invasion and the fact that the Reformation took place outside Italy prevented the development of a strong movement for Italian unity and independence at this time—though Petrarch's sentiment, with its ideal of political regeneration, finds a famous echo in the last chapter of *The Prince*, where Machiavelli actually quotes a verse of Petrarch:

Valour against fell wrath
Will take up arms; and be the combat quickly sped!
For, sure, the ancient worth,
That in Italians stirs the heart, is not yet dead.

(*The Prince*, 1935, Ch. 26, entitled 'Exhortation to liberate Italy from the Barbarians'.)

By Machiavelli's time, the 'possessive state' in France, England and Spain was beginning to have an impact; but it was as yet too weak and unable to homogenise the population or intervene effectively, i.e. scientifically, to provide a complete alternative to the old cosmic and universalist (Christian) image and ethic. The uneasy partial secularisation and reforming syncretism of the Renaissance intelligentsia does, however, throw some doubt on the validity of my argument; on the other hand, its muted character and the failure to evolve a nationalist movement (the emphasis on the vernacular was a response to the challenge of Neo-Latin Classicism) lends support to my model. Further research is clearly required, but it seems that this period, like its French late seventeenth/early eighteenth-century counterpart, represents a 'halfway' house between the common 'ethnocentric' and the novel 'polycentric' nationalism. The political similarity with ancient Greece (city-state divisions) was offset by a religious and cultural difference, i.e. the *divergence* between the 'territory' and population of the religious unit (Catholicism) and the linguistic (Italia), whereas in Greece they tended to coincide. The muted character of reform can be attributed to the overwhelming urge to look for the model of 'value' in a distant past only;

'value' could not, in comparison, be conceived of as an attribute of any other contemporary society. This overshadowing of the present by an idealised past was also at work in the case of the modern Greek nationalist revolt; except that by this time it was counterbalanced by the developed model of contemporary France: cf. PANOFSKY, 1970, Ch. 1, esp. pp. 9–11, 18–21, 22 (esp. note 2), 29–31.

The Renaissance confusion is apparent in the use of the other, related concept, 'modernity'; and it is Vasari who proposes to reserve 'moderno' for the art of the Renaissance, where previously it had been generally applied to the hitherto prevalent Gothic (architectural) style (ibid., pp. 34–5). What became, however, increasingly accepted was the tripartite division of history inaugurated by Petrarch.

Appendix E

SOME NATIONALIST MOVEMENTS

A. DEVELOPED

Europe	Asia and Middle East	Africa	America	Pan
French	Kazak	Algerian	Quebecois	Negroism
German	Uzbek	Tunisian	American	Arabism
Irish	Tatar	Moroccan	Mexican	Slavism
Belgian	Azeri	Egyptian	Haitian	Turkism
Basque	Georgian	Libyan	Cuban	Africanism
Catalan	Armenian	Sudanese	Jamaican	
Swiss	Indian	Somali	Trinidadian	
Flemish	Pakistani	Nigerian	Dominican	
Norwegian	Ceylonese	Yoruba	Republic	
Danish	Burmese	Biafran	Argentinian	
Swedish	Karen	Ewe	Brazilian	
Finnish	Sikh	Ghanaian	Chilean	
Icelandic	Naga	Ivory Coast	Peruvian	
Latvian	Bengali	Malian	Bolivian	
Estonian	Persian	Liberian	Guyana	
Lithuanian	Turkish	Cameroon	Uruguayan	
Byelorussian	Israeli	Congolese	Venezuelan	
Ukrainian	Palestinian	BaKongo		
Bulgarian	Kurd	Angolan		
Hungarian	Iraqi	Boer		
Polish	Syrian	Rhodesian		
Tyrolese	Yemeni	Kenyan		
Serbian	South Yemeni	Ugandan		
Croatian	Vietnamese	Tanzanian		
Slovenian	Cambodian	Malawi		

Macedonian	Indonesian	Zambian
Greek	Malayan
Cypriot	Filipino
Yugoslav	Chinese
Albanian	Japanese
Russian	Korean
Czech	Singapore
Slovak	Mongol
Rumanian

B. PRIMITIVE

Ancient and Medieval	Europe	Asia and Middle East	Africa	America
Egypt	Jurassiens	Turkmen	Hausa	Canada
Assyria	Bretons	Tadjiks	Berber	Red Indians
Persia	Corsicans	Bashkirs	Copts	Mormons
Zealots	Frisians	Uigurs	Ethiopia	Antilles
Hellenism	Manx	Yakuts	Ganda	(Dutch)
Carthage	Lapps	Mari	Kikuyu	Puerto
Rome (Italy)	Savoyards	Dagestani	Luo	Ricans
Urartians	Burgundians	Oirots	Chagga	Bermudans
Canaanites	Prussians	Tuvinians	Mozambique	Honduras
Philistines	Swabians	Chuvash	Lunda	San
Elamites	Serbs	Udmurts	Negroes	Salvador
Sumerians	Wends	Pathans	(Sudan)	Panama
Kassites	Scots	Druse	Arabs (Chad)	Ecuador
Lydians	Welsh	Assyrians	Ashanti	Araucan-
Parthians	19 c. Den-	(Christian)	Ibibio	ians
Mannaeans	mark	S. Arabia	Tiv	Anguillans
Hittites	16–17 c.	Afghans	Mossi	
Mitannians	England	Tibet	Fang	
Phoenicians	16 c.	Siam	Baluba	
Pagan Burma	Holland	Nepal	Lesotho	
T'ang China		Assam	Konzo	
		Andhrans	Tutsi	
		Keralans	Mongo	
		Marathis	Lulua	
Pan		Gujeratis	Botswana	
		Chin	Chad	
Europeanism		Shan	Niger	
Scandinavianism		Achinese	Sierra	
Dravidianism		Ambonese	Leone	
Latin Americanism		Batak	Gabon	
		Minangkabau	Congo (B.)	
		Maori	C. Afr. Rep.	
		Australia		
		New Zealand		

Bibliographical Note

The most important literature on Nationalism is:

1 K. DEUTSCH: *Interdisciplinary Bibliography on Nationalism, 1935-53*, Technology Press of M.I.T., 1956, which follows on K. PINSON's earlier *Selected Bibliography on Nationalism*, Columbia University Press, New York, 1935. Deutsch has brought this up to date in Chapter 1 of his *Nationalism and Social Communication*, Second Edition, John Wiley, New York, 1966.

2 B. AKZIN: *State and Nation*, Hutchinson, London, 1964, Ch. 2, and K. DEUTSCH & W. FOLTZ (eds.): *Nation-Building*, Atherton Press, New York, 1963 (pp. 132–50 by D. PUCHALA), contain shorter bibliographies of more recent titles.

3 An introductory Reader is L. SNYDER's *The Dynamics of Nationalism*, Van Nostrand, Princeton, 1964. On Asia and Africa, cf. I. WALLERSTEIN(ed.): *Social Change, The Colonial Situation*, Wiley, New York, 1966

4 The best brief critical bibliography on the vast topic of Modernisation is C. E. BLACK: *The Dynamics of Modernisation*, Harper & Row, New York, 1967 ('The Study of Modernisation: A Bibliographical Essay'); also the bibliography in J. P. NETTL & R. ROBERTSON: *International Systems and the Modernisation of Societies*, Faber & Faber, London, 1968.

5 A useful bibliography on African Politics is W. J. HANNA & J. L. HANNA: *Politics in Black Africa*, Michigan State University, Michigan, 1964. Also S. & P. OTTENBERG (eds.): *Cultures and Societies of Africa*, Random House, New York, 1960. Cf. also P. C. LLOYD: *Africa in Social Change*, Penguin, Harmondsworth, 1967, for further references.

6 For Latin American Nationalism see the bibliography in A. P. WHITAKER & D. C. JORDAN: *Nationalism in Contemporary Latin America*, Free Press, New York, 1966.

7 On the Middle East, cf. J. D. PEARSON: *Index Islamicus* 1906–55, Cambridge, 1958; with *Supplement* 1956–60, Cambridge, 1962.

8 For Russia, cf. E. J. SIMMONS: *USSR, A Concise Handbook*, 1947 and R. SCHLESINGER: *The Nationalities Problem and Soviet Administration*, RKP, London, 1956.

9 On India, an introductory bibliography is contained in W. H. MORRIS-JONES: *The Government and Politics of India*, Hutchinson, London, 1964.

10 Useful general reference works include E. R. SELIGMAN (ed.): *Encyclopaedia of the Social Sciences*, 1933, and UN 'Statistical Year-books'.

Bibliography

Small italic letters after a year date are used for differentiation in the References.

ACTON, LORD. *Essays in Freedom and Power*, Boston 1948.

ADENWALLA, M. 'Hindu concepts and the Gita in early Indian thought', in SAKAI, 1961.

AHMED, J. M. *The Intellectual Origins of the Egyptian Revolution*, London 1960.

AJAYI, J. F. A. *Christian Missions in Nigeria 1841–91; the Making of a New Elite*, London 1965.

——— 'The place of African history and culture in the process nation building in Africa South of the Sahara', *Journal of Negro Education* XXX, 3, 1960, 206–13.

AKZIN, B. *State and Nation*, London 1964.

ALMOND, G. A. & COLEMAN, J. S. (ed.). *The Politics of the Developing Areas*, Princeton 1960.

ALMOND, G. A. & PYE, L. W. (eds.). *Comparative Political Culture*, Princeton 1965.

ALMOND, G. A. 'A developmental approach to political systems', *World Politics* 17, 1965, 183–214.

ALNAES, K. 'Songs of the Rwenzururu rebellion: the Konzo revolt against the Toro in Western Uganda', in GULLIVER 1969.

ALWORTH, E. (ed.). *Central Asia, A Century of Russian Rule*, New York 1967.

ANCHOR, R. *The Enlightenment Tradition*, New York 1967.

ANDREWES, A. *The Greek Tyrants*, London 1960.

——— 'The growth of the city-state' in LLOYD-JONES 1965.

APTER, D. *The Politics of Modernisation*, Chicago 1965.

——— *Ghana in Transition*, New York 1963a.

——— *Some Conceptual Approaches to the Study of Modernisation*, Englewood Cliffs 1968.

APTER, D. (ed.). *Ideology and Discontent,* New York 1963*b*.
—— 'Ideology and discontent' in Apter (ed.) 1963*c*.
—— 'Political religion in the New Nations' in GEERTZ 1963*d*.
—— 'Political organisation and ideology' in MOORE & FELDMAN 1960*a*.
—— 'System, process and the politics of economic development', in HOSELITZ & MOORE 1963*e*.
—— 'The role of traditionalism in the political modernisation of Ghana and Uganda', *World Politics* XIII, 1960*b*, 45–68.
ARDREY, R. *The Territorial Imperative,* New York 1966.
ARENDT, H. *The Origins of Totalitarianism,* New York 1951.
ARGYLE, W. J. 'European nationalism and African tribalism', in GULLIVER 1969.
ARNAKIS, G. 'The role of religion in the development of Balkan nationalism', in JELAVICH, 1963.
AVERY, P. *Modern Iran,* London 1965.
AVINERI, S. *Karl Marx on Colonialism and Modernisation,* New York 1969.
AYAL, E. B. 'Nationalist ideology and economic development', *Human Organisation* 25, 3, 1966, 230–9.
BACON, H. *Barbarians in Greek Tragedy,* New Haven 1961.
BANKS, A. S. & TEXTOR, R. *A Cross-Polity Survey,* Cambridge Mass. 1963.
BANTON, M. (ed.). *Anthropological Approaches to the Study of Religion,* London 1966.
BARBU, Z. 'Nationalism as a source of aggression', in Ciba Foundation 1966.
BARNARD, F. 'Culture and political development: Herder's suggestive insights', *A.P.S.R.* LXII, 2, 1969, 379–97.
BARON, S. *Modern Nationalism and Religion,* New York 1960 (1947).
BASTIDE, R. 'Messianism and socioeconomic development', *Cahiers Internationales de Sociologie* 31, 1961.
BAUER, O. *Die Nationalitetenfrage und die Sozialdemokratie,* 2nd edn., Vienna 1924.
BECKER, C. *The Heavenly City of the Eighteenth Century Philosophers,* New Haven 1932.
BELLAH, R. *Tokugawa Religion,* New York 1957.
—— (ed.). *Religion and Progress in Modern Asia,* New York 1965.
—— 'Religious aspects of modernisation in Turkey and Japan', *A.J.S.* 64, 1958, 1–5.
BENDIX, R. *Nation Building and Citizenship,* New York 1964.
—— 'Tradition and modernity reconsidered', *Comparative Studies in Society and History* IX, 1966–7, 292–346.
BENNIGSEN, A. 'Problems of bilingualism and assimilation in the North Caucasus', *Central Asian Review* 15, 3, 1967, 205–11.
BENNIGSEN, A. & LEMERCIER-QUELQUEJAY, C. *Islam in the Soviet Union,* London 1966.
—— *Les Mouvements Nationaux chez les Musulmans de Russie,* Paris 1960.
BERGHE, G. VAN. 'Contemporary nationalism in the Western world', *Daedalus* 95, 3, 1966, 828–61.

BERGER, M. *The Arab World Today*, Garden City 1962.
BERGER, P. *The Social Reality of Religion*, London 1969.
BERGHE, P. VAN DEN (ed.). *Africa, Social Problems of Conflict and Change*, San Francisco 1965.
—— 'The sociology of Africa', in BERGHE, 1965.
BERKES, N. *The Development of Secularism in Turkey*, Montreal 1964.
BERLIN, I. 'Herder and the Enlightenment', in WASSERMAN, 1965.
BINDER, L. *The Ideological Revolution in the Middle East*, New York 1964.
BLACK, C. E. *The Dynamics of Modernisation*, New York 1966.
BLAU, J. *Varieties of Modern Judaism*, New York 1966.
—— *et al.* (ed.). *Essays in Jewish Life and Thought*, New York 1959.
—— 'Tradition and innovation', in BLAU *et al.*, 1959.
BOCK, K. 'Evolution, function and change', *A.S.R.* XXVIII, 1963, 229–37.
—— 'Theories of progress and evolution', in CAHNMANN & BOSKOFF (eds.) 1964.
BOROCHOV, B. *Nationalism and the Class Struggle*, tr. A. DUKER, New York 1937.
BOTTOMORE, T. B. *Elites and Society*, London 1964.
BOZEMAN, A. *Politics and Culture in International History*, Princeton 1960.
BRACEY, J. JR., MEIER, A. & RUDWICK, E. (eds.). *Black Nationalism in America*, Indianapolis & New York 1970.
BRANDON, S. G. F. *Jesus and the Zealots*, Manchester 1967.
—— *The Trial of Jesus of Nazareth*, London 1968.
BRINTON, C. *The Anatomy of Revolution*, rev. edn., New York 1952 (1938).
BROTZ, H. (ed.). *Negro Social and Political Thought, 1850–1920*, New York & London 1966.
BUJRA, A. S. 'Political conflict and social stratification in the Hadramaut', *Middle Eastern Studies* III, 4 & IV, 1, 1967, 355–75, 2–28.
BURKS, R. V. *The Dynamics of Communism in Eastern Europe*, Princeton 1965.
BURN, A. R. *The Lyric Age of Greece*, London 1960.
BURROW, J. W. *Evolution and Society*, Cambridge 1966.
BURY, J. *A History of Greece* (revised R. Meiggs), 3rd edn., London 1951.
CADY, J. *A History of Modern Burma*, Ithaca 1958.
CAHNMANN, W. 'Religion and nationality', *A.J.S.* 49, 1943/4, 524–9.
CAHNMANN, W. & BOSKOFF, A. (eds.). *Sociology and History*, London 1964.
CALVERT, P. 'Revolution, the Politics of Violence', *Political Studies* 15, 1967.
CAMUS, A. *The Rebel*, Harmondsworth 1962.
CARRERE D'ENCAUSSE, H. *Réforme et Révolution chez les Musulmans de l'Empire Russe*, Paris 1966.
CARTER, G. (ed.). *National Unity and Regionalism in Eight African States*, Ithaca 1966.
CIBA FOUNDATION. *Conflict*, London 1966.

COBBAN, A. *Rousseau and the Modern State*, London 1964.
—— *In Search of Humanity*, London 1960.
COHEN, P. *Modern Social Theory*, London 1968.
COHN, N. *The Pursuit of the Millennium*, London 1957.
COLBOURN, R. & STRAYER, J. 'Religion and the state', *Comparative Studies in Society and History*, I, 1, 1958, 38–57, 387–93.
COLEMAN, J. S. *Nigeria, Background to Nationalism*, Berkeley & Los Angeles 1958.
—— 'Nationalism in Tropical Africa', *A.P.S.R.* XVIII, 1954, 404–26.
CONQUEST, R. (ed.). *The Soviet Nationalities Policy in Practice*, London 1967.
COULTON, G. G. 'Nationalism in the Middle Ages', *Cambridge Historical Journal*, V, 1, 1935, 15–40.
COWAN, L. G. *The Dilemmas of Africa Independence*, New York 1964.
CRANSTON, M. *Freedom*, London 1954.
DANBY, H. (ed.). *The Mishnah*, London 1958.
DAVIES, I. *African Trade Unions*, Harmondsworth 1966.
DAVIS, H. B. *Nationalism and Socialism*, New York & London 1967.
—— 'Nations, colonies and classes: the position of Marx and Engels', *Science and Society* 29, 1965, 26–43.
DESAI, A. R. *The Social Background of Indian Nationalism*, Bombay 1948.
DEUTSCH, K. W. *Nationalism and Social Communication*, 2nd edn., New York 1966.
—— *Nationalism and its Alternatives*, New York 1969.
—— *The Nerves of Government*, New York 1966.
DEUTSCH, K. W. & FOLTZ, W. (eds.). *Nationbuilding*, New York 1963.
DOOB, L. *Patriotism and Nationalism*, New Haven & London 1964.
DORE, R. P. 'On the possibility and desirability of a theory of modernisation', *Communications Series No. 38*, University of Sussex, Institute of Development Studies, 1969.
DOSTOEVSKI, F. *The Brothers Karamazov*, tr. D. Magarshack, Harmondsworth, 1958.
DUBNOW, S. *A History of the Jews in Russia and Poland*, New York 1916.
DURKHEIM, E. *The Division of Labour in Society*, tr. G. Simpson, New York 1933.
—— *Socialism*, ed. with Introduction by A. Gouldner, New York 1960*b*.
—— *The Elementary Forms of the Religious Life*, New York 1941.
—— *Montesquieu and Rousseau, Forerunners of Sociology*, tr. R. Mannheim, Michigan 1960*a*.
—— *Professional Ethics and Civic Morals*, New York 1958.
EARLE, E. M. (ed.). *Nationalism and Internationalism*, New York 1950.
EHRENBURG, V. *The Greek State*, Oxford 1960.
—— *From Solon to Socrates*, London 1965.
EISENSTADT, S. N. *Modernisation; Protest and Change*, Englewood Cliffs 1966.
—— *The Political Systems of Empires*, New York 1963.

EISENSTADT, S. N. 'Modernisation and conditions of sustained growth', *World Politics* 16, 1964*c*, 576–94.

—— 'Social change, differentiation and evolution', *A.S.R.* 29, 1964*a*, 375–86.

—— 'Breakdowns of modernisation', *Economic Development and Cultural Change* XII, 1964*b*, 345–67.

ELIADE, M. *Myths, Dreams and Mysteries*, Chicago and London 1958.

ELKAN, W. *Migrants and Proletarians*, Oxford 1960.

ELLEMERS, J. E. 'The Revolt of the Netherlands: the part played by religion in the process of nation-building', *Social Compass* XIV, 1967, 93–103.

ELVIKEN, A. 'The genesis of Norwegian nationalism', *Journal of Modern History* III, 1931, 365–91.

EMERSON, R. 'Nationalism and political development', *Journal of Politics* 22, 1, 1960, 3–28.

EPSTEIN, K. 'A new study of Fascism', *World Politics* 16, 1964.

ETTINGER, S. 'Russian society and the Jews', I.J.A. lecture, 3.3.1970.

FEST, J. C. *The face of the Third Reich*, tr. M. Bullock, London 1970.

FIELDHOUSE, D. K. (ed.). *The Theory of Capitalist Imperialism*, London 1967.

FISHMAN, J. A. *et al.* (eds.). *Language Problems of Developing Countries*, New York 1968.

FISHMAN, J. A. 'Nationality-nationalism and nation-nationalism', in FISHMAN *et al.* (ed.) 1968.

FLORESCU, R. R. 'The Uniate Church: catalyst of Rumanian national consciousness', *Slavonic and East European Review*, 45, 1967, 324–42.

FONDATION HARDT. 'Grecs et Barbares', *Entretiens sur l'Antiquité classique* VIII, Geneva 1962.

FORREST, W. G. *The Emergence of Greek Democracy*, London & New York, 1966.

FORSTER, E. M. *A Passage to India*, Harmondsworth 1936.

FRANKFORT, H. *et al. Before Philosophy*, Harmondsworth 1951.

FRAZEE, C. A. *The Orthodox Church and Independent Greece, 1821–52*, Cambridge 1969.

FRYE, R. N. *The Heritage of Persia*, New York 1966.

—— (ed.). *Islam and the West*, The Hague 1957.

GASPARD, J. 'Palestine: Who's Who among the Guerillas', *New Middle East*, 18, March 1970, 12–16.

GEERTZ, C. (ed.). *Old Societies and New States*, New York 1963*a*.

—— 'The integrative revolution', in Geertz 1963*b*.

—— 'Ideology as a cultural system', in Apter (ed.), 1963*c*.

GEIGER, T. *The Conflicted Relationship*, New York 1967.

GELLNER, E. *Thought and Change*, London 1964.

—— 'Tribalism and social change', in LEWIS W. H. (ed.), 1965.

—— 'Nationalism', L.S.E. Development Seminar, November 1965.

GELLNER, E. & IONESCU, G. (eds.). *Populism*, London 1969.

GERSCHENKRON, A. *Economic Backwardness in Historical Perspective*, Cambridge, Mass. 1962.

GERTH, H. & MILLS, C. W. (eds.). *From Max Weber, Essays in Sociology*, London 1947.

GHIRSHMAN, I. *Iran*, Harmondsworth 1954.

GIBB, H. A. R. *Recent Trends in Islam*, Chicago 1947.

GIBB, H. A. R. & BOWEN, H. *Islamic Society and the West*, 2 vols., London 1957.

GINSBURG, M. *Nationalism, A Reappraisal*, Leeds 1961.

GREENBERG, L. *The Jews of Russia*, New Haven 1951.

GROUSSET, R. *The Civilisations of the East*, New York 1931.

GULLIVER, P. H. (ed.). *Tradition and Transition in East Africa*, London 1969.

GUSFIELD, J. R. 'Tradition and modernity: misplaced polarities in the study of social change', *A.J.S.* 72, 4, 1967, 351–62.

—— 'Mass society and extremist politics', *A.S.R.* XXVII, 1962, 19–30.

GUTHRIE, W. K. C. *The Greeks and their Gods*, London 1950.

GUTKIND, P. 'The African urban milieu', *Civilisations* 12, 2, 1962, 167–91.

HAIM, S. *Arab Nationalism*, Berkeley & Los Angeles 1962.

HALECKI, O. *A History of Poland*, revised edn., London 1955.

HALPERN, B. *The Idea of the Jewish State*, Cambridge 1961.

HALPERN, M. *The Politics of Social Change in the Middle East and North Africa*, Princeton 1963.

HALPERN, M. 'Towards further modernisation of the study of new nations', *World Politics*, 17, 1964, 157–81.

HANDELSMAN, M. 'Le role de la Nationalité dans l'histoire du Moyen Age', *Bulletin of the International Committee of Historical Sciences* II, 2, 1929, 235–46.

HANDMAN, S. 'The sentiment of nationalism', *Political Science Quarterly*, 36, 1921, 107–14.

HARRISON, S. *India, the Most Dangerous Decade*, Princeton 1960.

HAUGEN, E. 'Dialect, language, nation', *American Anthropologist* 68, 4, 1966, 922–35.

HAYES, C. *The Historical Evolution of Modern Nationalism*, New York 1931.

HEIMSATH, C. *Indian Nationalism and Hindu Social Reform*, Princeton 1964.

HERDER, J. G. *Werke*, Berlin 1877–1913.

HERTZ, F. *Nationality in history and politics*, London 1944.

HERTZBERG, A. *The Zionist Idea*, New York 1960.

HESS, R. 'Ethiopia' in CARTER, 1966.

HEYD, U. *The Foundations of Turkish Nationalism*, London 1950.

—— (ed.). *Studies in Islamic History and Civilisation* IX, 1961, Jerusalem, *Scripta Hierosolymitana*.

—— 'The Ottoman Ulema and Westernisation in the time of Selim III and Mahmud II', in HEYD, 1961.

HIGNETT, C. *A History of the Athenian Constitution*, Oxford 1958.

HILFERDING, R. *Finanzkapital*, tr. E. Bass & D. Adam, Vienna 1923 (1910).

HOBSON, J. A. *Imperialism, A Study*, London 1932 (1902).
HODGKIN, T. *Nationalism in Colonial Africa*, London 1956.
—— 'The relevance of "Western" ideas in the derivation of African nationalism' in PENNOCK, 1964.
—— 'A note on the language of African nationalism', *St. Antony's Papers* 10, 1961, 22–40.
HOFFER, E. *The True Believer*, New York 1951.
HOFFMAN, S. *Le Mouvement Poujade*, Paris 1956.
HOLLAND, W. L. (ed.). *Asian Nationalism and the West*, New York 1953.
HOPKINS, K. 'Civil-military relations in developing countries', *B.J.S.* XVII, 1966, 165–82.
HOSELITZ, B. & MOORE, W. (eds.). *Industrialisation and Society*, The Hague 1963.
HOURANI, A. *Arabic Thought in the Liberal Age, 1798–1939*, London 1962.
HOVANNISIAN, R. G. *Armenia, the Road to Independence*, Berkeley 1967.
HOWARD, R. C. 'The Chinese reform movement of the 1890s: a symposium', Introduction, *Journal of Asian Studies* XXIX, 1, 1969, 7–14.
HUNTER, G. *The New Societies of Tropical Africa*, Oxford 1962.
HYSLOP, B. *French Nationalism in 1789 according to the General Cahiers*, New York 1934.
JANSEN, M. B. (ed.). *Changing Japanese Attitudes to Modernisation*, Princeton 1965.
JELAVICH, B. & C. (eds.). *The Balkans in Transition*, Berkeley 1963.
JOHNSON, H. G. (ed.). *Economic Nationalism in Old and New States*, London 1968.
JOHNSON, H. G. 'A theoretical model of economic nationalism in new and developing states', *Political Science Quarterly*, LXXX, 1965, 169–85.
JOHNSON, J. J. 'The new Latin American nationalism', *Yale Review*, 54, 1965, 187–204.
JULY, R. *The Origins of Modern African Thought*, London 1968.
KANTOROWICZ, E. H. '*Pro patria mori* in medieval political thought', *American Historical Review*, 56, 3, 1951, 472–92.
KAPLOW, J. (ed.). *New Perspectives on the French Revolution*, New York 1965.
KATZ, J. 'Jews and Judaism in the 19th century', *Journal of World History* IV, 4, 1958, 881–900.
KAUFMANN, Y. *The Religion of Israel*, tr. M. Greenberg, London 1961.
KAUTSKY, J. H. (ed.). *Political Change in Underdeveloped Countries*, New York 1962.
KEDDIE, N. *Religion and Revolution in Iran*, London 1966.
KEDOURIE, E. *Nationalism*, London 1960.
—— *Afghani and Abduh*, London & New York 1966.
—— *Nationalism in Africa and Asia*, forthcoming.
KEDWARD, R. *The Dreyfus Affair*, London 1965.
KEMILAINEN, A. *Nationalism, Problems Concerning the Word, the Concept and Classification*, Yvaskyla 1964.

K

KIERNAN, V. 'The new Nation-States', *New Left Review* 30, 1964.

KILSON, M. 'Authoritarian and single-party tendencies in African politics', *World Politics* 15, 1963, 262–94.

—— 'The analysis of African nationalism', *World Politics*, 10, 3, 1958, 484–92.

KOHN, H. *The Idea of Nationalism*, New York 1967 (1944).

—— *Nationalism, Its Meaning and History*, Princeton 1955.

—— *Prophets and Peoples*, New York 1961.

—— *Panslavism*, 2nd rev. edn., New York 1960.

—— *A History of Nationalism in the East*, London 1929.

—— *The Mind of Germany*, London 1965.

—— *Nationalism and Liberty, the Swiss Example*, London 1957.

—— 'The origins of English nationalism', *Journal of the History of Ideas* I, 1940, 69–94.

KOLARZ, W. *Peoples of the Soviet Far East*, London 1954.

KORNHAUSER, W. *The Politics of Mass Society*, London 1959.

LASLETT, P. & RUNCIMAN, W. G. (eds.). *Philosophy, Politics and Society*, 2nd series, Oxford 1962.

LE BON, G. *The Crowd*, London 1947.

LEFEBVRE, G. 'Revolutionary Crowds', in KAPLOW, 1965.

LEGUM, C. *Pan-Africanism*, London 1962.

LEIDEN, C. & SCHMITT, K. *The Politics of Violence, Revolution in the Modern World*, Englewood Cliffs 1968.

LENIN, V. I. *Critical remarks on the national question*, Moscow 1951 (1913).

—— '*Preliminary draft of theses on the national & colonial questions*', *Selected Works*, II, 2, Moscow 1952 (1920).

—— *Imperialism, the Highest Stage of Capitalism*, Moscow 1947 (1916).

LE PAGE, R. B. *The National Language Question*, London 1964.

LERNER, D. *The Passing of Traditional Society*, New York 1964 (1958).

LEVENSON, R. *Li'ang Ch'i Ch'ao and the Mind of Modern China*, Berkeley & Los Angeles 1967.

LEVI, M. *Political Power in the Ancient World*, tr. J. Costello, London 1965.

LEWIS, B. *The Emergence of Modern Turkey*, 2nd edn., London 1968.

LEWIS, W. A. *Politics in West Africa*, London 1965.

LEWIS, W. H. (ed.). *French-Speaking Africa, The Search for Identity*, New York 1965.

LIJPHART, A. *The Politics of Accomodation*, Berkeley & Los Angeles 1968.

LIPSET, S. *Political Man*, London 1963.

LIPSKEY, G. *Ethiopia*, New Haven 1962.

LITTLE, K. *West African Urbanisation*, Cambridge 1965.

LIVELEY, J. (ed.). *The Enlightenment*, London 1966.

LLOYD, P. C. *Africa in Social Change*, Harmondsworth 1967.

—— (ed.). *The New Elites of Tropical Africa*, London 1966.

LLOYD-JONES, H. (ed.). *The Greek World*, Harmondsworth 1965.

LOWENTHAL, R. 'Communism versus nationalism', *Problems of Nationalism*, 11, 6, 1962, 37–44.

LUCKENBILL, D. D. *Ancient Records of Assyria and Babylonia*, Chicago 1926–7.

MACHIAVELLI, N. *The Prince*, tr. L. Ricci, rev. by E. R. P. Vincent, London 1935.

MACINTYRE, A. 'A Mistake about Causality in the Social Sciences', in LASLETT & RUNCIMAN, 1962.

MANNHEIM, K. *Ideology and Utopia*, London 1936.

—— *Man and Society in an Age of Reconstruction*, London 1940.

MANNONI, O. *Prospero and Caliban*, London 1956.

MARCUS, J. R. (ed.). *The Jew in the Medieval World*, New York 1965.

MARTIN, D. *Pacifism*, London 1965.

MARTINS, H. '"Developmental nationalism" in Brazil', *Sociological Review Monograph* No. 11, 1967, 153–72.

MARUYAMA, M. *Thought and Behaviour in Modern Japanese Politics*, expanded edn., ed. I. Morris, London 1968.

MARX, K. & ENGELS, F. *The German Ideology*, Moscow 1964.

—— *Basic Writings on Politics and Philosophy*, ed. L. S. Feuer, New York 1959.

MATOSSIAN, M. 'Ideologies of "delayed industrialisation": some tensions and ambiguities', *Economic Development and Cultural Change*, VI, 3, 1958, 217–228.

MAYER, P. *Townsmen and Tribesmen*, Oxford 1961.

MAZRUI, A. *Pax Africana*, London 1966.

MCCULLEY, B. T. *English Education and the Origins of Indian Nationalism*, New York 1940.

MEAD, G. H. *Mind, Self and Society*, Chicago 1934.

MEHDEN, F. VON DER. *Religion and Nationalism in South-East Asia*, Madison 1963.

MERRITT, R. L. & ROKKAN, S. (eds.). *Comparing Nations*, New Haven 1966.

MEYER, M. A. *The Origins of the Modern Jew*, Detroit 1967.

MILL, J. S. *Considerations on Representative Government*, London 1872.

MILLS, C. W. *The Power Elite*, New York 1956.

MINOGUE, K. *Nationalism,* London 1967.

MISRA, B. B. *The Indian Middle Classes*, Oxford 1961.

MONTAGNE, R. 'The "modern state" in Africa and Asia', *The Cambridge Journal* V, 1952, 583–602.

MONTESQUIEU, S. DE C., BARON DE. *The Spirit of the Laws*, tr. T. Nugent, New York & London 1966.

MOORE, W. & FELDMAN, A. (eds.). *Labour Commitment and Social Change in Developing Areas*, New York 1960.

MORRIS-JONES, W. H. *The Government and Politics of India*, London 1964.

MOSSE, G. L. 'The genesis of Fascism', *Journal of Contemporary History* I, 1, 1966, 14–26.

MUNGER, E. S. *Afrikaner and African Nationalism*, London 1967.

NALBANDIAN, L. Z. *The Armenian Revolutionary Movement*, Berkeley 1963.

NAMIER, L. B. *Avenues of History*, New York 1952.

NETTL, J. P. & ROBERTSON, R. *International Systems and the Modernisation of Societies,* London 1968.
—— 'Modernisation, industrialisation or development?', *B.J.S.* XVII, 3, 1966, 274–91.
NEUMANN, F. *Behemoth, the Structure and Practise of National Socialism, 1933–44,* New York 1944.
NISBET, R. A. *The Quest for Community,* New York 1953.
—— (ed.). *Emile Durkheim,* Englewood Cliffs 1965.
NORBECK, E. *Religion in Primitive Society,* New York 1961.
NOTH, M. *The History of Israel,* London 1960.
O'DEA, T. *The Sociology of Religion,* Englewood Cliffs 1966.
ORTEGA Y GASSET, J. *The Revolt of the Masses,* New York 1932.
OSSOWSKI, S. *Class Structure in the Social Consciousness,* London 1962.
PALMER, R. 'The national idea in France before the Revolution', *Journal of the History of Ideas* I, 1940, 95–111.
PANOFSKY, E. *Renaissance and Renascences in Western Art,* London 1970.
PARSONS, T. *Structure and Process in Modern Societies,* Illinois 1960.
—— *Societies, Evolutionary and Comparative Perspectives,* Englewood Cliffs 1965.
—— *Essays in Sociological Theory,* rev. edn., London 1964*a*.
—— 'Evolutionary universals in Society', *A.S.R.* XXIX, 1964*b*, 339–57.
—— *The Social System,* London 1951.
PEACOCK, J. L. 'Religion, communications and modernisation: a Weberian critique of some recent views', *Human Organisation,* 28, 1, 1966, 35–41.
PENNOCK, J. R. (ed.). *Self-Government in modernising societies,* Englewood Cliffs 1964.
PEPELASSIS, A. 'The image of the past and economic backwardness', *Human Organisation* 17, 1958, 9, 19–27.
PERHAM, M. *The Colonial Reckoning,* London 1963.
PINSON, K. S. (ed.). *Nationalism and History,* Philadelphia 1958.
PLAUT, W. G. *The Rise of Reform Judaism,* New York 1963.
POCOCK, D. 'Notes on the interaction of English and Indian thought in the 19th century', *Journal of World History,* IV, 4, 1958, 833–48.
POLIAKOV, L. *Harvest of Hate,* New York 1954.
POLK, W. R. 'The nature of modernisation: the Middle East and North Africa', *Foreign Affairs* 44, 1, 1965, 100–10.
POPPER, K. *The Open Society and its Enemies,* 4th edn., London 1962.
—— *The Poverty of Historicism,* London 1961.
POTTER, D. M. 'The Historian's use of nationalism and vice-versa', in RIASANOVSKY & RIJNIK, 1963.
PRITCHARD, J. B. (ed.). *The Ancient Near East,* Princeton 1958.
PYE, L. W. (ed.). *Communications and Political Development,* Princeton 1965.
PYE, L. W. & VERBA, S. *Political Culture and Political Development,* Princeton 1965.
RAMSAUR, E. *The Emergence of the Young Turks,* Princeton 1957.

REID, A. 'Nineteenth-century Pan-Islam in Indonesia and Malaysia', *Journal of Asian Studies* 26, 2, 1967, 267–83.

REISS, H. S. (ed.). *The Political Thought of the German Romantics, 1793–1815*, Oxford 1955.

RENAN, E. *Qu'est-ce qu'une Nation?*, Paris 1882.

RENIER, G. J. *The Dutch Nation, An Historical Study*, London 1944.

RIASANOVSKY, A. V. & RIJNIK, B. (eds.). *Generalisations in Historical Writing*, Philadelphia 1963.

ROFF, W. R. *The Origins of Malay Nationalism*, New Haven 1966.

ROKKAN, S. (ed.). *The Comparative Method, Transactions of the Fourth World Congress of Sociology* III, 1961.

RONDOT, P. 'Quelques Remarques sur le Ba'ath', *Orient* 31, 1964, 7–19.

ROOS, H. *A History of Modern Poland*, London 1966.

ROSDOLSKY, R. 'Friedrich Engels und das Problem der "Geschichts-loser Völker"', *Archiv für Sozialgeschichte IV, 1964*, Hanover, 87–282.

ROTBERG, R. 'African nationalism: concept or confusion?', *Journal of Modern African Studies* IV, 1, 1967, 33–46.

—— 'The rise of African nationalism: The Case of East and Central Africa', *World Politics* XV, 1, 1962, 75–90.

ROUCH, J. 'Second generation of migrants in Ghana and the Ivory Coast' in SOUTHALL, 1961.

ROUSSEAU, J.-J. 'Contrat Social, Projet Corse, Considerations sur le Gouvernement de Pologne', in *Political Writings of Rousseau*, ed. C. E. Vaughan, 2 vols., Cambridge 1915.

ROUX, G. *Ancient Iraq*, Harmondsworth 1964.

ROYAL INSTITUTE OF INTERNATIONAL AFFAIRS. *Nationalism, A Report*, London 1939.

RUNCIMAN, W. G. *Social Science and Political Theory*, Cambridge 1965.

RUSSETT, B. *et al. World Handbook of Political and Social Indicators*, New Haven 1964.

RUSTOW, D. *A World of Nations*, Washington D.C. 1967.

SACHAR, H. *The Course of Modern Jewish History*, New York 1958.

SAFRAN, N. *Egypt in Search of Political Community*, Cambridge, Mass. 1961.

SAKAI, R. (ed.). *Studies on Asia*, Vol. II, Lincoln 1961.

SARKISYANZ, E. *Buddhist Backgrounds of the Burmese Revolution*, The Hague 1964.

SCHAFER, B. C. *Nationalism, Myth and Reality*, New York 1955.

—— 'Bourgeois nationalism in the pamphlets on the eve of the French Revolution', *Journal of Modern History* X, 1938, 31–50.

SCHEUCH, E. K. 'Cross-national comparisons with aggregate data', in MERRITT & ROKKAN, 1966.

SCHREKER, J. 'The reform movement, nationalism and China's foreign policy', *Journal of Asian Studies* XXIX, 1, 1969, 43–53.

SCHLESINGER, R. *The Nationalities Problem and Soviet Administration*, London 1956.

SCHUMPETER, J. A. *Capitalism, Socialism and Democracy*, 3rd edn., London 1950.

SELZNICK, P. *The Organisational Weapon*, New York 1952.
SETON-WATSON, H. 'Fascism, Right and Left', *Journal of Contemporary History* I, 1, 1966, 183–97.
—— *Nationalism, Old and New*, London 1965.
—— *Neither War Nor Peace*, London 1960.
SETON-WATSON, R. *The Southern Slav Question and the Habsburg Monarchy*, London 1911.
SHAHEEN, S. *The Communist Theory of Self-Determination*, The Hague 1956.
SHERRARD, P. *The Greek East and the Latin West*, London 1959.
SHILS, E. *Political Development in the New States*, New York 1964.
—— 'Intellectuals in the Political Development of New States', *World Politics* XII, 1960, 329–68.
SIEGFRIED, A. *Switzerland*, London 1950.
SILVERT, K. (ed.). *Expectant Peoples: Nationalism and Development*, New York 1967.
SIMON, L. (ed.). *Achad Ha'am: Essays, Letters, Memoirs*, Oxford 1946.
SINGH, K. *Prophet of Indian Nationalism*, London 1963.
SKINNER, E. P. *The Mossi of Upper Volta*, Stanford 1964.
SKINNER, G. W. 'The nature of loyalties in rural Indonesia' in SKINNER, 1959.
—— (ed.). *Local, Ethnic and National Loyalties in Village Indonesia, A Symposium*, New Haven 1959.
SMELSER, N. J. *Essays in Sociological Explanation*, Englewood Cliffs 1968a.
—— *Theory of Collective Behaviour*, London 1962.
—— 'Towards a theory of modernisation' in SMELSER, 1968b.
—— 'Social and Psychological Dimensions of Collective Behaviour' in SMELSER, 1968c.
SMITH, A. D. 'Modernity and evil: some sociological reflections on the problem of meaning', *Diogenes* 71, 1970, 65–80.
SMITH, W. C. *Modernisation of a Traditional Society*, London 1965.
SMYTHE, H. H. & M. M. *The New Nigerian Elite*, California 1960.
SNYDER, L. *The Dynamics of Nationalism, A Reader*, Princeton 1964.
—— *The Meaning of Nationalism*, New Brunswick 1954.
—— *The New Nationalism*, Ithaca 1968.
SOUTHALL, A. (ed.). *Social Change in Africa*, Oxford 1961.
SOUTHERN, R. 'Two kinds of nationalism, England and the Continent', *Third Programme Talk*, 6.3.1967.
SPIRO, M. E. 'Religion: problems of definition and explanation', in BANTON, 1966.
STAVRIANOS, L. *The Balkans Since 1453*, New York 1961.
—— 'Antecedents to the Balkan revolutions of the 19th century,' *Journal of Modern History* 29, 1957, 335–48.
STOIANOVITCH, T. 'The pattern of Serbian intellectual evolution', *Comparative Studies in Society and History* I, 1958, 242–72.
SYKES, C. *Crossroads to Israel*, London 1965.
SYMMONS-SYMONOLEWICZ, K. 'Nationalist movements: an attempt at a comparative typology', *Comparative Studies in Society and History* VII, 1965, 221–30.

TACITUS. *Annals*, in *Tacitus on Imperial Rome*, tr. M. Grant, Harmondsworth, 1956.
TALMON, J. L. *The Origins of Totalitarian Democracy*, London 1952.
—— *Political Messianism, the Romantic Phase*, London 1960.
THUCYDIDES. *History of the Peloponnesian War*, tr. R. Warner, Harmondsworth 1954.
TOLSTOY, L. *War and Peace*, tr. R. Edmonds, Harmondsworth 1957.
TREVOR-ROPER, H. *Jewish and Other Nationalisms*, London 1961.
ULAM, A. *The Unfinished Revolution*, New York 1960.
UNESCO. *Social Implications of Industrialisation and Urbanisation in Africa South of the Sahara*, ed. D. Forde, Paris 1956.
VATIKIOTIS, P. J. *The Modern History of Egypt*, New York 1969.
—— *The Egyptian Army in Politics*, Bloomington, Indiana 1961.
—— (ed.). *Egypt Since the Revolution*, London 1968.
VIENNOT, J-P. 'Le Ba'ath entre Théorie et Pratique', *Orient* 30, 1964, 13–27.
VIRGIL. *Aeneid*, ed. T. E. Page, London 1938.
WAKIN E. *A Lonely Minority*, New York 1963.
WALEK-CZERNECKI, M. T. 'Le rôle de la Nationalité dans l'histoire de l'Antiquité', *Bulletin of the International Committee of Historical Science* II, 2, 1929, 305–20.
WALLERSTEIN, I. *Africa, the Politics of Independence*, New York 1961.
—— (ed.). *Social Change, The Colonial Situation*, New York 1966.
—— 'Elites in French-Speaking West Africa', *Journal of Modern African Studies* 3, 1, 1965, 1–33.
WASSERMAN, E. A. (ed.). *Aspects of the Eighteenth Century*, Baltimore 1965.
WAUTHIER, C. M. *The Literature and Thought of Modern Africa*, London 1966.
WEBER, M. *Economy and Society*, ed. G. Roth & C. Wittich, New York 1968.
—— *Theory of Social and Economic Organisation*, New York 1964.
—— *The Sociology of Religion*, tr. E. Fischoff, London 1965.
—— 'Social psychology of the world religions', in GERTH & MILLS, 1947.
—— 'Ethnic groups' in WEBER 1968, I, 2, Ch. 5.
WEINGROD, A. *Israel, Group Relations in a New Society*, London 1965.
WELCH, C. M. Jr. *Recent Attempts at Political Unification in West Africa*, D. Phil. thesis, St. Antony's College, Oxford 1964.
WERTHEIM, W. F. 'Religious reform movements in South and South East Asia', *Archives de Sociologie des Religions* 9, 1958, 53–62.
WHEELER, G. *The Modern History of Soviet Central Asia*, London 1964.
WHITAKER, A. P. *Nationalism in Latin America*, Gainsville, Fla. 1962.
WHITAKER, A. P. & JORDAN, D. C. *Nationalism in Contemporary Latin America*, New York 1966.
WILBER, D. N. *Afghanistan*, New Haven 1962.
WILENSKY, H. L. 'Mass Society and Mass Culture', *A.S.R.* XXIX, 1964, 173–97.

WILSON, D. A. 'Nation-Building and Revolutionary War' in DEUTSCH & FOLTZ, 1963.

WIRTH, L. 'Types of Nationalism', *A.J.S.* 41, 6, 1936, 723–37.

WOLIN, S. *Politics and Vision*, Boston 1960.

WOLLHEIM, R. (ed.). *Hume on Religion*, London & Glasgow 1963.

WORRELL, H. *A Short Account of the Copts*, Michigan 1945.

WORSLEY, P. *The Third World*, London 1964.

WORSLEY, P. 'The concept of Populism', in GELLNER & IONESCU, 1969.

WUORINEN, J. 'Scandinavia and national consciousness', in EARLE, 1950.

YADIN, Y. *Masada*, London 1966.

YINGER, J. M. *Religion, Society and the Individual*, New York 1957.

YOUNG, C. M. *Politics in the Congo*, Princeton 1965.

ZARTMANN, W. 'Characteristics of Developing Foreign Policies', in LEWIS, W. H. 1965.

ZENKOVSKY, S. *PanTurkism and Islam in Russia*, Cambridge, Mass. 1960.

—— 'A century of Tatar revival', *Slavic Review* 12, 1953, 303–18.

ZERNATTO, G. 'Nation: the history of a word', *Review of Politics* VI, 1944, 351–66.

ZNANIECKI, F. *Modern Nationalities*, Urbana, Illinois 1952.

Notes

Full bibliographical details for each book or article quoted below are given in the alphabetical bibliography on pages 275 ff and all references here are simply to author and date. Where an author has written more than one work in a single year such works are differentiated by italic letters following the year date.

INTRODUCTION

1 ALNAES, 1969.
2 Cf. ARGYLE, 1969. In this stimulating article Argyle argues that the many similarities between African 'tribal' movements and their European 'nationalist' counterparts override the difference in size of the units involved. Most nationalist movements in Central and Eastern Europe started from literary and historical associations, broke out into violence over the issue of cultural facilities, invented or rediscovered a common and glorious past, competed for salaried posts in the imperial bureaucracies, and so on. The same can be shown in the case of many African 'tribalist' movements—for example, the BaKongo A.B.A.K.O. of 1952 or the Kikuyu Central Association of 1928, the Soli Tribal Association in Northern Rhodesia, the Zulu Society of South Africa, the Ibo N.C.N.C. and the Luo Union in Kampala. In addition, the Lenje of Northern Rhodesia, the Budama of Uganda, the Luba and Mongo in the Congo, the Ganda, the Fang of Gabon, the Chagga of Tanganyika, and of course the Hausa, Yoruba, Ashanti, Lunda and Ewe, all at one time or another demanded a redistribution of posts and cultural facilities for their groups.

Argyle wants, from these examples, to assimilate African 'tribalism' to European 'nationalism'. This, to my mind, can only be done if we drop the kinship basis that is held to be one of the essential characteristics of a 'tribe'. The group would then retain its cultural distinctiveness as well as its territorial definition, and, if it evinced group sentiment and possessed external political relations with other groups, could be held to constitute what the French call an 'ethnie'. But this holds only for some of the many African 'tribes'. It is doubtful if a really small tribe, based on kinship role-structure, could evince that sentiment or enter into such relations with other like groups; hence size remains a rough-and-ready guide. This will be argued at length later (Chapter 7).

Argyle's point about the difficulty of using size is well taken—especially with regard to the ?400,000 Basques. And his explanation of nationalism in terms of growing competition for power and wealth, accompanied by democratic and egalitarian legitimations, which then take group form for effectiveness, needs to be further developed.

3 An illuminating study of this in Eastern Europe is BURKS, 1965, esp. Preface to the new edition. It is worth citing here the words of Nehru at a conference in Lucknow in 1950 (in HOLLAND 1953):

> Any other force, any other activity that may seek to function, must define itself in terms of this nationalism. . . . No other argument in any country of Asia is going to have weight if it goes counter to the national spirit of the country, Communism or no Communism.

This echoes Nkrumah's doctrine of the 'political kingdom' and its primacy, and Sekou Touré's position that there are no classes (and hence no Marxist class antagonisms) in Africa.

4 KEDOURIE, 1960, p. 90.

5 MONTESQUIEU, 1966, Book 19.

6 This is the approach of ZNANIECKI's *Modern Nationalities*, 1952. It is interesting that the sociology of knowledge, which might be expected to concern itself with nationalism, has once again been deflected by its Marxian-Mannheimian origins from attending to the social location and institutional influences on nationalism.

7 Cf. APTER, 'Political Organisation and Ideology', MOORE & FELDMAN, 1960a.

CHAPTER ONE   *The Doctrine and its Critics*

1 MILL, 1872.

2 RENAN, 1882. As Kedourie says, this favourable tradition stems from Locke's defence of liberty and representative government and Burke's insistence on the rights of the American colonies.

3 ACTON, 'Nationality', in ACTON, 1948. There is, of course, another equally radical critique of the dangers inherent in the slogans of nationalism and 'national culture', which it sees as the weapon of the bourgeoisie in alliance with the clergy and landlords—I mean, the Marxist. The *locus classicus* for the diametrical opposition of Marxism to *petit bourgeois* nationalism, in the name of proletarian internationalism, is Lenin's *Critical Remarks on the National Question*, (1913), Moscow 1951.

4 KEDOURIE, 1960, p. 18.
5 *Ibid.*, p. 138.
6 *Ibid.*, p. 140.
7 *Ibid.*, p. 133.
8 *Ibid.*, p. 80.
9 *Ibid.*, p. 70. Besides, there is an important empirical objection to Herder's arguments for the primacy of language in differentiating communities and individualising personalities. There is after all nothing 'natural' about linguistic nations, and 'the world is indeed diverse, much too diverse, for the classifications of nationalist anthropology. Races, languages, religions, political traditions and loyalties are so inextricably intermixed that there can be no clear convincing reason why people who speak the same language, but whose history and circumstances otherwise diverge, should form one state, or why people who speak two different languages and whom circumstances have thrown together should not form one state', *ibid.*, p. 79. It may be that this difficulty in securing agreement on the elements of a definition of the concept of the 'nation', which has weighed most heavily as an argument in the West, constitutes another reason for the lack of interest in nationalism among sociologists.
10 *Ibid.*, pp. 80–1.
11 *Ibid.*, p. 81.
12 *Ibid.*, p. 81.
13 *Ibid.*, p. 89.
14 HEINE, *Religion and Philosophy in Germany*, 1834, in KEDOURIE, 1960, p. 89.
15 Hume in particular castigated these examples of hatred which he believed were inevitable consequences of coercive monotheism, cf. his *Dialogues Concerning Natural Religion*, in WOLLHEIM, 1963. But monotheism is not the only cause of political violence. The dynastic principle kept Europe at war for large parts of the eighteenth century, cf. ANCHOR, 1967. Of course, the scale of violence has vastly increased; but that is the result of improved communications and technology rather than any ideological movements. All the evidence suggests that men would have committed violence on as large a scale before the advent of ideology or scientific techniques of destruction, had they possessed the means, and that Genghis Khan and Ashurnasirpal II would have matched the intensity of destructive violence of a Hitler or Stalin.
16 One thinks mainly of writers such as Cesaire, Senghor and Diop, or Taha Husain, Tawfiq al-Hakim and Abduh in Egypt, or Chatterjee, Tagore and Aurobindo in India. But there is also the new European interest in African art or Indian religion, which is closely associated with the rise of nationalism in these areas.
17 MINOGUE, 1967, Ch. 1.
18 F. JAHN, *Das Deutsche Volkstum*, Lübeck, 1810, tr. Snyder in SNYDER, 1964.

19 For the intellectual context of the formation of this German 'organic' theory, cf. REISS, 1955; for the social context, cf. KOHN, 1967, Ch. 7.

20 BARON, 1960, p. 6.

21 J. G. Fichte, *Addresses to the German Nation* (1807–8), tr. R. F. Jones and G. R. Turnbull, 1922, cited in KEDOURIE, 1960, p. 83.

22 KEDOURIE, 1960, p. 1.

23 *Ibid.*, pp. 71–3.

24 KEMILAINEN, 1964.

25 The Greco-Turkish exchange of populations in 1922, and the goals of Greek policy, were largely determined by Byzantine ideals and categories, cf. G. Arnakis in B. & C. JELAVICH, 1963. For Burma and Indonesia, cf. MEHDEN, 1963.

26 Cf. HODGKIN, 1964 and 1961. This will be argued more fully at various points.

27 KEDOURIE, 1960, p. 133.

28 This is one of the difficulties that Rousseau's General Will attempts to cope with. For most nationalists, collective will is *sui generis* and not just a macrocosm of individual will—except in the latter's 'true' or 'essential' nature, which is usually obscured. But this collective will is both the product and the producer of the exercise of many individual wills in history. As such, it is almost as stable and enduring as its prototype, 'nature'. This aspect of the doctrine has affinities with Durkheim's conscience collective.

29 ROUSSEAU, 1915 (II, 319, Projet Corse).

30 WEBER, 1968, Vol. I, Part 2, Ch. 5, 'Ethnic Groups'.

31 Some early nationalists did not draw the full conclusions from their doctrine, e.g. Herder and other so-called 'cultural nationalists'; they did not therefore subscribe to (5)–(7). But the difference is merely one of emphasis or degree. The only practical way of safeguarding the nation's individuality is through the use of power and planned policy, whose sole instrument, under modern conditions is the state. 'Political' and 'cultural' nationalists differ over means, *how* to preserve or create the 'nation', not over ends, *that* it be preserved.

32 We shall return to the language issue in greater detail, especially in Chapters 6 and 7. For the present, it is enough to note that language, if not literature, remains an attractive ingredient for nationalists because it is often the least disputable link with the ideal past, the most tangible element of the collective heritage, especially for those whom religious images and loyalties could no longer satisfy, like the Christians of the Lebanon, cf. HOURANI, 1962, Ch. 3–4.

33 Cf. DOOB, 1964, for some Tyrolean examples.

34 M. Aflaq, *On the Road to Resurrection*, 1963, cited in BINDER, 1964.

35 This Periclean ideal of the Funeral Speech expresses more aptly some, though not all, of the sentiments associated with nationalism, than the laws and spirit of the Sparta which served as Rousseau's model and inspiration. Cf. Thucydides, Book Two.

36 The Rousseauan contrast of 'nature' and 'civilisation' purports to

describe an empirical state of affairs 'within history', unlike the myths analysed by ELIADE, 1968. This is an example of the typical nationalist manner of unconsciously idealising a part of the past in order to attain a future harmony.

CHAPTER TWO   *The Imitation of Kant*

1 POPPER, 1962, Vol. II, Ch. 12/3, pp. 49–58, 60–4. Cf. his statement that Hegel 'saw that nationalism answers a need—the desire of men to find and to know their definite place in the world, and to belong to a powerful collective body' (p. 64). 'Nationalism appeals to our tribal instincts, to passion and to prejudice, and to our nostalgic desire to be relieved from the strain of individual responsibility which it attempts to replace by a collective or group responsibility' (p. 49).

For Popper, the 'principle of the national state is not only inapplicable but it has never been clearly conceived. It is a myth. It is an irrational, a romantic and Utopian dream, a dream of naturalism and of tribal collectivism' (p. 51).

I can find no explanation in all this as to why, after its long decline from the time of Alexander onwards, nationalism should suddenly and so dramatically reappear and sweep all before it at the time of the French Revolution and the German reaction to Napoleon. (The latter is written off as 'one of those typical tribal reactions against the expansion of a super-national empire', p. 55.) But of course if nationalism is simply equated with tribalism, the natural state of man, what need of further explanation? All we need to know is why it eventuated in Fascism, where before it had appeared as an ally of 'freedom and reason' in the French Revolution. Nationalism is really introduced into Popper's story to link tribalism to racial Fascism; and Hegel is made to serve as the main link (where Kedourie sees him as a theorist of the State, not the Nation). It is hardly surprising that Rousseau is denied the title (and to some extent the paternity) of nationalist; nationalists *cannot* be good democrats, or vice versa. (Popper seems to admit a certain doubt here.)

The real trouble in all this is that psychologistic and ideological explanations are substituted for sociological ones; and secondly that definitions of nationalism are not separable from explanations of it. The psychological categories are simply ethical labels. They are far too broad and simple to explain the incidence, varieties, intensities, scope, etc., of nationalism. Besides, if nationalism is simply a form of tribalism, why should tribalism take this peculiar form at this particular historical and social juncture?

Ethically, too, the case is a bit overstated. Of course, nationalism can provide a sense of security, relieve strain, evoke xenophobia, undermine freedom, etc., i.e. serve all kinds of individual needs, desirable or otherwise, according to preference or reasoned assessment of wider consequences. But its wider *social* and *political* consequences include not only war and terrorism, but political pluralism, recognition of the value of other groups, and an impetus to collective improvement and innovation. It rather depends on the nature and the qualities of the advanced nation which serves as a model...

2 Psychological theories of nationalism are described in HERTZ, 1944, Ch. 1/5, which reveals the vagueness of their categories and difficulty in testing their assumptions. Cf. also the review in SNYDER, 1954, Ch. 3. Evaluation of the various approaches and their fruitfulness is beyond the scope of this book and my competence.

3 TREVOR-ROPER, 1961.

4 Cf. for example, PERHAM, 1963. A much more realistic picture stressing the step-by-step growth of nationalism among the western-educated, but often marginal, elites in Africa is provided by WALLERSTEIN, 1961, Ch. 3, and LLOYD, 1967, esp. Chs. 9 and 11. The exclusive and hypocritical character of Nigerian mission preachers from the West from the 1870's onwards and the African separatist reaction, is brought out in AJAYI, 1965. But he is quite insistent that it is *local* inequities, not mesmerising foreign doctrines picked up at universities abroad, that gradually makes secession both desirable and possible. Rousseau, etc., as Hodgkin points out, could serve to legitimate conceptions and aspirations which had their origin in the local situation. Africans use the same language as the Levellers, not because they have read Sexby, but because similar conditions produce the idea that men are born with certain inalienable 'birthrights'. As Padmore puts it:

> When the Gold Coast Africans demand self-government today, they are, in consequence, merely asserting their birthright which they never really surrendered to the British who, disregarding their treaty obligations of 1844, gradually usurped full sovereignty over the country. (G. Padmore, *The Gold Coast Revolution*, London, 1953, p. 35)

a sentiment that found resonance at the third inter-territorial Congress of the Rassemblement Démocratique Africain at Bamako in late September, 1957 (résolution politique):

> Le Congrès (du RDA) considère que l'indépendance des peuples est un droit inaliénable leur permettant de disposer des attributs de leur souveraineté selon les intérêts des masses populaires. . . . Mais il considère que l'inter-dépendance est la règle d'or de la vie des peuples et se manifeste au 20ième siècle par la constitution des grands ensembles politiques et économiques. . . .

5 AHMED, 1960.
6 ALWORTH, 1967, Ch. 6.

7 WELCH, 1964, esp. Ch. 6.
8 STAVRIANOS, 1957.
9 STOIANOVITCH, 1958.
10 KEDOURIE, 1960, p. 33.
11 *Ibid.*, p. 24.
12 *Religion within the Limits of Pure Reason*, 1793, cited in KEDOURIE, 1960, p. 29.
13 *The Foundations of Natural Law*, 1796, cited p. 39.
14 *Ibid.*, p. 44.
15 *Letters on the Aesthetic Education of Man*, 1795, cited p. 45.
16 *Ibid.*, p. 99.
17 *Ibid.*, p. 101. It is not clear how far Kedourie thinks this need is universal, rather than merely widespread and strong. Nor is it clear how much explanatory power he attaches to this need. I incline to think, reading the passage in its context, that the appeal to needs is on the whole secondary, and that, as argued in the text, nationalism is portrayed as an irresistible (or nearly so) force, where enlightenment philosophies have paved the way for wholesale change.
18 *Ibid.*, p. 105.
19 Cf. ARDREY, 1966.
20 GELLNER, 1964, pp. 151–2 (footnote). Gellner contends that for Kant 'self-determination' 'lends itself to individualism and/or universalism, but hardly to a cult of national cultures', since the residual self is alone independent of external causes and blind forces, provided it is rational. All other parts of the self are contingent on external forces, and therefore cannot be identified with the 'true self'. And a nation's characteristics are, of course, likewise contingent.
21 KEDOURIE, forthcoming. I am indebted to Professor Kedourie for allowing me to allude to this work before its publication, introduced in the form of lectures given at the London School of Economics in 1967.
22 This remark applies solely to the earlier work. In the forthcoming book, an explanation of nationalism's appeal to the less educated but broader mass of the population is provided in terms of the elite's manipulation of traditionalist sentiments through the exploitation of chiliastic hopes generated by the impact of a levelling European administration and market economy. An example was the use of the traditional Shinto cult to bolster loyalty to the Emperor in Japan and so achieve national solidarity. Aflaq and Zurayck see in Islam merely a buttress for Arabism; and Tilak and Aurobindo were using elements of traditional Hinduism, such as the cult of Shivaji or Kali, or a special activist reading of the Gita, to foster an all-India nationalism, cf. ADENWALLA, 1961 (Vol. II).

This is part of his wider thesis that the 'cult of the Dark Gods' is as much an imitation of Europe as a revulsion from it; and that nationalism is the group-historical variant of the general notion of progress which originated in Europe, and which leads to unnecessary and dangerous contortions when it is imported into other areas of the world.

It is certainly true that in Kenya and India nationalist leaders found it necessary to appeal to traditional sentiments and hence religious symbols, if they desired a mass base. But quite often they decided that they could attain independence and other goals without such appeals, and that, as in Africa, such attempts to harness latent feelings would only result in awakening the micro-nationalism of the major ethnie. Instead, as in the Ivory Coast or Ghana, use was made of the urban associations and the modernist aspirations of the semi-educated school-leavers and urban workers; this was particularly true in Guinea, Togoland, Senegal and Dahomey, cf. WALLER-STEIN, 1965. Other countercases include Turkey, Egypt, Norway and Burma, where the nationalists achieved their objects without resorting to 'neo-traditionalism'. For a general delineation of the effects of the imposition of European rule on traditional agrarian societies, cf. MONTAGNE, 1952.

23 The key passage already cited is on p. 99 of Kedourie's *Nationalism*. It provides us with the only clue as to the genesis of the 'spirit of the age' (or perhaps it is that spirit itself?), which in turn necessitates the spread, if not the initial emergence, of nationalism.

24 BECKER, 1932; cf. Peter Gay's rebuttal in R. O. Rockwood (ed.), Ithaca, *Carl Becker's Heavenly City Revisited* 1958, cited in LIVELY, 1966, pp. 108–10.

25 Kedourie has developed this aspect of his thesis in his subsequent book (cited above), tracing the millenarian ideal from men like Joachim of Fiore in the twelfth century, through the New Covenant of the Middle Ages' Sectarians, through to Lessing's idea of evolutionary, purposive progress in his *Education of Humanity*, 1780. The plasticity of ideology is such that it is always possible to trace pedigrees, even where the total climate has changed as much as it did from Joachim to Lessing. Sociologically, however, the connection appears rather thin; Lessing drew from so many other sources than a secularised version of medieval millenarianism, and the certainty sought by the rationalists was quite different in kind from the terrestrial salvation awaited by the millennialist—exactly in its secularity. Moreover, the strata which were drawn towards millennialism or its messianic counterparts in the colonies (whether in the Congo or Brazil or New Guinea), were largely lower class and dis-privileged, or oppressed and peripheral, groups. Whereas the first nationalists, and the leadership in most instances, are drawn from the more privileged strata, even the upper classes—like the sons of Brahmins in India, or the creoles of Sierra Leone, the prestigious 'old families' of Ghana (Bannermans, Brews, Casely Heyfords) or the puritan Islamic chiefs and educated men of Guinea and Mali—not to mention the chiefs and wealthy planters who opposed French interests in the Ivory Coast. Cf. LLOYD, 1966, and APTER, 1963*a*, esp. pp. 148–50.

CHAPTER THREE *The Religion of Modernisation*

1 A concise statement can be found in COHEN, 1968.
2 EISENSTADT, 1966; see also his articles, 1964*a* and 1964*c*. Smelser, 1968.
3 Cf. SELZNICK, 1952, Ch. 7.
4 SMELSER, 1968, p. 118.
5 EISENSTADT, 1966, p. 15.
6 *Ibid.*
7 K. Davis, 'Social and demographic aspects of economic development in India', in S. Kuznets, W. E. Moore & J. J. Spengler (eds.), *Economic Growth: Brazil, India, Japan,* Duke University Press, Durham, N.C., 1955; cited by SMELSER, *op. cit.,* p. 134.
8 SMELSER, *op. cit.,* p. 134.
9 *Ibid.,* p. 135. '. . . in the early stages of a nation's development, nationalism is heady, muscular and aggressive; as the society evolves to an advanced state, however, nationalism tends to settle into a more remote and complacent condition, rising to fury only in times of national crisis.' This description is more convincing than the implicit explanation.
10 SMELSER, *op. cit.,* p. 97.
11 DURKHEIM, 1933.
12 NISBET, 1965, Introduction.
13 DURKHEIM, 1960; and the perceptive discussion in Sheldon Wolin, 1960, Ch. X.
14 A. Gouldner, in his Introduction to Durkheim's *Socialism,* 1960*b*, argues, against Parsons, that Durkheim's analysis was aimed at Comte's exaggeration of the role of moral consensus in stabilising society, and owed much to St. Simon's stress on discovering new ways to satisfy old and new needs in the new industrial order; a concern that accounts for his sympathy towards socialism.
15 DURKHEIM, 1958 and 1941.
16 J.-J. Rousseau, *Contrat Social* IV, 8, cited in BARON, *Modern Nationalism and Religion,* Meridian Books, New York, 1960, p. 26.
17 J.-J. Rousseau, 1915, esp. ii, p. 431, *Considérations sur le Gouvernement de Pologne.* The theoretical weakness in Rousseau, of course, is his conception that only in a territorially confined state can *l'amour de la patrie* flourish. Such a *'nationalisme de clocher',* exclusive and defensive, symbolises the sense of inner privacy under public assault, so ill-adapted to the scale and complexity of modern life. The strength of his conception lies in the broad characterisation of the elements of nationality ('*Où est-elle cette patrie? Ce ne sont ni les murs ni les hommes qui font la patrie; ce sont les lois, les moeurs, les coutumes, le Gouvernement, la constitution, la manière d'être qui résulte de tout cela. La patrie est dans les relations de L'Etat à ses membres; quand ses relations changent, ou s'anéantissent, la patrie s'évanouit', Correspondance Générale,* ed. T. Dufour, Paris, 1924–34, X, 337–8, cited in COBBAN, 1964), and in his sense of its close links with liberty and constitutionalism. Patriotism is the sole rampart for individual freedom, alone inspiring

consensus, its precondition. Nationalism is not solely a doctrine regulating the external relations of a community, but is both a theory of, and itself a product of, a certain type of state and society (*'Le peuple soumis aux lois en dit être l'auteur; il n'appartient qu'à ceux qui s'associent de régler les conditions de la société'*, Contrat Social, II, 6).

Good discussions of Rousseau's national sentiment and his nationalist doctrine can be found in Cobban, *op. cit.*, Ch. 4, and KOHN, 1967, Ch. 5, pp. 237–59.

18 APTER, 1963*d* (also 1960*b*, 1963*c* and more generally APTER, 1965).

19 TALMON, 1952. (The thesis has been criticised on historical grounds by COBBAN, 1960.)

20 APTER, 1960*a* (also 1963*e*).

21 The literature on functionalism and modernisation is large. For our purposes, the key works are PARSONS, 1964*b*; *idem* 1965 and 1960. BELLAH, 1958; also the works by Eisenstadt cited above; ALMOND, 1965 and SHILS, 1964.

22 For critical appraisals, see NETTL and ROBERTSON, 1968; BLACK, 1966; BENDIX, 1964; *idem* 1966–7.

23 BOCK, 1963, more generally, *idem* 1964; BURROW, 1966.

24 GELLNER, 1964, pp. 15–20. We are not saying that the 'structural differentiation' model is not useful as an ordering framework; but it only sets the stage for the action at any given point.

25 Eisenstadt's notion of 'dedifferentiation' (fusion of roles and collectivities previously differentiated) shows awareness of the problem, but only serves to point up the ethnocentrism of his model, cf. his article 1964*b*.

26 GEERTZ, 1963*c*.

27 SMELSER, 1962. The original 'structuralist' approach has recently been tempered under criticism: cf. Smelser's essay 'Social and psychological dimensions of collective behaviour', 1968*c*, but it still fails to answer the criticism in the text. For a revealing application of Smelser's 'value-added' schema, cf. ELLEMERS, 1967. By providing an alternative Weberian explanation in terms of the 'fit' between ideas and particular group interests, Ellemers renders the Smelserian framework nugatory. Not only does it not aid in explaining why it was Calvinism that proved so attractive, especially for the rising class of merchants, or why a new nation arose on its basis; it even distorts the situation, throwing together under one schematic heading completely unrelated elements, and then deducing the sequence of events by *a priori* elimination of alternatives (e.g. Protestant sectarianism *or* 'Erasmian' libertarianism) disallowed by the framework's assumptions (e.g. it *has* to be a 'generalised belief system' that harnesses opposition). It thereby minimises the role of coercion in war stressed by P. Geyl, *The Revolt of the Netherlands* (1932), London, 1958. Cf. also LIJPHART, 1968, Ch. 5.

28 The functionalist definition of religion, which provides the theoretical foundation for the argument, can be seen in O'DEA, 1966,

Ch. 1; and YINGER, 1957. Cf. also PARSONS, 1951, Chs. 5, 8; NORBECK, 1961, Ch. 8.

29 MINOGUE, 1967.

30 BELLAH, 1958 and *idem* 1957, pp. 6–7, drawing on Tillich's 'ultimate concern' notion.

31 SPIRO, 1966. Also FRANKFURT *et al.*, Harmondsworth, 1951.

32 ARNAKIS, 1963.

33 CAHNMANN, 1943/4, pp. 524–9.

34 FLORESCU, 1967, pp. 324–42.

35 MANNHEIM, 1940.

36 M. HALPERN, 1963.

37 RONDOT, 1964 and VIENNOT, 1964, pp. 13–27. More generally, BINDER, 1964.

38 BERGER, 1962. M. HALPERN, *op. cit.*; BINDER, *op. cit.*

39 KORNHAUSER, 1960.

40 *Ibid.*, p. 125.

41 *Ibid.*, p. 123.

42 DURKHEIM, 1958, pp. 62–3.

43 COHN, 1957, pp. 21–32.

44 HOFFMANN, *Le Mouvement Poujade*, Paris, 1956.

45 It stems from the concerns of de Tocqueville and Mill, and has more recently found vivid expression in the writings of Mannheim, Arendt, Mills, Selznick, Lederer, Le Bon and Ortega y Gasset. For a critique of the 'mass society' thesis, cf. GUSFIELD, 1962, pp. 19–30, in which he shows that the pluralist assumption of an overall 'harmony of interests' (drawing on Hamilton, Madison and Truman) is an ideological commitment with little sociological basis. The conflict of groups in a multicentred society can increase political alienation in rapid change, and hence militant activism, among the economically deprived and the culturally isolated. The solidary foundation of modern society ought rather to be sought in the effects of cultural homogenisation. Cf. also WILENSKY, 1964, pp. 173–97.

46 KORNHAUSER, *op. cit.*, p. 47.

47 POCOCK, 1958, pp. 833–48.

48 B. HALPERN, 1961, Ch. 2, provides an explanation in terms of the conflicts in Zionist conceptions of the problem itself. Cf. SYKES, 1965.

49 LITTLE, 1965, Chs. 6, 8; HODGKIN, 1956, II, 2.

50 Cf. LE BON, 1947; ARENDT, 1951; HOFFER, 1951; ORTEGA Y GASSET, 1932.

51 MILLS, 1956, p. 310.

52 LEFEBVRE, 1965.

53 ULAM, 1960. BARBU, 1966, sees in nationalism a collective reaction to (*a*) a deep crisis in the structure and self-image of a community, following modernisation, and (*b*) a series of disrupting social and psychological processes, triggered by a cultural lag. He thereby seeks to account for the aggressive nature of some nationalisms,

e.g. in France, Weimar and Russia, in terms of psychological variables. His cultural hypothesis is rather more convincing than his social-psychological: *why* were the members of the French community, or many of them, 'bound to look for a new social frame of reference, that is to say, a new consensus regarding authority and order, for a new system of legitimacy regarding their beliefs and aspirations, and for a new form of group identity'? (p. 187).

Once again, there is the unstated assumption about social needs.
54 KOLARZ, 1954. The Bolshevik victory prevented the spread of this nationalism to the less educated sectors. The Buryats, of course, were pan-Mongol, as were the Tuvinians; the Oirots and Khakhassians (not more than 100,000 together in 1939) in the High Altai also trace their lineage to descendants of Ghengis Khan, and share a Turkic bias. The Yakut language, too, is Turkic; their 'Yakut Union' founded as early as 1906, demanded the return of land alienated to Russian colonists, and the admission of Yakuts to the police!

CHAPTER FOUR   *Anticolonialism*

1 The term 'primary revolt' is used by J. S. Coleman to characterise the traditionalistic initial resistance to colonial intrusion, cf. his *Nigeria: Background to Nationalism*, 1958, and his article, 1954. The putting down of such resistance was generally seen as a war of pacification, and still is.
2 MEAD, 1934.
3 This kind of analysis features prominently in NETTL and ROBERTSON, 1968, especially 'The Inheritance Situation' (Part II).
4 WORSLEY, 1964.
5 *Ibid.*, p. 35.
6 *Ibid.*, p. 45.
7 *Ibid.*, p. 49.
8 *Ibid.*, p. 15.
9 *Ibid.*, p. 65.
10 *Ibid.*, p. 69.
11 *Ibid.*, pp. 83–4.
12 *Ibid.*
13 LENIN, 1947.
14 HOBSON, 1902; HILFERDING, 1923 (1910).
15 *Ibid.*, pp. 426–8, excerpt in FIELDHOUSE, 1967.
16 KAUTSKY, 1962.
17 *Ibid.*, p. 39. The methodological qualification is on p. 9.
18 *Ibid.*, p. 57.
19 *Ibid.*, p. 48.
20 This has been examined, in relation to the foreign policy of the *Neue Rheinische Zeitung*, by ROSDOLSKY, 1964.
21 The attitudes of Marxists towards nationalism are the subject of a few monographs: especially BLOOM, 1941, and DAVIS, 1967.
22 F. ENGELS, *Po und Rhein*, Werke, XIII, p. 267. The descriptions of Montenegrins and Mexicans are contained in letters from Marx to

Engels of Feb. 16, 1857 and Nov. 20, 1862, and Marx & Engels: *The Civil War in the United States*, International, 1937, p. 262. Marx's comment on the Chinese is in his 'Revolution in China and Europe', *Werke, IX*, p. 96, cited in DAVIS, 1967, 60–1.

23 For Engels' opinion of the Slavs and dependence on Hegel's theses, cf. DAVIS, *op. cit.* pp. 3, 22–3, 34–8.

24 DAVIS, *op. cit.*, p. 37, citing K. Marx, *Insemnari despre Romani*, Bucharest, 1964, p. 39; also note 31, p. 218.

25 MARX & ENGELS, 1964, p. 518.

26 K. Marx, 'Prospects in France and England' (*New York Tribune*, April 27, 1855), *Werke XI*, 182, cited in DAVIS, *op. cit.*, p. 74.

27 Marx & Engels, *The Communist Manifesto, 1848* in MARX and ENGELS, 1959, especially pp. 19, 26. Cf. Davis, 1965. Davis also raises the interesting question of Marx's conception of the role of the 'nation' after the withering away of the 'state', and points to a revealing passage in his essay 'Zur Judenfrage', Deutsch-Französische Jahrbücher, 1843–4, *Werke I*, p. 376, in which 'national' relationships are classed as 'human' ones (along with natural, moral and theoretical ones) linking 'men as a species'—as opposed to the egotistic, externalised relationships of bourgeois society bred by Christianity ('a world of atomized and mutually hostile individuals'). There are, however, many contradictions and ambivalences in Marx's position on nationalism—Engels seems to have been more consistent and more chauvinist.

28 K. Kautsky, 'Die Moderne Nationalität', *Neue Zeit*, V (Stuttgart), 1887, pp. 402–5, cited in DAVIS, 1967, p. 140.

29 K. Kautsky, in *Neue Zeit*, 1886, pp. 522–5, cited in DAVIS, *op. cit.*, p. 142.

30 R. Luxemburg, 'Der Sozialpatriotismus in Polen', *Neue Zeit*, XIV, 2, 1895–6, especially 212–16, 464–8. She continued to oppose the principle of self-determination, unlike even Lenin, in a series of articles of 1908–9. The whole question of Stalin's famous definition of the nation, and the development of Lenin's stand on nationalism in Europe, is thoroughly examined in SHAHEEN, 1956. It also analyses the Austro-Marxist schemes of 'personalist' cultural autonomy advanced by Karl Renner and Otto Bauer, which Stalin so bitterly attacked.

31 SCHUMPETER, 1950, pp. 49–55.

32 A. J. P. Taylor, *Englishmen and Others*, Hamish Hamilton, London, 1956, pp. 76–80, cited in FIELDHOUSE, *op. cit.*, pp. 125–9.

33 I owe these points to E. Kedourie in the first of a series of lectures delivered on Nationalism in Africa and Asia in 1967.

34 Their differences can be summarised as follows:
1 Worsley lays more stress on psychological and intellectual colonisation of the personality, 'filling out' the structural framework, yet remaining strictly within it.
2 Worsley is more conscious than Kautsky of the schisms within the intelligentsia—though less in relation to nationalism. He also

points to their links with the deruralised peasantry, leading to 'populism'.

3 Kautsky lays more store by intrasocietal divisions, whereas for Worsley the mass of the population are exploited peasants—he looks especially to Africa (see WORSLEY, 1964, pp. 162-4).

4 For Kautsky 'classes' happen to be the major 'interest groups' of agrarian societies undergoing industrialisation. He is a methodological Marxist only. Worsley sees class analysis as the only method of explaining international cleavages, so minimising intrasocietal divisions—while not quite endorsing Sekou Touré's 'there are no classes in Africa' position.

35 This does not exclude external borrowing, or attempts to model one's national development on that of some prestigious Other—be it the West, Japan, Russia, Yugoslavia, Israel, China, Cuba, etc. But like Kemalist Turkey, the greatest efforts are devoted to developing one's own territorial unit, and forgoing foreign adventures. There are, of course, some notable exceptions—Greece till 1922, Egypt today, Nkrumah's Ghana—where foreign policy objectives and military expenditures divert resources from internal development. For Kemal's 'ethnic', 'heartland' nationalism, cf. B. LEWIS, 1968, pp. 357-61 (on *vatan* concept) (and Ch. 2 of SYKES, 1965).

36 GERSCHENKRON, 1962.

37 What starts as a description of an empirical trend (based on the Indian case) tends, under the neo-Marxist evolutionism influence, to turn into a series of 'stages' of political development, a kind of 'natural', if not inevitable, progression. This fits with the Marxist tendency to evaluate nationalism as a 'progressive' or 'reactionary' force, according to its ability to promote the revolution of the workers and intellectuals, cf. LENIN, 1950.

38 CALVERT, 1967, p. 1.

39 This definition is drawn from an article by S. Neumann, 'The International Civil War', *World Politics*, I, 1949, pp. 335-6, cited in LEIDEN & SCHMITT, 1968.

40 Cf. the essays in GELLNER & IONESCU, 1968. Of course, the 'failure' of the Armenian case was due to the tragedy of external pressures, which cut short the revolutionising impact of the Dashnaks on this ancient and highly traditional community, cf. HOVANNISIAN, 1967.

41 Cf. BRINTON, 1952. Different scholars vary in the cases they are willing to include among the 'great Revolutions'; besides Brinton's four (England, France, America, Russia), most would include China, and possibly Cuba and Mexico, with Turkey and Vietnam and Algeria as candidates. For Smelser's 'value-added' logic, cf. his *Collective Behaviour*, 1962.

42 There is considerable evidence that, especially after 1937, the *Gleichschaltung* policy of the Nazis began to be applied to the industrial cartels, and that from about 1940 the Party, increasingly dominated by the SS, took over the direction of the State bureaucracy and army, the other pillars of the Nazi state—for the purpose of

creating a totally New Order in Europe. In fact, the ideology of the Party led directly to the revolutionising of the way of life, culture, and finally economic relations, of the vast mass of the German population. Success in war would have brought physical changes too, according to certain plans—of a biological, as well as territorial nature: cf. the essays of Mosse and Seton-Watson in *Journal of Contemporary History* I, 1, 1966, and NEUMANN, 1944. I therefore place Nazism among the 'revolutions', while not unmindful of its peculiarities.

43 In this I tend to disagree with the 'peaceful', legalist implications of J. Nettl's and R. Robertson's 'inheritance' concept in *op. cit.*, Pt. II (cf. note 3); a reformist orientation before a peaceful transfer of power may often conceal a threat of force.

CHAPTER FIVE *Transitional Man*

1 For a typical description of 'modernisation' processes, cf. BLACK, 1966.
2 Generally on this process, cf. BINDER, 1964. For attempts to reform the Ottoman Empire, cf. B. LEWIS, 1968 and BERKES, 1964 (esp. 'The Break-Through, 1826–78'), also HEYD, in *idem*, 1961. For Muhammad Ali, and his successors, cf. VATIKIOTIS, 1969 (Part I), and SAFRAN, 1961, Chs. 2, 3.
3 POLK, 1965, pp. 100–10.
4 LERNER, 1964 (1958), p. 23.
5 *Ibid.*, p. 24.
6 *Ibid.*, p. 75.
7 *Ibid.*, p. 132 and note 55, Ch. 4, where it is held that contact with the outside world is the principal solvent of the 'courage culture' founded on ignorance and immobility, which equates change with evil. For Lerner, the Middle East is really another 'Middle Worst'.
8 *Ibid.*, p. 46.
9 *Ibid.*, p. 46.
10 *Ibid.*, p. 47.
11 *Ibid.*, pp. 49–51.
12 *Ibid.*, pp. 49–50.
13 *Ibid.*, p. 55; but also 'no modern society functions efficiently without a developed system of mass media'. One is left to wonder whether this can be a simple empirical generalisation, or whether we are not already involved in certain teleological assumptions masquerading as causal explanations (final causes).
14 *Ibid.*, p. 46, a key passage.
15 *Ibid.*, p. 54.
16 *Ibid.*, pp. 46–7.
17 DEUTSCH, 1966 (1953), p. 101. Deutsch's study is subtitled 'An Inquiry into the foundations of Nationality', and is concerned with the much broader question of the formation of ethnic communities manifesting national sentiment (cf. Preface, p. v). While recognising the manifold links between the problem of the 'growth of nations' and that of the rise of 'nationalism' (the ideological movement), it

remains my firm conviction that there is greater analytic and empirical gain than loss in keeping these problems distinct, and that enquiries into these parallel problems should therefore be conducted separately first. This key methodological proposition will be argued later at greater length.

It is for this reason that I have chosen to focus on Lerner's account as representative of the general 'communications' approach; for, despite the apparently scant attention paid to 'nationalism' by Lerner overtly, when contrasted with the apparently central position which this phenomenon occupies in Deutsch's pages, the reality of the matter is the reverse. Closer reading shows that nationality is what interests Deutsch (and how you operationalise the concept), while nationalism is really only considered in Ch. 8 (and then blurred with Fascism—revealing the (I feel inadequate) premisses of 'communications' theory). Lerner, in the empirical accounts, is really interested in the immediate political concerns of his Middle Eastern participants, of which, it emerges, 'nationalism' is the most crucial. (Note his disagreement with Hocking on exactly this issue, pp. 74–5.) If his account is nevertheless unsatisfactory, it is for reasons to do with shortcomings in the theory, but also because Lerner fails to distinguish 'national sentiment' and 'nationalism'—a distinction elaborated later.

The elements common to both theorists are (a) their reliance on the 'communications' perspective, and (b) their teleological assumptions of the 'needs' of the developmental process itself.

18 For the concepts of 'mobilisation' and 'assimilation', cf. DEUTSCH, op. cit., Ch. 6, esp. pp. 126 sqq.

19 Other 'communications' theorists include Ithiel de Sola Pool, Wiener and to a certain extent McLelland. Political scientists like Pye, Verba and Almond have been heavily influenced by cybernetics and communications perspectives, cf. especially PYE, 1965, and ALMOND & PYE, 1965. All these ventures raise the major theoretical problem of the relationship between individual attitudes and societal institutions, and the methodological controversy over the uses of aggregate data starting with Robinson's so-called 'ecological fallacy' (data obtained from territorial units should not be used as measurements of individual units) and burgeoning into the so-called 'individualistic fallacy'. The difficulties of this latter fallacy are well put by SHEUCH, 1966, where it is argued that inferences from individual behaviour to group behaviour ignore the structural patterns of collectivities, and that, for example, a democratic political system may not correlate with a high incidence of non-authoritarian personalities. This tendency to confuse group and individual data in drawing inferences is a serious weakness in Lerner's 'correlational' and 'probabilistic' approach, but one which space precludes from further consideration.

20 GUSFIELD, 1967.

21 W. C. SMITH, 1965.

22 DORE, 1969.

23 NETTL & ROBERTSON, 1966.

24 DORE, *op. cit.* Other objections to the related concept of 'development' are suggested in GEIGER, 1967, pp. 10–13. This basically historical objection is roughly Smith's third objection to equating modernisation with westernisation, the difference in socio-cultural contexts of Asian, African and Latin American societies. At the same time, Geiger appears to take issue with Dore's 'piecemeal' approach in terms of the leaders' goals, by his insistence on a focus 'upon the social process as a whole so as to illuminate the complex relationships among its major aspects' (p. 11); and he refuses to regard the problems of these countries as 'autonomous, and therefore, as involving primarily technical problems'.

25 Metternichian reaction characterises the policies of Feisal of Saudi Arabia; the more subtle type of 'sealing off' policies practised in the Middle East or Latin America usually concern land reform and wealth redistribution questions—or, as in South Africa, the educational exclusion of the majority of the population. This of course involves the assumption that modernisation is a 'total' set of processes, affecting the mass of the population, and not just an elite preserve (though it may start among a minority), to be applicable as a *societal* description.

26 PEACOCK, 1966.

27 LERNER, *op. cit.*, p. 47.

28 There is considerable literature on the causes and consequences of urbanisation and migrant labour in Africa. The best-known works are LITTLE, 1965; ELKAN, 1960; and UNESCO, 1956. Cf. also MAYER, 1961; GUTKIND, 1962, and ROUCH, 1961.

29 Cf. ULAM, 1964.

30 LERNER, *op. cit.*, pp. 49–50.

31 This conflicts with the evaluation of NETTL & ROBERTSON, 1968, pp. 54–8; the difference follows from the opposed definitions of 'modernisation'.

32 PEACOCK, *op. cit.*, p. 41, referring to his *The Rites of Modernisation*, University of Chicago Press, Chicago, 1968.

33 KEMILAINEN, 1964, stresses this consciousness of 'national character' among all the writers of the Enlightenment, which all but a few (e.g. Rousseau, Herder, Zimmerman's *vom Nationalstolze*, Zurich 1779) denigrated. Even Zimmerman, and the others, were deeply influenced in their incipient nationalism by the *preceding* cosmopolitan values.

34 PEACOCK, *op. cit.*, makes this latter point against current emphasis on linguistic models of nationalism.

35 In 1963, I compared the two systems for a month. Nine out of twelve items of news on radio and television in Britain were local, or national, or introduced to highlight Britain's role in world affairs, e.g. the Test Ban Treaty.

36 LERNER, *op. cit.*, p. 229.

37 *Ibid.*, p. 261.
38 *Ibid.*, p. 228.
39 *Ibid.*, p. 292 and Table 3 on p. 290.
40 DEUTSCH, *op. cit.*, Ch. 8.

CHAPTER SIX   *Industrialisation*

1 MINOGUE, 1967, analyses Gellner's theory in terms of the idea that every man is now an immigrant.
2 GELLNER, 1964, Ch. 7, p. 171, note 2.
3 *Ibid.*, p. 179, Ch. 8.
4 *Ibid.*, p. 159, note 1, Ch. 7. I am not at all sure that the recent drive for decentralisation and devolution of power, even in modern conditions, is at bottom irrelevant. Nobody wants to give up recent technological benefits (with some anarchist exceptions); but many are increasingly alarmed, as a matter of practical and passionate democratic politics, at the problems raised by the scope and penetration of state bureaucracy. As Runciman points out, the main animus of the elitist theorists was aimed at the impossibility of maintaining libertarian democracy under modern territorial and technological conditions. If the term 'participation' is to have any meaning—and it *does* seem to evoke a strong response in Western societies—the Athenian (or Genevan) example must remain relevant for experiments with mechanisms for making the rulers more accountable, less remote, etc. (cf. RUNCIMAN, 1965, Ch. 4, especially the reference to ostracism, p. 78, as an example of the need for 'representativeness').

One could also argue that nationalism in the West today—in Scotland, Brittany, Wales, Flanders, etc.—is to a considerable extent an expression of this tension between 'participatory democracy' and the drive for technological efficiency and prosperity. This question was not completely foreign to the Athenians, whose democracy was rather less 'direct' than is often supposed, and had to compensate for the fairly unequal distribution of property, especially in the radical Thetic phase: cf. V. EHRENBURG, 1960. FORREST, 1966 (Ch. 1), argues against Hignett's stress on these internal socio-economic distinctions (HIGNETT, 1958, p. 260), but the point is that this fairer distribution of the fifth century was achieved *via* the democratic reforms from Solon on.
5 Importing factories within the indigenous scientific skills run into severe difficulties of 'cultural dualism'; indeed, such alien enclaves may foster an anti-technological bias, as Shils observes, 1960.
6 For some of those consequences, cf. MATOSSIAN, 1958. One is tempted to argue that this syndrome is the external precondition of nationalism—were it not for post-war Western cases.
7 GELLNER, *op. cit.*, p. 140, Ch. 6.
8 *Ibid.*, p. 28, Ch. 1, where the exogeneity of contemporary industrialisation is emphasised against the classical Evolutionist image of continuous, endogenous world growth.

9 *Ibid.*, p. 35, Ch. 2. Note that Gellner stresses the relevance and popularity of sociology, and not economics (except Myrdal and Galbraith), which tends to ignore the 'institutional, psychological and evaluative framework whose very conditions of emergence, and whose final forms, are *just* what is most problematical' (p. 37). One could hardly have a clearer statement of anti- 'economism'!

10 *Ibid.*, p. 150 sqq.

11 *Ibid.*, p. 155.

12 *Ibid.*, p. 157. How far, and in what sense, this is the case, will be examined in the next chapter.

13 *Ibid.*, p. 158; the 'human brand', or kind, is equated with 'culture'.

14 *Ibid.*, p. 159—another revealing passage (see below).

15 *Ibid.*, p. 173. The bracketed quote underlines Gellner's linguistic assumption.

16 *Ibid.*, p. 160.

17 *Ibid.*, p. 168. And yet, though the educational bases already existed in the Tokugawa or Bourbon epochs, a clearly 'reactive nationalism' did stimulate economic development in Japan and France. Ayal's argument supports Rostow in the Japanese, Turkish and Israeli cases, but one can cite the contrary example of post-independence Greece, whose 'backward-looking' nationalism hampered rapid development: cf. AYAL, 1966, and PEPELASSIS, 1958/9. This conflict suggests that we need to pare down our categories of analysis; this is one source of the need for a comprehensive typology of nationalisms.

18 *Ibid.*, p. 168. This will include African nationalisms, but what about the early nineteenth-century Latin American Creole cases, who did not seem to possess any cultural differentiae from their rulers? Yet a clear sense of the 'social organism', the 'cult of civic glory', and the twin desires for local-historical self-expression and popular sovereignty, all reminiscent of the French model, emerges from Argentina's 1810 'doctrina del Mayo' literature and Juan Egana's 1811 Chilean constitution; cf. WHITAKER, 1962.

19 *Ibid.*, p. 173.

20 Voltaire, *Dictionnaire Philosophique*, 'Patrie', cited in POTTER, 'The Historian's Use of Nationalism and Vice-Versa', in A. V. Riasanovsky & B. Rijnik (eds.), *Generalisations in Historical Writing*, University of Pennsylvania Press, Philadelphia, 1963.

21 Hector St. Jean de Crèvecoeur, *Letters of an American Farmer* (London, 1782), Everyman's Library, London and New York, 1912, pp. 41-4, cited in POTTER, 1963.

22 KEDOURIE, 1960. Its uncompromising claims revive old hatreds and upset political stability, pp. 115-17.

23 AKZIN, 1964, pp. 53 sqq., esp. 55-62, which also discusses the contrast between nationalism and emigration (but not colonisation), so dependent empirically on the reception accorded to the immigrant in the host country.

24 For the Balkan cases generally, cf. STAVRIANOS, 1957. The Burman

case differs from the other three in having attained the objective of
independence—but again it was largely the work of the urban
intelligentsia (and Japanese), with the traditional peasantry playing
a separate 'ethnocentric' role in the hinterland Saya San rebellion of
1930–1, cf. SARKISYANZ, 1964.

25 But—as of now, Barzani's Kurds seem to have forced Iraq to grant
their demand for regional autonomy (*Observer*, March 15, 1970).
There are, of course, Palestinian workers in the diaspora, but Fatah,
Habash's Popular Front for the Liberation of Palestine, and Hawat-
meh's strictly Marxist Popular Democratic Front for the Liberation
of Palestine, are all led by the westernised intelligentsia. Fatah was
started before the Six Day War 'under the influence of the Algerian
model, mainly amongst Palestinian students in German universities, many of them engineers'; it then attracted the nationalists
and Muslim activists, especially ex-members of the Muslim Brotherhood and of the extreme right wing Parti Populaire Syrien. If the
leadership is moving towards a more revolutionary left wing
orientation, 'the Fatah man fights against "the Jews", even though
officially Fatah has nothing against the Jews but only dislikes
"Zionists". Nevertheless, the basic feelings inside the Fatah ranks
seems to be largely one of Jihad'; 'the average Fatah member is a
man of the people, many of whom seem to be steeped in the
Islamic Jihad feeling'—recruitment is mainly from the refugee
camps of the unemployed, whom one might describe as an 'artificial
proletariat' in the respective Arab states. The Palestinian who has
found some work in another country tends to stay there. Cf.
GASPARD, 1970.

26 For the Caucasian groups, which number about fifty, and belong to
the Turkic, Iranian or Ibero-Caucasian language families, cf.
BENNIGSEN, 1967. Arabic was the only written tongue till 1900. Of
the others, Avar, Kumyk and Azeri tended to be secondary *lingua
francas*, till the Soviets started a Russification campaign after 1923;
even so, it is estimated that between 60% and 90% cling to their
mother tongue as their first language. Most of these tribes are very
small: there are some 11,463 Tats, 30,353 Cherkessians, 79,631
Adyges—but 418,756 Chechen and 944,213 Dagestanis, according
to the 1959 Soviet census, which probably was of some importance
in explaining the development of their nationalisms, primitive as
they were. Size, too, may be a factor in the Bashkir, Welsh, etc.,
cases—but here we are already in the presence of a more developed
sense of common political ties and history. However, the most
industrialised areas of Wales seem even now to be least affected by
nationalism—or by the language-retention movement.

27 GELLNER, *op. cit.*, p. 169, Ch. 7, note 1.

28 There are also cases, such as the current crisis of the East African
Asians or the Copts, who feel they cannot risk a reactive national-
ism at home, and decide to emigrate or remain quiescent: cf.
WAKIN, 1945.

29 MISRA, 1961.

30 DESAI, 1948; WORSLEY, 1964.

31 HODGKIN, 1956, Ch. 4, pp. 117–18, 124–32.

32 DAVIES, 1966, Ch. 5, p. 96.

33 *Ibid.*, p. 97.

34 JULY, 1968, esp. Chs. 6, 9–11, 13–14.

35 ROTBERG, 1962, pp. 75–90.

36 HUNTER, 1962, p. 285, with Table.

37 SMYTHE, 1960.

38 For Polish messianism of Krasinski, Slowacki, Towianski, Czieszowski, Trentowski and the historian Lelewel, cf. KOHN, 1960, Ch. 2 and references.

39 HALECKI, 1955, Ch. 23. After the 1906 split in the P.P.S., most workers followed Pilsudski into the patriotic Right against Dzierzynski's Left (internationalist); cf. ROOS, 1966.

40 Dubnow's writings are collected in PINSON, 1958. A general introduction to Zionism, stressing its bourgeois origins, is HERTZBERG, 1960.

41 BOROCHOV, 1937, a *tour de force* in providing a materialist (Marxist) basis for nationalism's necessity, drawing on Marx's concept of the 'conditions' of production (as opposed to the 'relations') in *Capital*, Vol. III. These *conditions*, to which Engels also refers, include natural environment, race and external historic influences, which result in the vertical differentiation of identical forces and relations of productions, i.e. different societies, and later nations. For Martov, cf. PINSON, 1945.

42 BARON, 1960, Ch. 7: 'Almost every third Jew living in Europe during the generation preceding the First World War left it for overseas' (p. 222), mainly for America, but also Britain, South Africa, and to some extent Latin America. This was largely due to their extraordinary demographic increase, and the bleak economic and political conditions in the Pale.

43 BENNIGSEN & LEMERCIER-QUELQUEJAY, 1966, Ch. 7; and ZENKOVSKY, 1953, on the bourgeois origins of Tatar nationalism, and on Sultan Galiev. For the Ishahist movement of 1904, the Berek, Tancy and 1917 Committee, cf. BENNIGSEN & L-QUELQUEJAY, 1960.

44 *Ibid.*, Part I, where it is pointed out that there were some 150,000 workers in 1914, but most were scattered in the Urals and Donetz and isolated from the skilled Russian proletariat there. The post-1905 'industrial bourgeoisie' were less pan-Turkist, more interested in the Tatar nation *per se*, a limited territorial nationalism.

45 Cf. AKZIN, *op. cit.*, and as applied to Russification, Professor Dr. S. ETTINGER, 1970, which brought out the significance and causes of this oscillation of both Tsarist and Soviet policies.

46 Cf. WHEELER, 1964, esp. Chs. V, VII–VIII, pp. 157 sqq.—in 1957, only 11% of the workers in the Tashkent textile combine were Uzbeks. Russian colonisation by skilled workers still remains the most important factor in the industrialisation of Central Asia; and

Bennigsen and Quelquejay (Islam in the Soviet Union) consider the unveiling policy a relative failure even among the intelligentsia, who reserve their first room for their Russian guests, but their second for those of their own nationality. On the other hand, Soviet policy has undermined the clan, tribe and joint-family, as well as the customs of *kalym* and *levirate*; but not the *aksakalism*, the 'exaggerated' respect for (the grey beards of) one's parents among Muslim intellectuals.

According to H. Carrere d'Encausse (in ALLWORTH, 1967, Chs. 6–7, pp. 180 sqq.), the Russian colonists numbered 332,000 in 1906, as against a native proletariat of 32,000 (15,000 in the railway industry, and 14,500 miners) in the whole Turkistan *guberniia* which contained some 5,378,000 Central Asians.

47 KOLARZ, 1954, Ch. 4. On *korenisatzia* and *mestnichestvo*, cf. BENNIGSEN & QUELQUEJAY, *op. cit.*

48 ZENKOVSKY, 1960, Ch. VII.

49 Cf. SHAFER, 1955, Ch. 9, esp. pp. 171–5, but note his analysis of the benefits of protectionism for farmers and workers, as well as the bourgeoisie, presupposes the existence of a nation-state with a 'national interest' to protect. Implicitly, the lower classes are held to swing over to nationalism only *after* independence is achieved, as the German Social-Democrat case proves. Such a post-independence 'integrationist' economic nationalism is explained in terms of economic benefits to key producer groups through redistribution of 'psychic' and material gains by JOHNSON, 1965, pp. 169–85; cf. the studies in *idem*, 1968.

50 Cf. WILSON, 1963, where revolutionary guerrilla warfare is likened to the levee *en masse* for moving the peasant masses 'from one kind of social structure to another through "emergency" measures and practices which ostensibly continue only "for the duration"' (p. 93)—in underdeveloped and 'immobilised' agrarian societies. Such revolutionary wars, especially in Asia, mobilise and organise and activate the latent energies of the masses. The mobilisation process 'uses human energy fully and educates the participants to understand new frames of mind, new beliefs, and new social organisations. A nation is being built' (p. 88). The last statement rather begs the question; it hardly follows from the previous one, even if 'nation' *is* defined as a 'special form of political community, associated . . . with the institution of the state' (p. 84). On the other hand, the nationalist character of Communist guerrilla movements is hardly open to dispute.

51 HOPKINS, 1966, questions the assumptions of Janowitz, that their modernising nationalism results from involvement with modern military techniques.

52 CADY, 1958.

53 WEBER, 1965, esp. Chs. 6–8; and his 'Social Psychology of the World Religions', in GERTH & MILLS, 1947.

54 There is a vast literature on intellectuals and intelligentsias. Cf.

LIPSET, 1963, Ch. 10; SETON-WATSON, 1960, Ch. VI; BOTTOMORE, 1964; OSSOWSKI, 1962, and the various writings of Shils, Kautsky, etc.

55 GELLNER, *op. cit.*, Ch. 7, p. 171.

56 MANNHEIM, 1936 (1960), pp. 3–4, and 1940, Part II.

57 MARUYAMA, 1968, Ch. 4. For the analogous 'self-strengthening' movement in China from the 1860's, cf. HOWARD, 1969, pp. 7–14, and pp. 43–53. In 1894, Li Ping-heng, governor of Shantung wrote to the Emperor: 'The proper way to defend against foreigners is still to use the concept of "Asia converting the barbarians",' a typical Sinocentric expression of the traditionalist culturalism.

58 Cf. Father Zossima's sermons in the *Brothers Karamazov*, and the legend of the Grand Inquisitor. The opposition to Western scientific liberalism and the universalism of the Roman Church comes out very clearly in the voice of Shatov in *The Possessed*, II, 1/7 (Modern Library Edition), who equates the Godhead with the Russian people and nation. In his youth, Solovyev too embraced this religious Slavophilism: cf. KOHN, 1961, Ch. 5.

59 The prototype of this evolutionary religious reformism is Lessing's *Education of Humanity*, 1780, which holds that Divine Providence uses both reason and revelation for the task of educating the human race from the Old Testament onwards—an argument that has weighed heavily in the recent history of Judaism and Islam; cf. GIBB, 1947, and BLAU, 1966, Chs. 2, 4.

60 DEUTSCH, 1966, Ch. 9, pp. 190–1.

61 GELLNER, *op. cit.*, p. 178.

62 H. SETON-WATSON, 1965, pp. 21–2.

63 BENTHEM VAN DER BERGHE, 1966.

64 G. Jahoda & H. Taifel at a meeting in Cambridge, Sept. 3, 1965, in *New York Herald Tribune* of September 4/5, 1965.

65 SNYDER, 1968, Ch. 13.

66 GELLNER, *op. cit.*, p. 155.

67 *Ibid.*

68 *Ibid.*, p. 159.

69 The process of 'homogenisation' in Tudor England and Bourbon France was disastrously imitated by Nicholas I and Alexander III in Russia, Mahmud II and Abdul Hamid in Ottoman Turkey, and the Germanisation policies of the eighteenth/nineteenth-century Habsburgs, themselves imitated by the Magyarisation of Croats, Slovenes, etc. More generally, we must take into account the significance of the rulers' orientations (and information) in mediating the impact of modernisation and westernisation—its pace, kind and direction, especially their perceived need for skills, etc.

70 GELLNER, 1965.

71 Cf. LE PAGE, 1964.

72 For the connections between language modernisation and nationalism, cf. FISHMAN *et al.*, 1968, esp. Fishman, Paden, Haugen. The

Turkish literary renascence of the 1860's, of which Sinasi, Ziya Pasha and Namik Kemal were the main exponents, coincided with the importation of the idea of *vatan* (fatherland); even if this still referred to an Islamic Ottomanism, it was undoubtedly inspired by the ideals of the French Revolution, Montesquieu and Rousseau, and applied to 'The Ottoman people' (cited in B. LEWIS, 1968, I, Ch. 5, p. 145).

The same holds for the Balkans. Korais tells how he identified himself as a 'Greek' to the incredulous Parisians during the French Revolution, while embarking on his philological labours. And Obradovic writes revealingly to Haralampije on April 13, 1783:

> Here I propose to remain at least a year, and with the help of God and of some kind Serbian, I intend to publish in our common Serbian language a book printed in the civil alphabet that shall be called the Counsels of Sound Reason, for the benefit of my nation, that my toil and my long wanderings may not be all in vain. My book will be written in pure Serbian, just as this letter, that all Serbian sons may understand it, from Montenegro to Smerdovo and the Banat... I shall be overpaid if any fellow countryman of mine says, when the green grass grows over me, 'Here lie his Serbian bones! He loved his people! May his memory be eternal!'

Cf. G. R. Noyes, *The Life and Adventures of Dimitrije Obradovic*, Berkeley, California, 1953, pp. 133-7.

This does not mean, however, that such 'cultural nationalists' had clear conceptions of political independence for their group; but the logic of their thought, as revealed in Herder's diaries, has a sole political result: overturning the existing non-national governments for more 'representative' ones. Herder's *Travel Diary* of 1769 reveals his desire to collect data on mythologies 'and to examine everything from the point of view of politics' (*Werke* IV, pp. 363-4, Suphan edn., Berlin, 1877-1913); but political censorship and the diffusion of his interests give his work the appearance of lack of interest in political nationalism. Herder's political goal was a decentralised democratic collectivism, encouraging diversity, participation and the competition of ideas, so as to express to the full the people's personality as revealed in language; this aided the process of societal Bildung.

Herder is usually cited as *the* example of a 'cultural nationalist' in opposition to later 'political nationalists' or to Rousseau. But the antithesis does not lie here. The tie up between politics and culture (but not necessarily language) is a *sine qua non* of all nationalists, according to the doctrine's internal logic—rather than the empirical predilections of its practitioners. Cf. BARNARD, 1969. I am indebted for this last point to Professor Kedourie.

CHAPTER SEVEN Definitions

1 Josephus, *Jewish War*, II, 118.
2 Josephus, *Antiquities of the Jews*, XVIII, 1–10, esp. 4–5. The passage ends significantly: 'The fourth philosophical sect was founded by this Judas the Galilaean. Its sectaries associated themselves in general with the doctrine of the Pharisees; but they had an invincible love of liberty, for they held God to be their only lord and master.' The other sects were the Sadducees, Pharisees and Essenes, but it is rather doubtful whether Zealotism was a fourth sect separate from Pharisaism, or simply its activist wing, since Josephus' own Pharisaic connections, coupled with his guilt feelings over Zealotism, makes his testimony on this matter suspect (see below).
3 BRANDON, 1968, pp. 31–4.
4 Josephus, *Jewish War*, VII, 323–333, cf. YADIN, 1966, for a full description of the circumstances.
5 BRANDON, 1967, Ch. 2, generally on Zealot ideals and the traditional *Heilsgeschichte*, esp. pp. 46–51, 62–4. There is less disagreement with this aspect of Brandon's thesis than with his attempt to connect Jesus and the Jerusalem Christians with Zealotism.
6 *Maccabees*, I, 1, 41–3, and 2, 26–7. From the italicised words, we see that the author conceived of cultural homogeneity in predominantly religious terms, as one would expect.
7 *Numbers*, 25, 6–13 confirmed by a passage of Tractate Sanhedrin 9.6. in DANBY, 1958. Elijah was accorded Messianic connections already in *Malachi*, 4, 5.
8 Josephus, *Jewish War*, II, 163, *Antiquities of the Jews*, XVIII, 5; cf. BRANDON, *op. cit.*, pp. 54, 110–13, 181, 320.
9 KOHN, 1967, Ch. 2.
10 EHRENBURG, 1965.
11 Thucydides, II, 36, 1, my italics; it is the land, rather than an ethnic or cultural group, which is free.
12 *Ibid.*, II, 71, 2. Here the ethnic concept and the territorial refer to two separate entities, Hellas and Plataea. Josephus uses a similar phrase to refer to the Jews' wish to preserve their national independence against Rome (*ten patrion autonomian*), *War*, II, 53.
13 EHRENBURG, 1960, and FORREST, 1966.
14 LEVI, 1965, pp. 47–8.
15 *Ibid.*, pp. 41–6, 51–8, on the oracles, Games, colonies and citizenship.
16 ANDREWES, 1965, esp. pp. 57–64. Cf. the study by BACON, 1961. The best introduction to the question of Greek unity is provided by the essays in FONDATION HARDT, 1962. I am much indebted to W. G. Forrest for drawing my attention to this book, and for a long discussion with him on nationalism in ancient Greece.
17 Cf. HALPERN, 1961. Ataturk's exact words are given in LEWIS, 1968, p. 292: 'The Turks are the friends of all civilised nations. Countries vary, but civilisation is one, and for a nation to progress it must take part in this single civilisation.'

18 Aristotle, *Poetics*, 1447–9. Cf. BURY, 1951, pp. 200–1, and BURN, 1960, pp. 251, 310, for its peasant origins and the Megaran democratic experiment.

19 Cf. the essay by Baldry in FONDATION HARDT, 1962, especially on the views of Eratosthenes and Polybius, who do seem to have entertained a 'polycentric' concept.

The Puritan Revolution's nationalism was predominantly ethnocentric: cf. KOHN, 1940. Of course, one should not overlook the universalistic element in ancient Judaism, e.g. *Amos*, 1, 3, where Yahweh self-evidently looks after all nations, the story of Sodom, Jonah and Nineveh, etc.: cf. KAUFMANN, 1961, II, 9, esp. pp. 295–301.

20 For the concept of 'primary resistance', cf. COLEMAN, 1958, Chs. 6–7.

21 COLEMAN, 1954, pp. 404–26, who subsumes these under the rubric 'nativism' in Linton's sense, citing the case of Mau Mau, and Chilembwe's uprising.

22 Cf. SHERRARD, 1959, Ch. 7. Cf. also STAVRIANOS, 1961, Ch. 15. The disastrous social, educational and economic consequences of the Byzantine political goose-chase in Greek development, of the persistence of the 'ethnocentric' ideal, are well brought out by PEPELASSIS, 1958/9, pp. 19–27.

23 PRITCHARD, 1958, VII, *passim*.

24 *Ibid.*, VI.

25 *Ibid.*, 'The War Against the Peoples of the Sea', pp. 185–6.

26 *Ibid.*, pp. 173–5, 195–201. Cf. the reference to the 'tribes of Tamud, Ibadidi, Marsimanu, and Haiapa, the Arabs who live, far away, in the desert (and) who know neither overseers nor official(s) and who had not (yet) brought their tribute to any king. I deported their survivors and settled (them) in Samaria.'

27 The criteria are those used to define the concept of the 'tribe' in Africa in the Introduction to GULLIVER, 1969.

28 Cf. FRYE, 1966, esp. Ch. 2. We should, however, beware of his modern practice of equating tribes and ethnie with linguistic units, simply because our main method of discovering the separate existence of an ethnic group is through the appearance of separate linguistic forms. If, for example, Urartian does turn out to be a form of earlier Hurrian, this linguistic identity should not blind us to their separate ethnic identities consequent upon very different geographical and political conditions. Just as there is a case for regarding Israel and Judah as separate ethnic entities, despite alleged common descent and shared language: cf. NOTH, 1960, esp. pp. 179 sqq.

29 PRITCHARD, *op. cit.*, VII, *passim*; and LUCKENBILL, 1926–7, I, 443.

30 LUCKENBILL, *op. cit.*, II, pp. 139–89, cited in ROUX, 1964, Ch. 19.

31 FRYE, *op. cit.*, pp. 88–92; and ROUX, *op. cit.*, p. 275 sqq. The archaeological and historical work on these interesting precursors of the Armenians is mainly Russian.

32 This is the picture that emerges from the survey by WALEK-CZERNECKI, 1929, pp. 305–20. He holds that Meyer's limited notion of nationality as pertaining to Greeks, Jews and Persians is inadequate, but then goes on to argue that, while the concept of nationality is widely applicable to the groupings of the ancient Near East, it is inappropriate to the classical world, which was composed of city-states, each with its fervent patriotism, excluding all other attachments. But the argument is based on an *a priori* assumption of the exclusiveness of 'patriotism', which we saw to be at least questionable in the Greek case. The argument seems to hold rather better in the Roman case, since neither Latium nor Italy ever achieved the necessary cultural homogeneity or citizenship rights. Yet the very fact that this was a key political issue for the Gracchi and eventuated in the bellum sociale suggests that the base for a common sentiment and polity existed.

33 PRITCHARD, *op. cit.*, pp. 226–30. This is the limit of transition to the 'polycentric' form; there is no suggestion that we can learn from foreign peoples, rather than God, for they possess no independent virtue of their own, no intrinsic value.

34 WEBER, 1965, p. 1, where he is still clearly thinking in terms of 'essences' rather than working definitions (nominalist).

35 POPPER, 1961, pp. 28 sqq., and *The Open Society and its Enemies*, I, 3 and II, II, 2. The scientific use of definitions is held to differ from the Aristotelian 'essentialist' one in its desire merely to sum up a long story by a shorthand symbol. Essentialism and historicism are mutually reinforcing positions: to speak of social change presupposes an unchanging essence undergoing it, but the essence, as the sum of the thing's hidden potentialities, is only actualised, and hence known, through its historical changes.

36 COLEMAN, 1958, Appendix. But Popper appears to think that emphasis on the 'qualitative character of social events' leads to essentialism, the search for real definitions.

37 Cf. SPIRO, 1966. It stands nearest to Popper's 'constitutions' or inductive definitions (*Open Society*, II, 11, notes 48, 50) and arises in the course of a discussion (on the emergence of nationalism) as a very natural request for clarification of the sense(s) in which key terms are being used. Since in this field there are very significant rival senses given to these terms, we need to make our choices of meanings, and the criteria for our choices, explicit. The 'penumbra of vagueness', otherwise, would be uncomfortably wide.

38 In fact, of course, this method lies behind the *construction* of the ideal-type, which always must involve an element of arbitrary selection, however many concrete instances it is based upon. All I have done is to construct my types of 'nationalism' and the 'nation' from the common features of the *ideals* of these concepts held by the great majority of so-called nationalists (self-styled and recognised as such by others).
   The assumption of normative rationality built into the method of

the ideal-type is subject to our knowledge of the 'ends of the participants'; Weber is explicit about this, cf. his comments on the 1866 Prussian campaign, *The Theory of Social and Economic Organisation*, Free Press, New York, 1964, pp. 92–112.

39 *Selected Works*, V, p. 510, 1891, cited by KEMILAINEN, 1964.

40 HYSLOP, 1934, p. 22.

41 KEMILAINEN, *op. cit.*, p. 50 sqq.

42 *Der Sprach-Brockhaus*, Wiesbaden, 1958, cited in KEMILAINEN, *op. cit.*, and SNYDER, 1954, Ch. 1, whose very similar list of meanings is indebted to *Webster's Dictionary*.

43 The significance of this distinction was impressed upon me by Professor Dore, to whom I am very grateful.

44 This, of course, is to some extent an argumentum *ex silentio*. Historians differ greatly as to the extent of 'nationalism' in ancient Greece, and of 'national sentiment' among the inhabitants of Seleucid and Roman Judaea. In the latter case, for example, Noth minimises the involvement of the mass of Jewry with Zealotism, following Josephus to the letter, while Brandon and Hengel suggest a widely diffused support. Some of their arguments might be thought to be retrospectively deterministic—as when they argue from the analogy of modern guerrilla movements gaining local sympathy in the countryside. In the Greek case, we are definitely hampered by lack of material which could throw light on sentiments of unity and motives for collective action against the Persians; also by expectations of modernity which we tacitly entertain in judging the ancient Greek form of nationalism. If we stick to the 'ethnocentric' pole for Greece, too, we will not be tempted to return the conventional verdict of 'no nationalism', upon *a priori* modernist assumptions.

45 A fifth term, 'state-nation', coined by Zartmann, will be useful in defining the characteristics of many African states today, which are intent on moulding their heterogeneous populations into distinctive nations, cf. ZARTMANN, 1965.

46 The dominant Eastern type of nationalism was also 'ethnocentric', —as in Japan, China and Burma. Even the mystical and monotheistic traditions in East and West are not genuinely 'polycentric' since the level of abstraction of their categories 'relativises' the issue to such an extent that the dichotomy becomes insignificant— all value being transferred on to the true Self, or God.

47 For the Persian case of 'renewal' nationalism, cf. KEDDIE, 1966, and AVERY, 1965. Other cases would include eighteenth-century Switzerland, nineteenth-century Denmark, post-1919 Turkey, Cuba, and to some extent, China.

48 The whole issue is analysed in SHAHEEN, 1956. Bauer's scheme is set out in his *Die Nationalitätenfrage und die Sozialdemokratie*, 1924.

49 Cf. HALPERN, *op. cit.*, esp. Chs. 2, 6; and SACHAR, 1958, Ch. 18.

50 I take Rousseau, not as an infallible textual guide to 'nationalism' or its 'correct' interpretation, but simply as representative of other

nationalist traditions of the 'voluntaristic' variety. Nationalism has been 'married' to many elements from other ideological traditions; Fascism was popular before the war, but the present favoured candidates are, of course, communism, 'socialism' and populism. This is testimony as much to the persistence of certain ideologies as to their 'plasticity' (see Introduction).

51 RUSTOW, 1967, Ch. 1, esp. pp. 21–8. Rustow's definition of the 'nation' as 'a self-contained group of human beings who place loyalty to the group as a whole above competing loyalties' suffers from the same lack of specificity as that of his model, Mill. Common sympathies, co-operation, 'desire to be under the same government', and to be governed 'by themselves, or a portion of themselves, exclusively' (*Considerations on Representative Government*, 1872, Ch. 16), is an adequate description of the concept of 'national sentiment', but leaves in complete vagueness the characteristics of the group with these desires, the definition of 'themselves' who want to be self-governing—i.e. the 'nation'. Rustow's self-contained group with primary loyalties to itself, fails equally to overcome this defect. Sects can be very self-contained, and, if anything, more exclusive in their demands for allegiance. So can class-parties, villages in a subsistence economy, district estates, and 'tribes'. It is interesting that Rustow is prepared to concede the title of 'nation' to the latter (p. 28), while uneasily noting the distinction between them and the French 1789 'nation' with its egalitarian and centralising tendencies. (He also inserts a new factor at this point, 'whether every individual was conceived as having a direct relationship to that group'— which in effect goes some way towards the French ideal, and contradicts the segmentary principle of the African 'tribes'.) And what is the value of a definition of the 'nation' which fails to distinguish the 'Arabian bedouin clans (both before and immediately after their unification through Muhammad)' in principle from the modern post-1789 nation-states?

52 ROYAL INSTITUTE OF INTERNATIONAL AFFAIRS, 1939.

53 KOHN, 1967 (1944), Ch. 1.

54 RENAN, 1882.

55 GERTH & MILLS, 1947; the Nation in the section on 'Structures of Power', pp. 171–9. The definition is uncomfortably retrospective, and very close to the Hegelian theory of 'historyless peoples'. Why Weber, of all sociologists, should have devoted so little attention to such an important European and global phenomenon as nationalism, is peculiar. Was it the 'ambiguity' of the concept of the nation, underlined in this passage, or the vastness of the task of 'analysing all sorts of community sentiments of solidarity in their genetic conditions and in their consequences for the concerted action of the participants' (pp. 175–6), that held him back? Or perhaps it was the fact that nationalism in the early twentieth century seemed to be a mere local (European) phenomenon, compared to such global topics as the rise of capitalism or bureaucracy, and that it had no

clear links with his major theoretical concerns, such as the conflict between materialism and idealism or positivism and the verstehen approach, etc. (On both issues, he is, I think, mistaken.)

56 This is not unduly complicated. Weber intimates that there can be an ideal-type of anything, even at one or more 'removes'. The range of ideals of the nation absolutely require us to abstract further, to arrive at a clearly formulated model of the major interrelated features. The 'empirical method', then, serves only the purpose of abstraction, which requires the most comprehensive possible survey as a starting-point. Later, of course, the definitional ideal-type itself becomes otiose, 'after understanding is reached', as it were. One must concede that in the field of nationalism, at any rate, this latter hope is utopian.

57 This distinction (and the connection) between the 'nation' and 'nationalism' is as crucial as, I feel, it is obvious; but even now it is not always observed, mainly because the catch-all concept of 'national sentiment' with its cloudy 'penumbra of vagueness' has been allowed to obscure the empirical distinction. Sometimes an author will admit the analytic distinction, only to succumb to his Europocentrism, and allow 'nationalism' only in the cases where there are (or might be in the very near future, e.g. the Somali case) 'nations'.

The definition in the text is somewhat compressed in the interests of simplicity and conciseness. The full definition reads: 'The nation is a large group of human beings, possessing vertical integration of the population around a common system of labour, a more-than-local territory with horizontal mobility throughout, direct member-ship of the group with equal citizenship rights, at least one mark of relative recognised dissimilarity by which members may distinguish themselves from those of another similar group, and relationships of alliance, competition or conflict with other similar groups, and a high level of group sentiment.' The seven characteristics of an ideal 'nation', then are size, economic integration, territorial mobility, a distinctive culture, external relationships, equal membership rights and group loyalty.

58 YOUNG, 1965, Ch. 11.

59 AKZIN, 1964, Ch. 3.

60 The phrase is Rotberg's, in ROTBERG, 1967. On the whole, I am in agreement with his argument, though I think it holds more for the ex-British colonial polities, and should not be taken to exclude the possibility (and existence) of the 'ethnie-based' nationalisms in Africa.

61 SILVERT, 1967, Introduction and Appendix, esp. pp. 440–1, 19.

62 GEERTZ, 1963b.

63 R. SETON-WATSON, 1911.

64 LEWIS, 1968, Ch. 10.

65 PALMER, 1940; and SCHAFER, 1938. The changes that occurred at the time of the Revolution were from the concepts of *pays* to that of

patrie, sujet to *citoyen* and *concitoyen,* and *état* to nation; typical titles of pamphlets at the time were *Catéchisme National, Essai du patriotisme, Questions d'un bon patriote.* The patriot is commonly defined in these works as a citizen who loves his country and countrymen, and wishes to make country great and countrymen happy through the well-known reforms. In the *Credo du tiers-état* (1789), we read: 'Je crois à l'esprit de patriotisme qui va remplacer l'esprit de corps, à l'union des campagnes, des villes, des provinces et de la France entière . . . union qui opérera le bien, sacrifiera l'intérêt personnel à l'intérêt général.' Of course, this was in fact the bourgeois union of propertied, but hitherto excluded, citizens, who owned, and therefore 'were' France. The superimposition of common interests upon common culture produces a nationalism of the bourgeoisie and intelligentsia, as Gellner has argued it does for the workers at a later stage (Ch. 6).

66 AKZIN, *op. cit.,* p. 39. In the British case, Norman cultural elements were gradually fused with Saxon through State action into a single nationality: cf. Third Programme talk by Southern, 1967. Till 1204, the traffic was two-way, since the Anglo-Norman aristocracy were supreme politically in 'France'.

67 GERTH & MILLS, *op. cit.,* p. 78.

68 One should include here the ethnic territories of the Feudal Orders, e.g. the Teutonic Knights. Some of these principalities were or are tiny, e.g. Weimar with some 6,000 members or the 15,000 strong San Marino. They have not followed the current fashion of proclaiming themselves nations as well as states.

69 SIEGFRIED, 1950.

70 For the 'Young Turk' movement, cf. RAMSAUR, 1957.

71 Such uses are apparent in Africa and Asia today; any ethnically-based movement is automatically dubbed 'separatist'. The leaders of the African states are in Kossuth's position; having just acquired self-government, its precarious quality makes them cling to its forms meticulously, and given the economic resources of Africa (and Eastern Europe), they feel they cannot afford to split up their territories. But such readily understandable attitudes should not be allowed to impinge on the question of the definition of the 'nation'; as is the case with a number of political scientists. One example is David Apter, 1963*d.*

72 COLEMAN, 1958, Appendix. One should, I feel, lay more stress on the isolation of the tribe, and on the characteristic segmentation of power at each level within the tribe. Cf. GELLNER, 1965.

73 For the Turkish case, cf. GIBB & BOWEN, 1957, and STAVRIANOS, *op. cit.,* Ch. 15. For the Khazars, cf. MARCUS, 1965, III, B, containing the letters of Hasdai Ibn Shaprut and King Joseph *c.* 960, and DUBNOW, 1916, I, pp. 19–29. For the German case and Treitschke's dismissal of the 'doctrine of the right of self-determination for all branches of the German race' for the 'right of the sword', cf. KOHN, 1965, Ch. 7, pp. 162–7.

74 CONQUEST, 1967.
75 *Werke*, 1877–1913, V, 117–36 (*On the Origin of Language*, 1772).
76 This is Fichte's contribution. Folk poetry and music are as important in defining the national character to Herder: 'But music, however rude and simple, speaks to every human heart, and this with the dance constitutes Nature's general festival throughout the earth . . . for the music of a nation, in its most imperfect form and favourite tunes, displays the internal character of the people. . . .' Folk poetry is valuable 'because of its constant and international elements'. Cf. R. T. Clark, Jr., *Herder, His Life and Thought*, Berkeley, 1955, p. 431. In Herder's *Werke*, IX, pp. 528–9, we read: 'It will remain eternally true that if we have no Volk, we shall have no public, no nationality, no literature of our own which shall live and work in us.'
77 *Werke*, XVIII, p. 206, cited in BERLIN, 1965, pp. 47–104.
78 *Ibid.*, p. 76.
79 BARNARD, *op. cit.*, who thinks Herder substitutes common language for Rousseau's general will, but only in the broadest sense, i.e. 'culture'.
80 Cf. W. H. LEWIS, *op. cit.*, and JULY, 1968, Ch. 19; 1965, pp. 1–33. For the intelligentsia, the linguistic dilemma is psychologically and practically particularly difficult. Senghor puts it thus:

> Sentez-vous cette souffrance
> Et ce désespoir à nul autre égal
> d'apprivoiser, avec les mots de France,
> Ce cœur qui m'est venu du Sénégal?
> (*Anthologie de la nouvelle poésie nègre et malgache*, p. 108)

And Gandhi replied to the Macaulay educational doctrine similarly:

> Is it not a painful thing that, if I want to go to a court of justice, I must enploy the English language as a medium, that when I become a barrister, I may not speak my mother-tongue and that someone else should have to translate to me in my own language? Is not this absolutely absurd? Is it not a sign of slavery? Am I to blame the English for it, or myself? It is we, the English-knowing Indians, that have enslaved India. The curse of the nation will rest not upon the English but upon us.
> (Gandhi, *Collected Works*, X, p. 156)

Both are cited in WAUTHIER, 1966.
81 Cf. AKZIN, *op. cit.*, p. 129.
82 HAUGEN, 1966, pp. 922–35.
83 *Ibid.* Ionic tended to be the medium for historical writing, Doric for choral lyric and Attic for tragedy.
84 H. Wolff, 'Intelligibility and Interethnic Attitudes', *Anthropological Linguistics*, I, 3, pp. 34–41; cited in FISHMAN, 1968.

85 This appears to be the motivation behind the present compromise proposals before the Government. This suggests a conflict between two circles of allegiance, the first based on linguistic ties among the previously disprivileged Flemish and then the numerically inferior and downwardly mobile (relatively) Walloons, the second on common history, religion and political institutions. The concept of 'political culture' would accord with the latter all-Belgian circle of loyalty, were it not so inherently vague, and oblivious of the religious tie here.

86 *War and Peace*, 1957, I, p. 3.

87 FISHMAN, *op. cit.*, and J. Paden in *idem*, pp. 199–213.

88 This follows Durkheim's stress on the distinctiveness of the type of 'organic solidarity', but goes on to add another necessary trait, minimal democratisation in the sense of *some* rights and duties which are both important and not mediated by groups which intervene between the individual and the State. Durkheim tends to see this relationship as one of 'nakedness' of the individual to State power; cf. Ch. 2.

89 KOHN, 1957, and cf. the comments on (British and) Swiss 'territorial' nationality in NAMIER, 1952. Kohn makes it clear that the cantons after Confederation were a loose alliance, like Israelites and Medes, i.e. an 'ethnie' in our terminology. Only in the eighteenth century, did a regenerative or 'renewal' nationalism spread from France to induce a distinctively *Swiss* patriotism, extolling Swiss virtues, institutions, history, etc., and bringing with it a new set of direct relationships in certain areas between the member of the commune and canton and the federal state. From this point, we witness the growth of a Swiss 'nation', accelerated by nineteenth-century industrialisation.

90 Ironically, she furnished the basis (with Rome and Sparta) for the very different Rousseauan conception. People imagined they were reviving her glory by distilling the 'essence' (here *l'esprit*) of her peculiar institutions and laws. Pericles' patriotism-of-the-polis was, however, set within a definite pan-Greek framework. In resorting to force to retain her Confederacy, Athens did indeed break to some extent with this religiously sanctioned framework (but then the Spartan-controlled Delphic oracle was hostile), but we find no trace of a 'secessionist' impulse, or a desire to set up a truly 'Attic/Ionic' state.

For a brief review of the 'racial factor' in Peloponnesian politics of the sixth and seventh centuries B.C., cf ANDREWES, 1960, Ch. 5. The conclusion is that the issue was secondary, and in Athens non-existent. The first of these contentions is at least open to doubt.

91 This relativity of tribe, ethnie and nation, and yet the basic difference between them, is exemplified by the debate over detribalisation and supertribalisation in the literature on African urbanisation. The sense of 'ethnicity' in the city, as opposed to its absence in the traditional isolation of the countryside, which characterises the

uprooted African migrant, is, I would argue, an attribute of the growth of the 'ethnie', which leads to 'ethnic politics' and 'ethnic arithmetic' at the national level. Another indication is the role of the so-called 'tribal association', really an ethnie-one. On the whole, this is quite compatible with 'national' loyalty, but sometimes it becomes transformed into an ethnie-based nationalism, as with the Ibo.

92 I am indebted to Mr. J. Winkler for pointing out the importance of autarchy on the economic level as a separate dimension in the thinking and aspirations of nationalists. A certain minimal territory and population is necessary to make this a realistic proposition. The exact limits of this unit vary with changes in the degree of international cooperation and interdependence, the advance of technology, the opportunities for acquiring skills and education cheaply, the internal homogeneity and consensus of the population, its strategic position, etc. (Czechoslovakia is an obvious case of the latter difficulty, as Masaryk's prophecy was so strikingly vindicated; so in a different way is Israel.) It is, on the whole, somewhat easier to make a reasonable attempt at moulding and running a nation-state today than in the last century, if one can use the Cold War rivalries and U.N. agencies to advantage, as does Tunisia, but very much more difficult to reach self-sustaining growth for the most backward areas.

93 The test of the half-million mark is somewhat arbitrary in view of the Nigerian civil war, and the size of Gabon (400,000) or Yakutia (237,000). One wonders if oil rather than size will bring the 1,200,000 Libyans nationhood quicker than to the Basques or half-million Chuvash or Mari? Is it on grounds of size that we dismiss the claims of the Iban, Lapps and Aborigines (respectively 190,000, 32,000 and 140,000)? Do numbers make the one and a half millions of Togolese, Liberians, Nicaraguans and Costa Ricans more like 'nations' than the 238,000 Buryat Mongols or the 600,000 Shans?

As a definitional feature rather than an explanatory precondition, size of population is the most variable of the seven traits. In fact, there is a strong suspicion that it is really a precondition only. The nationalist picture of the 'nation' involves the dimensions of external political relations and economic integration; and these are difficult to envisage, under modern conditions even more than before, without a sufficiently strong supporting population with enough differentiated skills to be a factor in the political (international) arena; i.e. to retain your independence, you must be large enough *relative to your neighbours* to resist encroachments. In Eastern Europe, this implies many millions to counter Germany and Russia; in Africa you can get away with a few millions; and in Siberia and the Caribbean, you may manage with hundreds of thousands, if you tacitly accept Great Power domination. You must also be large enough to show you can run a modern state and society at home with efficiency; the ensuing political stability serves to discourage attacks.

The reason why it has become a definitional feature is, I think, historical: France and England, the first nation-states and the models for all others, were large in scale and size, *and* in all respects, 'successful'.

94 *De l'Esprit des Lois*, XXVIII, 9: 'Sous les deux premières races on assembla souvent la nation, c'est à dire, les seigneurs et les évêques; il n'était point des communes.' Cited in *Zernatto*, 1944.

95 *Ibid.* The Rumanian-speaking 'people' (ethnie) could not be represented, as they didn't have their *own* lords and clergy. The reason why for us they are an ethnie and not a nation is not, of course, because they didn't possess their own or anybody else's lords and clergy, but because they had no common political rights and no common division of labour, as subsistence farmers in Wallachia!

96 Jacobinism was a premonition of things to come, in this sense as in others; cf. KILSON, 1963.

CHAPTER EIGHT *Typologies*

1 CRANSTON, 1954, distinguishes such arbitrary or 'stipulative' definitions from the usual dictionary or 'lexicographical' ones.

2 Cf. SNYDER, 1954, for a similar but rather more pessimistic scheme of total world-engulfing decline. In his recent *The New Nationalism*, Cornell University Press, Ithaca, 1968, pp. 64–7, Snyder elaborates Kohn's dichotomy into seven continental/regional types of nationalism, to encompass the post-1945 'new nationalism' of the developing countries. These are:

1 Europe: 'fissiparous' nationalism, which repeats the old-style small-nation nationalism characteristic of the area.

2 Africa: Black nationalism, based on a hard racial core but wearing a Western-style democratic coating.

3 Middle East: a politico-religious nationalism, that is, a religious nationalism tinged with political overtones.

4 Asia: 'Anticolonial' nationalism, opposing Western imperialism, whose mainspring is the psychological need to 'save face', typical of the Orient.

5 Latin America: Populist nationalism, a revolutionary process which is 'a combination of Spanish pride, fickleness and fierce sense of independence', coupled with opposition to Yankee domination.

6 United States: a 'melting-pot' nationalism, mixing spiritual idealism and materialism with moralistic overtones.

7 Soviet Union: messianic nationalism, which is simply a global expansion of the Czarist messianism.

The psychologism of these 'types' is readily apparent, and some of the distinctions are vague. Does 'anti-colonial' nationalism and face-saving not occur in Africa and Latin America, not to mention the Middle East? Was Indian (Hindu) nationalism or

Burmese (Buddhist) resistance any less 'politico-religious' than Arab nationalism? Do Spaniards possess a monopoly of pride, etc., and isn't revolutionary populism to be found in China, Vietnam, Algeria and Yugoslavia? These characterisations do not take us far; and they preclude any useful comparisons, as do all historical typologies. As for the implicit notion that geographical location determines the type of nationalism, this would lead, if carried through, to a cult of the unique, which would satisfy every idealist's dream.

3 TREVOR-ROPER, 1962.

4 HAYES, 1931. For Hayes, the 'humanitarian' is the primary type, and the earliest. Its 'aristocratic' version is represented by Bolingbroke, its 'democratic' by Rousseau, and its 'cultural' by Herder. The extension of the 'democratic' leads to the Jacobin variety, and the Liberal type of nationalism is the product of both the aristocratic and the democratic versions. Such genealogies may be of use in tracing the connections and differences of thought and style in the writings of certain late eighteenth-century West European nationalists; they certainly reveal the rich diversity of ideas among its earliest exponents—a point which I have been at pains to stress throughout. But if these pedigrees are extended outside Europe and into the nineteenth and twentieth centuries, they become distorting straitjackets.

5 BINDER, 1964, Ch. 6, gives a penetrating analysis of these strands of thought in the writings of Michal Aflaq.

6 KOHN, 1967 (1944).

7 KEDOURIE, 1960, p. 43.

8 KEDWARD, 1965, Part II, Ch. 1. He points up this conflict in terms of the distinction between the *pays réel* and the *pays légal*, or Integralism and Republicanism.

9 In his later *Nationalism, Its Meaning and History*, 1955, Hans Kohn recognises this distinction, within his two 'horizontal' types, and indicates his preference for the Anglo-Saxon subvariety—as do Cranston and Minogue.

10 A good account of this distinction is given in BINDER, *op. cit.*, Ch. 4. Cf. HERTZ, 1944.

11 Renan's celebrated essay 'Qu'est-ce qu'une Nation?' of 1882, contains elements drawn from both ideological kinds of nationalism, the plebiscitarian and the traditional-organic. This explains the rather different conclusions drawn by pupils; contrast the common Western interpretation with that of the Crimean Tatar, Akchurin, who recommended an ethnic pan-Turkism to the Turks and Russian Muslims in 1904. Cf. ZENKOVSKY, 1960, Ch. 3.

12 MARTINS, 1967.

13 HANDMAN, 1921.

14 WIRTH, 1936.

15 DEUTSCH, 1966. The same holds for his recent *Nationalism and Its Alternatives*, 1969.

16 GINSBERG, 1961. He presents a complex typology of the causal factors at work in generating national consciousness. The upshot of his argument is that no single factor constitutes a sufficient or necessary condition for the formation of a nation. Even such a process as secularisation is only a contributory cause, as the example of Norway demonstrates. There priests were among the leaders of the nationalist movement (the same is true of Burma). Here at least Ginsberg is rather too sweeping. An incipient secularisation coupled with the growth of an intelligentsia and the influence of Montesquieu and Rousseau in the eighteenth century (e.g. on Gunnerus' Norwegian Scientific Society of 1767 or Ludvig Holberg's *Danmarks og Norges*) led to a full-blown linguistic nationalism of the Herderian variety in the 1830's under Henrik Wergeland's 'Young Norway' pro-peasant party. ELVIKEN, 1931, holds that the secular French doctrines of popular sovereignty and collective self-determination form the bridge between a traditional national consciousness ('ethnocentrism') and modern (nineteenth-century 'polycentric') nationalism. The Norwegian case remained predominantly democratic (unlike the otherwise similar Burmese case). This analysis is extended to Finland, Denmark and Sweden in WUORINEN, 1950. The whole process forms a fairly common sequence, and the factors Ginsberg enumerates need to be related to such a framework.

17 H. SETON-WATSON, 1965.

18 WORSLEY, 1964, Ch. 2.

19 MINOGUE, 1967, p. 12, uses this rather unsatisfactory residual category. It presupposes a unified 'Third World', and I have already made my criticisms of this concept in Chapter 4.

20 KAUTSKY, 1962, Ch. 2. Kautsky also makes room for an 'integration' nationalism which he defines as loyalty to an existing territorial state. Such a nationalism is to be found equally in the West and in the underdeveloped world—in the latter case, after independence has been attained. (Cf. also Chapter 4.)

21 SYMMONS-SYMONOLEWICZ, 1965, pp. 221–30.

22 Cf. MERRITT & ROKKAN, 1966, *passim*; and ROKKAN, 1961.

23 Cf. the criticisms of this methodological dualism by MACINTYRE, 1962.

24 Cf. NISBET, 1953, Ch. 7; WOLIN, 1960, Ch. X, and CRANSTON, 1954, Ch. 7—for philosophical accounts of this crucial transition.

25 As ULAM, 1964, and KAUTSKY, 1962, point out.

CHAPTER NINE   The Varieties of Nationalism

1 E. P. SKINNER, 1964.

2 REID, 1967.

3 COLEMAN, 1958, Ch. 7.

4 HODGKIN, 1956; and the discussion of this contrast in KILSON, 1958, pp. 484–92.

5 RENIER, 1944.

6 This is the term used by Coleman (above) and in his article 'Nationalism in Tropical Africa', 1954.

7 For an analysis of 'messianisms' as a kind of half-way house between a traditional cyclical and a modern 'Promethean' or linear-progressive mentality, cf. BASTIDE, 1961.

8 WORSLEY, 1964, uses these terms, but we need to supplement his 'achievement' criterion by one of 'intensity', i.e. did the group manage to develop a strong nationalist movement?

9 *The Times*, March 25, 1967, and April 3–6, 1967.

10 Cf. KOLARZ, 1954, and WHEELER, 1964.

11 Cf. C. McGlashlan in the *Observer*, October 30, 1966, and J. Morgan in the *Sunday Times*, March 12, 1967.

12 The best study of linguistic and regional nationalism within India is HARRISON, 1960.

13 I do not wish to minimise this element, especially in settler areas, but agree with Kautsky that the 'racial' division is less important in most cases than the 'colonial' situation.

14 Zionism's debates over priorities provide a classical example. Even Jabotinsky's extension of Herzl's 'political Zionism' based on 'Judennot' (the physical need of homeless Jews) tacitly recognises the logical priority of the cultural survival of a group defined in solely cultural terms. (Only Zangwill's 'territorialism'—a numerically insignificant strand—did not espouse the cultural Palestinian homeland.) Hence the fear in Israel today of a deep *Kulturkampf*; it isn't just a question of offending the influential Orthodox minority, it expresses a real hesitation to expose the underlying bases of statehood, especially now. (Cf. the cited works of B. Halpern and Hertzberg.)

15 Cf. YOUNG, 1965, Chs. 9–12.

16 G. W. SKINNER, 1959a.

17 The 'mixed' variety has been further subdivided by Geertz in his excellent essay 'The Integrative Revolution', 1963.

18 This statement should be construed only as an ideal-typical construct of possibilities, and not a kind of situational determinism.

19 Here I agree with ROTBERG, 1967. This category, which Symmons-Symonolewicz's Europocentrism neglects, is particularly important in the African context; though here again, we have to note the 'racial' element, i.e. both the ethnic nationalisms of the Kikuyu or Ibo or Somali, and the pan-Africanism which remains an elusive but powerful ideal. Cf. MAZRUI, 1966, esp. Ch. III. The ensuing dilemmas of ethnicity are brilliantly analysed in W. A. LEWIS, 1965.

20 This is classically portrayed in Forster's *Passage to India,* 1936, and Mannoni's *Prospero and Caliban,* 1956.

21 Cf. TALMON, 1960, pp. 265–8.

22 There seems to be an inverse correlation between the intensity of 'Pan' and 'Secession' types, which appear in oscillating phases.

23 In some of these cases, the majority of the group is located in the 'ancestral' homeland; yet even in this case, the movement starts in

the exiled communities, e.g. Korais in Paris or Obradovic in the Habsburg domains or Emin and Bagramian in Madras in the late eighteenth century: cf. NALBANDIAN, 1963. Kachatur Aborian, the father of Armenian nationalism (1804/10–1810), was also an exile in Georgia and a wanderer in Europe. The only cases of groups returning to an ancestral homeland where hardly any co-nationals were living at the time, were, as far as I can gather, the Liberian and the Jewish. A new Reader on Negro nationalism with sections on the Back-to-Africa movements from Cuffe and Turner to Garvey is BRACEY, MEIER, & RUDWICK, 1970; and cf. on Delaney and Holley, BROTZ, 1960, Pt. I.

24 This is one of the chief motifs of pan-Arabism, and this example highlights the continuity between ordinary 'irredentism' and 'pan' Movements.

25 The Swabians provide an excellent example of what I mean. Till the Hitlerian pan-Germanist element in Nazism became a political factor in Europe, they led a quiet group-preserving existence. Suddenly, the Nazi party offered them status, bread, jobs, etc., and they were swept into the wider Nazi movement, with its use of irredentism for political purposes.

26 HESS, 1966. Cf. also LIPSKEY, 1962, and WILBER, 1962.

27 Of course, 'regeneration' is a hall-mark of all nationalisms. The point here is the social context, which is characterised by 'disintegration' and social divisions of an acute type. The recent Cambodian revolution against Sihanouk, according to Mark Frankland in the *Observer* of May 17, 1970, is such a 'renewal' nationalism, bringing to power a new elite of the wealthy and educated, the first since Cambodia's independence. The highly nationalistic intelligentsia provides the movement's social base. (Its involvement in the Vietnam conflict is another matter.) Even if this example is inaccurate, it illustrates the theoretical point I wish to make in separating the 'renewal' type.

28 A good analysis of the problems facing such movements is to be found in COWAN, 1964. See also WEINGROD, 1965.

29 Cf. WHITAKER & JORDAN, 1966. As Kubitschek put it: 'We want to be on the side of the West, but we do not want to be its proletariat.' The modern populist nationalism is worker-oriented and concerned with autarchy and domestic development, especially in Brazil, Argentina and Mexico. Cf. J. J. JOHNSON, 1965.

30 On the Nasserist Free Officer Revolution cf. VATIKIOTIS, 1961, and more recently VATIKIOTIS, 1968 and 1969. On Japanese 'renewal' activities, cf. JANSEN, 1965.

CHAPTER TEN   'Dual Legitimation'

1 I owe this formulation to Mr. M. Hickox, to whom I am grateful for his criticisms of these ideal-types.

2 Cf. GROUSETT, 1931; GHIRSHMAN, 1954, esp. pp. 142–46. On empires generally, cf. EISENSTADT, 1963.

3 Tacitus, *Annals*, XI, 23–4.

4 BOZEMAN, 1960, Ch. 13, p. 447 sqq.

5 On Dubois and Philip IV, cf. KANTOROWICZ, 1951. After the defeat of Courtrai (1302), Philip, we learn, levies taxes *ad tuitionem patriae et ad defensionem patriae*: '. . . for the defence of the native fatherland which the venerable antiquity of our ancestors ordered to fight for, because they preferred the care for the fatherland even to the love of their descendants.' This was party a return to the territorial concept of classical antiquity, of Virgil's Ausonia and Italia; but it also includes now a Christian view of the State as the *corpus mysticum*. Both notions were increasingly attached to the royal domain of the personal monarch. The dynastic and religious nature of 'national sentiment' in the regions of France (Lorraine, Normandy, Burgundy, Brittany, and France (Paris) proper) is borne out by HANDELSMAN, 1929, pp. 235–46. On the question of national sentiment generally during this period, cf. COULTON, 1935, pp. 15–40.

6 R. Tagore, *Nationalism*, 1917, cited in KEDOURIE, 1960, pp. 110–11.

7 For some contrasts between European and African political evolution, cf. KIERNAN, 1964. On European states, cf. BENDIX, 1964.

8 Cf. the classic analysis in GREENBERG, 1951. The Tatars were singled out for religious repression from 1556 onwards, especially by Peter who used Kievan missionary monks to convert them. But from 1766, Catherine II reversed the policy: cf. ZENKOVSKY, 1960.

9 For a phenomenological account of this process of 'cosmisation', cf. P. BERGER, 1969. The citation is from Weber's *Social Psychology of the World Religions*, in GERTH & MILLS, 1947.

10 For a fuller account, cf. A. D. SMITH, 1970.

11 DOSTOEVSKY, 1958, *The Brothers Karamazov*, Vol. I, p. 287, and Camus' comments in *The Rebel*, 1962, pp. 50–58.

12 WEBER, *op. cit.*, pp. 275–6, and his *Sociology of Religion*, 1965, pp. 138–50.

13 Cf. MARTIN, 1965.

14 COLBOURN & STRAYER, 1958.

15 A good example is the various pretexts trumped up as justifications for starting the Peloponnesian War in 431. Thucydides' cynicism here is, as far as one can tell, sociologically unrepresentative.

16 AVINERI, 1969, esp. p. 29.

17 Cf. the works cited by B. Lewis & Berkes; also FRYE, 1957 (esp. essay by Berkes).

18 It will be understood that a particular case of nationalism may well fall under more than one category or 'type'; for example, Burma could be placed under the 'Mixed' rubric, and Turkey and Persia under the 'Ethnic'. However, there is usually one category which fits each case somewhat better than others for purposes of further research and comparison, and this is the consideration guiding my choice here. (This is not an exhaustive list.)

19 Here I depart somewhat from Wittfogel's analysis, and agree that

large-scale political interventionism on an enduring basis is a specifically modernising development: cf. M. HALPERN, 1964.

20 O'DEA, 1966, Ch. 1.

21 ROFF, 1967.

22 Cf. FRAZEE, 1969, and the article by Arnakis in B. & C. JELAVICH, 1963.

23 This is the subject of much recent controversy: cf. KEDOURIE, 1966; HAIM, 1962; and HOURANI, 1970, Ch. V.

24 The Zealot ideal is, of course, the subject of the Israeli Nationality Law dispute in the recent Shalit case, with the traditionalist rabbis consistently upholding the 'ethnocentric' outlook in their descent-based definition of Jewishness. A religious parallel, with this time a linguistic twist, can be found in the Catholic monarchism of Maurras and Barrès: cf. KEDWARD, 1965.

25 For these three aspects of the 'problem of meaning', cf. Geertz's brilliant essay in BANTON, 1966.

26 GUTHRIE, 1950, Chs. 6, 11, esp. pp. 157–9, where he cites the parallel Montanist and Mevlevi Dervishes heresies in the identical region of Anatolia. A good introduction to the Mu'tazilite heresy and its relevance to modern Islamic evolution is given in the opening pages of SAFRAN, 1961. The orthodox Sunni (Ash'arite) doctrine was partly a reaction to this attempted reform.

27 BUJRA, 1967, pp. 355–75, 2–28.

28 Cf. the excellent analysis in MEYER, 1967.

29 *Othello*, V, 2:

> If heaven would make me such another world
> Of one entire and perfect chrysolite,
> I'd not have sold her for it.

30 Perhaps Namik Kemal typifies this dual allegiance best, and Abduh and Moses Mendelssohn and their followers in Islam and Judaism have their Eastern counterparts in the Buddhist Lakhshmi Narasu, the Hindu Roy and Chandra Sen and the Chinese (Confucian) K'ang Yu-wei and Li'ang Ch'i Ch'ao. Cf. McCULLEY, 1940 and LEVENSON, 1967. Cf. also SINGH, 1963, Ch. 2, on Aurobindo's forerunners.

31 No attempt is made to document what is admittedly an ideal-typical picture of the religious thought of the 'unhistorical enlightenment'—and a highly composite one at that. In European history, it would cover the period from the late seventeenth to early nineteenth centuries. But the general deist pattern in which God gradually recedes into the empyrean after completing His work to leave man to fulfil his part of His plan through the use of reason, is clear enough and globally relevant.

32 Cf. BLAU, 1959*b*, supporting the favoured etymological derivation (from *religare*, to bind again).

33 A brief account of Baha'ullah's development of Babism in Akko after 1868 is to be found in KOHN, 1929, Ch. 2, esp. p. 33.

34 This is the meaning given in Kohn, *ibid.*, p. 23, referring to Islam and Judaism: 'In this respect the Wahabi movement resembles certain tendencies in ancient Jewish religious history which centred on the sect of the Rechabites and the circles influenced by the early prophets. Elijah and Amos, in their dress and mien and teaching, stood for the ancient austerity of the primitive desert religion as opposed to the emasculating influence of Canaan's city civilisation and the abuse and idolatry which had crept in in consequence. It seems that the Rechabites aimed at a like return to the ancient ideal: they were Puritan nomads who scorned wine and the cultivation of the soil. But at the same time this early prophetic movement involved a national protest against alien ways.' The renovation envisaged in my sense of 'revivalism' is basically future-oriented and willing to find a *modus vivendi* with the power of the 'scientific state'. It revives a lost consciousness and will to face the difficult tasks of the future.

35 If the community to be renovated is not the 'primary bearer' of the religious tradition, but a latecomer like Turks or Kazakhs, the attack on degenerate and burdensome tradition may well turn into a full-scale assault on *all* forms of religion. Gokalp's ethnic-linguistic 'revivalism' which plays down religion paved the way for Ataturk's Sun Language theory and interest in Oguz Khan, to bolster self-confidence: cf. HEYD, 1950.

36 Ahad Ha'am is a fine example of the secularisation of the 'chosen people' concept. Cf. SIMON, 1946, and the Introduction in HERTZBERG, 1960. This 'agnostic rabbi', so influenced by British empiricism, was one of a whole class of men excluded by the traditional hierarchy, and who as a result shifted their focus to a historical-linguistic concept of their group. Their failure to find an adequate definition of the quality of group uniqueness, shorn of religious sanction, haunts all nationalisms. Political nationalism remains largely external until this question is resolved. Till then, nationalism remains a 'cultural journey', a continual migration of the spirit, solving some problems only to raise fresh ones. Thesis and antithesis reappear in ever new guises.

37 As this brief list indicates, the division between the rationalist and the 'revivalist' wings of the 'reformist' movements is more of an analytic than an empirical distinction. In a given case, e.g. Kemal or Iqbal, one can find the two wings stressed at different phases of the author's development. Or we may witness an actual institutional schism, as at the 'conservative' walk-out of Zechariah Frankel from the Frankfurt Reform Synod in 1845, or the founding of the Arya Samaj in 1875 by Dayananda in opposition to Roy's and Chandra Sen's earlier Brahmo Samaj. But the historical permutations are complex, cf. POCOCK, 1958 and DESAI, 1954, esp. Chs. 13, 17. On the Jewish case, cf. BLAU, 1966, and KATZ, 1958.

38 Cf. for example PERHAM, 1963, Ch. 2.

39 The stereotypical imitation-rejection mechanism has been severely

criticised by HODGKIN, 1964. For him, the psychoanalytic version of nationalism's emergence is an example of residual 'intellectual colonialism'; we should rather focus on the historical situation and the social movement in which particular leaders played their roles, otherwise each case of nationalism would have to be treated as *sui generis*.

A sentiment such as Blyden's below owes as much to Montesquieu, Burke or Rousseau as to Herder, Fichte or Mazzini—if a 'respectable' pedigree really needs to be sought for an ideal that I would argue has a clear sociological matrix without need for recourse to diffusionism or psychologism:

> Every race has a soul, and the soul of the race finds expression in its institutions, and to kill those institutions is to kill the soul. . . . No people can profit or be helped under institutions which are not the outcome of their own character.

(in *West Africa before Europe and Other Addresses*, 1903, p. 140, p. 101, cited in AJAYI, 1960.)

40 I know of no full-scale comparative study of religious reform and nationalism, or of religious reform movements *per se*, only case studies. For two brief regional interpretations cf. WERTHEIM, 1958, and BELLAH, 1965, esp. Epilogue. See also GIBB, 1947; MEHDEN, 1968; PLAUT, 1963; BERKES, 1964; CARRERE d'ENCAUSSE, 1966; HEIMSATH, 1964; HOWARD *et al*, 1969.

APPENDIX A

1 See Note (2) of Chapter 2, and SNYDER, 1968.
2 Cf. especially ALMOND & COLEMAN, 1960; PYE & VERBA, 1965; EMERSON, 1960, pp. 3-28; ALMOND, 1965.
3 Cf. DEUTSCH & FOLTZ, 1963, and APTER, 1968.
4 The two most important recent works on nationalist economics and language development in relation to nationalism are JOHNSON, 1968; and FISHMAN, *et al.*, 1968. Cf. also LE PAGE, 1964.
5 KAUTSKY, 1962; and the critique by LOWENTHAL, 1962, pp. 37-44.
6 Cf. the works of Deutsch and Lerner, especially in Chapter 5, but also MERRIT & ROKKAN, 1966, and the quantitative data and correlations in BANKS & TEXTOR, 1963, and especially RUSSETT *et al.*, 1964. Also DEUTSCH, 1966*b*, Parts II & III, esp. Ch. 7, 12, still operates with a notion of autonomy of the 'system' (political or personal); it does not explain either how such systems come into being, or why men come to demand sovereignty for 'their' political system. The functionalist model of transactional power remains at the level of description and analysis.
7 The best recent psychological theory of nationalism, as a development of patriotism which is universal because based on the stimuli of land, people and culture, is that of DOOB, 1964. I would take issue, however, on two points. First, we need evidence to back the assertion that these stimuli operate universally (as well as closer

definition of their scope and meaning). Secondly, the strong case for separating nationalism from any group solidarity sentiments is overlooked in the standard psychological approach, and Doob is no exception. What is at stake is why allegiances and attachments should be focused on the 'nation' rather than on other collectivities like clan, village, congregation, dynasty or city. The tie-up of land, culture and 'people' with sovereignty is what has to be explained, over and above group loyalty.

It is interesting that when Doob comes to his explanation of the rise of both patriotism and nationalism, he resorts to clear sociological factors, culture, language, geographical isolation, the common enemy, etc.

APPENDIX B

1 M. WEBER, 1965, Ch. 4–8.
2 Virgil (*Aeneid VI*, 853) and Darius' inscriptions attest the antiquity of such single-nation imperialisms. In the Roman case, however, there was never much cultural homogeneity in the seven villages of the original confederation; it was nicknamed the 'asylum of Romulus' on account of its ethnic heterogeneity.
3 Cf. EPSTEIN, 1964.
4 H. SETON-WATSON, 1966.
5 *Ibid.*, MOSSE, 1966, who stresses the organic instinctualist revolt against positivism and liberalism and its taming through identification of the individual will with that of the movement, Leader and State. It was in Western Fascism that the corporate State (of the bourgeoisie) was prized: Eastern Fascism stressed the racial aspect, and was more revolutionary and activist.
6 MUNGER, 1967. BERGHE, 1965b.
7 LEGUM, 1962. But the humanist vision is still preserved by Césaire, Senghor and Présence Africaine.
8 POLIAKOV, 1954. Cf. also PARSONS, 1964a, Chs. VI, VII. FEST, 1970. LIPSET, 1963, Ch. 4.
9 KEDOURIE, 1960.
10 GELLNER & IONESCU, 1969: I follow MacRae's characterisation in the main.
11 WORSLEY, 1969.

Index of Names

Index of Topics